T0331576

Feature Dimension Reduction for Content–Based Image Identification

Rik Das
Xavier Institute of Social Service, India

Sourav De
Cooch Behar Government Engineering College, India

Siddhartha Bhattacharyya
RCC Institute of Information Technology, India

A volume in the Advances in Multimedia and
Interactive Technologies (AMIT) Book Series

Published in the United States of America by
    IGI Global
    Information Science Reference (an imprint of IGI Global)
    701 E. Chocolate Avenue
    Hershey PA, USA 17033
    Tel: 717-533-8845
    Fax: 717-533-8661
    E-mail: cust@igi-global.com
    Web site: http://www.igi-global.com

Library of Congress Cataloging-in-Publication Data

Names: Das, Rik, 1978- editor. | De, Sourav, 1979- editor. | Bhattacharyya,
  Siddhartha, 1975- editor.
Title: Feature dimension reduction for content-based image identification /
  Rik Das, Sourav De, and Siddhartha Bhattacharyya, editors.
Description: Hershey, PA : Information Science Reference, an imprint of IGI
  Global, [2019] | Includes bibliographical references and index.
Identifiers: LCCN 2017055700| ISBN 9781522557753 (hardcover) | ISBN
  9781522557760 (ebook)
Subjects: LCSH: Optical pattern recognition. | Image analysis--Data
  processing. | Data reduction. | Computer vision.
Classification: LCC TA1650 .F43 2019 | DDC 006.4/2--dc23 LC record available at https://lccn.loc.gov/2017055700

This book is published in the IGI Global book series Advances in Multimedia and Interactive Technologies (AMIT) (ISSN: 2327-929X; eISSN: 2327-9303)

British Cataloguing in Publication Data
A Cataloguing in Publication record for this book is available from the British Library.

All work contributed to this book is new, previously-unpublished material. The views expressed in this book are those of the authors, but not necessarily of the publisher.

For electronic access to this publication, please contact: eresources@igi-global.com.

Advances in Multimedia and Interactive Technologies (AMIT) Book Series

Joel J.P.C. Rodrigues
National Institute of Telecommunications (Inatel),
Brazil & Instituto de Telecomunicações, University
of Beira Interior, Portugal

ISSN:2327-929X
EISSN:2327-9303

MISSION

Traditional forms of media communications are continuously being challenged. The emergence of user-friendly web-based applications such as social media and Web 2.0 has expanded into everyday society, providing an interactive structure to media content such as images, audio, video, and text.

The **Advances in Multimedia and Interactive Technologies (AMIT) Book Series** investigates the relationship between multimedia technology and the usability of web applications. This series aims to highlight evolving research on interactive communication systems, tools, applications, and techniques to provide researchers, practitioners, and students of information technology, communication science, media studies, and many more with a comprehensive examination of these multimedia technology trends.

COVERAGE

- Multimedia Streaming
- Web Technologies
- Mobile Learning
- Multimedia Technology
- Social Networking
- Digital Games
- Digital Images
- Audio Signals
- Digital Watermarking
- Gaming Media

IGI Global is currently accepting manuscripts for publication within this series. To submit a proposal for a volume in this series, please contact our Acquisition Editors at Acquisitions@igi-global.com or visit: http://www.igi-global.com/publish/.

Titles in this Series

For a list of additional titles in this series, please visit: www.igi-global.com/book-series

Real-Time Face Detection, Recognition, and Tracking System in LabVIEW™ Emerging Research and Opportunities
Manimehala Nadarajan (Universiti Malaysia Sabah, Malaysia) Muralindran Mariappan (Universiti Malaysia Sabah, Malaysia) and Rosalyn R. Porle (Universiti Malaysia Sabah, Malaysia)
Information Science Reference • copyright 2018 • 140pp • H/C (ISBN: 9781522535034) • US $155.00 (our price)

Empirical Research on Semiotics and Visual Rhetoric
Marcel Danesi (University of Toronto, Canada)
Information Science Reference • copyright 2018 • 312pp • H/C (ISBN: 9781522556220) • US $195.00 (our price)

Exploring Transmedia Journalism in the Digital Age
Renira Rampazzo Gambarato (National Research University Higher School of Economics, Russia) and Geane C. Alzamora (Federal University of Minas Gerais, Brazil)
Information Science Reference • copyright 2018 • 348pp • H/C (ISBN: 9781522537816) • US $195.00 (our price)

Image Retrieval and Analysis Using Text and Fuzzy Shape Features Emerging Research and Opportunities
P. Sumathy (Bharathidasan University, India) P. Shanmugavadivu (Gandhigram Rural Institute, India) and A. Vadivel (SRM University, India)
Information Science Reference • copyright 2018 • 183pp • H/C (ISBN: 9781522537960) • US $145.00 (our price)

Multimedia Retrieval Systems in Distributed Environments Emerging Research and Opportunities
S.G. Shaila (National Institute of Technology, India) and A. Vadivel (National Institute of Technology, India)
Information Science Reference • copyright 2018 • 140pp • H/C (ISBN: 9781522537281) • US $165.00 (our price)

Handbook of Research on Advanced Concepts in Real-Time Image and Video Processing
Md. Imtiyaz Anwar (National Institute of Technology, Jalandhar, India) Arun Khosla (National Institute of Technology, Jalandhar, India) and Rajiv Kapoor (Delhi Technological University, India)
Information Science Reference • copyright 2018 • 504pp • H/C (ISBN: 9781522528487) • US $265.00 (our price)

Transforming Gaming and Computer Simulation Technologies across Industries
Brock Dubbels (McMaster University, Canada)
Information Science Reference • copyright 2017 • 297pp • H/C (ISBN: 9781522518174) • US $210.00 (our price)

Feature Detectors and Motion Detection in Video Processing
Nilanjan Dey (Techno India College of Technology, Kolkata, India) Amira Ashour (Tanta University, Egypt) and Prasenjit Kr. Patra (Bengal College of Engineering and Technology, India)
Information Science Reference • copyright 2017 • 328pp • H/C (ISBN: 9781522510253) • US $200.00 (our price)

701 East Chocolate Avenue, Hershey, PA 17033, USA
Tel: 717-533-8845 x100 • Fax: 717-533-8661
E-Mail: cust@igi-global.com • www.igi-global.com

Rik Das would like to dedicate this book to his father, Mr. Kamal Kumar Das, his mother, Mrs. Malabika Das, his better half, Mrs. Simi Das, and his kids, Sohan and Dikshan.

Sourav De would like to dedicate this book to loving wife, Debolina, beloved son, Aishik, and grandmother, Late Kamalabala De.

Siddhartha Bhattacharyya would like to dedicate this book to his father, Late Ajit Kumar Bhattacharyya, his mother, Late Hashi Bhattacharyya, his beloved wife, Rashni, and his cousin sisters-in-law, Nivedita, Madhuparna, Anushree, and Swarnali.

Table of Contents

Detailed Table of Contents

Chapter 1

Rik Das, Xavier Institute of Social Service, India
S. N. Singh, Xavier Institute of Social Service, India
Mahua Banerjee, Xavier Institute of Social Service, India
Shishir Mayank, Xavier Institute of Social Service, India
T. Venkata Shashank, Xavier Institute of Social Service, India

Image data has portrayed immense potential as a resourceful foundation of information in current context for numerous applications including biomedicine, military, commerce, education, and web image classification and searching. The scenario has kindled the requirement for efficient content-based image identification from the archived image databases in varied industrial and educational sectors. Feature extraction has acted as the backbone to govern the success rate of content-based information identification with image data. The chapter has presented two different techniques of feature extraction from images based on image binarization and morphological operators. The multi-technique extraction with radically reduced feature size was imperative to explore the rich set of feature content in an image. The objective of this work has been to create a fusion framework for image recognition by means of late fusion with data standardization. The work has implemented a hybrid framework for query classification as a precursor for image retrieval which has been so far the first of its kind.

Chapter 2

Sourav De, Cooch Behar Government Engineering College, India
Madhumita Singha, Xavier Institute of Social Service, India
Komal Kumari, Xavier Institute of Social Service, India
Ritika Selot, Xavier Institute of Social Service, India
Akshat Gupta, Xavier Institute of Social Service, India

Technological advancements in the field of machine learning have attempted classification of the images of gigantic datasets. Classification with content-based image feature extraction categorizes the images based on the image content in contrast to conventional text-based annotation. The chapter has presented a feature extraction technique based on application of image transform. The method has extracted meaningful features and facilitated feature dimension reduction. A technique, known as fractional coefficient of transforms, is adopted to facilitate feature dimension reduction. Two different color spaces, namely RGB and YUV, are considered to compare the classification metrics to figure out the best possible reduced feature dimension. Further, the results are compared to state-of-the-art techniques which have revealed improved performance for the proposed feature extraction technique.

Chapter 3

Rose Bindu Joseph P., VIT University, India
Ezhilmaran Devarasan, VIT University, India

Content-based image retrieval aims to acquire images from huge databases by analyzing their visual features like color, texture, shape, and spatial relationship. The search for superior accuracy in image retrieval has resulted in concentrating more on semantic gap reduction between the low-level features and high level human reasoning. Fuzzy theory is a prevailing methodology which helps in attaining this goal by using attributes and interpretations similar to human reasoning. The vagueness and impreciseness in image data and the retrieval process can be modeled by fuzzy sets. This chapter analyses fuzzy theoretic approaches in various stages of content-based image retrieval system. Various fuzzy-based feature descriptors are discussed along with different fuzzy classification and indexing algorithms for content-based image retrieval. This chapter also presents an overview of various fuzzy distance and similarity measures for image retrieval. A novel fuzzy theoretic retrieval for finger vein biometric images is also proposed in this chapter with experiment and analysis.

Chapter 4

Vivek K. Verma, Manipal University Jaipur, India
Tarun Jain, Manipal University Jaipur, India

This is the age of big data where aggregating information is simple and keeping it economical. Tragically, as the measure of machine intelligible data builds, the capacity to comprehend and make utilization of it doesn't keep pace with its development. In content-based image retrieval (CBIR) applications, every database needs its comparing parameter setting for feature extraction. CBIR is the application of computer vision techniques to the image retrieval problem that is the problem of searching for digital images in large databases. In any case, the vast majority of the CBIR frameworks perform ordering by an arrangement of settled and pre-particular parameters. All the major machine-learning-based search algorithms have discussed in this chapter for better understanding related with the image retrieval accuracy. The efficiency of FS using machine learning compared with some other search algorithms and observed for the improvement of the CBIR system.

Chapter 5

Mohammad Atique, Sant Gadge Baba Amravati University, India
Leena Homraj Patil, Priyadarshini Institute of Engineering, India

Attribute reduction and feature selection is the main issue in rough set. Researchers have focused on several attribute reduction using rough set. However, the methods found are time consuming for large data sets. Since the key lies in reducing the attributes and selecting the relevant features, the main aim is to reduce the dimensionality of huge amount of data to get the smaller subset which can provide the useful information. Feature selection approach reduces the dimensionality of feature space and improves the overall performance. The challenge in feature selection is to deal with high dimensional. To overcome the issues and challenges, this chapter describes a feature selection based on the proposed neighborhood positive approximation approach and attributes reduction for data sets. This proposed system implements for attribute reduction and finds the relevant features. Evaluation shows that the proposed neighborhood positive approximation algorithm is effective and feasible for large data sets and also reduces the feature space.

Chapter 6
    Madan U. Kharat, MET Institute of Engineering, India
    Ranjana P. Dahake, MET Institute of Engineering, India
    Kalpana V. Metre, MET Institute of Engineering, India

Image retrieval is gaining significant attention in areas such as surveillance, access control, etc. The content-based feature extraction plays a very crucial role in image retrieval. For the characterization of a specific image, mainly three features (i.e., color, texture, and shape) are used. Multimedia can store text, image, audio, and video which can be processed and retrieved. The various techniques are used for image retrieval such as textual annotations, content-based image retrieval in many application areas like medical imaging, satellite imaging, etc. However, most of these techniques were designed for specific domains and universally accepted method is yet to be designed; hence, CBIR is a field of active research. Similar output images indicate efficiency of search and retrieval process. In this chapter, the authors have discussed various image feature extraction techniques and clustering approaches for content-based feature extraction from image and specifically focused on color based CBIR techniques.

Chapter 7
    Saugata Bose, University of Liberal Arts Bangladesh, Bangladesh
    Ritambhra Korpal, Savitribai Phule Pune University, India

In this chapter, an initiative is proposed where natural language processing (NLP) techniques and supervised machine learning algorithms have been combined to detect external plagiarism. The major emphasis is on to construct a framework to detect plagiarism from monolingual texts by implementing n-gram frequency comparison approach. The framework is based on 120 characteristics which have been extracted during pre-processing steps using simple NLP approach. Afterward, filter metrics has been applied to select most relevant features and supervised classification learning algorithm has been used later to classify the documents in four levels of plagiarism. Then, confusion matrix was built to estimate the false positives and false negatives. Finally, the authors have shown C4.5 decision tree-based classifier's suitability on calculating accuracy over naive Bayes. The framework achieved 89% accuracy with low false positive and false negative rate and it shows higher precision and recall value comparing to passage similarities method, sentence similarity method, and search space reduction method.

Chapter 8

Segmentation of Multiple Touching Hand Written Devnagari Compound Characters: Image
Segmentation for Feature Extraction 140

Prashant Madhukar Yawalkar, MET Institute of Engineering, India
Madan Uttamrao Kharat, MET Institute of Engineering, India
Shyamrao V. Gumaste, MET Institute of Engineering, India

One of the most widely used steps in the process of reducing images to information is segmentation, which divides the image into regions that hopefully correspond to structural units in the scene or distinguish objects of interest. Segmentation is often described by analogy to visual processes as a foreground/background separation, implying that the selection procedure concentrates on a single kind of feature and discards the rest. Machine-printed or hand-drawn scripts can have various font types or writing styles. The writing styles can be roughly categorized into discrete style (handprint or boxed style), continuous style (cursive style), and mixed style. We can see that the ambiguity of character segmentation has three major sources: (1) variability of character size and inter character space; (2) confusion between inter character and within-character space; and (3) touching between characters.

Chapter 9

Logo Matching and Recognition Based on Context 164

Tapan Kumar Das, VIT University, India

Logos are graphic productions that recall some real-world objects or emphasize a name, simply display some abstract signs that have strong perceptual appeal. Color may have some relevance to assess the logo identity. Different logos may have a similar layout with slightly different spatial disposition of the graphic elements, localized differences in the orientation, size and shape, or differ by the presence/absence of one or few traits. In this chapter, the author uses ensemble-based framework to choose the best combination of preprocessing methods and candidate extractors. The proposed system has reference logos and test logos which are verified depending on some features like regions, pre-processing, key points. These features are extracted by using gray scale image by scale-invariant feature transform (SIFT) and Affine-SIFT (ASIFT) descriptor method. Pre-processing phase employs four different filters. Key points extraction is carried by SIFT and ASIFT algorithm. Key points are matched to recognize fake logo.

Chapter 10

Detecting and Tracking Segmentation of Moving Objects Using Graph Cut Algorithm 177

Raviraj Pandian, GSSS Institute of Engineering and Technology for Women, India
Ramya A., KalaignarKarunanidhi Institute of Technology, India

Real-time moving object detection, classification, and tracking capabilities are presented with system operates on both color and gray-scale video imagery from a stationary camera. It can handle object detection in indoor and outdoor environments and under changing illumination conditions. Object detection in a video is usually performed by object detectors or background subtraction techniques. The proposed method determines the threshold automatically and dynamically depending on the intensities of the pixels in the current frame. In this method, it updates the background model with learning rate depending on the differences of the pixels in the background model of the previous frame. The graph cut segmentation-based region merging algorithm approaches achieve both segmentation and optical flow computation accurately and they can work in the presence of large camera motion. The algorithm makes use of the shape of the detected objects and temporal tracking results to successfully categorize objects into pre-defined classes like human, human group, and vehicle.

Alzheimer's is the most common form of dementia in India and it is one of the leading causes of death in the world. Currently it is diagnosed by calculating the MSME score and by manual study of MRI scan. In this chapter, the authors develop and compare different methods to diagnose and predict Alzheimer's disease by processing structural magnetic resonance image scans (MRI scans) with deep learning neural networks. The authors implement one model of deep-learning networks which are convolution neural network (CNN). They use four different architectures of CNN, namely Lenet-5, AlexNet, ZFNet, and R-CNN architecture. The best accuracies for 75-25 cross validation and 90-10 cross validation are 97.68% and 98.75%, respectively, and achieved by ZFNet architecture of convolution neural network. This research will help in further studies on improving the accuracy of Alzheimer's diagnosis and prediction using neural networks.

Humans make object recognition look inconsequential. In this chapter, scale-invariant feature extraction and shape-index depiction are used on a range of images for identifying objects. The shape-index is attained and used as a local descriptor or key-point descriptor. First surface properties for shape index identification and second as 2D scale invariant feature transformed for key-point detection and feature extraction. The object recognition classification is compared results with shape-index identification and 2D scale-invariant feature transform for key-point detection with SIFT and SURF. The authors are using images from the ImageNet dataset, and with use of shift-index + SIFT descriptors, they are finding better accuracy at the classification stage.

Chapter 13

This chapter explores the prevailing segmentation methods to extract the target object features, in the field of plant pathology for disease diagnosis. The digital images of different plant leaves are taken for analysis as most of the disease symptoms are visible on leaves apart from other vital parts. Among the different phases of processing a digital image, the substantive focus of the study concentrates mainly on the methodology or algorithms deployed on image acquisition, preprocessing, segmentation, and feature extraction. The chapter collects the existing literature survey related to disease diagnosis methods in agricultural plants and prominently highlights the performance of each algorithm by comparing with its counterparts. The main aim is to provide an insight of creativeness to the researchers and experts to develop a less expensive, accurate, fast and an instant system for the timely detection of plant disease, so that appropriate remedial measures can be taken.

Preface

Image data has portrayed immense potential as a resourceful foundation of information in current context for numerous applications including biomedicine, military, commerce, education, and Web image classification and searching. It has been considered as an important part of Big Data. Mass affinity to converse using images and graphics has been observed. Recently, broad applications of image identification have been recognized for autonomous vehicles. Hence, the domain is considered to be contemporary as well as of interest to the funding agencies for developing advanced applications in robotics and artificial intelligence in future. Researchers from assorted domain have shown consistent urge to explore the rich contents in image data and to design new techniques to exploit the usefulness of the images. Numerous methods for feature extraction from image data have been proposed by the scholars to facilitate timely identification of image data which can combat a terminal disease or a natural calamity. It is an essential component for achieving the sustainable development goals for our future generation and to make the earth a better place to live.

The book is going to be based on contemporary trends and techniques in content based image recognition. The domain of research has been contemporary to recent trends in multimedia computing that have witnessed a surge in rapid growth in digital image collections. The publication will be about managing, archiving, maintaining and extracting information from these huge repositories. Two specific drawbacks have been observed in contemporary literatures regarding the dimension of feature vectors extracted from the images which in turn increase the time for convergence of classification and/or retrieval results. The aforesaid scenario can be threatening in real time. Late identification may result in delayed decision making for treatment of a terminal disease or to take remedial action against catastrophe. Therefore, the extracted features must be reduced in dimension to minimize time consumption for recognition of image data. Reduced feature size facilitates fusion of multiple features which allow rich exploration of image data. This also increases the classification rate which in turn enhances accuracy. On the other hand, smaller feature dimension decrease time consumption. Thus, the publication will propose innovative solutions to all the above-mentioned problems and will offer new research directions. The publication will cover segmentation techniques for feature reduction, clustering techniques for feature reduction, early fusion of extracted features, late fusion of classification decision, supervised learning and unsupervised learning techniques.

The book would come to the benefits of several categories of students and researchers. At the students' level, this book can serve as a treatise/reference book for the special papers at the masters level aimed at inspiring possibly future researchers. Newly inducted PhD aspirants would also find the contents of this book useful as far as their compulsory course works are concerned.

At the researchers' level, those interested in interdisciplinary research would also be benefited from the book. After all, the enriched interdisciplinary contents of the book would always be a subject of interest to the faculties, existing research communities and new research aspirants from diverse disciplines of the concerned departments of premier institutes across the globe. This is expected to bring different research backgrounds (due to its cross platform characteristics) close to one another to form effective research groups all over the world. Above all, availability of the book should be ensured to as much universities and research institutes as possible through whatever graceful means it may be.

The book comprises thirteen well versed chapters. Chapter 1 presents two different techniques of feature extraction from images based on image binarization and morphological operators. The multi technique extraction with radically reduced feature size was imperative to explore the rich set of feature content in an image. The objective of this work has been to create a fusion framework for image recognition by means of late fusion with data standardization. The work has implemented a hybrid framework for query classification as a precursor for image retrieval which has been so far the first of its kind.

Chapter 2 presents a feature extraction technique based on application of image transform. The method has extracted meaningful features and facilitated feature dimension reduction. A technique, known as fractional coefficient of transforms is adopted to facilitate feature dimension reduction. Two different color spaces, namely RGB and YUV are considered to compare the classification metrics to figure out the best possible reduced feature dimension. Further, the results are compared to state-of-the-art techniques which have revealed improved performance for the proposed feature extraction technique.

Content based image retrieval aims to acquire images from huge databases by analyzing their visual features like color, texture, shape and spatial relationship. The search for superior accuracy in image retrieval has resulted in concentrating more on semantic gap reduction between the low level features and high level human reasoning. Fuzzy theory is a prevailing methodology which helps in attaining this goal by using attributes and interpretations similar to human reasoning. The vagueness and impreciseness in image data and the retrieval process can be modeled by fuzzy sets. In Chapter 3, the authors analyze fuzzy theoretic approaches in various stages of content based image retrieval system. Various fuzzy based feature descriptors are discussed along with different fuzzy classification and indexing algorithms for content based image retrieval. This chapter also presents an overview of various fuzzy distance and similarity measures for image retrieval. A novel fuzzy theoretic retrieval for finger vein biometric images is also proposed in this chapter with experiment and analysis.

This is the age of Big data where aggregating information is simple and keeping it economical. Tragically, as the measure of machine intelligible data builds, the capacity to comprehend and make utilization of it doesn't keep pace with its development. In content-based image retrieval (CBIR) applications, every database needs its comparing parameter setting for feature extraction. CBIR is the application of computer vision techniques to the image retrieval problem that is the problem of searching for digital images in large databases. In any case, the vast majority of the CBIR frameworks perform ordering by an arrangement of settled and pre-particular parameters. All the major machine learning based search algorithm has discussed in Chapter 4 for better understanding related with the image retrieval accuracy. The efficiency of FS using machine learning compared with some other search algorithms and observed for the improvement of the CBIR system.

Attribute Reduction and Feature selection is the main issue in Rough set. Researchers have focused on several attribute reduction using Rough set. However the methods found are time consuming for large data set since the key lies in reducing the attributes and selecting the relevant features. The main aim is to reduce the dimensionality of huge amount of data to get the smaller subset which can provide the useful information. Feature Selection approach reduces the dimensionality of feature space and improves the overall performance. The challenge in feature selection is to deal with high dimensional. To overcome the issues and challenges, Chapter 5 describes a feature selection based on the proposed neighborhood positive approximation approach and attributes reduction for data sets. This proposed system implements for attribute reduction and finds the relevant features. Evaluation shows that the proposed Neighborhood Positive Approximation Algorithm is effective and feasible for large data sets and also reduces the feature space.

Nowadays image retrieval is gaining significant attention in the area such as surveillance, access control etc. The content-based feature extraction plays a very crucial role in image retrieval. For the characterization of a specific image, mainly three features i. e. color, texture and shape are used. Multimedia can store text, image, audio and video which can be processed and retrieved. The various techniques are used for image retrieval such as textual annotations, Content Based Image Retrieval in many application areas like medical imaging, satellite imaging etc. However most of these techniques were designed for specific domains and universally accepted method is yet to be designed hence CBIR is a field of active research. Similar output images indicate efficiency of search and retrieval process. In Chapter 6, the authors have discussed various image feature extraction techniques and clustering approaches for content based feature extraction from image and specifically focused on color based CBIR techniques.

In Chapter 7, an initiative is proposed where Natural Language Processing techniques and supervised machine learning algorithms have been combined to detect external plagiarism. The major emphasis is on to construct a framework to detect plagiarism from monolingual texts by implementing n-gram frequency comparison approach. The framework is based on 120 characteristics which have been extracted during pre-processing steps using simple NLP approach. Afterward, filter metrics has been applied to select most relevant features and supervised classification learning algorithm has been used later to classify the documents in four levels of plagiarism. Then, confusion matrix was built to estimate the false positives and false negatives. Finally, we have shown C4.5 decision tree based classifier's suitability on calculating accuracy over Naive Bayes. The framework achieved 89% accuracy with low false positive and false negative rate and it shows higher precision and recall value comparing to Passage Similarities method, Sentence Similarity method, and Search Space Reduction method.

One of the most widely used steps in the process of reducing images to information is segmentation: which divides the image into regions that hopefully correspond to structural units in the scene or distinguish objects of interest. Segmentation is often described by analogy to visual processes as a foreground/background separation, implying that the selection procedure concentrates on a single kind of feature and discards the rest. Machine-printed or hand-drawn scripts can have various font types or writing styles. The writing styles can be roughly categorized into discrete style (handprint or boxed style), continuous style (cursive style), and mixed style. Chapter 8 shows that the ambiguity of character segmentation has three major sources: (1) Variability of character size and inter character space; (2) Confusion between inter character and within-character space, and; (3) Touching between characters.

Logos are graphic productions that recall some real-world objects or emphasize a name, simply display some abstract signs that have strong perceptual appeal. Color may have some relevance to assess the logo identity. Different logos may have a similar layout with slightly different spatial disposition of the graphic elements, localized differences in the orientation, size and shape, or differ by the presence/absence of one or few traits. In Chapter 9, the authors use ensemble based frame work as it choose the best combination of preprocessing methods and candidate extractors. The proposed system has reference logos and test logos which are verified depending on some features like regions, pre-processing, key points. These features are extracted by using gray scale image by scale-invariant feature transform (SIFT) and Affine-SIFT (ASIFT) descriptor method. Pre-processing phase employs four different filters. Key points extraction is carried by SIFT and ASIFT algorithm. Key points are matched to recognize fake logo.

Real-time moving object detection, classification and tracking capabilities are presented in Chapter 10 with its system operating on both color and gray scale video imagery from a stationary camera. It can handle object detection in indoor and outdoor environments and under changing illumination conditions. Object detection in a video is usually performed by object detectors or background subtraction techniques. The proposed method determines the threshold automatically and dynamically depending on the intensities of the pixels in the current frame. In this method, it updates the background model with learning rate depending on the differences of the pixels in the background model of the previous frame. The graph cut segmentation based region merging algorithm approaches achieve both segmentation and optical flow computation accurately and they can work in the presence of large camera motion. The algorithm makes use of the shape of the detected objects and temporal tracking results to successfully categorize objects into pre-defined classes like human, human group and vehicle.

Alzheimer's is the most common form of dementia in India and it is one of the leading cause of death in the world. Currently it is diagnosed by calculating the MSME score and by manual study of MRI Scan. In Chapter 11, the authors develop and compare different methods to diagnose and predict Alzheimer's disease by processing structural Magnetic Resonance Image Scans (MRI Scans) with deep learning neural networks. We implement one model of deep learning networks which are Convolution Neural Network (CNN). We use four different architectures of CNN namely Lenet-5, AlexNet, ZFNet and R-CNN Architecture. The best accuracies for 75-25 cross validation and 90-10 cross validation are 97.68% and 98.75% respectively and is achieved by ZFNet architecture of convolution neural network. This research will help in further studies on improving the accuracy of Alzheimer's diagnosis and prediction using neural networks.

Humans make object recognition look inconsequential. In Chapter 12, scale-invariant feature extraction and shape-index depiction are used of range images for identifying objects. The shape-index is attained and used as a local descriptor or key-point descriptor. First surface properties for shape index identification and second as 2D scale invariant feature transformed for key-point detection and feature extraction. The object recognition classification is compared results with shape-index identification and 2D scale-invariant feature transform for key-point detection with SIFT and SURF. We are using images from the ImageNet dataset and with use of shift-index + SIFT descriptors, we are finding the better accuracy at classification stage.

Chapter 13 explores the prevailing segmentation methods to extract the target object features, in the field of plant pathology for disease diagnosis. The digital images of different plant leaves are taken for analysis as most of the disease symptoms are visible on leaves apart from other vital parts. Among the different phases of processing a digital image, the substantive focus of the study concentrates mainly on the methodology or algorithms deployed on image Acquisition, Preprocessing, Segmentation and Feature Extraction. The chapter collects the existing literature survey related to disease diagnosis methods in agricultural plants and prominently highlights the performance of each algorithm by comparing with its counterparts. The main aim is to provide an insight of creativeness to the researchers and experts to develop a less expensive, accurate, fast and an instant system for the timely detection of plant disease, so that appropriate remedial measures can be taken.

The objective of the book is to bring a broad spectrum of artificial intelligence and its applications under the purview of 3D image processing so that it is able to trigger further inspiration among various research communities to contribute in their respective fields of applications thereby orienting these application fields towards 3D image processing and analysis. Once the purpose, as stated above, is achieved a larger number of research communities may be brought under one umbrella to ventilate their ideas in a more structured manner. In that case, the present endeavor may be seen as the beginning of such an effort in bringing various research applications in the complementary fields of 3D image processing and analysis close to one another.

Rik Das
Xavier Institute of Social Service, India

Sourav De
Cooch Behar Government Engineering College, India

Siddhartha Bhattacharyya
RCC Institute of Information Technology, India

February 2018

Chapter 1
An Integrated Framework for Information Identification With Image Data Using Multi-Technique Feature Extraction

Rik Das
Xavier Institute of Social Service, India

S. N. Singh
Xavier Institute of Social Service, India

Mahua Banerjee
Xavier Institute of Social Service, India

Shishir Mayank
Xavier Institute of Social Service, India

T. Venkata Shashank
Xavier Institute of Social Service, India

ABSTRACT

Image data has portrayed immense potential as a resourceful foundation of information in current context for numerous applications including biomedicine, military, commerce, education, and web image classification and searching. The scenario has kindled the requirement for efficient content-based image identification from the archived image databases in varied industrial and educational sectors. Feature extraction has acted as the backbone to govern the success rate of content-based information identification with image data. The chapter has presented two different techniques of feature extraction from images based on image binarization and morphological operators. The multi-technique extraction with radically reduced feature size was imperative to explore the rich set of feature content in an image. The objective of this work has been to create a fusion framework for image recognition by means of late fusion with data standardization. The work has implemented a hybrid framework for query classification as a precursor for image retrieval which has been so far the first of its kind.

DOI: 10.4018/978-1-5225-5775-3.ch001

INTRODUCTION

Information identification has been guided by a fresh perspective with the intensification of digital era. The popularity and growth of image capturing devices have prioritized images as a familiar media of communication for the mass (Korytkowski, Rutkowski, & Scherer, 2016). The image datasets have been archived and maintained as rich sources of valuable information (Ahmadian, & Mostafa, 2003). Traditional means of information identification with images have been based on text-based recognition system. The process used to map images with text-based annotations. However, text or keywords based mapping of images has insufficient information about image contents and is based on the perception of the individual performing the job of annotation (Walia, Goyal, & Brar, 2014). These are major drawbacks for recognition of information with images and to escalate the success rate.

The discovery of a object of interest or locating the region of interest in a picture or an arrangement of pictures, which has applications in confront acknowledgment and in addition to video conferencing frameworks, is a testing assignment and has been considered by numerous researchers (Das, & Walia, 2017). Once the test picture is removed from the scene, its gray level and size are standardized before putting away or testing. In a few applications, for example, distinguishing proof of international ID pictures or drivers' licenses, conditions of picture obtaining are typically so controlled that a portion of the pre-processing stages may not be essential.

Firmly attached to the assignment of feature extraction is the intelligent and sensible meaning of closeness amongst test and known examples. The undertaking of finding a pertinent distance measure in the chosen highlighted space, and consequently and adequately using the embedded information to distinguish test objects precisely is one of the principle challenges in image identification. The process of content based image identification has evolved as an efficient alternative for the above mentioned limitations. The success of the aforesaid methodology has been dependent on designing efficient feature extraction techniques. Content based system operates with the combination of diverse low level and high level features namely, color, shape and texture (Zhu, & Shyu, 2015). The authors felt that image has diverse set of features which can hardly be described with a single feature extraction technique. Therefore, two different techniques of feature extraction have been proposed based on feature extraction with image binarization and feature extraction with morphological operator respectively. Binarization of images has been considered as an efficient means for feature extraction from images. Shape feature has also been well understood for content-based identification as human perception has been based on shape of an object. The main contribution of the paper has been to carry out content-based image identification with a hybrid framework by fusion of two different feature extraction techniques with reduced feature vector size. The dimension of the feature vectors are made independent of the image size. The classification results with the individual techniques are fused by means of Z score normalization to obtain higher recognition rate. Further, a retrieval system is designed with classified query for content based image retrieval. Even though, the contemporary literatures have enlisted different techniques of feature extraction based on image content, but the feature dimension has remained a major cause of concern (Dawn, & Shaikh, 2016; Iosifidis, Tefas, & Pitas, 2013). The bulky signatures extracted from images have resulted in slow convergence for classification and retrieval results. On the other hand, content-based image identification with single set of feature vectors is unable to produce satisfactory outcomes in several occasions. The authors have addressed both the above-mentioned limitations and have proposed a fused architecture for the recognition process with multi feature extraction techniques. Although, the work bears some technical similitude with prior approaches, as they have extracted features based on binarization and morphological operators. But, we have taken a step further by drastically reducing the feature vector size and making it independent of the image dimensions. Even though, fusion of multi techniques has been implemented earlier for retrieval purpose, but, to the best of our knowledge, designing a fusion framework with multiple features for query classification as a precursor of retrieval has not been accomplished before. Moreover, the claimed superiority for recognition results over the existing techniques has hardly shown any statistical significance in the previous works. Hence, one can hardly comprehend that whether the increase in results has happened as a matter of chance. We have validated the statistical significance of our research findings to show the robustness of our proposed methodologies in information identification with image data. The classification and retrieval results have shown an improvement of 27% and 20.44% in Precision values, respectively, over state-of-the art techniques. The experiments are carried out with two well-known public datasets namely Wang dataset and Oliva and Torralba (OT-Scene) dataset.

The organization of the paper is as follows. Section II has reviewed the Related Work. Our Approach has been discussed in Section III. Experimental Setup is elaborated in Section IV, followed by Results and Discussions in Section V. Conclusion is given in Section VI.

BACKGROUND

This work has developed fusion based architecture for content-based image classification and retrieval with two different techniques of feature extraction based on image binarization and morphological operators. Hence, it is in correlation with research on binarization based feature extraction and morphology-based feature extraction from images. It is also in connection with research on multi technique fusion for content-based image identification. Hence, the following subsections have reviewed some contemporary and earlier works on these three topics.

Image Binarization Techniques for Feature Extraction

Feature extraction from images has been largely carried out by means of image binarization. Appropriate threshold selection has been imperative for execution of efficient image binarization. Nevertheless, various factors including uneven illumination, inadequate contrast etc. can have adverse effect on threshold computation (Valizadeh, Armanfard, Komeili, & Kabir, 2009). Contemporary literatures on image binarization techniques have categorized three different techniques for threshold selection namely, mean threshold selection, local threshold selection and global threshold selection to deal with the unfavorable influences on threshold selection. Enhanced classification results have been comprehended by feature extraction from mean threshold and multilevel mean threshold based binarized images (Kekre, Thepade, Das, & Ghosh, 2013; Thepade, Das, & Ghosh, 2013). Eventually, it is identified that selection of mean threshold has not dealt with the standard deviation of the gray values and has concentrated only on the average which has prevented the feature extraction techniques to take advantage of the spread of data to distinguish distinct features. Therefore, image signature extraction is carried out with local threshold selection and global threshold selection for binarization, as the techniques are based on calculation of both mean and standard deviation of the gray values (Liu, 2013; Yanli, & Zhenxing, 2012; Ramirez-Ortegon, & Rojas, 2010; Otsu, 1979; Shaikh, Maiti, & Chaki, 2013).

Use of Morphological Operators for Feature Extraction

Commercial viability of shape feature extraction has been well highlighted by systems like Image Content (Thepade, Das, & Ghosh, 2014), PicToSeek (Flickner, Sawhney, Niblack, Ashley, Huang, Dom, & Steele, 1995).Two different categorization of shape descriptors namely, contour-based and region-based descriptors have been elaborated in the existing literatures (Gevers, & Smeulders, 2000; Mehtre, Kankanhalli, & Lee, 1997). Emphasize of the contour-based descriptors has been on boundary lines. Popular contour-based descriptors have embraced Fourier descriptor (Zhang, & Lu, 2004), curvature-scale space (Zhang, & Lu, 2003), and chain codes (Mokhtarian, & Mackworth, 1992). Feature extraction from complex shapes has been well carried out by means of region-based descriptors, since the feature extraction has been performed from whole area of object (Dubois, & Glanz, 1986).

Fusion Methodologies and Multi Technique Feature Extraction

Information recognition with image data has utilized the features extracted by means of diverse extraction techniques to harmonize each other for enhanced identification rate. Recent studies in information fusion have categorized the methodologies typically into four classes, namely, early fusion, late fusion, hybrid fusion and intermediate fusion. Early fusion combines the features of different techniques and produces it as a single input to the learner. The process inherently increases the size of feature vector as the concentrated features easily correspond to higher dimensions. Late fusion applies separate learner to each feature extraction technique and fuses the decision with a combiner. Although it offers scalability in comparison to early fusion, still, it cannot explore the feature level correlations, since it has to make local decisions primarily. Hybrid fusion makes a mix of the two above mentioned techniques. Intermediate fusion integrates multiple features by considering a joint model for decision to yield superior prediction accuracy. Color and texture features are extracted by means of 3 D color histogram and Gabor filters for fusion based image identification. The space complexity of the feature is further reduced by using genetic algorithm which has also obtained the optimum boundaries of numerical intervals (Kim, & Kim, 2000). Local descriptors based on color and texture is calculated from Color moments and moments on Gabor filter responses. Gradient vector flow fields are calculated to capture shape information in terms of edge images. The shape features are finally depicted by invariant moments. The retrieval decisions with the features are fused for enhanced retrieval performance (ElAlami, 2011). Feature vectors comprising of color histogram and texture features based on a co-occurrence matrix are extracted from HSV color space to facilitate image retrieval (Hiremath, & Pujari, 2007). Visually significant point features chosen from images by means of fuzzy set theoretic approach. Computation of some invariant color features from these points is performed to gauge the similarity between images (Yue, Li, Liu, & Fu, 2011). Recognition process is boosted up by combining color layout descriptor and Gabor texture descriptor as image signatures (Banerjee, Kundu, & Maji, 2009). Multi view features comprising of color, texture and spatial structure descriptors have contributed for increased retrieval rate (Jalab, 2011). Wavelet packets and Eigen values of Gabor filters are extracted as feature vectors by the authors in (Shen, & Wu, 2013) for neural network architecture of image identification. Higher retrieval results have been apprehended with intra-class and inter-class feature extraction from images (Irtaza, Jaffar, Aleisa, & Choi, 2014). In (Rahimi, & Moghaddam, 2015), extraction of color and texture features through color co-occurrence matrix (CCM) and difference between pixels of scan pattern (DBPSP) has been demonstrated and an artificial neural network (ANN) based classifier is designed. In (ElAlami, 2014), content-based image retrieval is carried out by integrating the modified color motif co-occurrence matrix (MCMCM) and difference between the pixels of a scan pattern (DBPSP) features withequal weights. Fusion of retrieval results obtained by capturing colour, shape and texture withthe color moment (CMs), angular radial transform descriptor and edge histogram descriptor (EHD) features respectively had outclassed the Precision values of individual techniques (Subrahmanyam, Maheshwari, & Balasubramanian, 2013). Color histogram and spatial orientation tree has been used for unique feature extraction from images for retrieval purpose (Walia, Vesal, & Pal, 2014). A recent technique has implemented early fusion of extracted feature vectors.

Techniques discussed in the contemporary literatures have yielded hefty feature vectors which have resulted in sluggish image identification process. The authors have addressed the limitation and have proposed techniques to extract feature vectors with considerably smaller dimension which is independent image size. Late fusion architecture of content-based image identification with the novel feature extraction techniques has revealed superior performance compared to existing techniques and has exhibited statistical significance of improvement (Subrahmanyam, Maheshwari, & Balasubramanian, 2012).

PROPOSED APPROACH

Feature extraction is carried out with two different techniques namely, image binarization with local threshold selection by Feng's method and morphological operator for shape feature extraction. The multi technique feature extraction process is carried out to explore the rich feature set of the image data for superior classification and retrieval results by implanting fusion framework. Each of the techniques for feature extraction has been enlisted in the following subsections along with the architecture for fusion.

Feature Extraction by Image Binarization

A given image is separated into three color components namely Red (R), Green (G) and Blue (B) respectively. Binarization of each color component is carried by means of Feng's local threshold selection technique (Yıldız, Aslan, & Alpaydın, 2011). The binarization decision is formulated in terms of image contrast. Initially, the technique has shifted a primary local window to compute the local mean (m), minimum grey level (M) and the standard deviation (s). The value of M is calculated by considering the value of minimum grey level. The effect of illumination is compensated by computing the dynamic of standard deviation (Rs) for a larger local window named as the secondary local window as shown in Figure 1. The appropriate size of the local window has been governed by the variation of illumination and the set up of the image capturing equipment. The window is shifted left to right and top to bottom across the entire image for threshold selection. The threshold value is calculated as in Equation 1.

$$T = (1 - \alpha_1) \cdot m + \alpha_2 \cdot \left(\frac{s}{R_s}\right) \cdot (m - M) + \alpha_3 \cdot M \qquad (1)$$

where

Figure 1. Process of local threshold selection with Feng's Method

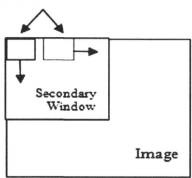

$$\alpha_2 = k_1 \cdot \left(\frac{s}{R_s} \right)^{\gamma}$$

and

$$\alpha_3 = k_2 \cdot \left(\frac{s}{R_s} \right)^{\gamma}$$

where, α_1, γ, k_1, and k_2 are positive constants.

The equation has three corresponding coefficients α_1, α_2 and α_3 for three elements to allow more flexible and versatile control on the weight of different equation elements. Formulation of α_2 and α_3 have been carried out adaptively based on normalized local standard deviation (s/Rs) as it is assumed that windows having the foreground image has larger standard deviation compared to the background. Hence inclusion of (s/Rs) ratio in coefficients α_2 and α_3 has permitted the computed threshold to separate the foreground and the background image efficiently without much subsequent knowledge of the input image.

The effect of binarization applying Feng's local threshold selection has been shown in Figure 2.

The Table in the figure is the sample of the feature values extracted from the images in the test dataset. The gray values are compared to the corresponding threshold values and two clusters are formed comprising of gray values higher than the corresponding local threshold and gray values lower than the corresponding local threshold. The values of μ_{hi} and μ_{lo} are calculated by computing the means of the cluster higher than the local threshold and lower than the local threshold respectively. The mean and standard deviation of each cluster is computed to derive two feature vectors x_{hi} and x_{lo} for each color component as shown in Equations 2 and 3, where x stands for Red (R), Green (G) and Blue (B) components.

$$x_{hiF.V.} = \left(\left(\frac{1}{(m*n)} \right)* \right) \left(\sum_{i=1}^{m} \sum_{j=1}^{n} x_{hi}(i,j) \right) + \left(\sqrt{\frac{1}{(m*n)} \sum_{i=1}^{m} \sum_{j=1}^{n} \left(x_{hi}(i,j) - \mu_{hi} \right)^2} \right) \right) \tag{2}$$

Figure 2. Process of feature extraction with binarization

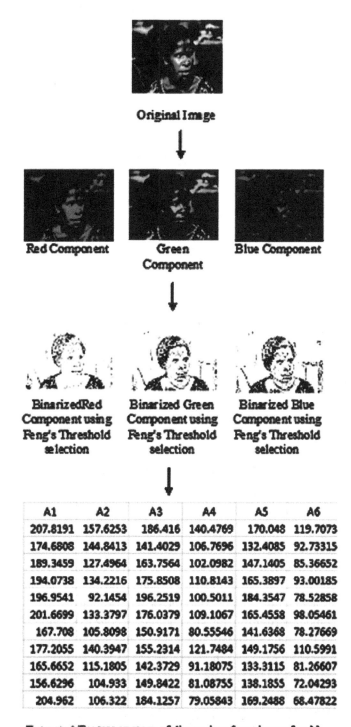

A1	A2	A3	A4	A5	A6
207.8191	157.6253	186.416	140.4769	170.048	119.7073
174.6808	144.8413	141.4029	106.7696	132.4085	92.73315
189.3459	127.4964	163.7564	102.0982	147.1405	85.36652
194.0738	134.2216	175.8508	110.8143	165.3897	93.00185
196.9541	92.1454	196.2519	100.5011	184.3547	78.52858
201.6699	133.3797	176.0379	109.1067	165.4558	98.05461
167.708	105.8098	150.9171	80.55546	141.6368	78.27669
177.2055	140.3947	155.2314	121.7484	149.1756	110.5991
165.6652	115.1805	142.3729	91.18075	133.3115	81.26607
156.6296	104.933	149.8422	81.08755	138.1855	72.04293
204.962	106.322	184.1257	79.05843	169.2488	68.47822

Extracted Feature vectors of dimension 6 per image for 11 images

$$x_{loF.V.} = \left(\left(\frac{1}{(m*n)} \right) * \sum_{i=1}^{m} \sum_{j=1}^{n} x_{lo}(i,j) \right) + \left(\sqrt{ \frac{1}{(m*n)} \sum_{i=1}^{m} \sum_{j=1}^{n} \left(x_{lo}(i,j) - \mu_{lo} \right)^2 } \right) \qquad (3)$$

where,

$$\mu = \left(\frac{1}{(m*n)} * \sum_{i=1}^{m} \sum_{j=1}^{n} x(i,j) \right)$$

and

$$\sigma = \left(\sqrt{ \frac{1}{(m*n)} \sum_{i=1}^{m} \sum_{j=1}^{n} \left(x(i,j) - \mu \right)^2 } \right)$$

μ = mean

σ = standard deviation

x = R, G and B for individual components, T_x = threshold value for each pixel

Therefore, each color component comprised of two feature vectors which sums up to 6 feature vectors for three color components per image.

Feature Extraction by Morphological Operator

Object based information identification has remarkably utilized the shape feature for extraction of meaningful signatures from the image data. The contour of the region of interest within an image can be well referred by shape. A vital genre of morphological transform has been represented by the hat-transforms. For a 1-D structuring element K if a signal f is assumed, then the maximum signal value over a circular neighbor-hood of a given radius can be calculated by dilation, whereas, the minimum signal value can be computed by erosion.

An important morphological transform called opening is represented by erosion followed by dilation. Dilation followed by an erosion is named as closing, which is the dual of opening. Top hat transform is defined as the residual of the opening compared to the original signal.

The authors have implemented Bottom-Hat Morphological edge extraction (BHMEE) (Feng, & Tan, 2004). The area of interest for feature extraction in each of the Red, Green and Blue color component of the images has been located by means of the technique as in Figure 3.

Two different clusters are formed by grouping gray values of the contour region and the background portion of individual color components of the image. The mean and standard deviation for the two clusters are derived for computing the feature vectors of the images as in Equations 2 and 3. The feature vector size is 6 for each image with 2 feature vectors for each color component.

Figure 3. Process of feature extraction with Bottom-Hat Operator

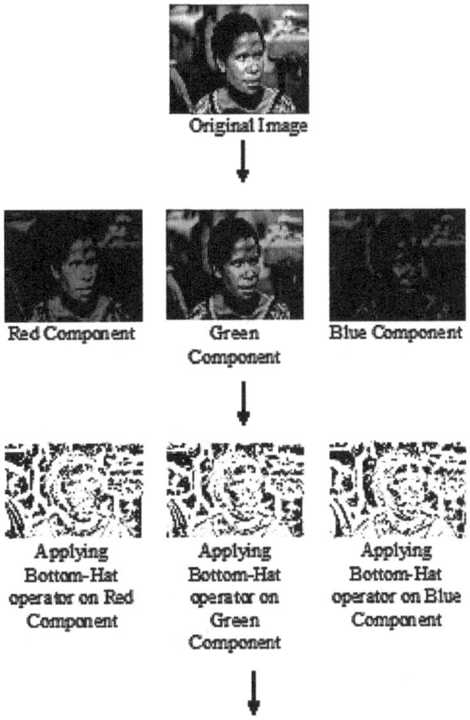

A1	A2	A3	A4	A5	A6
194.199	265.2042	197.9297	254.3438	198.5614	249.8848
165.8493	185.8176	164.5048	186.4736	164.7283	187.8101
173.8784	195.872	173.3776	199.7014	173.2536	202.2475
191.0568	186.4965	190.2741	193.6895	189.7467	199.3988
164.9518	212.1557	165.6821	201.9095	164.7116	210.2983
188.1826	206.1521	188.3149	211.9614	187.8604	217.8292
141.5851	186.1117	142.3193	199.7941	141.1129	205.074
158.6744	217.6613	159.4312	227.6686	159.7629	227.935
151.6588	206.0519	153.2293	223.35	152.7841	223.6446
144.7347	176.2047	146.4593	172.4763	145.4499	177.2157
193.553	210.5932	192.7885	216.7935	191.1233	220.8147

Extracted Feature vectors of dimension 6 per image for 11 images

Framework for Classification

At the outset, classification is carried out with individual feature extraction techniques separately to measure the performance of each technique independently. Two different distance measures namely, mean squared error (*MSE*) measure and city block distance measure are used for two different techniques of feature extraction. The working formulae for two distance measures have been given in Equations 4 and 5 respectively.

$$D_{MSE} = \frac{1}{mn} \sum_{i=1}^{n} (Q_i - D_i)^2 \qquad (4)$$

$$D_{cityblock} = \sum_{i-1}^{n} \left| Q_i - D_i \right|$$ (5)

where, Q_i is the query image and D_i is the database image. Further, the classification decisions inferred from each of the techniques are normalized with Z score normalization as in Equation 6.

$$dist_n = \frac{dist_i - \mu}{\sigma}$$ (6)

where, μ is the mean and σ is the standard deviation.

The weighted sums of the normalized distances are added to calculate the final distance measure as in Equation 7.

$$dist = w_1 d_n^{binarization} + w_2 d_n^{morphological}$$ (7)

The weights are calculated from individual average Precision rates of each of the proposed techniques. The normalization process has been implemented to avoid dependence of the classification decision on a feature vector with higher values of attributes which have the possibilities to have greater effect or "weight." The process has normalized the data within a common range such as [-1, 1] or [0.0, 1.0].

Framework for Retrieval

Two different retrieval techniques have been designed and compared for retrieval results. The first one has fused the retrieval results of individual techniques with Z score normalization for a generic query and has retrieved the top 20 matches from the dataset. The second technique has classified the query by fusion of classification decisions of two different feature extraction techniques, before forwarding it for retrieval purpose. The classified query has been put forward to retrieve the top 20 matches only from the class of interest. In contrast to the conventional process, it has restricted the query only to the classified category to look for desired results and has limited the search space.

The process of classification and retrieval has been illustrated in Figure 4.

PROPOSED APPROACH

Two widely used public datasets are used for the experimental purpose, namely Wang Dataset (10 categories, 1000 images) and Oliva and Torralba (OT-Scene) dataset (8 categories, 2688 images).

Datasets

Wang Dataset

It is a widely used public dataset provided by Wang et al. (Jalba, Wilkinson, & Roerdink, 2004). It has 10 different categories of 1000 images. Every image is of dimension 256x384 or 384x256 and each

Figure 4. Classification and retrieval with fusion framework

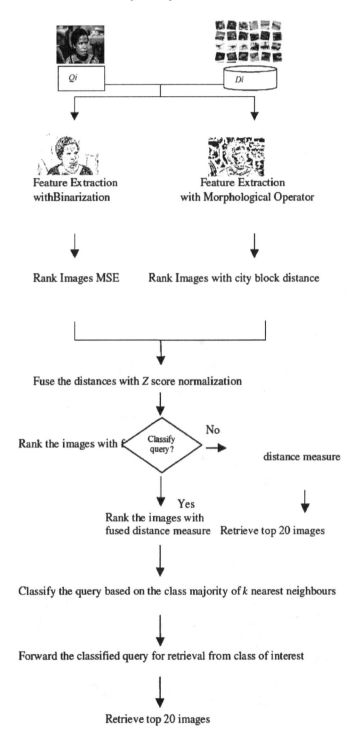

category comprises of 100 images. The different classes in this dataset are Tribals, Sea Beaches, Gothic Structures, Buses, Dinosaur, Elephants, Flowers, Horses, Mountains and Food. A sample collage for Wang's dataset has been given in Figure 5.

Oliva and Torralba (OT-Scene) Dataset

This dataset comprises of 2688 images and is divided into eight different categories (Li, & Wang, 2003). The dataset is provided by MIT. The different categories in the dataset are Coast and Beach (with 360 images), Open Country (with 328 images), Forest (with 260 images), Mountain (with 308 images), Highway (with 324 images), Street (with 410 images), City Centre (with 292 images) and Tall Building (with 306 images). A sample collage for OT Scene dataset is given in Figure 6.

Evaluation of classification performances are carried out primarily by means of k-fold cross validation (Walia, & Pal, 2014; Thepade, Das, & Ghosh, 2015). Two different distance measures are utilized for matching the image contents, namely, mean squared error measure and city block distance. A value

Figure 5. Sample collage for Wang dataset

Figure 6. Sample collage for Oliva and Torralba (OT-Scene) dataset

of 10 has been assigned as an integer value to k. In this process the, entire dataset is divided into 10 subsets. 1 subset is considered as the testing set and the rest 9 subsets are considered to be training set. The method is repeated for 10 trials and the performance of the classifier is evaluated by combining the 10 results thus obtained after evaluating the 10 folds. The value 10 is chosen randomly as the number of subdivisions and has been generally preferred in other literatures also for carrying out the task of cross validation. The repeated random sub sampling property of the technique has used all the images in the datasets for both training and validation purposes. Henceforth, fusion based architecture is implemented for boosting up the classification results. Precision, Recall, F1 Score and Misclassification Rate (MR) are considered to measure the classification performances. The retrieval performance is measured by mean of Precision and Recall values for different techniques of feature extraction. The metrics have followed the standard definitions and the working formulae for each of the metrics have been given in Equations 8, 9, 10 and 11:

$$Precision = \frac{Total\ Number\ of\ Relevant\ Images\ Identified}{Total\ Number\ of\ identified\ Images} \tag{8}$$

$$Recall = \frac{Total\ Number\ of\ Relevant\ Images\ Identified}{Total\ Number\ of\ Images\ in\ the\ Relevant\ Class} \tag{9}$$

$$F1score = \frac{2 * Precision * Recall}{Precision + Recall} \tag{10}$$

$$MR = \frac{FP + FN}{TP + TN + FP + FN} \tag{11}$$

True Positive (TP) = Number of instances classified correctly.
True Negative (TN) = Number of negative results created for negative instances
False Positive (FP) = Number of erroneous results as positive results for negative instances
False Negative (FN) = Number of erroneous results asnegative results for positive instances

RESULTS AND DISCUSSIONS

The experimental setup is comprised of Matlab 7.11.0(R2010b) on Intel core i5 processor with 4 GB RAM.

To begin with, evaluation of classification performances is carried out for the two different datasets, namely, Wang dataset and OT-Scene dataset for binarization based feature extraction technique and morphological feature extraction technique. The classification results are calculated for 10 fold cross validation for each of the feature extraction techniques and the category wise Precision and Recall values for classification are given in Table 1 and Table 2 for Wang and OT Scene datasets respectively.

Table 1. Comparison of precision and recall for Wang dataset with two different feature extraction techniques using 10-fold cross validation

Categories	Precision (Feature Extraction With Binarization)	Recall (Feature Extraction With Binarization)	Precision (Feature Extraction With Morphological Operator)	Recall (Feature Extraction With Morphological Operator)
Tribals	0.606	0.63	0.708	0.75
Sea Beach	0.72	0.59	0.667	0.3
Gothic Structure	0.467	0.056	0.761	0.51
Bus	0.669	0.79	0.543	0.94
Dinosaur	1	1	0.99	1
Elephant	0.98	1	0.839	0.99
Roses	1	0.82	0.653	0.47
Horses	0.846	0.99	0.74	0.94
Mountains	0.797	0.63	0.69	0.69
Food	0.854	0.82	0.769	0.7
Average	0.794	0.783	0.736	0.729

Table 2. Comparison of precision and recall for ot-scene dataset with two different feature extraction techniques using 10-fold cross validation

Categories	Precision (Feature Extraction With Binarization)	Recall (Feature Extraction With Binarization)	Precision (Feature Extraction With Morphological Operator)	Recall (Feature Extraction With Morphological Operator)
Coast	0.563	0.333	0.771	0.7
Forest	0.617	0.625	0.652	0.628
Highway	0.568	0.785	0.67	0.508
Inside City	0.444	0.688	0.653	0.88
Mountain	0.355	0.46	0.709	0.535
Open Country	0.725	0.468	0.51	0.434
Street	0.377	0.328	0.349	0.427
Tall Building	0.488	0.419	0.462	0.575
Average	0.526	0.506	0.602	0.589

It is observed in Table 1 that classification with binarization based feature extraction technique has higher Precision and Recall values compared to the feature extraction with morphological operator in case of Wang dataset. The categories named Dinosaur and Roses have shown maximum Precision and Recall values and the Gothic Structure category has shown the minimum for feature extraction technique using binarization. Feature extraction with morphological operator has resulted in highest Precision and Recall values for the category named Dinosaur and least values for the category named Buses.

The scenario is reversed in case of OT Scene dataset in Table 2 which has shown better classification results for feature extraction with morphological operator compared to the binarization technique.

The category named Forest has shown the highest Precision and Recall values for feature extraction with binarizaiton and the least values are exhibited by the Street category. On the other hand, feature extraction with morphological operator has the highest Precision and Recall values for the category named Coast and the minimum value for the category named Street which is common in case of both the feature extraction techniques in case of OT Scene dataset.

The individual techniques have shown different values for successful classification which is based on the robustness of the feature extraction techniques for each dataset. Further, a fusion based approach is designed and is aimed to attain higher degree of successful classification by standardization of classification decision of each of the participating feature extraction techniques with Z score normalization as discussed using feature scaling in (Das, R., & Walia, E, 2017). The comparison of average Precision and Recall values for the individual techniques and the fused approach has been given in Figure 7.

The experimentation is carried out with Wang dataset.

The confusion matrix for classification with feature extraction by binarization is shown in Table 3-5.

Figure 7. Comparison of precision and recall values for individual techniques and fused approach for Wang dataset

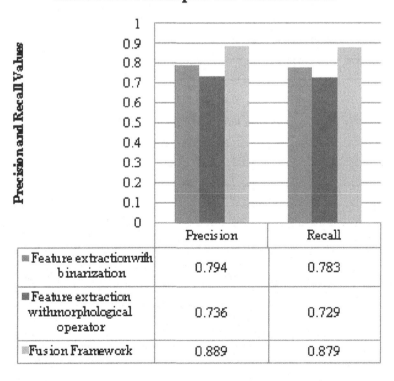

	Precision	Recall
■ Feature extraction with binarization	0.794	0.783
■ Feature extraction with morphological operator	0.736	0.729
■ Fusion Framework	0.889	0.879

Table 3. Confusion matrix for classification with feature extraction with binarization

a	b	c	d	e	f	g	h	I	J	Classified as
63	7	16	4	0	0	0	1	3	6	a=Tribals
14	59	17	4	0	0	0	0	6	0	b=Sea Beach
9	6	56	19	0	0	0	0	6	4	c=Gothic Structure
2	0	16	79	0	0	0	0	0	3	d=Bus
0	0	0	0	100	0	0	0	0	0	e=Dinosaur
0	0	0	0	0	100	0	0	0	0	f=Elephant
2	1	0	0	0	1	82	14	0	0	g=Roses
1	0	0	0	0	0	0	99	0	0	h=Horses
6	9	9	9	0	0	0	3	63	1	i=Mountains
7	0	6	3	0	1	0	0	1	82	j=Food

Table 4. Confusion matrix for classification with feature extraction with morphological approach

a	b	c	d	e	f	g	h	i	j	Classified as
75	2	2	6	0	6	4	4	1	0	a=Tribals
12	30	14	33	0	0	5	5	0	1	b=Sea Beach
8	7	51	24	0	0	1	2	6	1	c=Gothic Structure
0	5	0	94	0	0	0	1	0	0	d=Bus
0	0	0	0	100	0	0	0	0	0	e=Dinosaur
0	0	0	0	1	99	0	0	0	0	f=Elephant
11	1	0	15	0	13	47	8	4	1	g=Roses
0	0	0	0	0	0	5	94	0	1	h=Horses
0	0	0	1	0	0	7	6	69	17	i=Mountains
0	0	0	0	0	0	3	7	20	17	j=Food

Table 5. Confusion matrix for classification with multi technique fusion

a	b	c	d	e	F	g	h	i	j	Classified as
84	4	0	7	0	1	0	0	2	2	a=Tribals
12	70	7	10	0	0	0	0	1	0	b=Sea Beach
8	0	60	23	0	0	0	0	8	1	c=Gothic Structure
0	0	1	99	0	0	0	0	0	0	d=Bus
0	0	0	0	100	0	0	0	0	0	e=Dinosaur
0	0	0	0	0	100	0	0	0	0	f=Elephant
1	0	0	0	0	2	89	8	0	0	g=Roses
0	0	0	0	0	0	0	100	0	0	h=Horses
0	2	2	3	0	0	0	8	82	3	i=Mountains
1	0	0	1	0	0	0	0	3	95	j=Food

Although, the Precision and Recall values for comparison of the multi technique fusion methodology have outclassed the individual technique of feature extraction, a null hypothesis has been designed in Hypothesis 1 based on the Precision values of the techniques to validate the statistical significance of the performance improvement.

Hypothesis 1

There is no significant difference among the Precision values of the individual techniques with respect to the multi technique fusion approach for classification results.

A paired t-test (2 tailed) is conducted to find out the p-values of the existing techniques with respect to the proposed technique. The test has conducted a comparative measure of the variation in the Precision value of the proposed and the existing techniques to evaluate the actual difference between two means. The results have been displayed in Table 6.

The p values have calculated the strength of evidences against the null hypothesis and are found to be significant. Hence, the null hypothesis is rejected and it is established that the multi technique fusion framework of classification has improved classification performance over individual techniques.

The classification results with fusion framework are compared to the classification results of state-of-the art techniques using four different metrics, namely, Precision, Recall, F1 Score and Misclassification Rate (MR) in Figure 8.

It is clearly observed that the proposed technique of classification has outclassed all the existing techniques. It has shown an average increase of 27%, 26% and 18% in Precision, Recall and F1 Score respectively and an average decrease of 6% in Misclassification Rate (MR) with respect to the existing techniques.

Henceforth, the feature extraction techniques are tested for the retrieval performances with Wang dataset. The retrieval is carried out in two different ways, namely, by generic query and by classified query. Random selection of 5 different images is performed from each category of Wang dataset. On the whole, 50 images are selected as query images from all the 10 categories of the Wang dataset. Firstly, a generic query is fired at the dataset and top 20 matches are selected based on the Z score standardized distance of individual ranking done by each of the feature extraction techniques. Further, the query is classified to its nearest matching class by means of the fusion based classification technique and is forwarded to search for results only within the class of interest.

A comparison of category wise Precision and Recall values for retrieval with generic query and classified query has is shown in Table 7 and Table 8.

Sample retrieval has been illustrated in Figure 9 which has compared retrieval with generic query with respect to classified query.

Figure 9 has evidently exposed that retrieval with classified query has identified all the 20 images from the same category of the query image, whereas, retrieval with generic query has recognized 17

Table 6. Paired t-test for significance of fusion based classification over individual techniques

Techniques	p Value	t calc	Significance
Feature extraction with binarization	0.0438	2.3425	Significant
Feature extraction with morphological operator	0.0006	5.1906	Significant

Figure 8. Comparison of precision, recall, F1 score and MR values for proposed technique and existing approaches with Wang dataset for content based image classification

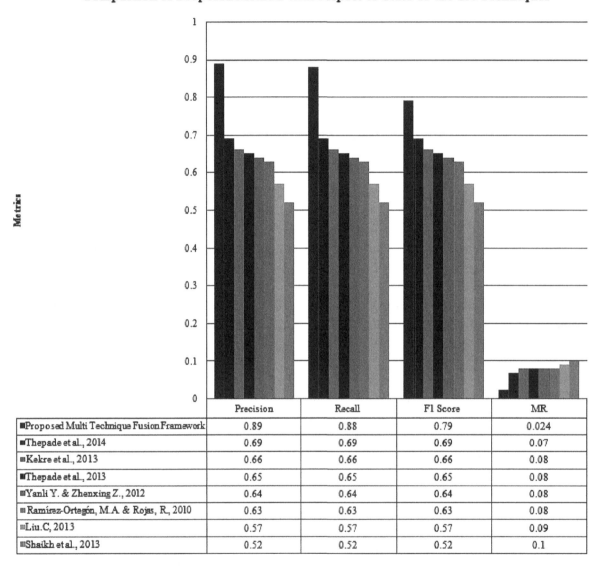

Comparison of Proposed Method with respect to State-of-the art Techniques

	Precision	Recall	F1 Score	MR
■Proposed Multi Technique Fusion Framework	0.89	0.88	0.79	0.024
■Thepade et al., 2014	0.69	0.69	0.69	0.07
■Kekre et al., 2013	0.66	0.66	0.66	0.08
■Thepade et al., 2013	0.65	0.65	0.65	0.08
■Yanli Y. & Zhenxing Z., 2012	0.64	0.64	0.64	0.08
■Ramírez-Ortegón, M.A. & Rojas, R., 2010	0.63	0.63	0.63	0.08
■Liu.C, 2013	0.57	0.57	0.57	0.09
■Shaikh et al., 2013	0.52	0.52	0.52	0.1

images from the category of query image and 3 different images from the category Flowers, Elephant and Gothic Structure.

Hence, the Precision values for retrieval by fusion technique with classified query have been compared to state-of-the art techniques in Figure 10.

The results in Tables 7 and Table 8 have clearly revealed that retrieval with fusion framework has higher Precision and Recall values compared to individual techniques. However, while comparing the retrieval outcomes with generic query and classified query, it is inferred that the results of the later one has visibly outperformed.

Table 7. Comparison of precision values for retrieval with individual techniques, multi technique fusion with generic query and multi technique fusion with classified query for Wang dataset

Categories	Precision (Feature Extraction With Binarization)	Precision (Feature Extraction With Morphological Operator)	Precision (Multi Feature Fusion Technique With Generic Query)	Precision (Multi Feature Fusion Technique With Classified Query)
Tribals	45	79	84	100
Sea Beach	55	35	61	60
Gothic Structure	43	46	51	80
Bus	67	62	84	100
Dinosaur	100	100	100	100
Elephant	100	95	100	100
Roses	93	46	86	100
Horses	99	92	99	100
Mountains	44	25	43	40
Food	58	69	73	80
Average	70.4	64.9	78.1	86

Table 8. Comparison of recall values for retrieval with individual techniques, multi technique fusion with generic query and multi technique fusion with classified query

Categories	Recall (Feature Extraction With Binarization)	Recall (Feature Extraction With Morphological Operator)	Recall (Multi Feature Fusion Technique With Generic Query)	Recall (Multi Feature Fusion Technique With Classified Query)
Tribals	9	15.8	16.8	20
Sea Beach	11	7	12.2	12
Gothic Structure	8.6	9.2	10.2	16
Bus	13.4	12.4	16.8	20
Dinosaur	20	20	20	20
Elephant	20	19	20	20
Roses	18.6	9.2	17.2	20
Horses	19.8	18.4	19.8	20
Mountains	8.8	5	8.6	8
Food	11.6	13.8	14.6	16
Average	14.08	12.98	15.62	17.2

Figure 9. Comparison of retrieval with classified query and generic query

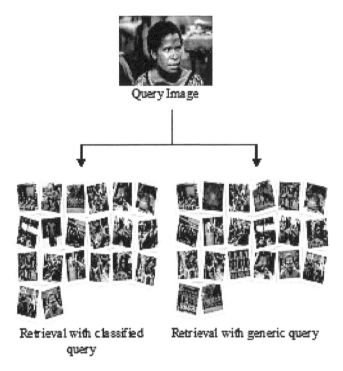

The comparison in Figure 10 has undoubtedly established the dominance of the proposed retrieval methodology in contrast to the benchmarked techniques. The proposed technique has shown an average increase of 20.44% in Precision value. A paired t test is conducted to validate the statistical significance of the research findings for retrieval results.

Hypothesis 2

There is no significant difference among the Precision values of the state-of-the art techniques with respect to the fusion approach of retrieval with classified query. Table 6 has enlisted the p values and t-calc for the paired t test. The Precision value of our technique is compared to that of the existing techniques to obtain the computed values in Table 9.

The p values have clearly indicated that Precision values for our technique has significant difference with respect to the state-of-the art techniques. Hence, the null hypothesis is rejected and the supremacy of the proposed method is established.

CONCLUSION

The paper has carried out exhaustive comparison of different feature extraction techniques and the usefulness of the techniques to predict classification and retrieval results. Consequently, the following conclusions have been enlisted:

Figure 10. Comparison of proposed retrieval technique with respect to state-of-the art fusion based retrieval techniques

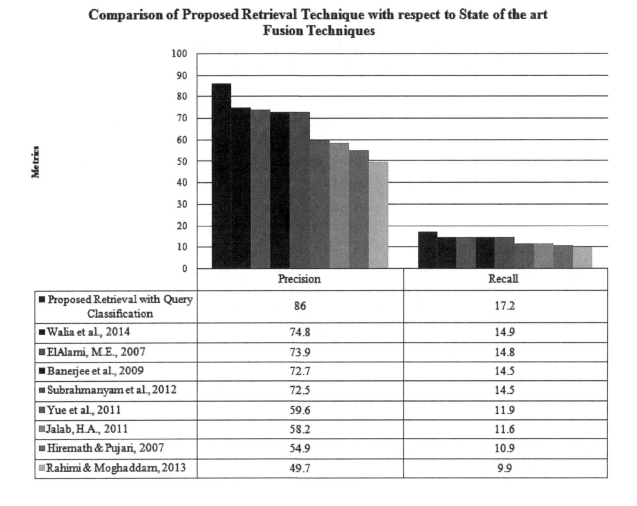

Table 9. Paired t test for significance of retrieval with classified query over state-of-the-art techniques

Techniques	p Value	t Calc	Significance
M.E. Elami, 2011	0.0231	2.7324	*Significant*
Hiremath&Pujari, 2007	0.0004	5.3913	*Significant*
Yue et al., 2011	0.0002	6.1721	*Significant*
Banerjee et al., 2009	0.0474	2.2952	*Significant*
Jalab, 2011	0.0117	3.1496	*Significant*
Rahim & Moghaddam, 2015	0.0003	5.5841	*Significant*
Subrahmanyam et al. 2013	0.0287	2.6017	*Significant*
Walia et al., 2014	0.0277	2.6224	*Significant*
Subrahmanyam et al., 2012	0.0146	3.0167	*Significant*

- Successful proposition of two different feature extraction techniques based on image binarization and morphological operators.
- The dimension of feature vectors is radically reduced for each feature extraction technique.
- The feature size is independent of the magnitude of the image.
- Designing the fusion framework for both classification and retrieval methods.
- Establishing the statistical significance of our research findings.

The importance of classification has been clearly established by using it as a precursor for query categorization for retrieval. It is inferred that the fusion framework with multi feature extraction techniques has enhanced capabilities for content-based information identification with image data. Nevertheless, we are aiming to design global feature vectors for individual image categories to further reduce the training time of the learner.

REFERENCES

Ahmadian, A., & Mostafa, A. (2003). An efficient texture classification algorithm using Gabor wavelet. In *Engineering in Medicine and Biology Society, 2003. Proceedings of the 25th Annual International Conference of the IEEE* (*Vol. 1*, pp. 930-933). IEEE. 10.1109/IEMBS.2003.1279918

Banerjee, M., Kundu, M. K., & Maji, P. (2009). Content-based image retrieval using visually significant point features. *Fuzzy Sets and Systems*, *160*(23), 3323–3341. doi:10.1016/j.fss.2009.02.024

Das, R., & Walia, E. (2017). Partition selection with sparse autoencoders for content based image classification. *Neural Computing & Applications*, 1–16.

Das, R., & Walia, E. (2017). Partition selection with sparse autoencoders for content based image classification. *Neural Computing & Applications*. doi:10.100700521-017-3099-0

Dawn, D. D., & Shaikh, S. H. (2016). A comprehensive survey of human action recognition with spatio-temporal interest point (STIP) detector. *The Visual Computer*, *32*(3), 289–306. doi:10.100700371-015-1066-2

Dubois, S. R., & Glanz, F. H. (1986). An autoregressive model approach to two-dimensional shape classification. *IEEE Transactions on Pattern Analysis and Machine Intelligence*, *PAMI-8*(1), 55–66. doi:10.1109/TPAMI.1986.4767752 PMID:21869323

ElAlami, M. E. (2011). A novel image retrieval model based on the most relevant features. *Knowledge-Based Systems*, *24*(1), 23–32. doi:10.1016/j.knosys.2010.06.001

ElAlami, M. E. (2014). A new matching strategy for content based image retrieval system. *Applied Soft Computing*, *14*, 407–418. doi:10.1016/j.asoc.2013.10.003

Feng, M. L., & Tan, Y. P. (2004). Adaptive binarization method for document image analysis. In *Multimedia and Expo, 2004. ICME'04. 2004 IEEE International Conference on* (Vol. 1, pp. 339-342). IEEE.

Flickner, M., Sawhney, H., Niblack, W., Ashley, J., Huang, Q., Dom, B.& Steele, D. (1995). Query by image and video content: The QBIC system. *Computer, 28*(9), 23-32.

Gevers, T., & Smeulders, A. W. (2000). Pictoseek: Combining color and shape invariant features for image retrieval. *IEEE Transactions on Image Processing*, *9*(1), 102–119. doi:10.1109/83.817602 PMID:18255376

Hiremath, P. S., & Pujari, J. (2007). Content based image retrieval using color, texture and shape features. In *Advanced Computing and Communications, 2007. ADCOM 2007. International Conference on* (pp. 780-784). IEEE. 10.1109/ADCOM.2007.21

Iosifidis, A., Tefas, A., & Pitas, I. (2013). Multi-view human action recognition: A survey. In *Intelligent Information Hiding and Multimedia Signal Processing, 2013 Ninth International Conference on* (pp. 522-525). IEEE. 10.1109/IIH-MSP.2013.135

Irtaza, A., Jaffar, M. A., Aleisa, E., & Choi, T. S. (2014). Embedding neural networks for semantic association in content based image retrieval. *Multimedia Tools and Applications*, *72*(2), 1911–1931. doi:10.100711042-013-1489-6

Jalab, H. A. (2011). Image retrieval system based on color layout descriptor and Gabor filters. In *Open Systems (ICOS), 2011 IEEE Conference on* (pp. 32-36). IEEE. 10.1109/ICOS.2011.6079266

Jalba, A. C., Wilkinson, M. H., & Roerdink, J. B. (2004). Morphological hat-transform scale spaces and their use in pattern classification. *Pattern Recognition*, *37*(5), 901–915. doi:10.1016/j.patcog.2003.09.009

Kekre, H. B., Thepade, S., Das, R. K. K., & Ghosh, S. (2013). Multilevel Block Truncation Coding with diverse color spaces for image classification. In *Advances in Technology and Engineering (ICATE), 2013 International Conference on* (pp. 1-7). IEEE 10.1109/ICAdTE.2013.6524718

Kim, W. Y., & Kim, Y. S. (2000). A region-based shape descriptor using Zernike moments. *Signal Processing Image Communication*, *16*(1), 95–102. doi:10.1016/S0923-5965(00)00019-9

Korytkowski, M., Rutkowski, L., & Scherer, R. (2016). Fast image classification by boosting fuzzy classifiers. *Information Sciences*, *327*, 175–182. doi:10.1016/j.ins.2015.08.030

Li, J., & Wang, J. Z. (2003). Automatic linguistic indexing of pictures by a statistical modeling approach. *IEEE Transactions on Pattern Analysis and Machine Intelligence*, *25*(9), 1075–1088. doi:10.1109/TPAMI.2003.1227984

Liu, C. (2013). A new finger vein feature extraction algorithm. In *Image and Signal Processing (CISP), 2013 6th International Congress on* (Vol. 1, pp. 395-399). IEEE. 10.1109/CISP.2013.6744026

Mehtre, B. M., Kankanhalli, M. S., & Lee, W. F. (1997). Shape measures for content based image retrieval: A comparison. *Information Processing & Management*, *33*(3), 319–337. doi:10.1016/S0306-4573(96)00069-6

Mokhtarian, F., & Mackworth, A. K. (1992). A theory of multiscale, curvature-based shape representation for planar curves. *IEEE Transactions on Pattern Analysis and Machine Intelligence*, *14*(8), 789–805. doi:10.1109/34.149591

Otsu, N. (1979). A threshold selection method from gray-level histograms. *IEEE Transactions on Systems, Man, and Cybernetics*, *9*(1), 62–66. doi:10.1109/TSMC.1979.4310076

Rahimi, M., & Moghaddam, M. E. (2015). A content-based image retrieval system based on Color Ton Distribution descriptors. *Signal, Image and Video Processing*, *9*(3), 691–704. doi:10.100711760-013-0506-6

Ramirez-Ortegon, M. A., & Rojas, R. (2010). Unsupervised evaluation methods based on local gray-intensity variances for binarization of historical documents. In *Pattern Recognition (ICPR), 2010 20th International Conference on* (pp. 2029-2032). IEEE. 10.1109/ICPR.2010.500

Shaikh, S. H., Maiti, A. K., & Chaki, N. (2013). A new image binarization method using iterative partitioning. *Machine Vision and Applications*, 1–14.

Shen, G. L., & Wu, X. J. (2013). *Content based image retrieval by combining color, texture and CENTRIST*. Academic Press.

Subrahmanyam, M., Maheshwari, R. P., & Balasubramanian, R. (2012). Expert system design using wavelet and color vocabulary trees for image retrieval. *Expert Systems with Applications*, *39*(5), 5104–5114. doi:10.1016/j.eswa.2011.11.029

Subrahmanyam, M., Wu, Q. J., Maheshwari, R. P., & Balasubramanian, R. (2013). Modified color motif co-occurrence matrix for image indexing and retrieval. *Computers & Electrical Engineering*, *39*(3), 762–774. doi:10.1016/j.compeleceng.2012.11.023

Thepade, S., Das, R., & Ghosh, S. (2013). Performance comparison of feature vector extraction techniques in RGB color space using block truncation coding for content based image classification with discrete classifiers. In *India Conference (INDICON), 2013 Annual IEEE* (pp. 1-6). IEEE. 10.1109/INDCON.2013.6726053

Thepade, S., Das, R., & Ghosh, S. (2014). A novel feature extraction technique using binarization of bit planes for content based image classification. *Journal of Engineering*.

Thepade, S., Das, R., & Ghosh, S. (2015). A novel feature extraction technique with binarization of significant bit information. *International Journal of Imaging and Robotic*, *15*(3), 164–178.

Thepade, S. D., Das, R. K. K., & Ghosh, S. (2013). Image classification using advanced block truncation coding with ternary image maps. In *Advances in Computing, Communication, and Control* (pp. 500–509). Berlin: Springer. doi:10.1007/978-3-642-36321-4_48

Valizadeh, M., Armanfard, N., Komeili, M., & Kabir, E. (2009, October). A novel hybrid algorithm for binarization of badly illuminated document images. In *Computer Conference, 2009. CSICC 2009. 14th International CSI* (pp. 121-126). IEEE. 10.1109/CSICC.2009.5349338

Walia, E., Goyal, A., & Brar, Y. S. (2014). Zernike moments and LDP-weighted patches for content-based image retrieval. *Signal, Image and Video Processing*, *8*(3), 577–594. doi:10.100711760-013-0561-z

Walia, E., & Pal, A. (2014). Fusion framework for effective color image retrieval. *Journal of Visual Communication and Image Representation*, *25*(6), 1335–1348. doi:10.1016/j.jvcir.2014.05.005

Walia, E., Vesal, S., & Pal, A. (2014). An effective and fast hybrid framework for color image retrieval. *Sensing and Imaging*, *15*(1), 93. doi:10.100711220-014-0093-9

Yanli, Y., & Zhenxing, Z. (2012). A novel local threshold binarization method for QR image. *IET International Conference on Automatic Control and Artificial Intelligence (ACAI)*, 224-227. 10.1049/cp.2012.0959

Yıldız, O. T., Aslan, O., & Alpaydın, E. (2011). Multivariate statistical tests for comparing classification algorithms. *Lecture Notes in Computer Science, 6683*, 1–15. doi:10.1007/978-3-642-25566-3_1

Yue, J., Li, Z., Liu, L., & Fu, Z. (2011). Content-based image retrieval using color and texture fused features. *Mathematical and Computer Modelling, 54*(3), 1121–1127. doi:10.1016/j.mcm.2010.11.044

Zhang, D., & Lu, G. (2003). A comparative study of curvature scale space and Fourier descriptors for shape-based image retrieval. *Journal of Visual Communication and Image Representation, 14*(1), 39–57. doi:10.1016/S1047-3203(03)00003-8

Zhang, D., & Lu, G. (2004). Review of shape representation and description techniques. *Pattern Recognition, 37*(1), 1–19. doi:10.1016/j.patcog.2003.07.008

Zhu, Q., & Shyu, M. L. (2015). Sparse linear integration of content and context modalities for semantic concept retrieval. *IEEE Transactions on Emerging Topics in Computing, 3*(2), 152–160. doi:10.1109/TETC.2014.2384992

Chapter 2
Dimension Reduction Using Image Transform for Content-Based Feature Extraction

Sourav De
Cooch Behar Government Engineering College, India

Madhumita Singha
Xavier Institute of Social Service, India

Komal Kumari
Xavier Institute of Social Service, India

Ritika Selot
Xavier Institute of Social Service, India

Akshat Gupta
Xavier Institute of Social Service, India

ABSTRACT

Technological advancements in the field of machine learning have attempted classification of the images of gigantic datasets. Classification with content-based image feature extraction categorizes the images based on the image content in contrast to conventional text-based annotation. The chapter has presented a feature extraction technique based on application of image transform. The method has extracted meaningful features and facilitated feature dimension reduction. A technique, known as fractional coefficient of transforms, is adopted to facilitate feature dimension reduction. Two different color spaces, namely RGB and YUV, are considered to compare the classification metrics to figure out the best possible reduced feature dimension. Further, the results are compared to state-of-the-art techniques which have revealed improved performance for the proposed feature extraction technique.

DOI: 10.4018/978-1-5225-5775-3.ch002

INTRODUCTION

A vast growth for image datasets is noticed due to easy availability of high end image capturing devices for which the requirement for feature extraction efficiency to promptly identify the database images has also seen a steep rise (Thepade, 2017). Hence, the computational capabilities need to be increased by leaps and bounds in order to save time and resources and also speed up the applications. The process of image identification has been governed predominantly by text-based annotation for assorted applications in diverse domains (Das, 2017a). The classification results are computed based on the text representation of the image content which is often dependent on the vocabulary of the data entry operator and frequently turns out to be inconsistent. The business functions also get adversely affected by the inappropriate classification result generation which results in adverse effects on its revenue generation. The idea of content based image classification has emerged as a fruitful alternative and has considered the content of the image as image features in contrast to the text based annotation process to identify image data (Das, 2017b).This feature may represent a single attribute of the image or may be a composition of different attributes (Lee, 2013; Shaikh, 2013; Liu, 2013; Yanli, 2012; Thepade, 2015).The process of applying image transform reduces the image to its compact form and thus reduces the feature vector size of the image. The reduced size of feature vectors in turn diminishes computational overhead for classification process (Jing, 2004). Content based image classification has assorted applications in criminology, computer aided diagnosis, military, GIS and various other fields. It is proved to be productive in the engineering and architectural projects. It is an aid for the advertising and publishing sector where the journalists keep a record of the various events and advertisements. In archaeology and historical research, maintaining such records assists in research as reference can be drawn for the final image obtained post excavation (Das, 2015a). The custom-built image feature extraction process may include interference with the complete image surface. The paper represents a technique to maneuver only a small part of the actual image and work upon the same to make the match more accurate. The image is broken into its constituent component colors namely, red (R), green (G) and blue (B), which are the primary color components. Discrete Cosine Transform (DCT) is applied on each of the components for feature extraction using image transformation (Kekre, 2010; Das, 2015b). The test images are augmented by a technique named odd image formation on which DCT is applied to extract partial coefficients of transforms as image features (Thepade, 2013). The image preprocessing part using odd image formation increases the efficiency of feature extraction and helps in achieving elevated accuracy in classification outputs. Therefore, the authors have attempted to figure out essential and necessary feature components contributing to the classification accuracy by eliminating the features which are not significant to improve classification results. Thus the classification of images is performed on the basis of content of the images represented by features extracted with partial energy coefficients. The results of classification are compared to that of the benchmarked content-based feature extraction techniques and the proposed technique has outperformed based on classification metrics.

The objectives of this work can be summarized as follows:

1. Designing an efficient content-based feature extraction process.
2. Feature dimension reduction for decreased computational complexity.
3. Comparing the results to the state-of-the-art.

BACKGROUND

Feature extraction begins from an initial set of image data and builds informative features thus leading to better machine learning and interpretations (Thepade, 2014). Feature extraction along with feature selection is a part of Dimension Reduction. Taking the previous studies and researches into consideration, Glaucoma images have been extracted by the use of Discrete Wavelet Transform as using this technique reduced features are obtained in three directions (vertical, horizontal, and diagonal) (Mookiah, 2012). Thereafter Contourlet Transform is also used for more directions and better resolution and for classification the Contourlet images are sent to Support vector Machine (SVM) classifier (Do, 2005). Various approaches employed for dimensional reduction have been deployed including the pattern recognition framework for face recognition with Radon and Fourier transforms and classifying the results using minimum distance classifier (Sanjay, 2016). To support this, when results were contrasted with FERET and the ORL databases, the former transform results were found superior in terms of recognition rate. In addition to these, PCA (Principle Component Analysis) is juxtaposed with LDA (Linear Discriminant Analysis). PCA transforms the high dimensional input space onto the feature space where the maximal variance is displayed. It leads to derivation of maximum axes with maximum variance on whole data set. On the other hand, LDA is obtained by maximizing the difference between classes and minimizing the distance within classes (Ravi, 2015). It finds axes for best class separation. On evaluation with Precision and Recall methods, PCA was found better. PCA has also been used to reduce both noise contained in the original image features and dimensionality of feature spaces by extraction of features for the class of images represented by the positive images provided by subjective RF. The method increases the retrieval speed and reduces the memory significantly without sacrificing the retrieval accuracy.

The current technique used in this paper illustrates the feature extraction and dimension reduction using image transform technique. Discrete Cosine Transform (DCT) is considered as the transform technique from which partial coefficients are chosen as content-based features of the test images. The results of classification have outperformed the state-of-the art and have shown improved recognition accuracy.

ISSUES WITH TEXT ANNOTATION BASED IMAGE IDENTIFICATION

Time complexity, dissimilar outcomes, large number of options Inaccuracy & inefficacy have been used as determining factors by the authors to discover the reasons for user dissatisfaction as given in Table 1 (Chen 2014). These factors also relate to image identification.

Phi is used as a test variable as de-identification of Phi, according to Privacy Rule standards may enable many research activities and is permitted by a covered entity or by a business associate.

Chi square test says there is a significant relationship between the variables. However, it does not say how significant this may be. Phi correlation and Cramer's V are post-test to give this additional information about the significance of the relationship.

Phi varies between -1 and 1.

- Close to 0 it shows little association between variables.
- Close to 1, it indicates a strong positive association.
- Close to -1 it shows a strong negative correlation.

Table 1. Chi square test for user dissatisfaction analysis

Chi-Square Tests				
Raw Variable→ User dissatisfaction in image retrieval at in different medias				
Column Variables ↓	Likelihood Ratio	Sig. (2-Sided)	Phi	Cramer's V
Time taken in searching process	266.819	.000	1.28	0.905
Dissimilar outcome with searching key word	54.004	.000	0.5	0.354
Large number of options as output	1.55	0.818	0.091	0.065
Inaccuracy & inefficacy	91.656	.000	0.674	0.477

Number of samples: 185.

Cramer's V is used for calculation of correlation in tables with more than 2x2 rows and columns. Cramer's V varies between 0 and 1.

- Close to 0 it shows little association between variables.
- Close to 1, it indicates a strong association.

PROPOSED TECHNIQUES

During the initial years of image processing in 1979, Block Truncation Coding (BTC) is developed as a successful image coding algorithm that involves an image to be segmented into nxn blocks such that they do not imbricate. BTC makes computation simpler as there are smaller complexities involved. It even preserves the edges of the images and each block can be compressed separately according to its variance (Guo, 2015a; Guo, 2014; Guo, 2015b; Hu, 2013). Coding of small image blocks are done one at a time. It is used widely for image compression. The significance of the technique is the value of mean and standard deviation of the reconstructed image remain same to that of the original image. In our approach, we have considered the different color components, namely, R, G and B as the blocks and have implemented the concept of block truncation coding to assist the process of content-based feature extraction.

COLOR SPACES

Colour perception is the process of the brain that triggers the cone receptors of the eye. Hue, saturation, and brightness are the properties of the colours that are inherently distinguished by the human eye. The spectral colours can be distinguished as they have different wavelength. However, perception of colours constituting of multiple wavelengths is complex (Tokarczyk, 2015; El-Latif, 2013). A computer recognises a particular colour by the phosphor emissions of red, green and blue. Hence, three coordinates are required to specify a colour. Colour space is a mathematical model that describes the colour range in the form of tuples of numbers. It helps to visualize a colour. The colour spaces considered over here are: RGB and YUV.

RGBCOLOR SPACE (R-RED, G-GREEN, B-BLUE)

The RGB colour space consists of the primary colours: red, green and blue that are the base colours used to elaborate this colour space. If none of the base colours are used, the resultant is black and if all three are used in full intensities, the resultant would be white. The desired colours may be produced by the combination of the intensities of the base colours in varied proportions. Each pixel of an image in RGB is assigned intensity values of the range of 0-255. Hence it can be inferred that there can be as many as 16,777,216 colours on the screen just my mixing these three colours in differing ratios (Ganesan, 2014).

YUV COLOR SPACE

Y stands for Luminance (brightness) component and the U and V signify the chrominance (colour) components.YUV colour model is utilised by composite colour video tutorials such as PAL, NTSC, and SECAM. YUV colour space consists of two components: One luminance, i.e. brightness and two chrominance i.e. colour. RGB can be converted to YUV colour space using equation 1 (Podpora, 2014).

$$
\begin{bmatrix} Y \\ U \\ V \end{bmatrix} = \begin{bmatrix} 0.299 & 0.587 & 0.144 \\ -0.14713 & -0.22472 & 0.436 \\ 0.615 & -0.51498 & 0.10001 \end{bmatrix} \begin{bmatrix} R \\ G \\ B \end{bmatrix} \tag{1}
$$

IMAGE PRE-PROCESSING

Generation of Odd Images

Initially a normal image was horizontally flipped across X and Y axis. Formation of Odd Image is performed by:

1. Flipping a normal image horizontally, and
2. Subtracting the flipped image from the normal image as done in Equation (2) (Thepade, 2013).

$$
I_{Odd} = \frac{I_N - I_F}{2} \tag{2}
$$

where,

I_N = Normal Image
I_F = Flipped Image

The odd image created by the flipped version of the same image is helpful in extracting more information from the given set of data.

Some bits may contribute significantly while some others may have insignificant contribution, but each bit has some or the other role to play in the formation of the image (Nigam, 2015; Kao, 2015). Hence, separation of the image into its constituent bits helps in understanding the importance and contribution of each bit in the image.

Intensity value of each pixel was represented by an 8 bit binary vector Figure 1 and a binary matrix was used to represent each bit plane Figure 2. The bit plane is exploited to generate the image slices Figure 3 (a) – 3(k).

Amalgamated image with bit planes 5, 6, 7 and 8 is prominent with significant image information as it contains less noise. Therefore, bit plane 5, 6, 7 and 8 are identified as significant bit planes and are binarized using a local threshold selection method for feature vector generation.

FEATURE EXTRACTION USING DISCRETE COSINE TRANSFORM (DCT)

Reduction of the dimension of the feature vector of the images helps in shortening the time consumed in the comparison of feature vectors during classification process (Li, 2016). This dimension reduction results in exclusion of insignificant coefficients and is performed by allocating the high frequency component to the upper end of the image and the low frequency component to the lower end of the image. DCT is primarily being chosen to design the technique of feature dimension reduction for the content based features extracted from the test images.

Figure 1. Odd image generation

Original Image   Flipped Image   Odd Image

Figure 2. Bit binary vector

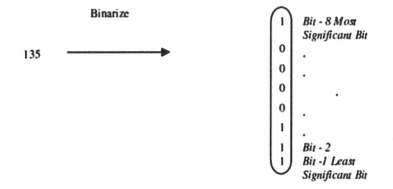

Figure 3.

Fig. 3(a) Odd Image

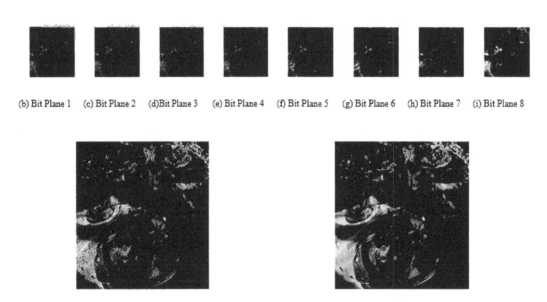

(b) Bit Plane 1   (c) Bit Plane 2   (d)Bit Plane 3   (e) Bit Plane 4   (f) Bit Plane 5   (g) Bit Plane 6   (h) Bit Plane 7   (i) Bit Plane 8

(k) Amalgamated Image of Bit Plane 1,2,3 and 4

(l) Amalgamated Image of Bit Plane 5,6,7 and 8

Differentiation of the Red, Green and Blue colour components in a test image is followed by application of image transform (DCT) to each of the color components to extract the feature vectors of each component. Feature vector database is prepared by extracting partial coefficients from this feature vector set as in Figure 4.

Feature vectors are being extracted using 14 different steps from the transformed images. Each of the steps has extracted different transform coefficients ranging from 100% to 0.06% as shown in Figure 2.

The feature vectors of the query image are then compared with the database images for classification. This is done for the whole set of feature vectors and for partial coefficients of feature vectors. There is an entire set of query images and classification is carried out for this entire set and the results of the

Figure 4. Extraction of features with fractional DCT coefficients

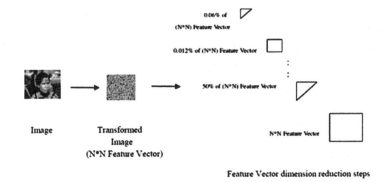

classification are compared aiming for the highest results in order to find out the best percentage of partial coefficient for feature extraction technique. This best percentage is obtained by applying image transform on the feature vector set.

The general equation for a 1D (*N* data items) DCT is defined by the following Equations 3 and 4.

$$F\left(u\right) = \sqrt{\left(\frac{2}{N}\right)} \sum_{i=0}^{N-1} \Lambda\left(i\right) \cdot \cos\left[\frac{\pi}{2}\frac{u}{N}\left(2i+1\right)\right] f\left(i\right) \tag{3}$$

where,

$$\Lambda\left(i\right) = \begin{cases} \dfrac{1}{\sqrt{2}} & for\ \xi = 0 \\ 1 & otherwise \end{cases} \tag{4}$$

The general equation for a 2D (*N* by *M* image) DCT is defined by the following Equations 5 and 6.

$$F\left(u,v\right) = \sqrt{\frac{2}{N}}\sqrt{\frac{2}{M}} \sum_{i=0}^{N-1}\sum_{j=0}^{M-1} \Lambda\left(i\right) \cdot \Lambda\left(j\right) \cdot \cos\left[\frac{\pi}{2}\frac{u}{N}\left(2i+1\right)\right] \cdot \cos\left[\frac{\pi}{2}\frac{v}{M}\left(2j+1\right)\right] \cdot f\left(i,j\right) \tag{5}$$

where,

$$\Lambda\left(\xi\right) = \begin{cases} \dfrac{1}{\sqrt{2}} & for\ \xi = 0 \\ 1 & otherwise \end{cases} \tag{6}$$

WANG DATASET

A sample collage for Wang's dataset has been given in Figure 5. The dataset comprises of different images arranged in 10 different classes. Each of the class is represented by 100 images which gives a total count of 1000 images for the entire dataset (Walia, 2014).

CLASSIFICATION TECHNIQUE

Tenfold Cross Validation

Cross validation is a technique that scrutinizes anticipating models by means of dividing the original sample into training sets and test sets. Training set is designed to train the model and the test set is designed to evaluate the model.

There are also other methods for model evaluation. One is Residuals. However, the problem with residuals is that it does not give a signal of how well the learner will perform when it is asked to give predictions on the data it has not previously seen or worked upon. One way to overcome this problem is to not handover the entire dataset at once and only exposes the learner to a limited portion of dataset during the training phase and disclose the rest of the dataset during the test phase.

The method adopted for evaluation of classification results in this work is k-fold cross validation. Here, the data set is divided into training set and test set for k different times. The process of cross validation is repeated for 10 different times and the average of all the results is considered as the final accuracy (Triba, 2015; Krstajic, 2014; Poursepanj, 2013). Let k is any variable that holds natural numbers. In k-fold cross validation, the original sample will be partitioned into k-equal sized sub samples and out of these sub samples, a single subsample is recognised and preserved for testing the model and the rest k-1 sub samples are used for training purpose. This cross-validation process is repeated k times for all k sub samples used once as the validation data, and this repetition is termed as Folds. The average of the

Figure 5. Sample Wang data set

k results is used to produce a single estimation. The advantage of this method is that all observations are used for both training and validation purpose and each observation is used exactly once for validation.

For classification problems, a strategically layered k-fold cross validation is used where folds are selected in such a manner that each fold consists almost the same number of class labels.

Here, 10 fold cross validation has been used. This implies that the data is broken into 10 sets of size=n/10. Training set consists of 9 datasets (k-1 observations) and 1 is used for validation purpose at a time. This is done for all 10 observations and the mean accuracy is calculated.

ANALYSIS AND DISCUSSIONS

Feature extraction is performed on the odd image variety of test images formed in Wang data set in two different color spaces, namely, RGB and YUV. This is done with the help of a common numerical programming environment namely, MATLAB. Fractional coefficients of DCT are evaluated for F1 Score and Misclassification Rate. The coefficient percentage showing highest F1 Score and lowest MR is chosen as the feature vector. Further, dimension reduction of these feature vectors gives the following results in the form of F1 score and MR score. Further, the precision and recall of for classification with the chosen fractional coefficient as feature vector is compared to state-of-the-art techniques. The expressions for each metric are given in Equations 7-10.

$$\text{Precision is given by: } \frac{number\ of\ correct\ positive\ results}{number\ of\ all\ positive\ results} \tag{7}$$

$$\text{Recall is given by: } \frac{number\ of\ correct\ positive\ results}{number\ of\ positive\ results\ that\ should\ have\ been\ returned} \tag{8}$$

The F1 score is the Harmonic mean of the precision and Recall.

$$\text{F1 Score}= 2 \cdot \frac{1}{\dfrac{1}{precision}+\dfrac{1}{recall}} = \frac{precision \cdot recall}{precision + recall} \tag{9}$$

Misclassification Rate (MR) can be defined as under.

Let X is a feature space with a finite number of elements. Moreover, let C be a set of classes, let y: X → C be a classifier, and let c be the target concept to be learned. Then the true misclassification rate, denoted as Err ∗ (y), is defined as follows:

$$Err^{*}\left(y\right) = \frac{\left|\left\{x \in X : c\left(x\right) \neq y\left(x\right)\right\}\right|}{\left|X\right|} \tag{10}$$

Lowest misclassification rate is desirable feature that is looked for in an Image Transform using Discrete Cosine Transform.

When 100% feature size was considered, the F1 score for RGB was found to be 0.23 and its MR score was 0.169. While, for the same feature size, F1 score and MR score for YUV colour space was found to be 0.34 and 0.145 respectively.

Now, the feature size was continuously being reduced and F1 Score and MR is recorded for each reduction step. A comparison of F1 Score and MR in two different color spaces are shown in Table 2.

Table 2. Comparison of F1 Score and MR for different feature dimensions

Feature Dimensions	Metrics for Classification	RGB Color Space	YUV Color Space
100% feature Size	F1 Score	0.23	0.34
	MR	0.169	0.145
50% feature Size	F1 Score	0.36	0.44
	MR	0.135	0.103
25% of (N*N) feature size for N*N Image	F1 Score	0.45	0.45
	MR	0.103	0.102
12.5% of feature Size	F1 Score	0.45	0.46
	MR	0.103	0.101
6.25% of feature Size	F1 Score	0.45	0.46
	MR	0.102	0.101
3.125% of feature Size	F1 Score	0.45	0.47
	MR	0.102	0.099
1.5625% of feature Size	F1 Score	0.46	0.5
	MR	0.101	0.094
0.7813% of feature Size	F1 Score	0.47	0.53
	MR	0.101	0.092
0.39% of feature Size	F1 Score	0.5	0.58
	MR	0.098	0.083
0.195% of feature Size	F1 Score	0.52	0.65
	MR	0.095	0.073
0.097% of feature Size	F1 Score	0.54	0.7
	MR	0.093	0.064
0.048% of feature Size	F1 Score	0.58	0.73
	MR	0.087	0.058
0.024% of feature Size	F1 Score	0.6	0.74
	MR	0.083	0.057
0.012% of feature Size	F1 Score	0.63	0.76
	MR	0.078	0.052
0.006% of feature Size	F1 Score	0.62	0.73
	MR	0.079	0.06

Till the Feature size been taken as 0.012%, the accuracy (F1 score) has been increasing along with continuous fall in the MR score until Feature size is reduced to 0.006%. Post this phase, the accuracy begins to fall. The results are recorded previous to this stage.

It is observed that 0.012% of full feature dimension is having the highest F1 Score and lowest MR for both the color spaces. This is an indication that the maximum optimum value is reached and the stage for recording the final results and the state for conclusion has arrived for feature dimension selection.

Further, the Precision and Recall Values of the proposed technique is compared to that of the state-of-the-art techniques as in Figure 6.

The comparison shown in Figure 6 has established that the classification with proposed technique of feature extraction has surpassed the accuracy of benchmarked techniques.

Thus the following objectives are met after performing the experiment.

1. An efficient content-based image classification system s designed.
2. Reduction of feature dimension is effectively carried out.
3. Comparison with state-of-the-art techniques has revealed superiority of the proposed technique.

CONCLUSION

The paper has discussed about Dimension Reduction using Image Transforms for Content Based Feature Extraction. The type of image transformation deployed here is Discrete Cosine Transform. Efforts have been made to first reduce the dimensions of the image by extracting the feature vectors of the image in

Figure 6. Classification comparison of proposed technique to state-of-the-art

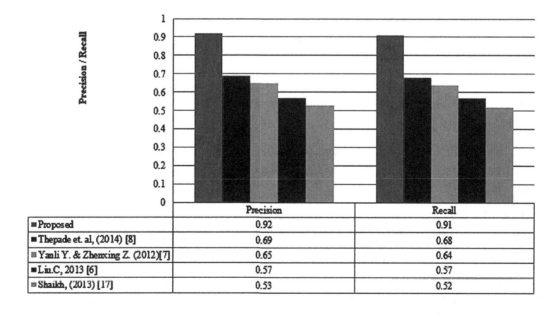

	Precision	Recall
■ Proposed	0.92	0.91
■ Thepade et. al, (2014) [8]	0.69	0.68
▥ Yanli Y. & Zhenxing Z. (2012)[7]	0.65	0.64
■ Liu.C, 2013 [6]	0.57	0.57
▥ Shaikh, (2013) [17]	0.53	0.52

the RGB and YUV colour spaces. Post this dimension reduction, the images have been classified with content-based features. Wang data set used in this experiment classification metrics used is F1 score, MR score, precision and recall. The final results of classification with reduced feature dimension have made the feature extraction technique useful for real world applications. The research can be further extended towards designing of fusion based framework to explore combination of diverse features for boosting classification accuracy.

REFERENCES

Chen, G., & Chen, L. (2014). Recommendation based on contextual opinions. In *International Conference on User Modeling, Adaptation, and Personalization* (pp. 61-73). Springer.

Das, R., & Bhattacharya, S. (2015a). A Novel Feature Extraction Technique for Content Based Image Classification in Digital Marketing Platform. *American Journal of Advanced Computing*, 2(1), 17–24. doi:10.5923/j.ac.20120201.04

Das, R., Thepade, S., & Ghosh, S. (2015b). Content based image recognition by information fusion with multiview features. *International Journal of Information Technology and Computer Science*, 7(10), 61–73. doi:10.5815/ijitcs.2015.10.08

Das, R., Thepade, S., & Ghosh, S. (2017a). Decision Fusion for Classification of Content Based Image Data. In Transactions on Computational Science XXIX (pp. 121-138). Springer Berlin Heidelberg. doi:10.1007/978-3-662-54563-8_7

Das, R., & Walia, E. (2017b). Partition selection with sparse autoencoders for content based image classification. *Neural Computing & Applications*, 1–16.

Do, M. N., & Vetterli, M. (2005). The contourlet transform: An efficient directional multiresolution image representation. *IEEE Transactions on Image Processing*, 14(12), 2091–2106. doi:10.1109/TIP.2005.859376 PMID:16370462

El-Latif, A. A. A., Li, L., Wang, N., Han, Q., & Niu, X. (2013). A new approach to chaotic image encryption based on quantum chaotic system, exploiting color spaces. *Signal Processing*, 93(11), 2986–3000. doi:10.1016/j.sigpro.2013.03.031

Ganesan, P., & Rajini, V. (2014). Assessment of satellite image segmentation in RGB and HSV color space using image quality measures. In *Advances in Electrical Engineering (ICAEE), 2014 International Conference on* (pp. 1-5). IEEE.

Guo, J. M., & Liu, Y. F. (2014). Improved block truncation coding using optimized dot diffusion. *IEEE Transactions on Image Processing*, 23(3), 1269–1275. doi:10.1109/TIP.2013.2257812 PMID:23591493

Guo, J. M., & Prasetyo, H. (2015a). Content-based image retrieval using features extracted from halftoning-based block truncation coding. *IEEE Transactions on Image Processing*, 24(3), 1010–1024. doi:10.1109/TIP.2014.2372619 PMID:25420264

Guo, J. M., Prasetyo, H., & Chen, J. H. (2015b). Content-based image retrieval using error diffusion block truncation coding features. *IEEE Transactions on Circuits and Systems for Video Technology*, *25*(3), 466–481. doi:10.1109/TCSVT.2014.2358011

Hu, Y. C., Lo, C. C., Chen, W. L., & Wen, C. H. (2013). Joint image coding and image authentication based on absolute moment block truncation coding. *Journal of Electronic Imaging*, *22*(1), 013012–013012. doi:10.1117/1.JEI.22.1.013012

Jing, X. Y., & Zhang, D. (2004). A face and palmprint recognition approach based on discriminant DCT feature extraction. *IEEE Transactions on Systems, Man, and Cybernetics. Part B, Cybernetics*, *34*(6), 2405–2415. doi:10.1109/TSMCB.2004.837586 PMID:15619939

Kao, C. C., & Lin, H. Y. (2015). Performance Evaluation of Bit-plane Slicing based Stereo Matching Techniques. VISAPP, 365-370. doi:10.5220/0005260203650370

Kekre, H. B., Thepade, S. D., Athawale, A., Shah, A., Verlekar, P., & Shirke, S. (2010). Energy compaction and image splitting for image retrieval using kekre transform over row and column feature vectors. *International Journal of Computer Science and Network Security*, *10*(1), 289–298.

Krstajic, D., Buturovic, L. J., Leahy, D. E., & Thomas, S. (2014). Cross-validation pitfalls when selecting and assessing regression and classification models. *Journal of Cheminformatics*, *6*(1), 10. doi:10.1186/1758-2946-6-10 PMID:24678909

Lee, Y. H., Kim, B., & Rhee, S. B. (2013). Content-based image retrieval using spatial-color and Gabor texture on a mobile device. *Computer Science and Information Systems*, *10*(2), 807–823. doi:10.2298/CSIS120716035L

Li, Y., Miao, Z., Xu, Y., Li, H., & Zhang, Y. (2016). Combining Nonlinear Dimension Reduction and Hashing Method for Efficient Image Retrieval. In *Semantics, Knowledge and Grids (SKG), 2016 12th International Conference on* (pp. 126-130). IEEE

Liu, C. (2013) A new finger vein feature extraction algorithm. In *Image and Signal Processing (CISP), 2013 6th International Congress on* (Vol. 1, pp. 395-399). IEEE. 10.1109/CISP.2013.6744026

Mookiah, M. R. K., Acharya, U. R., Lim, C. M., Petznick, A., & Suri, J. S. (2012). Data mining technique for automated diagnosis of glaucoma using higher order spectra and wavelet energy features. *Knowledge-Based Systems*, *33*, 73–82. doi:10.1016/j.knosys.2012.02.010

Nigam, A., & Kushwaha, V. K. (2015). *Secure Transaction of Medical Images using bit plane slicing and integer wavelet transform approach*. Academic Press.

Podpora, M., Korbas, G. P., & Kawala-Janik, A. (2014). YUV vs RGB-Choosing a Color Space for Human-Machine Interaction. In FedCSIS Position Papers (pp. 29-34). Academic Press.

Poursepanj, H., Weissbock, J., & Inkpen, D. (2013). Ottawa: System description for SemEval 2013 Task 2 Sentiment Analysis in Twitter. In SemEval@ NAACL-HLT (pp. 380-383). Academic Press.

Ravi, K., & Ravi, V. (2015). A survey on opinion mining and sentiment analysis: Tasks, approaches and applications. *Knowledge-Based Systems*, *89*, 14–46. doi:10.1016/j.knosys.2015.06.015

Sanjay, G. (2016). A Comparative Study on Face Recognition using Subspace Analysis. In *International Conference on Computer Science and Technology Allies in Research* (p. 82). Academic Press.

Shaikh, S. H., Maiti, A. K., & Chaki, N. (2013). A new image binarization method using iterative partitioning. *Machine Vision and Applications*, 1–14.

Sonka, M., Hlavac, V., & Boyle, R. (2014). *Image processing, analysis, and machine vision*. Cengage Learning.

Thepade, S., Das, R., & Ghosh, S. (2013) Performance comparison of feature vector extraction techniques in RGB color space using block truncation coding for content based image classification with discrete classifiers. In *India Conference (INDICON), 2013 Annual IEEE* (pp. 1-6). IEEE. 10.1109/INDCON.2013.6726053

Thepade,S., Das, R. & Ghosh, S. (2015). A Novel Feature Extraction Technique Using Bi-narization of Bit Planes for Content Based Image Classification. *Journal of Engineering*. doi:10.1155/2014/439218

Thepade, S., Das, R., & Ghosh, S. (2017). Decision fusion-based approach for content-based image classification. *International Journal of Intelligent Computing and Cybernetics*, *10*(3), 310–331. doi:10.1108/IJICC-07-2016-0025

Tokarczyk, P., Wegner, J. D., Walk, S., & Schindler, K. (2015). Features, color spaces, and boosting: New insights on semantic classification of remote sensing images. *IEEE Transactions on Geoscience and Remote Sensing*, *53*(1), 280–295. doi:10.1109/TGRS.2014.2321423

Triba, M. N., Le Moyec, L., Amathieu, R., Goossens, C., Bouchemal, N., Nahon, P., ... Savarin, P. (2015). PLS/OPLS models in metabolomics: The impact of permutation of dataset rows on the K-fold cross-validation quality parameters. *Molecular BioSystems*, *11*(1), 13–19. doi:10.1039/C4MB00414K PMID:25382277

Walia, E., Vesal, S., & Pal, A. (2014). An effective and fast hybrid framework for color image retrieval. *Sensing and Imaging*, *15*(1), 93. doi:10.100711220-014-0093-9

Yanli, Y., & Zhenxing, Z. (2012). A novel local threshold binarization method for QR image. *IET International Conference on Automatic Control and Artificial Intelligence*, 224-227. 10.1049/cp.2012.0959

Chapter 3
Fuzzy Techniques for Content–Based Image Retrieval

Rose Bindu Joseph P.
VIT University, India

Ezhilmaran Devarasan
VIT University, India

ABSTRACT

Content-based image retrieval aims to acquire images from huge databases by analyzing their visual features like color, texture, shape, and spatial relationship. The search for superior accuracy in image retrieval has resulted in concentrating more on semantic gap reduction between the low-level features and high level human reasoning. Fuzzy theory is a prevailing methodology which helps in attaining this goal by using attributes and interpretations similar to human reasoning. The vagueness and impreciseness in image data and the retrieval process can be modeled by fuzzy sets. This chapter analyses fuzzy theoretic approaches in various stages of content-based image retrieval system. Various fuzzy-based feature descriptors are discussed along with different fuzzy classification and indexing algorithms for content-based image retrieval. This chapter also presents an overview of various fuzzy distance and similarity measures for image retrieval. A novel fuzzy theoretic retrieval for finger vein biometric images is also proposed in this chapter with experiment and analysis.

INTRODUCTION

During the past few decades, volume of digital image databases has grown exponentially because of the rapid advancement of internet, modern cameras and technologies. The quick surge of image data has amplified efficient accessibility in various fields such as security, medical image archives, multimedia encyclopedia, geographical information systems and biometric databases. In view of this, many content-based image retrieval (CBIR) systems have been established by utilizing color descriptors, texture or shape features for recovering preferred images from an assortment.

DOI: 10.4018/978-1-5225-5775-3.ch003

Even though many disadvantages of the outdated text-based retrieval systems have been overcome by CBIR systems, only low-level features are extracted by them to denote image data. The basic nature of subjective and fuzzy understanding and intuition of individuals cannot be handled by these rigid low-level measures. Also, for a visual content, different inferences and descriptions would be given by different individuals. In practical situations, high level reasoning and features are used by individuals for interpreting and recalling similar images and measuring the similarities between them. The need for improving the accuracy in retrieval process has forced to shift the focus of research in image retrieval into semantic gap reduction that lies among lower grade visual structures and competent semantics possessed by human. Fuzzy theory is a powerful tool to realize this goal which uses attributes and inferences similar to human reasoning. Furthermore, image data, specifications for image query and measures of similarity in retrieval problems comprise of fuzziness and imprecision. The concepts modeled by fuzzy set theory have no exact boundary between membership and non-membership and the change is gradual rather than abrupt. Fuzzy approaches can be used to model the vagueness and to represent and process imprecise and uncertain data. Fuzzy techniques provide a data model which is intuitive and user friendly that can take into account subjectivity and uncertainties. Human thinking and decision-making skills can be emulated in machines using the powerful reasoning algorithms of fuzzy theory.

Different researchers have proposed different fuzzy feature descriptors by replacing low level visual features for retrieving images similar to query image. Fuzzy attributed relational graphs are fuzzy image descriptors that can robustly represent objects in images along with their attributes and spatial relations. Another fuzzy descriptor that is used in CBIR is Fuzzy color histogram (FCH) which been proposed as a competent feature descriptor that can overcome the drawbacks of traditional non-fuzzy descriptors efficiently.

Traditional techniques for image classification classify images mainly into discrete classes. A pixel is allocated into a class having highest degree of similarity. But it is not preferable in practical problems to allocate membership of image data completely into one class. Representation of images into continuous classes is the best alternative approach to this discrete representation. This can be effectively achieved by assigning a membership degree indicating the relative strength of inclusion into one particular class. A fuzzy support vector machine (FSVM) is an efficient alternative to classical SVM which reduces the effects of outliers and noises by using an appropriate fuzzy membership function. Fuzzy SVM performs powerfully even when the data is small in size. Fuzzy inference system is another fuzzy classifier widely used in image classification and retrieval which uses a series of appropriate fuzzy inference commands to classify images into fuzzy classes. Fuzzy c-means clustering (FCM) is a prevalent algorithm that works with the concepts of fuzzy theory. In this, each image feature is assigned a fuzzy membership of belongingness to a cluster.

Fuzzy theory offers a wide range of distance measures as well as similarity functions such as fuzzy Minkowsky distance, fuzzy Euclidean distance and fuzzy set theoretic similarity measures. The extracted visual features are transformed into fuzzy plane before calculating the appropriated fuzzy distance or similarity measures between them.

Fuzzy theory enables CBIR to pose a query in terms of linguistic variables which represents the various features of images under consideration. Fuzzy techniques have been used comprehensively at different image retrieval stages such as feature extraction, classification and indexing as well as in measuring the similarity among images. This chapter consolidates the various approaches in CBIR using fuzzy techniques. Back ground and related works in the various stages of fuzzy based CBIR is discussed first in this chapter, followed by a brief overview of the theory of image processing in fuzzy theoretic environment. Detailed descriptions on fuzzy feature descriptors, fuzzy classifiers and fuzzy distance measures are presented in the following sections. A fuzzy theoretic retrieval is introduced in the next part for finger vein biometric images with experiment and analysis and the book chapter is concluded with conclusion and directions for future research.

BACKGROUND AND RELATED WORKS

Content based image retrieval makes use of the traits of an image that are visually significant to characterize and index the images. These feature vectors are compiled as a database which is used for comparison with the query. Image retrieval is executed using an indexing system after calculating the similarity measures or distance measures.

Earlier systems of image retrieval used written annotation about images instead of visual elements. Advancement of internet and digital image technologies gave rise to urgent need of replacement of the manual annotation with a faster and efficient system after 1990, which is the content based image retrieval system. Comprehensive reviews about content-based image retrieval have been given by Smeulders et al. (2000), Rui et al. (1999) and Long et al. (2003). Numerous image retrieval systems have been established effectively in the recent era, like different versions of QBIC Systems (Flickner, Sawhney, Niblack, Ashley, Huang, Dom,... & Steele, 1995), SIMPLIcity System (Wang & Wiederhold, 2001), Blobworld System (Carson, Thomas, Belongie, Hellerstein, & Malik,1999) and VisualSEEK (Smith & Chang,1997).

Fuzzy set theory put forward by Zadeh (1965), has been adopted by image retrieval systems in the recent years because it makes the process simpler by applying a reasoning similar to that of human. The two major approaches in fuzzy inference are Mamdani method proposed by Mamdani and Assilian (1975) in which consequent of rules is fuzzy set and Takagi-Sugeno-Kang method by Takagi and Sugeno (1985) where consequent of rules is a linear combination of inputs. It was Prewitt who introduced fuzzy set theoretic concepts into image processing (Prewitt, 1970). Pal and King (1983) as well as Rosen field (1984) carried out many researches on fuzzy theory in image processing.

Krishnapuram et al.(2004) used fuzzy attributed relational graphs (FARG) for a fuzzy image retrieval system(FIRST) by extending the concept of fuzzy attributed graphs (FAG) introduced by Chan and Cheung (1992). A node is used in this approach for representing an object or region of images and characteristics like size or color. Edges are representatives of relations among regions with features such as spatial relation and adjacency. Aboulmagd et al. (2009) implemented matching algorithm for graphs with FARG as feature descriptor which uses similarity of color attributes for image retrieval. A fuzzy conceptual graph was proposed as matching feature descriptor by Mulhem et al. (2001). Fuzzy concepts, fuzzy relational attributes and fuzzy relations are the main components of the directed graphs used in this. Chen and Wang (2002) introduced a fuzzy matching which is region-based for CBIR named unified feature matching (UFM).

Han and Ma (2002) developed fuzzy color histogram (FCH) as a descriptor for color image retrieval using fuzzy c-means clustering (FCM) algorithm which provided membership grades. A novel fuzzy linking algorithm with fuzzy color histogram (FCH) was introduced by Konstantinidis et al. (2005) on the L*a*b* color space having a histogram which created less number of bins using a set of fuzzy inference rules. Chamorro-Martínez et al. (2007) implemented fuzzy object-relational database systems (FORDBMS) for fuzzy data by constructing a fuzzy HSI color space by extracting dominant fuzzy colors from images.

Fuzzy c-means clustering (FCM) is a one of the most widely used classification and indexing algorithm in CBIR which was introduced by Bezdek et al. (1984). Krishnapuram and Keller (1993) extended the concept of FCM using possibility theory where possibilistic partitions are attained by minimizing an appropriate objective function. Gath and Geva (1989) produced an unsupervised fuzzy partition optimal number of class algorithm (UFP-ONC) which is free from cluster names assumed initially. Li et al. (2008) discussed an innovative fuzzy weighted c-means algorithm (FWCM) by implementing the concept of weighted means using nonparametric weighted feature extraction (NWFE) for replacing the cluster centers in the FCM.

Fuzzy support vector machines (FSVM) was presented by Lin and Wang (2002) for image classification where input points of SVM were given a degree of fuzzy membership. The influence of noises and outliers in data points was reduced by allowing to contribute different learning decisions by different input points. A fuzzy SVM in which each sample is considered as positive as well as negative was given by Wang et al. (2005). Jiang et al. (2006) introduced a unique fuzzy SVM classification which takes the distance of class center to the data point into account. A pseudo label fuzzy SVM (PLFSVM) was developed by Wu and Yap (2006) in which pseudo labelled images for active learning were fuzzified.

Theory of fuzzy rules has been applied widely in various image classification algorithms which use either Mamdani FIS (Mamdani & Assilian, 1975) or Sugeno FIS (Takagi & Sugeno, 1985). Adaptive network based fuzzy inference system (ANFIS) is an extensively used FIS in image classification which was introduced by Jang (1993). Some image classification applications of FIS can be seen in (Nedeljkovic, 2004) and (Athanasiadis, Simou, Papadopoulos, Benmokhtar, Chandramouli, Tzouvaras,... & Huet, 2009).

Fuzzy based distance measures have been proposed in several works for retrieval of images similar to the query images. An overview of various fuzzy distance measures is given by Bloch (1999) and Zwick et al. (1987). Fan et al. (2001) presented some relations between distance measures and metric defined on fuzzy sets.

During the past few decades, significant advancement has been made in implementation and development of fuzzy theory in content-based image retrieval. However several challenges and issues continue to exist in this research area that still draw attraction from researchers in various disciplines.

IMAGE PROCESSING IN FUZZY THEORETIC ENVIRONMENT

Statistical models handle random events and outcomes whereas non-random imprecision are captured and quantified with fuzzy models. Vagueness and ambiguity in complex systems are efficiently modelled by fuzzy logic. Conventional set theory is extended using the concept of partial truth in fuzzy set theory. A grading that explains the level of affiliation of an element to a specific set is assigned by a fuzzy set. There has been a sturdy upsurge in the use of fuzzy techniques in image processing applications during the past few decades. Difficulties on object recognition and scene analysis is overcome with expert knowledge in many image processing applications. Human knowledge is processed and represented using fuzzy if then rules in the powerful tools provided by fuzzy set theory and fuzzy logic. But then the uncertainty in image data, process and results in image processing pose many difficulties. However, most of the time, it is the ambiguity and vagueness that causes uncertainty and not randomness. There are other types of imperfections that exist in image processing like geometrical fuzziness, ambiguity in greyness and ill-defined data even when the randomness is managed using probability theory. These glitches which are fuzzy in nature are often present in content-based image retrieval. The brightness or darkness level of a pixel or deciding the boundary level of two image sections or similar issues can be managed more efficiently using a fuzzy approach.

Fuzzy sets are the sets on the Universal set X which can assume degrees of membership which is between 0 and 1. The fuzzy set A can be stated as

$$A = \left\{ \left(t, \mu_A(t) \right), t \in X \right\}$$

where the membership function

$$\mu_A(t) = \begin{cases} 1 & if \ t \in A \\ 0 & if \ t \notin A \end{cases}.$$

Clearly the membership function $\mu_A(x)$ of an element x in A is a real number such that $0 \leq \mu_A(t) \leq 1$.

Fuzzy image processing (FIP) comprises of the various methodologies that comprehend, symbolize and develop the images, their fragments and characteristics as fuzzy sets. Fuzzy geometry such as fuzzy metric and topology, measures of fuzziness like divergence and entropy, fuzzy inference systems that works with image fuzzification, fuzzy rules and image defuzzification, fuzzy c-mans and possibile c-means clustering and fuzzy mathematical morphology using fuzzy erosion and dilation etc. are some of the important tools in fuzzy image processing. Depending on the problem to be solved, different processes and representations are chosen with appropriate fuzzy techniques. Image fuzzification, membership modification and image defuzzification are the three major stages in fuzzy image processing.

Intensity levels of images are converted into real numbers between 0 and 1 by shifting them to a fuzzy plane for using fuzzy measures in a problem. During fuzzification process crisp values of image intensity are transformed into fuzzy membership values of linguistic variables of fuzzy sets. A grade is associated to a linguistic variable using a membership function. A crisp object is converted into a fuzzy object by the process of fuzzification.

An image A can be characterized in fuzzy set theory as:

$$\sum_{i=0}^{M-1} \sum_{j=0}^{N-1} \left[g_{ij}, \mu_A \left(g_{ij} \right) \right], \ x \in A$$

where $\mu_A \left(g_{ij} \right)$ denote the membership value of the pixel of the image A with $0 \leq \mu_A \left(g_{ij} \right) \leq 1$. Here A is of size M x N having L levels and g_{ij} is the grey level at the pixel position

$$\left(i, j \right), i = 0, 1, 2, \dots M - 1, j = 0, 1, 2, \dots N - 1.$$

Fuzzy systems treat image pixels as fuzzy sets. There can be many overlapping fuzzy sets to describe the same image like black set, white set, edge set or dark, medium and light based on intensity levels as shown in Figure 1.

Figure 1. Example of fuzzy sets of an image

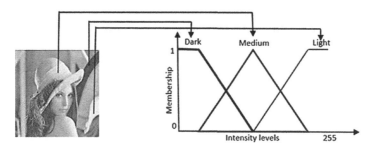

FUZZY BASED IMAGE DESCRIPTORS FOR CBIR

Classical approaches in CBIR make use of visual feature descriptors of images for recovering images from large scale databases depending on the interest of the users. But quite often, a set of these descriptors are not sufficient to represent the diverse aspects of an image completely.

Fuzziness and imprecision associated with individual understanding and perceptions cannot be managed efficiently with these rigid low-level measures. Moreover, accurate identification is difficult as many entirely different objects can share similar or same features. Fuzzy descriptors which are known for its tolerance to imprecise data. The use of fuzzy descriptors in content-based image retrieval allows more flexibility in the process and offers linguistic description for the features by replicating human reasoning and decision making in machines.

Fuzzy Attributed Relational Graphs (FARG)

Fuzzy attributed relational graphs are image descriptors that can robustly represent objects in images along with their attributes and spatial relations. Each region in an image is described using a node in the graph and the relation between the regions is characterized by an edge. The graph of query image is used for obtaining the best matches from database.

For using FARG descriptors for image retrieval the database images and the query image are converted into FARG nodes and edges by converting the image into different regions. For each region j a set of attributes are defined as,

$$A = \left\{ a_i, i = 1, 2, \ldots n_A \right\}$$

For example, some attributes can be defined as $a_1 = size$, $a_2 = contrast$, $a_3 = intensity$ and so on. Now, corresponding to each attribute a_i assign a set of linguistic labels given by,

$$\Lambda_i = \left\{ L_{ik}, k = 1, 2, \ldots n_{a_i} \right\}$$

For example, for attribute $a_1 = size$, set of linguistic label can be assigned as $\Lambda_1 = \{large, medium, small\}$ and for attribute $a_2 = contrast$ linguistic labels cane be given by $\Lambda_2 = \{low, high\}$.

Now define the fuzzy membership value of the attribute a_i at region or node j as μ_{ji}. For example, $a_1 = size$ of node j can be assigned as $\{0.7, 0.2, 0.9\}$. Now the node label of node j is denoted by,

$$\lambda(j) = \left\{ \left(a_i, \mu_{ji}\right), \mu_{ji} \in \mathcal{F}\left(\Lambda_i\right), i = 1, 2, \ldots n_A \right\}$$

Here $\mathcal{F}\left(\Lambda_i\right)$ is the power set of Λ_i. Each a_i can appear only once in Λ_i. In a similar way, attributes for the edges are defined as,

$$R = \left\{ r_i, i = 1, 2, \ldots n_R \right\}$$

For edge attribute r_i define the corresponding set of linguistic labels as,

$$\Sigma_i = \left\{ S_{ik}, k = 1, 2, \ldots n_{r_i} \right\}$$

Now define the fuzzy membership value of the attribute r_i for the edge e as v_{ji}. Now the edge label of edge e is denoted by,

$$\rho(e) = \left\{ \left(r_i, v_{ji}\right), v_{ji} \in \mathcal{F}\left(\Sigma_i\right), i = 1, 2, \ldots n_R \right\}$$

An illustration of FARG with fuzzy nodes and edges is given by Figure 2.

A leader approach is used for clustering the FARGs of database images incrementally forming FARG database of clusters of similar images. One leader FARG corresponds to each of the clusters. The database is formed gradually with a minimum cost. The query image is compared with the leader FARGs after converting it into an FARG. This is done using fuzzy graph matching algorithm. The FARG database is then reduced to a set of FARGs belonging to the clusters corresponding to the closest leaders to the query. Only these are ranked for image retrieval.

Figure 2. Representation of fuzzy nodes and edges in FARG

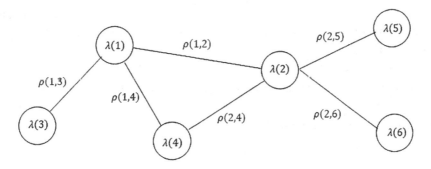

Fuzzy Color Histogram

Color histogram is one of the most commonly used feature descriptor for content-based image retrieval because of their easiness in implementation and invariance to translation and rotation. However, when the image database is very large, image discrimination using color histogram come to a saturation. In addition, spatial information of pixels are not taken into consideration giving similar color distributions for entirely different images. Also, it yields high computational cost due to its high dimensionality on representation. Being a one dimensional descriptor with less number of bins, fuzzy color histograms(FCH) helps in reducing the size of the feature database and hence the computational cost whereas three dimensional color histogram with more than 1000 bins is used in conventional algorithm. As human reasoning is used in FCH extraction, understanding and modification of query image FCH as well as submission of modified FCH back to the CBIR system becomes easier for the CBIR users. FCH spreads membership value of each pixel to all the histogram bins by considering the color similarity information whereas conventional color histogram allocates a pixel to only one of the bins.

Fuzzy color histogram (FCH) has been proposed as a competent feature descriptor for content based image retrieval which can overcome these drawbacks efficiently. Overall membership value is spread over all the histogram bins in FCH and information on the color similarity is considered. Noisy interference and quantization errors do not affect FCH seriously.

For an image I with a total number of N pixels, consider a color space with n color bins. The color histogram is given as, $\mathcal{H}(I) = [\hbar_1, \hbar_2, \ldots, \hbar_n]$. Here $\hbar_i = \frac{\aleph_i}{N}$ where $\aleph_i$ is the number of pixels in the ith color bin. Then the fuzzy color histogram (FCH) is defined as, $\mathcal{F}(I) = [f_1, f_2, \ldots, f_n]$. If μ_{ij} is the fuzzy membership value of the jth pixel in the ith color bin, then $f_i = \frac{1}{N} \sum_{j=1}^{N} \mu_{ij}$.

Fuzzy color histogram is formed from conventional color histogram by applying suitable fuzzy membership functions on histogram of each color component. For high dimensional spaces, dimension can be reduced by set of fuzzy inference rules or fuzzy c-means clustering algorithms.

Very large histograms having huge disparities among adjacent bins are created while using the classical method of color histograms. Hence excessive variations in the histogram are produced with some minor changes in the image. As each color space comprises of three components, this results in 3-dimensional histograms. It is comparatively complex and computationally costly procedure to operate and relate three dimensional histograms. Thus an efficient approach would be to reduce the dimension of histogram to one. Histogram linking is the process of projecting three-dimensional histogram into one dimensional histogram. The fuzzy linking method on L*a*b* color space (Konstantinidis, Gasteratos, & Andreadis, 2005) is explained below.

A color space is divided into a number of bins and number of image pixels belonging to each bin is counted for creating a histogram. The L*a*b* color space is used for creating the histogram by treating the color components as fuzzy sets. A predefined set of fuzzy rules are used for linking of these fuzzy sets to form the histogram. Use of less number of bins to describe the color distribution of images results in making the comparison of histograms much quicker and deliver more robustness to the algorithm. L*a*b* is one of the perceptually even color spaces and it has an approach similar to human in perceiving colors and hence is preferred commonly over other color spaces.

L*, a* and b* signifies luminance, greenness-redness and blueness-yellowness respectively in the L*a*b* color space. Typically the combination of a* and b* components that provides the color information of an image and hence more weight is assigned to a* and b* than L*. The L* space is divided into 3 sub regions namely dark, dim, and bright while a* and b* into 5 regions each in a similar way. The range of L* is from 0 to 100 and a* space range is between -86.1813 and 98.2352 while b* coordinate range is between -107.8617 and 94.4758. 20 prevalent colors in L*a*b* color space are chosen for experiment.

The input variables are fuzzified using triangular membership functions for each of the components. Using the fuzzy membership functions each image pixel in L*a*b* color space is assigned a degree of membership. A Mamdani FIS is used with a set of predefined fuzzy rules for linking the three components. The outputs of fuzzy rules are combined by MAX aggregation operator. 15 color bins are obtained in generating the final color histogram using trapezoidal membership functions. The final output of the inference system is produced by de-fuzzifying the resulting fuzzy set to get a crisp value. Overview of the proposed fuzzy inference system is shown in Figure 3.

Stability of fuzzy color histograms over other color based methods has been verified with experiments using images with different illumination settings. It has been observed that retrieval accuracy is the major benefit of the FCH using fuzzy inference rules.

Figure 3. Fuzzy rule set for fuzzy color histogram

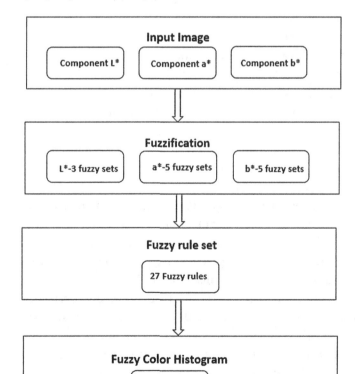

FUZZY BASED IMAGE CLASSIFICATION AND RETRIEVAL

Diverse aspects of Content-Based Image Retrieval (CBIR) have been studied robustly in the recent years.

Image classification is one of the most decisive stages of content-based image retrieval in an image database. It is necessary to extract the underlying semantics for the efficient management and utilization of image databases. Fuzzy reasoning can be combined competently with various techniques of image classification and labelling for semantic indexing and retrieval of images.

Statistical algorithms for classification are usually applied in the cases where the functional expression for the density functions are known beforehand. They also require a large collection of training samples for estimating the parameters. But in practical situations sufficiently large training sample with enough statistical data are often not available. Also, the nature of the sample points and the features are often fuzzy than stochastic. Because of these reasons fuzzy theory-based classification algorithms tend to give more appropriate and accurate result in more complex decision-making problems with less availability of statistics.

Fuzzy SVM

Support vector machines (SVM) are prevailing machine learning algorithms that are employed frequently in content-based image retrieval. This supervised learning technique ingrained in statistical learning model was introduced by Vladimir Vapnik at AT&T Bell Laboratories using the perception of minimizing structural risk. SVM algorithm reveals rationally handpicked samples for labeling so that supreme information gain is achieved in decision making. For feedback, the most informative images are selected by the SVM that are closest to the decision hyperplane.

The foremost perception behind SVM is separation of image samples into different classes after mapping the input image into a feature space of high dimension so that the margin between the classes is a maximum when separated by a surface. The separating surface could be a hyperplane or hypersurface depending on whether the classes are linearly separable or not. A quadratic programming problem is used for maximization of margin and its solution is obtained by its dual problem using Lagrange multipliers. The dot product of functions in feature space known as kernels are used for finding the optimal hyperplane without knowing the mapping. Support vectors are the input points whose combination is utilized for writing the solution of the maximal hyperplane.

Traditional SVM for two class classification treats each training image equally and assign them to two unique classes. But in reality, it is often seen that some of the training images are degraded due to noise. Furthermore, there could be cases of assigning the training images into the wrong classes accidentally. These points which do not belong completely to one class clearly are known as outliers. The traditional SVM algorithm which is sensitive to outliers produces a concluding margin that deviate rigorously from the ideal hyperplane. A fuzzy support vector machine (FSVM) is an efficient alternative to classical SVM which reduces the effects of outliers and noises by using an appropriate fuzzy membership function. Fuzzy SVM performs powerfully even when the number of data is small in size.

In FSVM, the outlook of each sample towards one class is quantified by assigning a fuzzy membership value. The importance of each sample towards the decision plane is represented by the corresponding membership function. A sample point with higher membership value is considered as more important. This gives the input points the freedom to make different contributions in formation of decision plane. FSVM algorithm makes sure that the important training points are classified correctly without giving much importance to some insignificant training points. The theory of Fuzzy SVM can be briefly explained as shown below.

Consider a training sample of k elements given by

$$T = \left\{ \left(\chi_\iota, \psi_\iota \right), \iota = 1, 2, \dots k \right\}$$

where $\chi_\iota \in \Re^l$ is an l-dimensional sample and ψ_ι is the class label which takes the value either -1 or 1. Let $Z = \theta\left(\chi \right)$ be the mapping from input space $\Re^l$ to high dimensional feature space Z. The optimal separating hyperplane with the minimal classification errors can be given by,

$$W \cdot Z + b = 0$$

Here the vector normal to the hyperplane is W and b is the bias that is a scalar.

The problem for optimization using conventional SVM is as follows.

$$Minimize : \frac{1}{2} W^2 + \mathbb{C} \sum_{\iota=1}^{k} \zeta_\iota$$

$$Subject\ to : \psi_\iota \left(W \cdot Z_\iota + b \right) \geq 1 - \zeta_\iota$$

$$\zeta_\iota \geq 0, \iota = 1, 2, \dots k$$

Here a balance between optimization of margin and violations in classification can be attained by tuning the regularization parameter $\mathbb{C}$. $\zeta_\iota, \iota = 1, 2, \dots k$ are the non-zero slack variables that are introduced for adjusting the amount of constraint violation.

In Fuzzy SVM, a fuzzy membership value υ_ι is assigned to each training sample χ_ι such that $0 \leq \upsilon_\iota \leq 1$ and it gives a measure of belongingness of χ_ι in class ψ_ι. Then the training sample takes the form

$$T = \left\{ \left(\chi_\iota, \psi_\iota, \upsilon_\iota \right), \iota = 1, 2, \dots k \right\}.$$

Now the problem for optimization in Fuzzy SVM can be stated as follows:

$$Minimize : \frac{1}{2} W^2 + \mathbb{C} \sum_{\iota=1}^{k} \upsilon_\iota \zeta_\iota$$

$$Subject\ to : \psi_\iota \left(W \cdot Z_\iota + b \right) \geq 1 - \zeta_\iota$$

$\zeta_\iota \geq 0, \iota = 1, 2, \ldots k$

In the optimization problem of Fuzzy SVM, υ_ι acts as the weightage for parameter ζ_ι. If a smaller membership value is chosen for υ_ι then the effect of the parameter ζ_ι is reduced accordingly and the point corresponding to that is considered as less significant.

The Lagrangian $\mathcal{L}\left(W, b, \zeta_\iota, \alpha, \beta\right)$ is constructed for solving the optimization problem and it is given by,

$$\mathcal{L}\left(W, b, \zeta_\iota, \alpha, \beta\right) = \frac{1}{2}W^2 + \mathbb{C}\sum_{\iota=1}^{k}\upsilon_\iota\zeta_\iota - \sum_{\iota=1}^{k}\alpha_\iota\left(\psi_\iota\left(W \cdot Z_\iota + b\right) - 1 + \zeta_\iota\right) - \sum_{\iota=1}^{k}\beta_\iota\zeta_\iota$$

The saddle points of $\mathcal{L}\left(W, b, \zeta_\iota, \alpha, \beta\right)$ are determined keeping the following conditions.

$$W - \sum_{\iota=1}^{k}\alpha_\iota\psi_\iota Z_\iota = 0$$

$$-\sum_{\iota=1}^{k}\alpha_\iota\psi_\iota = 0$$

$$\upsilon_\iota\mathbb{C} - \alpha_\iota - \beta_\iota = 0$$

The decision function is obtained by solving the dual problem with a set of support vectors and corresponding weights.

Fuzzy SVM has a parameter corresponding to each of the training sample whereas conventional SVM has only one free parameter altogether. The importance of a training point χ_ι is controlled with different value of the corresponding υ_ι. Therefore, selection of appropriate fuzzy membership function play an important role in Fuzzy SVM.

Fuzzy Inference System for Classification

Fuzzy inference system has been be used effectively for content based image retrieval as it provides simpler analysis and better design for the classification system. Fuzzy inference system employs fuzzy reasoning that includes some linguistic variables. The linguistic definition of the fuzzy rule-based classification model provides more flexibility and a parameter tuning closer to human reasoning. Moreover, fuzzy logic can handle the uncertainties and ambiguity in image classification more effectively. Several limitations of classical content-based image retrieval systems can be overcome by fuzzy rule based system which utilizes better understanding of image semantics. A fuzzy inference system can determine the relative importance of one image feature over the other, by assigning appropriate weight factor. The rules deployed in the inference system can constructed by user himself by analyzing the parameters and constraints present in the problem in hand. In the case of more complex problems where direct determination of fuzzy rules would be difficult, a training algorithm can be used for deriving the fuzzy rules indirectly from the collected information.

The most prevalent fuzzy inference systems are Mamdani FIS and Takagi-Sugeno FIS which differ in the nature of the consequent of the fuzzy rule base which are the output membership functions. Output of Mamdani fuzzy inference system gives fuzzy sets that do not depend on the input membership functions as the output, based on the predefined fuzzy rules. In Takagi-Sugeno FIS, output membership function is either a linear combination of the input fuzzy sets or a constant. Adaptive neuro fuzzy inference system (ANFIS) is another fuzzy inference system that is popularly used for image classification which adapts the parameters of the FIS using neural networks.

Fuzzy inference system formulates suitable rules and based on the rules, decision is made. A fuzzy inference system has the following components: fuzzification phase, inference phase, and defuzzification phase. Figure 4 shows the main components of a fuzzy inference system that can implemented for image classification.

During fuzzification stage, the number of input variables as well as output classes are decided along with their linguistic variable names based on the image data set. Each variable is assigned a fuzzy membership function such as triangle, trapezoidal, Gaussian etc. depending on the problem so that the crisp inputs are transformed into corresponding fuzzy values.

Inference phase of the system has a database which consists of fuzzy membership values of the variables used in the rule base. The main component of this phase is the predefined rule base based on which the decision-making unit performs the inference operations and decide the fuzzy output class. A general form of a fuzzy rule in Mamdani method can be written as:

$$\text{IF}\left(\text{fuzzy input } x_1 = a_1\right)\text{AND}\,/\,\text{OR}\left(\text{fuzzy input } x_2 = a_2\right)$$
$$\text{AND}\,/\,\text{OR}\cdots\text{THEN}\left(\text{fuzzy output } y = b\right)$$

A general rule in a Sugeno fuzzy system has the following form:

Figure 4. Stages of a fuzzy inference system for image classification

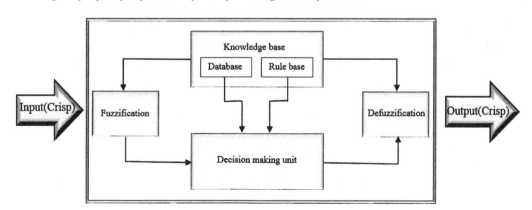

$$\text{IF}\left(\text{fuzzy input } 1 = x\right) \text{AND} / \text{OR}\left(\text{fuzzy input } 2 = y\right)$$
$$\text{THEN}\left(\text{fuzzy output } z = ax + by + c\right)$$

Depending on the image data set and the classification problem the number of rules in the rule base can be determined.

During the defuzzification interface, fuzzy output classes are transformed into crisp outputs which forms the final classification outputs.

Fuzzy C-Means Clustering (FCM)

Clustering is a well-recognized unsupervised classification technique which can be used efficiently in content-based image retrieval even when there is no prior understanding about the image data available. Fuzzy c-means clustering (FCM) is a one of the most commonly used clustering algorithm that works with the concepts of fuzzy theory. In this clustering technique, each image feature point is assigned a fuzzy membership of belongingness to a cluster. Fuzzy c-means algorithm aims at minimizing the cost function of dissimilarity measure by partitioning a group of n-vectors into c-fuzzy classes each having a cluster center. Some of different measures used for discriminating the classes are distance measures, similarity measures, connectivity measure and centroid. The image data set is allocated into disjoint crisp clusters in traditional non-fuzzy clustering methods where exactly one cluster is fixed for each data element. However, in fuzzy c-means clustering one image point can belong to more than one cluster simultaneously. This is regulated by a fuzzy membership degree with which each point fit into the various classes. An appropriate heuristic methodology is implemented in determining the fuzzy membership function.

A general form of a fuzzy c-means clustering can be explained as given below.

Consider an image data sample of $\mathbb{N}$ items given by,

$$A = \left\{a_1, a_2, \ldots, a_j, \ldots, a_{\mathbb{N}}\right\}.$$

Let this data be partitioned into $\mathbb{C}$ clusters given by,

$$U = \left\{U_1, U_2, \ldots, U_k, \ldots, U_{\mathbb{C}}\right\}$$

by assigning a fuzzy membership μ_{kj} for sample a_j to be in cluster U_k such that

$$\bigcup_{k=1}^{\mathbb{C}} U_k = A$$

and

$$U_p \bigcap U_q = \phi, 1 \leq p \neq q \leq \mathbb{C}.$$

Thus the fuzzy c-partition of the data set can be displayed in terms of the membership grade using a $\mathbb{C} \times \mathbb{N}$ matrix given by,

$$\begin{bmatrix} \mu_{11} & \cdots & \mu_{1\mathbb{N}} \\ \vdots & \ddots & \vdots \\ \mu_{\mathbb{C}1} & \cdots & \mu_{\mathbb{C}\mathbb{N}} \end{bmatrix}$$

This fuzzy c-partition satisfies the following conditions.

$$\mu_{kj} \in [0,1]$$

$$\sum_{k=1}^{\mathbb{C}} \mu_{kj} = 1, 1 \leq j \leq \mathbb{N}$$

$$\sum_{j=1}^{\mathbb{N}} \mu_{kj} > 0, 1 \leq k \leq \mathbb{C}$$

An iterative minimization of objective function is used in FCM algorithm for reaching the optimal fuzzy c-partition.

The input samples are considered along with their fuzzy membership as weights in calculating the distance to the corresponding cluster centers. When the membership grade of a sample is smaller, influence of the corresponding sample will become lesser in the calculation. Out of the different clustering measures to determine the optimal fuzzy c-partitions the most popular generalized least-squared errors functional is given by,

$$z_m(U,V) = \sum_{j=1}^{\mathbb{N}} \sum_{k=1}^{\mathbb{C}} (\mu_{kj})^m \, a_j - v_k^2$$

Here $V = \{v_1, v_2, \ldots, v_k, \ldots, v_\mathbb{C}\}$ is the space of cluster centers and m is a weighting exponent such that $1 \leq m \leq \infty$.

With more and more iterations, the optimal fuzzy c-partition becomes better and better and the final partition is determined when the difference between the consecutive partitions is less than a very small predetermined threshold value.

FUZZY MEASURES FOR CONTENT BASED IMAGE RETRIEVAL

Content based image retrieval depends on visual features of database images and their similarity to the query image features for retrieving the best matches. Selection of an appropriate similarity or distance measure plays a key role in efficient image retrieval. Fuzzy theory-based similarity or distance measures are finding applications popularly in CBIR in recent years. The reason for this can be mainly attributed not merely to the vast toolset they possess for efficiently handling imprecise spatial information, but also to the expert knowledge and differentiability that they offer. The extracted visual features are transformed into fuzzy plane before calculating the appropriated fuzzy distance or similarity measures between them. Fuzzy theory offers a wide range of distance measures as well as similarity functions.

Fuzzy Distance Measures

Consider a universal set X of feature vectors and let $\mathcal{F}$ be set of all fuzzy sets on X where $\wp$ be set of all crisp or ordinary sub sets of X. Then a fuzzy distance measure $\mathfrak{D} : \mathcal{F} \times \mathcal{F} \rightarrow [0,1]$ has the following properties (Xuecheng, 1992):

- $\mathfrak{D}(U,V) = \mathfrak{D}(V,U), \forall U, V \in \mathcal{F}$
- $\mathfrak{D}(U,U) = 0, \forall U \in \mathcal{F}$
- $\mathfrak{D}(A, A^c) = \max_{\forall U,V \in \mathcal{F}} \mathfrak{D}(U,V), \forall A \in \wp$
- $\mathfrak{D}(U,V) \leq \mathfrak{D}(U,W)$ and $\mathfrak{D}(V,W) \leq \mathfrak{D}(U,W), \forall U, V, W \in \mathcal{F}$ such that $U \subset V \subset W$.

Fuzzy Minkowsky Distance

Let U and V be two fuzzy sets on the universal set $X = \{x_1, x_2, ..., x_L\}$. Then Minkowsky distance between U and V is given by,

$$\mathfrak{D}_r(U,V) = \left(\sum_{j=1}^{L} \left| \mu_U(x_i) - \mu_V(x_i) \right|^r \right)^{1/r}, r \geq 1$$

Fuzzy Euclidean Distance

When $r = 2$ in the Minkowsky distance formula, we get Fuzzy Euclidean distance which is given by,

$$\mathfrak{D}_E(U,V) = \sqrt{\sum_{j=1}^{L} \left| \mu_U(x_i) - \mu_V(x_i) \right|^2}$$

Fuzzy Manhattan Distance

Fuzzy Manhattan distance (City block distance or Hamming distance) is obtained by putting $r = 1$ in the Minkowsky distance formula and it is given by,

$$\mathfrak{D}_M(U,V) = \sum_{j=1}^{L} \left| \mu_U(x_i) - \mu_V(x_i) \right|$$

Manhattan distance is called Hamming distance when all features are binary in the case of crisp sets.

Distance Measure With Fuzzy Entropy

Amount of uncertainty obtained from a fuzzy set can be measured by fuzzy entropy which is similar to traditional Shannon entropy. Different researchers have proposed different distance measures depending on the corresponding fuzzy entropies used. De Luca and Termini (1972) defined a fuzzy distance measure based on fuzzy entropy. It is given as follows:

$$\mathfrak{D}_E(U,V) = \left| \mathbb{E}(\mu_U) - \mathbb{E}(\mu_V) \right|$$

Here the fuzzy entropy is based on Shannon probabilistic entropy and is defined as follows, with a normalization constant K.

$$\mathbb{E}(\mu_U) = -K \sum_{j=1}^{L} \left[\mu_U(x_i) \log \left(\mu_U(x_i) \right) + \left(1 - \mu_U(x_i) \right) \log \left(1 - \mu_U(x_i) \right) \right]$$

Fuzzy Similarity Measures

Consider a universal set X of feature vectors and let $\mathcal{F}$ be set of all fuzzy sets on X where $\wp$ be set of all crisp or ordinary sub sets of X. Then a fuzzy similarity measure $\mathcal{S} : \mathcal{F} \times \mathcal{F} \to [0,1]$ has the following properties (Xuecheng, 1992):

- $\mathcal{S}(U,V) = \mathcal{S}(V,U), \forall U,V \in \mathcal{F}$
- $\mathcal{S}(U,U) = \max_{\forall U,V \in \mathcal{F}} \mathcal{S}(U,V), \forall U \in \mathcal{F}$
- $\mathcal{S}(A,A^c) = 0, \forall A \in \wp$
- $\mathcal{S}(U,V) \geq \mathcal{S}(U,W)$ and $\mathcal{S}(V,W) \geq \mathcal{S}(U,W), \forall U,V,W \in \mathcal{F}$ such that $U \subset V \subset W$.

The relation between fuzzy similarity measures and fuzzy distance measures is studied by various researchers. Johanyák and Kovács (2005) and Kóczy and Tikk (2000) define fuzzy similarity measure $S(U,V)$ using fuzzy distance measure $\mathfrak{D}(U,V)$ as follows:

$$S(U,V) = \frac{1}{1 + \mathfrak{D}(U,V)}$$

S. H. Lee proposed the following fuzzy similarity measure using fuzzy distance measure.

$$S(U,V) = 1 - \mathfrak{D}\left(U \cap V^c, [0]_X\right) - \mathfrak{D}\left(U \cup V^c, [1]_X\right)$$

Here, $[0]_X$ and $[1]_X$ are fuzzy sets in X with membership values 0 and 1.

AN EFFICIENT RETRIEVAL ALGORITHM FOR FINGER VEIN BIOMETRIC IMAGES BASED ON FUZZY THEORY

Finger vein recognition is explored extensively in the modern era as a competent biometric. The uncertainties and ambiguities in finger vein image retrieval can be handled more efficiently using fuzzy theory-based techniques. A fuzzy set theoretic image retrieval is presented in this session for retrieving finger vein images. After assigning fuzzy membership values to grey level histogram of images, the images are retrieved based on a fuzzy similarity measure using Einstein T norm from the database. Evaluation of the performance of the system is executed using precision rates and recall rates.

Before the image retrieval stage, the database images and the query image undergo fuzzification using gamma membership function. For this, grey level histogram of images are converted into fuzzy sets by applying the membership values

In set theoretic approach similarity measures are defined in terms of union or intersection of fuzzy sets. These approaches are based on the concept that if two fuzzy sets intersect weakly, then similarity between them can be considered to be less. Most of these similarity measures are based on the model proposed by Tversky (1977). Let the entities under investigation be represented by $W = \{p, q, r...\}$. Let the objects p, q, and r be characterized by the set of attributes denoted by P, Q, and R. Then Tversky defined the similarity function as given in the following equation.

$$S(p,q) = af(P \cap Q) - bf(P - Q) - cf(Q - P)$$

In the equation $a, b, c \geq 0$ and they are parameters leading to different kinds of measures. Another form of this can be given in ratio model as follows:

$$S(p,q) = \frac{f(P \cap Q)}{f((P \cap Q)) + bf(P - Q) + cf(Q - P)}$$

Using laws of set theory, $P - Q = P \cap Q^c$ where Q^c is the compliment of Q. Then the equation changes to the form:

$$S(p,q) = \frac{f(P \cap Q)}{f((P \cap Q)) + b\, f(P \cap Q^c) + c\, f(Q \cap P^c)}$$

Using this equation, similarity measure between the fuzzified database images $\mu_D(i)$ and query image $\mu_Q(i)$ can be obtained as given below.

$$S(p,q) = \frac{\sum_{i=1}^{L} \mu_D(i) \cap \mu_Q(i)}{\sum_{i=1}^{L} \mu_D(i) \cap \mu_Q(i) + b\sum_{i=1}^{L} \mu_D(i) \cap (1 - \mu_Q(i)) + c\sum_{i=1}^{L} \mu_Q(i) \cap (1 - \mu_D(i))}$$

Using algebra of fuzzy sets, intersection $\cap$ can be replaced by any triangular norm (T-norm) operators for better results. Here Einstein T-norm is used as intersection operator whose general form is given as follows:

$$E(d,q) = \frac{dq}{1 + (1 - d)(1 - q)}$$

In the case of the database and query fuzzy sets, it takes the form as shown below:

$$\mu_D(i) \cap \mu_Q(i) = \frac{\mu_D(i)\mu_Q(i)}{1 + ((1 - \mu_D(i))(1 - \mu_Q(i)))}$$

$$\mu_D(i) \cap (1 - \mu_Q(i)) = \frac{\mu_D(i)(1 - \mu_Q(i))}{1 + ((1 - \mu_D(i))\mu_Q(i))}$$

$$\mu_Q(i) \cap (1 - \mu_D(i)) = \frac{\mu_Q(i)(1 - \mu_D(i))}{1 + ((1 - \mu_Q(i))\mu_D(i))}$$

For each database image, the similarity measure $S(p,q)$ is calculated using these three equations, where the parameter values $b = 0.5$ and $c = 0.5$ as the relative importance to the distinctive features are the same. After calculating similarity for all the images in the database, a subset R of image database D is retrieved based on the similarity value which consists of the best matches to the query image.

Experiment and Analysis

Some standard distance measures are considered for comparing the performance of the suggested measure using finger vein image database. The image data set used is the open database by Hong Kong Polytechnic University.

The accuracy has been measured by calculating precision and recall for 10, 20, 30 and 40 retrieved images. Precision rate and recall rate are evaluated for the system, where number of images retrieved which are close to query is N_R, number of images in database that are close to the query is N_S and the number of retrieved images is N. Non-fuzzy method used for comparison is retrieval using hamming distance between the histogram values of images. Fuzzy hamming distance measure is the second method that is compared with the proposed method. Table 1 shows the precision rates of the different methods while retrieving 10, 20, 30 and 40 images. Table 2 gives a comparison between the recall rates of different methods. From the results it is evident that the proposed method retrieves the images much competently than the existing algorithms.

A fuzzy set theoretic algorithm is introduced in this session for image retrieval from a database of finger vein images. The efficiency of the proposed method is verified by calculating precision and recall. The designed fuzzy system is an attractive solution in efficiently retrieving the images relevant to query images. This method can also be beneficial in saving time during feature matching

Table 1. Precision rates for different number of retrieved images

N	Precision		
	Non Fuzzy Measure	**Fuzzy Distance**	**Proposed Method**
10	0.63	0.84	0.91
20	0.56	0.71	0.79
30	0.43	0.49	0.58
40	0.38	0.43	0.47

Table 2. Comparison of recall rates for different methods

N	Recall		
	Non Fuzzy	**Fuzzy Distance**	**Proposed Method**
10	0.31	0.36	0.40
20	0.39	0.46	0.59
30	0.45	0.56	0.64
40	0.55	0.63	0.72

CONCLUSION AND FUTURE DIRECTIONS

The requirement for competent access to image data is emerging swiftly in many fields, extending from digital libraries, art gallerias and medicine to education and military. An effective way of get into image data that been developed is Content-Based Image Retrieval (CBIR). Visual features are taken out from the images as the system interprets user information.

The ambiguity in image similarity can be addressed by fuzzy logic while also modeling the linguistic understanding in a qualitative and measured manner. This chapter analyses various techniques of fuzzy theory in different stages of CBIR. Using fuzzy descriptors like fuzzy attributed relational graphs or fuzzy color histograms which can represent query and database images in a more realistic way, low level feature descriptors in CBIR can be effectively replaced. Another area which boosts the effectiveness in CBIR compared with the classical methods are Fuzzy image classification and indexing algorithms. Fuzzy SVM, fuzzy c-means clustering and fuzzy inference system are some of the popular fuzzy image classification techniques. A competent toolset in terms of distance and similarity measures is also offered by Fuzzy theory which efficiently handles imprecise spatial information and uncertainty associated with image data.

User interaction is what Image retrieval systems heavily trust in. On the one hand, query specifications by user determines images to be retrieved. On the other hand, through the relevant feedback of users the system can refine the results into more relevant retrieval. Future research in CBIR needs more focus on utilizing the human reasoning ability of fuzzy theory in developing convenient and fool proof relevance feedback systems for CBIR. Based on fuzzy theory, prevailing and easy to use smart interfaces can be set up. That way user can evaluate the result of the current retrieval and notify the computer.

There is a high demand for search engines based on web, as it is crucial to index and recover the unlimited image data. Assimilated access to image libraries spread across the web has been investigated by several research systems on image megaservers. However, speed of retrieval is an important criteria in the case of retrieval using huge databases of images. Although some progress has been made in indexing methods of high dimensional features, it still needs more exploration.

Existing performance evaluation criterion and standard tests are still far from satisfactory. Judgement of image content can be subjective which may cause accurate evaluation difficult. It is necessary to implement objective evaluation and accurate feedback for competent performance of a retrieval system.

With fuzzy based image retrieval algorithms it is easier to achieve semantically meaningful retrievals by developing image features and metrics based on human perception.

REFERENCES

Aboulmagd, H., El-Gayar, N., & Onsi, H. (2009). A new approach in content-based image retrieval using fuzzy. *Telecommunication Systems*, *40*(1), 55–66. doi:10.100711235-008-9142-9

Athanasiadis, T., Simou, N., Papadopoulos, G., Benmokhtar, R., Chandramouli, K., Tzouvaras, V., ... Huet, B. (2009). Integrating image segmentation and classification for fuzzy knowledge-based multimedia indexing. *Advances in Multimedia Modeling*, 263-274.

Bezdek, J. C., Ehrlich, R., & Full, W. (1984). FCM: The fuzzy c-means clustering algorithm. *Computers & Geosciences*, *10*(2-3), 191–203. doi:10.1016/0098-3004(84)90020-7

Bloch, I. (1999). On fuzzy distances and their use in image processing under imprecision. *Pattern Recognition*, *32*(11), 1873–1895. doi:10.1016/S0031-3203(99)00011-4

Carson, C., Thomas, M., Belongie, S., Hellerstein, J. M., & Malik, J. (1999, June). Blobworld: A system for region-based image indexing and retrieval. In *International Conference on Advances in Visual Information Systems* (pp. 509-517). Springer. 10.1007/3-540-48762-X_63

Chamorro-Martínez, J., Medina, J. M., Barranco, C. D., Galán-Perales, E., & Soto-Hidalgo, J. M. (2007). Retrieving images in fuzzy object-relational databases using dominant color descriptors. *Fuzzy Sets and Systems*, *158*(3), 312–324. doi:10.1016/j.fss.2006.10.013

Chan, K. P., & Cheung, Y. S. (1992). Fuzzy-attribute graph with application to chinese character recognition. *IEEE Transactions on Systems, Man, and Cybernetics*, *22*(1), 153–160. doi:10.1109/21.141319

Chen, Y., & Wang, J. Z. (2002). A region-based fuzzy feature matching approach to content-based image retrieval. *IEEE Transactions on Pattern Analysis and Machine Intelligence*, *24*(9), 1252–1267. doi:10.1109/TPAMI.2002.1033216

De Luca, A., & Termini, S. (1972). A definition of a nonprobabilistic entropy in the setting of fuzzy sets theory. *Information and Control*, *20*(4), 301–312. doi:10.1016/S0019-9958(72)90199-4

Fan, J. L., Ma, Y. L., & Xie, W. X. (2001). On some properties of distance measures. *Fuzzy Sets and Systems*, *117*(3), 355–361. doi:10.1016/S0165-0114(98)00387-X

Flickner, M., Sawhney, H., Niblack, W., Ashley, J., Huang, Q., Dom, B., ... Steele, D. (1995). Query by image and video content: The QBIC system. *Computer, 28*(9), 23-32.

Gath, I., & Geva, A. B. (1989). Unsupervised optimal fuzzy clustering. *IEEE Transactions on Pattern Analysis and Machine Intelligence*, *11*(7), 773–780. doi:10.1109/34.192473

Han, J., & Ma, K. K. (2002). Fuzzy color histogram and its use in color image retrieval. *IEEE Transactions on Image Processing*, *11*(8), 944–952. doi:10.1109/TIP.2002.801585 PMID:18244688

Jang, J. S. (1993). ANFIS: Adaptive-network-based fuzzy inference system. *IEEE Transactions on Systems, Man, and Cybernetics*, *23*(3), 665–685. doi:10.1109/21.256541

Jiang, X., Yi, Z., & Lv, J. C. (2006). Fuzzy SVM with a new fuzzy membership function. *Neural Computing & Applications*, *15*(3-4), 268–276. doi:10.100700521-006-0028-z

Johanyák, Z. C., & Kovács, S. (2005). Distance based similarity measures of fuzzy sets. *Proceedings of SAMI*.

Kóczy, L. T., & Tikk, D. (2000). Fuzzy rendszerek. TypoTEX.

Konstantinidis, K., Gasteratos, A., & Andreadis, I. (2005). Image retrieval based on fuzzy color histogram processing. *Optics Communications*, *248*(4), 375–386. doi:10.1016/j.optcom.2004.12.029

Krishnapuram, R., & Keller, J. M. (1993). A possibilistic approach to clustering. *IEEE Transactions on Fuzzy Systems*, *1*(2), 98–110. doi:10.1109/91.227387

Krishnapuram, R., Medasani, S., Jung, S. H., Choi, Y. S., & Balasubramaniam, R. (2004). Content-based image retrieval based on a fuzzy approach. *IEEE Transactions on Knowledge and Data Engineering*, *16*(10), 1185–1199. doi:10.1109/TKDE.2004.53

Li, C. H., Huang, W. C., Kuo, B. C., & Hung, C. C. (2008). A novel fuzzy weighted c-means method for image classification. *International Journal of Fuzzy Systems*, *10*(3), 168–173.

Lin, C. F., & Wang, S. D. (2002). Fuzzy support vector machines. *IEEE Transactions on Neural Networks*, *13*(2), 464–471. doi:10.1109/72.991432 PMID:18244447

Long, F., Zhang, H., & Feng, D. D. (2003). Fundamentals of content-based image retrieval. In *Multimedia Information Retrieval and Management* (pp. 1–26). Springer Berlin Heidelberg. doi:10.1007/978-3-662-05300-3_1

Mamdani, E. H., & Assilian, S. (1975). An experiment in linguistic synthesis with a fuzzy logic controller. *International Journal of Man-Machine Studies*, *7*(1), 1–13. doi:10.1016/S0020-7373(75)80002-2

Mulhemý, P., Leowþ, W. K., & Leeþ, Y. K. (2001). Fuzzy conceptual graphs for matching images of natural scenes. *IJCAI*, 1.

Nedeljkovic, I. (2004). Image classification based on fuzzy logic. *The International Archives of the Photogrammetry, Remote Sensing and Spatial Information Sciences*, *34*, 685.

Pal, S. K., & King, R. A. (1983). On edge detection of X-ray images using fuzzy sets. *IEEE Transactions on Pattern Analysis and Machine Intelligence*, *PAMI-5*(1), 69–77. doi:10.1109/TPAMI.1983.4767347 PMID:21869086

Prewitt, J. M. (1970). Object enhancement and extraction. *Picture Processing and Psychopictorics*, *10*(1), 15-19.

Rosenfeld, A. (1984). The fuzzy geometry of image subsets. *Pattern Recognition Letters*, *2*(5), 311–317. doi:10.1016/0167-8655(84)90018-7

Rui, Y., Huang, T. S., & Chang, S. F. (1999). Image retrieval: Current techniques, promising directions, and open issues. *Journal of Visual Communication and Image Representation*, *10*(1), 39–62. doi:10.1006/jvci.1999.0413

Smeulders, A. W., Worring, M., Santini, S., Gupta, A., & Jain, R. (2000). Content-based image retrieval at the end of the early years. *IEEE Transactions on Pattern Analysis and Machine Intelligence*, *22*(12), 1349–1380. doi:10.1109/34.895972

Smith, J. R., & Chang, S. F. (1997, February). VisualSEEk: a fully automated content-based image query system. In *Proceedings of the fourth ACM international conference on Multimedia* (pp. 87-98). ACM.

Takagi, T., & Sugeno, M. (1985). Fuzzy identification of systems and its applications to modeling and control. *IEEE Transactions on Systems, Man, and Cybernetics*, *SMC-15*(1), 116–132. doi:10.1109/TSMC.1985.6313399

Tversky, A. (1977). Features of similarity. *Psychological Review*, *84*(4), 327–352. doi:10.1037/0033-295X.84.4.327

Wang, J. Z., Li, J., & Wiederhold, G. (2001). SIMPLIcity: Semantics-sensitive integrated matching for picture libraries. *IEEE Transactions on Pattern Analysis and Machine Intelligence*, *23*(9), 947–963. doi:10.1109/34.955109

Wang, Y., Wang, S., & Lai, K. K. (2005). A new fuzzy support vector machine to evaluate credit risk. *IEEE Transactions on Fuzzy Systems*, *13*(6), 820–831. doi:10.1109/TFUZZ.2005.859320

Wu, K., & Yap, K. H. (2006). Fuzzy SVM for content-based image retrieval: A pseudo-label support vector machine framework. *IEEE Computational Intelligence Magazine*, *1*(2), 10–16. doi:10.1109/MCI.2006.1626490

Xuecheng, L. (1992). Entropy, distance measure and similarity measure of fuzzy sets and their relations. *Fuzzy Sets and Systems*, *52*(3), 305–318. doi:10.1016/0165-0114(92)90239-Z

Zadeh, L. A. (1965). Fuzzy sets. *Information and Control*, *8*(3), 338–353. doi:10.1016/S0019-9958(65)90241-X

Zwick, R., Carlstein, E., & Budescu, D. V. (1987). Measures of similarity among fuzzy concepts: A comparative analysis. *International Journal of Approximate Reasoning*, *1*(2), 221–242. doi:10.1016/0888-613X(87)90015-6

KEY TERMS AND DEFINITIONS

Fuzzy Attributed Relational Graphs: Image descriptors in the form of graphs that represent objects in images along with their attributes and spatial relations.

Fuzzy C-Means Algorithm: A clustering algorithm for partitioning a group of n-vectors into c-fuzzy classes each having a cluster center.

Fuzzy Color Histograms: A color histogram in which fuzzy membership of each pixel is spread of all histogram bins.

Fuzzy Inference System: A decision making system based on a set of predefined fuzzy rules.

Fuzzy Set: A set with fuzzy membership grades for each of its elements.

Fuzzy Similarity Measures: Similarity measures for classification using fuzzy theory.

Fuzzy Support Vector Machine: A support vector machine that uses fuzzy membership functions for classification.

Chapter 4
Machine–Learning–Based Image Feature Selection

Vivek K. Verma
Manipal University Jaipur, India

Tarun Jain
Manipal University Jaipur, India

ABSTRACT

This is the age of big data where aggregating information is simple and keeping it economical. Tragically, as the measure of machine intelligible data builds, the capacity to comprehend and make utilization of it doesn't keep pace with its development. In content-based image retrieval (CBIR) applications, every database needs its comparing parameter setting for feature extraction. CBIR is the application of computer vision techniques to the image retrieval problem that is the problem of searching for digital images in large databases. In any case, the vast majority of the CBIR frameworks perform ordering by an arrangement of settled and pre-particular parameters. All the major machine-learning-based search algorithms have discussed in this chapter for better understanding related with the image retrieval accuracy. The efficiency of FS using machine learning compared with some other search algorithms and observed for the improvement of the CBIR system.

INTRODUCTION

In the last few decades, the dimensionality of the data associated with machine learning and information mining errands has hugely expanded. Information with high degree and dimensionality has becomes major challenge with classical learning techniques (Belarbi, Mahmoudi, & Belalem, 2017). With the expansive number of features, a learning model can be non-fitted, and it results poor accuracy. To address the information mining challenges and issue of the FS, a wide range of research reference are available. Image feature descriptors selection is the best way to eliminate noisy and redundant set from feature to be used in the classification. Major purpose of any FS method is to choose a subset of features that reduce the redundancy and maximize the significance to the target set. FS is used for refining learning performance, reducing computation, and shrinking required space. To discriminate one class object

DOI: 10.4018/978-1-5225-5775-3.ch004

from another for any pattern recognition algorithm features takes a major role. This chapter focuses on CBIR systems in which image features are extracted, and classified accordingly with one aspect of the relevancy of features with desired outcome. As a consequence FS plays a significant role CBIR and the improved selection process usually results in greater retrieval precision. Image classification is a generally contemplated issue in the analysis of images and also with, computer vision. Most of the classification frameworks can be separated into two major stages, include extraction of each image feature by a high-dimensional element vector. Next, these vectors are selected by help of classifier based on various search algorithms. Among feature extraction and the feature classification, an additional step can take place that is feature selection. This step, is about selection of a subset of features to improve the accuracy of information retrieval. Then again, include selection techniques have presently increased significant role to lessen semantic gap. Machine learning gives instruments by which vast amounts of information can be naturally examined. Feature Selection (FS) by distinguishing the most remarkable elements for learning, concentrates a learning computation on those parts of the information most helpful for investigation and future expectation. In such manner, this chapter is dedicated to show an idea of ways to deal with decrease the semantic gap using machine learning between low level visual components and irregular state semantics, through concurrent feature adjustment and highlight FS. To solve Feature Selection problem, a type of heuristic search algorithm can be used. Machine learning based search method is attractive intelligence optimization technique and many of the powerful method that has motivated and discussed in this chapter. Image feature subset selection is the way toward distinguishing and expelling however much immaterial and excess data as could reasonably be expected. This decreases the dimensionality of the information and may enable learning computations to work quicker and all the more adequately. Now and again, exactness on future characterization can be enhanced; in others, the outcome is a more reduced, effortlessly deciphered portrayal of the objective idea. On the basis of evaluation environments, FS procedures are divided into three major models as filter model, wrapper model and embedded model.

Importance of FS

Any machine learning based classification works on the simplest rule if set of features are waste (noisy data) it gives only waste as outcome. In case when size of feature set is large this becomes necessary for the relevant outcome. In most of the cases it is not necessary to include all the feature set for creating efficient algorithm. Only few set of features should be use for efficient and optimal result of the algorithms. Sometimes less is more accurate but accuracy depends on the optimal number of features i.e. not more or less but accurate. An optimal number of feature set generally reduces the time train as well as the performance time.

- **Faster Training:** One of the toughest difficulties in machine learning is getting the right data in the optimal size. An efficient CBIR system need machine learning algorithm and it commonly needs good size of training set for more accurate result but it upturns the complexity as well. If FS methods utilizes while constructing the training data set it improves the time complexity of algorithm.

- **Reduces Complexity:** Generally features selection procedures effort to discover the finest set of features that can isolate the classes but there is no open concern for problematic or informal samples and what should be used as training data. In enhancing, the algorithm picks out the features that reduce the error. Therefore, the best set of feature reduces the processing time as well it gives accurate result.

- **Improves Accuracy:** As FS is a procedure to discover the best optimal subset of characteristics which well explains the association of independent data with target data. Based on field knowledge, this techniques select feature(s) and it may have higher effect on target data. This helps to visualize the relationship between data, which makes selection process easier and improves the accuracy.

Characteristics of FS Algorithms

FS algorithms with a few remarkable exceptions perform a search through the space of feature subsets and, as a result must address four elementary issues affecting the nature of the search:

- **Starting Point:** Direction of the search is affected by the starting point in the feature subset space from where one need to begin the search. First choice is to start with zero features and after that consecutively add more attributes. In this scenario, the search is said to proceed forward through the search space. On the contrary, the search can start by considering all features and consecutively remove them. In this scenario, the search proceeds backward through the search space. Another choice is to start somewhere in the middle and move outwards from this point.

- **Search Organization:** An exhaustive search of the feature subspace is prohibitive for all but a small initial number of features. For N features there exist 2^N possible subsets from N features. Heuristic search approaches are more feasible than exhaustive approaches and can provide better results, although they do not guarantee finding the optimal subset.

- **Evaluation Strategy:** How subsets of the features are evaluated is the only one main distinguishing factor among FS algorithms for machine learning. One model, dubbed the filter (Min, Hu, & Zhu, 2014) works independent of any learning algorithm—before learning begins undesirable features are filtered out of the data. These algorithms utilize heuristics based on common characteristics of the data to evaluate the merit of feature subsets. Another school of thought argues that the bias of a particular induction algorithm should be taken into consideration when selecting features. This approach, called the wrapper, utilizes an induction algorithm along with a statistical re-sampling method such as cross-validation to estimate the final accuracy of feature subsets.

- **Stopping Criterion:** When to stop searching through the space of feature subsets is the decision of feature selector. Depending on the evaluation approach, a feature selector might stop adding or removing features when none of the alternatives improves upon the merit of a current feature subset. Alternatively, the algorithm might continue to revise the feature subset as long as the merit does not degrade. A further option could be to continue generating feature subsets until reaching the opposite end of the search space and then select the best.

FEATURE SELECTION FOR CBIR

CBIR is the application of computer vision techniques to the image retrieval problem that is the problem of searching for digital images in large databases. In CBIR search don't considers the metadata such as keywords, tags, or descriptions associated with the image. It only considers contents of the image. The term "content" means here are colors, shapes, textures, or some other related information that can be directly derived from the image itself. CBIR is necessary because searches that based completely on metadata are dependent on annotation quality and completeness. The effectiveness of traditional keyword image search is subjective and it cannot be well-defined. CBIR systems also have similar challenges in defining success. Many of the FS method was utilized to choose the optimal set of features that take full advantage of the detection level and make simpler the computation of the image retrieval processing (Nikkam & Reddy, 2016). Most of the system selects the best suitable feature set from a large image features, generally includes shape, color, and textual features with some classification technique. Therefore, FS is takes a vital role for the greater accuracy of the retrieval system.

MACHINE LEARNING BASED TECHNIQUES

Many components influence the achievement of machine learning on a given undertaking. The portrayal and nature of the case information is most importantly. Hypothetically, having more elements should bring about all the more segregating power. Nonetheless, down to earth involvement with machine learning computations has demonstrated this is not generally the situation. Many learning computations can be seen as making a gauge of the likelihood of the class mark given an arrangement of components. This is an intricate, high dimensional conveyance. Acceptance is frequently performed on restricted information. This makes assessing the numerous probabilistic parameters troublesome. Keeping in mind the end goal to maintain a strategic distance from over fitting the preparation information, numerous computations utilize the predisposition to fabricate a basic model that still accomplishes some satisfactory level of execution on the preparation information. This inclination frequently drives a computation to favor few prescient properties over a substantial number of components that, if utilized as a part of the best possible mix, are completely prescient of the class mark. In the event that there is excessively superfluous and repetitive data exhibit or the information is boisterous and questionable, at that point getting the hang of amid the preparation stage is more troublesome. Image feature subset selection is the way toward distinguishing and expelling however much immaterial and excess data as could reasonably be expected. This decreases the dimensionality of the information and may enable learning computations to work quicker and all the more adequately. Now and again, exactness on future characterization can be enhanced; in others, the outcome is a more reduced, effortlessly deciphered portrayal of the objective idea.

Genetic Algorithms (GA)

The GA are productive techniques for variable minimization. In feature set choice setting, the expectation mistake of the model based upon an arrangement of highlights is streamlined. The hereditary computation imitates the characteristic development by displaying a dynamic populace of arrangements. The individuals from the populace, alluded to as chromosomes, encode the chose highlights. The encoding more often than not takes type of bit strings with bits relating to choose highlights set and others cleared.

Every chromosome prompts a model manufactured utilizing the encoded highlights. By utilizing the preparation information, the blunder of the model is measured and fills in as a wellness work. Over the span of development, the chromosomes are subjected to hybrid and change. By permitting survival and proliferation of the fittest chromosomes, the computation viably limits the mistake work in ensuing ages. The achievement of GA relies upon a few variables. The parameters guiding the hybrid, change and survival of chromosomes ought to be deliberately enabled the populace to investigate the arrangement space and to forestall early meeting to homogeneous populace involving a neighborhood least. The decision of beginning populace is additionally imperative in hereditary element choice. To address this issue, e.g. a technique in view of Shannon's entropy joined with chart investigation can be utilized. Hereditary computation in light of the Darwinian survival of the fittest hypothesis, is a proficient and comprehensively material worldwide advancement computation. Rather than customary pursuit methods, hereditary computation begins from a gathering of focuses coded as limited length letters in order strings rather than one genuine parameter set. Moreover, hereditary computation isn't a slope climbing computation thus the subordinate data and step estimate count are not required. The three fundamental administrators of hereditary computations are: determination, hybrid and change. It chooses a few people with more grounded flexibility from populace as indicated by the wellness, and afterward chooses the duplicate number of individual as per the determination strategies, for example, Backer stochastic all-inclusive inspecting. It trades and recombines a couple of chromosome through hybrid. Transformation is done to change certain point state through likelihood. By and large, one needs to pick reasonable hybrid and change likelihood over and over through genuine issues.

Support Vector Machine (SVM)

SVM is based on the auxiliary hazard minimization guideline to look for a choice surface that can isolate the information focuses into two classes with a maximal edge between them. The decision of the correct piece work is the principle challenge when utilizing a SVM (Wei, Zhang, Yu, Hu, Tang, Gui, & Yuan, 2017). It could have distinctive structures, for example, Radial Function part and polynomial bit. The benefit of the SVM is its ability of learning in scanty, high dimensional spaces with not very many preparing cases by limiting a bound on the experimental mistake and the intricacy of the classifier in the meantime. Some of the mining tools utilizes the sequential minimal computation for SVM. The SVM frame a gathering of techniques coming from the basic hazard minimization standard, with the straight help vector classifier as its most fundamental part. The SVC goes for making a choice hyper plane that boosts the edge, i.e., the separation from the hyper plane to the closest cases from each of the classes. This takes into account defining the classifier preparing as an obliged streamlining issue. Essentially, the target work is unimodal, as opposed to e.g. neural systems, and in this manner can be enhanced successfully to worldwide ideal. In the easiest case, mixes from various classes can be isolated by straight hyper plane; such hyper plane is characterized exclusively by its closest mixes from the preparation set. Such mixes are alluded to as help vectors, giving the name to the entire strategy. Much of the time, in any case, no direct division is conceivable. To assess this issue, slack factors are presented. These factors are related with the misclassified mixes and, in conjunction with the edge, are liable to improvement. Along these lines, despite the fact that the mistaken grouping can't be stayed away from, it is punished. Since the misclassification of mixes firmly impacts the choice hyper plane, the misclassified mixes additionally move toward becoming help vectors.

Heuristic Search Base Algorithm (HSBA)

Searching the space of feature subsets within sensible time constraints is necessary if a FS algorithm is to operate on data with a large number of features. One simple search strategy is hill climbing using greedy approach, it considers local changes to the current feature subset. Often, a local change is simply the addition or deletion of a single feature from the subset which can give the optimal subset. When the algorithm considers only additions to the feature subset it is known as forward selection; considering only deletions is known as backward elimination (Vergara, & Estévez, 2014). Another approach, known as stepwise bi-directional search, uses both addition of features and deletion of features. Within each of these variations, the search algorithm may consider all possible local changes to the current subset and then select the best, or may simply choose the first change that improves the merit of the current feature subset. In either case, once a change of choice is accepted, it is never reconsidered in any step. If scanned from top to bottom, the diagram shows all local additions to each node; if scanned from bottom to top, the diagram shows all possible local deletions from each node.

MODELS OF FS

On the basis of evaluation conditions, FS algorithms are divided into three major models as filter model and wrapper model and embedded model.

Filter Model

The Filter Model for FS process is done as a pre-processing step with no induction algorithm. To select features the general characteristics of the training data are used i.e. distances between classes or statistical dependencies. This model performance is faster than the wrapper approach because filters methods usually involves less computation than wrappers and results in a better generalization because it works independently of the induction algorithm. Feature set produced by filter method is not tuned to a specific type of predictive model. It means feature set produced by this approach are more general as compare to wrapper and gives lower prediction performance. It is more valuable for showing the relationships between the features because the output feature set does not contain the assumptions of a prediction model. Many filter approaches provide output as feature ranking than an explicit best subset feature and cross validation is used to choose the cut-off point in the ranking.

Wrapper Model

This model features subset selection that can be done by utilizing the induction algorithm as a black box which means no knowledge of the algorithm is needed it just need the interface only. In this feature subset selection algorithm by utilizing the induction algorithm performs a search for a good subset itself as part of the evaluation function. In this accuracy of the induced classifiers is estimated using accuracy estimation techniques.

Embedded Model

The Embedded Model is a catch-all group of techniques which implement FS as part of the learning procedure i.e. model construction process. LASSO method is example of this approach which penalizes the regression coefficients with an L1 penalty, shrinking many of them to zero for constructing a linear model. LASSO algorithm select the any feature dataset which have non-zero regression coefficients. Bolasso is improvement over LASSO with bootstraps samples, and FeaLect which scores all the features based on combinatorial analysis of regression coefficients (Hansen, Reynaud-Bouret, & Rivoirard, 2015). Another approach is the Recursive Feature Elimination algorithm which is more popular and remove features with low weights and commonly used with Support Vector Machines (SVM) to repeatedly construct a model. Embedded approaches lie between filters and wrappers in terms of computational complexity.

Table 1. Pros and cons of FS techniques

S. No.	Modeling Used	Pros	Cons	Related Algorithms	Machine Learning Algorithm
1.	Filter Model (Wang, Zhang, Liu, Lv, & Wang, 2014; Javed, Maruf, & Babri, 2015; Roffo, Melzi, & Cristani, 2015; Roffo, & Melzi, 2016; Oreski & Oreski, 2014; Saeys, Inza, & Larrañaga, 2007)	Not dependent over classifier, Rapid, Accessible, Faster computation than wrapper method	Not domain feature based, Less Accessible	Classical FS Algorithm, Markov Algorithm, Welch's t-test, Infinite FS, Symmetrical Tau, Eigenvector Centrality	Decision Tree, Correlation-based Algorithms
2.	Wrapper Model (Diao & Shen, 2012; Zhang, Wang, Phillips, & Ji, 2014; Bermejo Gámez, J. A., & Puerta, 2014) Wrapper	Simple, Relates with classifier, feature related dependencies	Over fitting problem, Not guarantee for optimal solution as it uses greedy search	Harmony search, Binary PSO with Mutation, Iterated Local Search	Genetic algorithm, Ants colony
3.	Embedded Model(Tabakhi, Moradi, & Akhlaghian, 2014; Hansen, Reynaud-Bouret, & Rivoirard, 2015; Wei, Zhang, Yu, Hu, Tang, Gui, & Yuan, 2017)	Relates with classifier, Faster computation than wrapper methods, Models feature dependencies	FS only based on classifier	Lasso, Bo-Lasso	Naïve Bayes, SVM based Algorithm
4.	Hybrid Model (Chuang, Ke, & Yang, 2016; Jing, 2014)	Faster as Filter Model, Knowledge of learning algorithms as Wrapper Model	Not efficient for small feature set	Hill-Climbing	Hybrid Genetic Algorithm

71

CONCLUSION

This chapter concluded as conducted analysis of different methods of FS by using different search algorithm especially machine learning based techniques. The numerous FS techniques proposed by different authors has been discussed depend on very extraordinary standards. The major focus area of this work is to analyses the use of FS within image retrieval context. The efficiency of FS using machine learning compared with some other search algorithms and observed for the improvement of the CBIR system. A comparison has been included for various search algorithms with different models of FS in context of related pros and cons. It can be considered that machine learning based FS techniques gives better performance for image retrieval system. The result accuracy always depends on the desired outcome from image retrieval system with the nature of training data set.

REFERENCES

Belarbi, M. A., Mahmoudi, S., & Belalem, G. (2017). PCA as Dimensionality Reduction for Large-Scale Image Retrieval Systems. *International Journal of Ambient Computing and Intelligence*, *8*(4), 45–58. doi:10.4018/IJACI.2017100104

Bermejo, P., Gámez, J. A., & Puerta, J. M. (2014). Speeding up incremental wrapper feature subset selection with Naive Bayes classifier. *Knowledge-Based Systems*, *55*, 140–147. doi:10.1016/j.knosys.2013.10.016

Chuang, L. Y., Ke, C. H., & Yang, C. H. (2016). *A hybrid both filter and wrapper Feature Selection method for microarray classification*. Academic Press.

Diao, R., & Shen, Q. (2012). FS with harmony search. *IEEE Transactions on Systems, Man, and Cybernetics. Part B, Cybernetics*, *42*(6), 1509–1523. doi:10.1109/TSMCB.2012.2193613

Hansen, N. R., Reynaud-Bouret, P., & Rivoirard, V. (2015). Lasso and probabilistic inequalities for multivariate point processes. *Bernoulli*, *21*(1), 83–143. doi:10.3150/13-BEJ562

Javed, K., Maruf, S., & Babri, H. A. (2015). A two-stage Markov blanket based Feature Selection algorithm for text classification. *Neurocomputing*, *157*, 91–104. doi:10.1016/j.neucom.2015.01.031

Jing, S. Y. (2014). A hybrid genetic algorithm for feature subset selection in rough set theory. *Soft Computing*, *18*(7), 1373–1382. doi:10.100700500-013-1150-3

Min, F., Hu, Q., & Zhu, W. (2014). Feature selection with test cost constraint. *International Journal of Approximate Reasoning*, *55*(1), 167–179. doi:10.1016/j.ijar.2013.04.003

Nikkam, P. S., & Reddy, E. B. (2016). A Key Point Selection Shape Technique for Content based Image Retrieval System. *International Journal of Computer Vision and Image Processing*, *6*(2), 54–70. doi:10.4018/IJCVIP.2016070104

Oreski, S., & Oreski, G. (2014). Genetic algorithm-based heuristic for Feature Selection in credit risk assessment. *Expert Systems with Applications*, *41*(4), 2052–2064. doi:10.1016/j.eswa.2013.09.004

Roffo, G., & Melzi, S. (2016). Features selection via eigenvector centrality. Proceedings of New Frontiers in Mining Complex Patterns-NFMCP 2016, 1-12.

Roffo, G., Melzi, S., & Cristani, M. (2015). Infinite Feature Selection. *Proceedings of the IEEE International Conference on Computer Vision*, 4202-4210.

Saeys, Y., Inza, I., & Larrañaga, P. (2007). A review of Feature Selection techniques in bioinformatics. *Bioinformatics (Oxford, England)*, *23*(19), 2507–2517. doi:10.1093/bioinformatics/btm344 PMID:17720704

Tabakhi, S., Moradi, P., & Akhlaghian, F. (2014). An unsupervised Feature Selection algorithm based on ant colony optimization. *Engineering Applications of Artificial Intelligence*, *32*, 112–123. doi:10.1016/j.engappai.2014.03.007

Vergara, J. R., & Estévez, P. A. (2014). A review of Feature Selection methods based on mutual information. *Neural Computing & Applications*, *24*(1), 175–186. doi:10.100700521-013-1368-0

Wang, D., Zhang, H., Liu, R., Lv, W., & Wang, D. (2014). t-Test Feature Selection approach based on term frequency for text categorization. *Pattern Recognition Letters*, *45*, 1–10. doi:10.1016/j.patrec.2014.02.013

Wei, J., Zhang, R., Yu, Z., Hu, R., Tang, J., Gui, C., & Yuan, Y. (2017). A BPSO-SVM algorithm based on memory renewal and enhanced mutation mechanisms for Feature Selection. *Applied Soft Computing*, *58*, 176–192. doi:10.1016/j.asoc.2017.04.061

Zhang, Y., Wang, S., Phillips, P., & Ji, G. (2014). Binary PSO with mutation operator for Feature Selection using decision tree applied to spam detection. *Knowledge-Based Systems*, *64*, 22–31. doi:10.1016/j.knosys.2014.03.015

Chapter 5
Feature Selection Using Neighborhood Positive Approximation Rough Set

Mohammad Atique
Sant Gadge Baba Amravati University, India

Leena Homraj Patil
Priyadarshini Institute of Engineering, India

ABSTRACT

Attribute reduction and feature selection is the main issue in rough set. Researchers have focused on several attribute reduction using rough set. However, the methods found are time consuming for large data sets. Since the key lies in reducing the attributes and selecting the relevant features, the main aim is to reduce the dimensionality of huge amount of data to get the smaller subset which can provide the useful information. Feature selection approach reduces the dimensionality of feature space and improves the overall performance. The challenge in feature selection is to deal with high dimensional. To overcome the issues and challenges, this chapter describes a feature selection based on the proposed neighborhood positive approximation approach and attributes reduction for data sets. This proposed system implements for attribute reduction and finds the relevant features. Evaluation shows that the proposed neighborhood positive approximation algorithm is effective and feasible for large data sets and also reduces the feature space.

INTRODUCTION

A huge amount of documents on internet is growing immensely. To manage such a huge volume of data, data mining yield an important skill. Rapidly growth in the document preprocessing tool, database increases rapidly in rows and in column. Feature selection, called as attribute reduction turn out to be difficult in the field of pattern recognition machine learning and data mining. Pawlak proposed a specific conceptual structure rough set model for feature selection (Liu & Yu, 2005). Hundreds of attributes are available in the database. A major issue lies executing attribute reduction in rough set theory. Rough set

DOI: 10.4018/978-1-5225-5775-3.ch005

theory is considered soft computing approach to examine data, and defines a structure which becomes difficult to recognize the task of relevant attributes (Liang, Wang, Dang, & Qian, 2012). It also declines the performance of machine learning problem. Features selection means sustaining the unfair influence of features. Hence, it becomes significant to decrease dimensions of the data to smaller size. It also reduces the appropriate information for declining the storage cost and time. Attribute reduction recommended a logical approach for consistency-based feature selection (Lingras & Peters, 2012). To overcome such a large issue of feature selection and attribute reduction, few attributes are eliminated.

To overcome the issue of feature selection and attribute reduction, few attributes can be omitted, which will not seriously effect on classification accuracy. Much work has been done on the subject of attribute reduction, both theoretical and experimental.

The main theme of this scheme is to propose an Neighborhood feature selection positive approximation algorithm (NFSPA) using rough set technique. This algorithm is based on the proposed neighborhood positive approximation approach. Most of the researchers have focused on several attribute reduction using Rough set. However, it has been found that none of the attribute reduction algorithm is the best. It has been observed that the several issues of attribute reduction can be overcome by suggesting the algorithm. Since the key lies in reducing the attributes and selecting the relevant features. For this purpose, we proposed and demonstrated neighborhood positive approximation approach. The idea behind using this approach is to optimize the number of feature and improves the computational time. It has been demonstrated that the proposed scheme outperforms the high dimensionality of data. Hence achieves the curse of dimensionality.

The proposed system implements for attribute reduction and finds the relevant features. An experimental result shows that the proposed neighborhood positive approximation provides the improvement in computational time and reduces the number of feature.

RELATED WORK

Feature selection, known as attribute reduction has turn out to be a significant step. In rough set theory, features selection aims to maintain the discriminatory power of original features. Hence, it is therefore important to reduce dimensionality of the data to smaller set of features and relevant information for decreasing the cost in storing and reduction in the processing time. To overcome the issue of feature selection and attribute reduction, few attributes can be omitted, which will not seriously effect on classification accuracy (Patil & Atique, 2015). Rough set theory handles data sets with imprecision and uncertain information. It utilizes a study of attribute reduction information system. It achieves concept approximation from the universe through which two defined subsets are produced. So far, many researchers have studied an attribute reduction algorithm.

Pawlak's Rough Set Model

Rough set was initially instigated by Pawlak as a efficient approach which deals with uncertainty. It works on decision analysis, knowledge discovery, and conflict analysis. The two-defined subset lower and upper are obtained through concept approximation. These two operators define an equivalence relation (Pawlak, 1991). Rough set utilizes the similarity to partition space data and create jointly equivalence class as the essential concepts. It's applicable only to data with small attributes.

Heuristic Attribute Reduction Algorithm

The most recent research topic and fastest development in attribute reduction, which produced widely. Last twenty years many researchers have worked on attribute reduction techniques. Reduction algorithm by applying discernibility matrix is studied. In this it obtains decision table, it turn out to be natural processing problem. An approach computes the small attribute set, which determine a decision attribute table (Miao, Duan, Zhang, & Jiao, 2009). To conquer the problem arisen while reduction, algorithms has implemented. These algorithms pull out a reduct in a moderate period. Accelerator has designed in heuristic search process (Qian, Liang, Pedrycz, & Dang, 2011). In the accelerator, every time objects are removed from the space and added into the core when a new attribute is chosen. However, there is no effect on the time, if the core becomes reduct for large data, the time requires more. Besides, this it is space consuming for volume dataset. It is preferred to have computational time and space saving algorithm for volume data sets.

Rough Set Attribute Reduction (RSAR)

RSAR utilizes to diminish the dimension of dataset. It is considered as a preprocessing for learning system (Jensen & Shen, 2004). RSAR indiscernibility concept provides filter-based technique. In this the knowledge gets extraction. It retains some information even after reduction of knowledge. RSAR works only on relevant features and attempts neither transforming nor removing information (Chen, Zhao, Zhang, Yang, & Zhang, 2012). The high efficient approach relies simply on operators, suitable for complex techniques (Wang, Liang, & Qian, 2013). RSAR requires no human interference and no fine-tuning parameters. The advantage for RSAR analysis is that it requires no extra parameter to operate on data.

Neighborhood Rough Set Model

A neighborhood relation generates granules with statistical features. These granules are used to estimate the decision class. Hence, considering this idea, a neighborhood rough set was created. Basically, it is comparable to tolerance model. A kind of tolerance relation is associated with neighborhood. Presently no work deals with features and tolerance model up till now (Hu, Liu, & Yu, 2008). Assurance with neighborhood rough set is expected as a generalization process. It deals with heterogeneous features together with attributes of numerical and categorical.

Classical Rough Set Model

It is a statistical means with vagueness and deals a decision with representational attributes (Jensen & Shen, 2004). Simplifying the dependency function and compactness of fuzzy information, a classical rough set model attains a Quickreduct algorithm. Attribute reduction of classical rough set keeps the positive region unchanged which does not effect on attributes. Classical rough sets also use to address separate data.

Probabilistic Rough Set Model

It changes rough set dimension. Probabilistic model for rough sets form two model. Variable precision, the one who creates the regions that makes user-provided probabilities as constraint. Decision theoretic, another one who create the regions through cost of object classification appropriately.

Variable Precision Rough Set Model (VPRS)

VPRS, obtained from classical model for categorizing the objects (Shen & Wang, 2011). Pawlak's model is moderately perceptive to raw data. Therefore (Pawlak, 1991) VPRS model deals with vague and noisy information. It permits degree of uncertainty and misclassification. VPRS deals partial classification by instigation a probability value β.

Decision Theoretic Rough Set Model

Attribute reduction produces an optimization idea. In this model, a optimization concept typically illustrate three regions. The positive region means accepting, negative region means rejecting, and boundary region means non-committed. Decision theoretic rough set model considers bayesian procedure. These procedures offer efficient methods for obtaining the threshold value. These threshold value prospect for creating regions and minimizes cost (Yao & Zhao, 2008; Qian, Liang, Pedrycz, & Dang, 2011).

Covering Rough Set Model

The concepts of decision systems model is based on their reducts and a discernibility matrix for each type of covering decision system. Discernibility matrix develops subset that approximates a minimal reduct. Covering model is a natural expansion of classical model which effectively handles uninterrupted data (Zhang, Leung, & Zhou, 2013). The advantage of this model is that, it is an effective technique for numerical and categorical data and is more efficient one. The computational difficulty of the covering decision system greatly reduces.

However, in practical application, a great amount of data set cannot be directly hold by classical rough sets. For such reason, neighborhood, dominance, and similarity relation models are broadly used.

PROPOSED NEIGHBORHOOD ROUGHT SET

The essential perception of rough set is demonstrated in neighbourhood model. The universe data information system is $IS = \langle U, A \rangle$, U represents non-empty finite set of samples $\{s_1, s_2, s_3, ..., s_n\}$. A represents attribute set $\{a_1, a_2, a_3 ..., a_n\}$.

$\langle U, A \rangle$ is a decision table when $A = C \cup D$, C and D is condition and decision attribute. An variable $s_i \in U$ and $B \subseteq C$ the neighbourhood

$$\delta_B(s_i) = \left\{ s_j \mid s_j \in U, \Delta^B(s_i, s_j) \leq \delta \right\},$$

Δ a distance function when $\forall_{s_1,s_2,s_3} \in U$, satisfies,

1. $\Delta(s_1, s_2) \geq 0, \Delta(s_1, s_2) = 0 \ if \ and \ only \ if$;
2. $\Delta(s_1, s_2) = \Delta(s_1, s_2)$;
3. $\Delta(s_1, s_3) \leq \Delta(s_1, s_2) + \Delta(s_1, s_3)$.

These three metric distance function are mostly used in data mining task. Minkowsky distance is identified as: consider two objects s_1, s_2 in *M*-dimensional space. $A = \{a_1, a_2, a_3 ..., a_n\}$, $f(s, a_i)$ represents s in i^{th} attribute a_i . Therefore

$$\Delta_P(s_1, s_2) = \left(\sum_{i=1}^{N} \left| f(s_1, a_i) - f(s_2, a_i) \right|^P \right)^{1/p}$$

where If i) $p = 1$ called as manhattan distance $\Delta_1 = 1$ ii) $p = 2$, euclidean distance $\Delta_1 = 2$ iii) if $p = \infty$ called as chebychev distance for $\Delta_1 = \infty$.

$\delta_B(s_i)$ is the neighbourhood center with sample s_i and neighbourhood size on threshold δ . If δ is greater, then samples get connected in neighbourhood s_i .

In Neighbourhood Rough set model the two key factors play an important role in distance and threshold δ .

Shape of neighbourhood determines by distance. δ manages the range of neighbourhood. If $\delta = 0$, then the neighbourhood samples degrades and degenerates to one. Hence, the neighbourhood model is ordinary process (Patil & Atique, 2014). Different attributes deal with the different definitions compute neighbourhood samples $(s_0, s_1, ..., s_n)$.

Let $B_1 \subseteq A$ and $B_2 \subseteq A$ the different attributes, so the neighbourhood granules for sample s for B_1, B_2 and $B_1 \cup B_2$ are:

1. $\delta_{B_1}(s) = \left\{ s_i \mid \Delta_{B_1}(s, s_i) \leq \delta, s_i \in U \right\}$,
2. $\delta_{B_2}(s) = \left\{ s_i \mid \Delta_{B_2}(s, s_i) = 0, s_i \in U \right\}$,
3. $\delta_{B_1 \cup B_2}(s) = \left\{ s_i \mid \Delta_{B_1}(s, s_i) \leq \delta^\wedge \Delta_{B_2}(s, s_i) = 0, s_i \in U \right\}$.

$\wedge$ denotes '*and*' operator.

1. Represents numerical attribute,
2. Represents categorical attribute, and;
3. Represents mixed categorical and numerical attribute.

Other distance functions for numerical and categorical attributes are HVDM, IVDM, HEOM, and VDM.

HVDM is defined as:

$$HVDM\left(x,y\right) = \sqrt{\sum_{i=1}^{m} w_{a_i} \times d_{a_i}^{\;2}\left(x_{a_i}, y_{a_i}\right)}$$

where

$$d_{a_i}\left(x_{a_i}, y_{a_i}\right) = \begin{cases} 1, & x \text{ or } y \text{ is not known} \\ normalize\; d\_vdm_a\left(x,y\right), & a \text{ is nominal} \\ normalize\; d\_diff_a\left(x,y\right), & a \text{ is linear} \end{cases}$$

$$normalize\; d_{diff\,a}\left(x,y\right) = \frac{|x-y|}{4\sigma_a}$$

where σ_a standard deviation attribute a.

$$N1, normalize\; d\_vdm1_a\left(x,y\right) = \sum_{c=1}^{C}\left| \frac{N_{a,x,c}}{N_{a,x}} - \frac{N_{a,y,c}}{N_{a,y}} \right|.$$

$$N2, normalize\; d\_vdm2_a\left(x,y\right) = \sqrt{\sum_{c=1}^{C}\left| \frac{N_{a,x,c}}{N_{a,x}} - \frac{N_{a,y,c}}{N_{a,y}} \right|^2}.$$

$$N3, normalize\; d\_vdm3_a\left(x,y\right) = \sqrt{C * \sum_{c=1}^{C}\left| \frac{N_{a,x,c}}{N_{a,x}} - \frac{N_{a,y,c}}{N_{a,y}} \right|^2}$$

A set of object and neighbourhood relation N over U is neighbourhood space. For $S \subseteq C$, two object upper and lower, approximation S in $\langle U,N \rangle$ is:

$$\underline{N}S = \left\{ s_i \mid \delta\left(s_i\right) \subseteq S, s_i \in \cup \right\}$$

$$\bar{N}S = \left\{ s_i \mid \delta\left(s_i\right) \cap S \neq \varnothing, s_i \in \cup \right\}$$

Obviously $\underline{N}S \subseteq S \subseteq \bar{N}S$. The boundary of S in space is $BNS = \bar{N}S - \underline{N}S$. Boundary size affects the roughnesses of S in space $\langle U,N \rangle$. Boundary region is decided by X to hold U and δ.

Feature Selection Based on Neighborhood Positive Region (NPR)

NPR concept measures the significance of condition attribute from decision table (Patil & Atique, 2015).

Definition 1: Decision table $IS = \langle U, C \cup D, N \rangle S_1, S_2, \ldots, S_N$ be the subsets with decision 1 to N; $\delta_B(s_i)$ the neighborhood particle produced attribute $B \subseteq C$, the two approximation of decision D with subset attribute B is represented:

$$\underline{N}_B D = \bigcup_{i=1}^{N} \underline{N}_B S_i, \overline{N}_B D = \bigcup_{i=1}^{N} \overline{N}_B S_i,$$

where

$$\underline{N}_B S = \left\{ s_i \mid \delta_B(s_i) \subseteq S, s_i \in U \right\}, \overline{N}_B S = \left\{ s_i \mid \delta_B(s_i) \cap S \neq \varnothing, s_i \in U \right\}$$

The boundary region D with subset B is represented:

$$BN(D) = \overline{N}_B D - \underline{N}_B D$$

The lower approximation is said to be neighborhood positive region, represented as $POS_B(D)$. It is subset whose particle strictly belongs to the decision class. Classification task performance differently for different boundary region and different feature space.

Definition 2: Decision table $IS = \langle U, C \cup D \rangle$, Δ, and δ, dependency of D to NP_i is

$$\gamma_{NP_i}(D) = \frac{\left| POS_{NP_i}^{U}(D) \right|}{|U|}. \ \gamma_{NP}(D)$$ is ability of NP to approximate D. As $POS_{NPi}(D) \subseteq U$ we

have $0 \leq \gamma_{NP}(D) \leq 1$. D completely depends on NP and the decision system.

If $\gamma_{NP}(D) = 1$; otherwise, D depends on NP in the degree of γ.

Dependency function depends on size of region and returns approximation power (16). It also measures the significance. Attribute selection explore subset of attributes that have minimal and preserve power original features (Wang, 2006).

Three parameters are considered to design an algorithm: the significance measures, searching strategy and termination criteria. Forward greedy search algorithm is introduced which improves the searching strategy. Two significant measure inner and outer are used. The inner determines the significance of each attribute whereas the outer measures searching strategy. Attribute with maxima inner significance is consider and then assign the attribute with maxima outer significance into the subset of loop, until the stopping criteria satisfies.

Consider $IS = \langle U, C \cup D \rangle$, condition partition can be obtain as

$$U\!\!\Big/\!\!_C = \left\{ X_1, X_2, X_3 \dots, X_m \right\}$$

and the decision partition as

$$U\!\!\Big/\!\!_D = \left\{ Y_1, Y_2, Y_3 \dots, Y_n \right\}.$$

Definition 3: Decision table $IS = \langle U, C \cup D \rangle, B \subseteq C$ and $\forall a \in B$. The significance measure of a in B is:

$$SIG_1^{inner}\left(a, B, D\right) = \gamma_B\left(D\right) - \gamma_{B-a}\left(D\right)$$

$$\gamma_B\left(D\right) = \frac{\left|POS_B\left(D\right)\right|}{\left|U\right|}$$

Definition 4: Decision table $IS = \langle U, C \cup D \rangle, B \subseteq C$ and $\forall a \in C - B$. The significance measure of a in B is:

$$SIG_1^{outer}\left(a, B, D\right) = \gamma_{B \cup a}\left(D\right) - \gamma_B\left(D\right).$$

Attribute reduction algorithm is selected and intersection is indispensable and is known as core. The core sometimes remain an empty.

Definition 5: Decision table $IS = \langle U, C \cup D \rangle, B \subseteq A, \forall a \in B$, say a is surplus in B if $\gamma_{B-a}\left(D\right) = \gamma_B\left(D\right)$; otherwise, a and attribute B is indispensable.

The forward greedy search algorithm is shown in Figure 1.
The algorithm for forward greedy is described as shown in Algorithm 1.

Neighborhood Feature Selection Positive Approximation (NFSPA)

A chain of granulation enlarge simple to fine granulation. This series is called positive granulation world. A proposed approach has examined properties positive granulation (Leena & Atique, 2015).

Decision table $IS = \langle U, CUD \rangle, \dfrac{U}{D} = \left\{ Y_1, Y_2, \dots Y_r \right\}$ considered as target decision.

Definition 6: Decision table $IS = \langle U, C \cup D \rangle$ $X \subseteq U$ and $NP = \left\{ R_1, R_2, \dots, R_n \right\}$ a family of attribute sets with $R_1 \succeq R_2 \succeq \dots \succeq R_n \left(R_i \in 2^c \right)$. Given $NP_i = \left\{ R_1, R_2, \dots, R_i \right\}$, we define NP_i- lower ap-

Figure 1. Forward greedy search algorithm

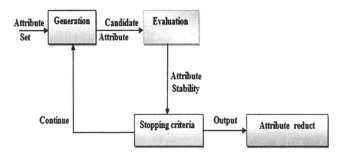

proximation sets $\underline{NP}_i(S)$ and NP_i- upper approximation sets $\overline{NP}_i(S)$ of NP_i- neighborhood positive approximation of X as:

$$\begin{cases} \underline{NP}_i(S) = \bigcup_{k=1}^{i} \underline{R_k S_k}, \\ \overline{NP}_i(S) = \overline{R_i S} \end{cases}$$

where

$$S_1 = S \text{ and } S_k = S - \bigcup_{j=1}^{k=1} \underline{R_j S_j}, k = 2,3,\ldots i, i = 1,2,\ldots n.$$

likewise, the boundary of *S* is:

$$BN_{NP_i}(S) = \overline{NP}_i(S) - \underline{NP}_i(S).$$

Definition 7: Decision table $IS = \langle U, C \cup D \rangle$, $NP_i = \{R_1, R_2, \ldots, R_n\}$ a family of attribute sets with

$$R_1 \succeq R_2 \succeq \ldots \succeq R_n \left(R_i \in 2^c\right) \text{ and } \frac{U}{D} = \{Y_1, Y_2, \ldots Y_r\}.$$

Two approximation of *D* with respect to NP_i is:

$$\begin{cases} \underline{NP}_i(D) = \left\{\underline{NP}_i(Y_1), \underline{NP}_i(Y_2), \ldots, \underline{NP}_i(Y_r)\right\} \\ \overline{NP}_i(D) = \left\{\overline{NP}_i(Y_1), \overline{NP}_i(Y_2), \ldots, \overline{NP}_i(Y_r)\right\} \end{cases}$$

$\underline{NP}_i D$ is neighborhood positive region of *D* with respect to the granulation order NP_i, denotes

$$POS_{NP_i}^U(D) = \bigcup_{k=1}^{r} \underline{NP_i Y_k}.$$

Algorithm 1. Forward greedy search algorithm based on NPR

`Input:`

`1: Decision Table` $IS = \langle U, C \cup D \rangle$

`2. Delta` δ `//` δ `size of neighborhood.`

`Output: reduct` *red*

`Step 1:` *red* $\leftarrow \varnothing$ `//` *red* `selected attributes`

`Step 2: For each` $a_k \in C - red$

`Step 3:    Compute` $\gamma_{red \cup a_k}(D) = \dfrac{\left| POS_{B \cup a_k}(D) \right|}{|U|}$

`Step 4: Compute` $SIG^{inner}(a_k \cdot red, D) = \gamma_{red \cup a_k}(D) - \gamma_{red}(D)$

`Step 5: End.`

`Step 6: Compute` $Sig^{inner}(a_k, C, D, U); k \leq |C|$ `//` $Sig^{inner}(a_k, C, D, U)$ `inner attribute` a_k`.`

`Step 7: Put` a_k `into` *red*`, where` $Sig^{inner}(a_k, C, D, U) > 0$`;`

`Step 8: While` $EF(red, D) \neq EF(C, D) do$ `// stopping criteria`

`{`

$red\ red \cup \{a_0\}$

`where`

$Sig^{outer}(a_0, red, D) = \max\left\{ Sig^{outer}(a_k, red, D), a_k \in C - red \right\}$ `//` $Sig^{outer}(a_k, C, D)$ `outer attri-`

`bute` a_k `.`

`Step 9: Return` *red*

`Step 10: End`

Definition 8: Decision table $IS = \langle U, C \cup D \rangle, B \subseteq A$, attribute set B is a relative reduct if

1. $\gamma_B(D) = \gamma_A(D)$;
2. $\forall a \in B, \gamma_B(D) > \gamma_{B-a}(D)$.

A first criterion says $POS_B(D) = POS_A(D)$ and a second criterion says there is no surplus attribute. Hence a reduct has the same power as the whole attribute set.

To improve searching strategy, rank preservation significance measures for neighborhood feature selection positive approximation from the decision table is introduced. The rank perpetuation of the significance attribute is based on the dependency measure and represents:

$$SIG_\Delta^{outer} = \left(a, B, D, U\right)$$

This proves as:

Definition 9: Let decision table $S = \left\langle U, C \cup D \right\rangle, B \subseteq C$ and $U^1 = U - POS_B^U(D)$. For

$$\forall a, b \in C - B, if\ SIG_1^{outer}\left(a, B, D, U\right) \geq SIG_1^{outer}\left(b, B, D, U\right),$$

then

$$SIG_1^{outer}\left(a, B, D, U^1\right) \geq SIG_1^{outer}\left(b, B, D, U^1\right).$$

Proof: From the definition 9 of:

$$SIG_1^{outer}\left(a, B, D\right) = \gamma_{B \cup a}\left(D\right) - \gamma_B\left(D\right).$$

The value depends on dependency function

$$\gamma_B\left(D\right) = \frac{\left|POS_B\left(D\right)\right|}{\left|U\right|},$$

since

$$U^1 = U - POS_B^U\left(D\right).$$

we know that

$$POS_B^U\left(D\right) = \varnothing\ and\ POS_{B \cup a}^{U^1}\left(D\right) = POS_{B \cup a}^{U^1} = POS_{B \cup a}^U\left(D\right) - POS_B^U\left(D\right).$$

Therefore we have,

$$\frac{SIG_1^{outer}\left(a,B,D,U\right)}{SIG_1^{outer}\left(a,B,D,U^1\right)} = \frac{\gamma_{B\cup a}^{U}\left(D\right)-\gamma_{B}^{U}\left(D\right)}{\gamma_{B\cup a}^{U^1}\left(D\right)-\gamma_{B}^{U^1}\left(D\right)}$$

$$= \frac{\left|U^1\right|\left|POS_{B\cup a}^{U}\left(D\right)-POS_{B}^{U}\left(D\right)\right|}{\left|U\right|\left|POS_{B\cup a}^{U^1}\left(D\right)-POS_{B}^{U^1}\left(D\right)\right|}$$

$$= \frac{\left|U^1\right|\left|POS_{B\cup a}^{U}\left(D\right)-POS_{B}^{U}\left(D\right)\right|}{\left|U\right|\left|POS_{B\cup a}^{U}\left(D\right)-POS_{B}^{U}\left(D\right)\right|}$$

$$= \frac{\left|U^1\right|}{\left|U\right|}$$

Because

$$\frac{\left|U^1\right|}{\left|U\right|} \geq 0 ,$$

and if

$$SIG_1^{outer}\left(a,B,D,U\right) \geq SIG_1^{outer}\left(b,B,D,U\right),$$

then

$$SIG_1^{outer}\left(a,B,D,U^1\right) \geq SIG_1^{outer}\left(b,B,D,U^1\right).$$

Hence it completes proof.

The significance measure of attribute is computed from step 6 and the time complexity requires is $O\left(\left|U\right|\right)$. Hence time complexity for core attributes in step 6 is

$O\left(\left|C\right|\left|U\right|\right)$. In step 9, the core attributes counts up the significance attribute till the reduct. The time complexity of forward attribute search algorithm, becomes

$$O\left(\sum_{i=1}^{\left|C\right|}\left|U_i\right|\left(\left|C\right|-i+1\right)\right)$$

Algorithm 2. An improved Neighborhood Feature Selection Positive Approximation algorithm (NFSPA)

Input:

1. Decision Table $IS = \langle U, C \cup D \rangle$

2. Delta δ // δ range of neighborhood.

Output: One reduct *red*

Step 1: $red \; \varnothing$; //*red* collection of special attribute.

Step 2: For each $a_k \in C - red$

Step 3: Compute $\gamma_{red \cup a_i}(D) = \dfrac{\left| POS_{B \cup a_i}(D) \right|}{|U|}$

Step 4: Compute $Sig_1^{inner}(a, B, D) = \gamma_B(D) - \gamma_{B-\{a\}}(D)$

Step 5: Compute $Sig_1^{outer}(a, B, D) = \gamma_{B \cup \{a\}}(D) - \gamma_B(D)$

Step 6: end

Step 7: Compute $Sig^{inner}(a_k, C, D, U), k \leq |C|$

Step 8: Put a_k into red where $Sig^{inner}(a_k, C, D, U) > 0$; // core attributes

Step 9: $i = 1; R_1 = red; P_1 = \{R_1\}$ and $U_i \leftarrow U$

Step 10: While $EF^{U_i}(red, D) \neq EF^{U_i}(C, D) \, do$

{

Compute positive region of neighborhood positive approximation $POS_{NP_i}^{U}(D)$,

$U_i = U - POS_{NP_i}^{U}(D)$

$i \leftarrow i + 1; red \leftarrow red \cup \{a_0\}$,

where

$Sig^{outer}(a_0, red, D) = \max\{Sig^{outer}(a_k, red, D), a_k \in C - red$

continued on following page

Algorithm 2. Continued

$$R_i \leftarrow R_i \cup \{a_0\}_{,}$$

$$NP_i \leftarrow \{R_1, R_2, \ldots, R_i\}$$

```
};
```

Step 11: Return *red*

Step 12: end.

and the time complexity of NFSPA becomes

$$O\left(|U||C| + \sum_{i=1}^{|C|} |U_i|(|C| - i + 1)\right).$$

However the time complexity for general attribute reduction algorithm is

$$O\left(|U||C| + \sum_{i=1}^{|C|} |U|(|C| - i + 1)\right).$$

The time complexity of NFSPA becomes much lower as compared to the general attribute reduction algorithm (NPR) which reduces the computation time.

EXPERIMENTAL ANALYSIS

Evaluation performance of general forward greedy search algorithm is accomplished and neighborhood feature selection positive approximation is proposed. Analysis is made on computational time, entropy measure and classification accuracy. These three methods are considered and compared on the number of feature of general algorithm with proposed. The experimental result shows the features on documents preprocessing, and features subset on algorithms. The objective is to compute the time efficiency of proposed feature selection algorithm. The data sets used in experimentation are outlined in Table 1 where the three datasets are downloaded from UCI machine learning. These algorithms executed on Windows XP Personal Computer and Intel® Core™ i7 CPU 2.66 GHz, 4.00 GB memory and MATLAB R2010b. The last two columns of Table 1 show features and classes used for preprocessing. These features are extensively used for feature extraction method.

Table 1. Dataset description

Dataset	Cases	Features	Classes
Reuters-21578	21	5677	04
Classic 04	54	1411	06
Newsgroup 20	52	976	04

Figure 2. Preprocess features on three data sets

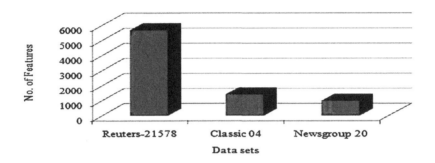

Time Efficient Analysis

Selected features for NPR and Improved NFSPA are equivalent. Hence the strength of Improved NFSPA algorithm retains the systematic power of unique features. The time of NFSPA basically decreases in compare to general NPR algorithm. The specific time and features for threshold values are shown in Table 2, 3, 4 Threshold delta has a significant task in NFSPA. It measures a parameter to manage neighborhood size. The time is skilled for two algorithms on three datasets Reuters-21578, Classic 04 and Newsgroup 20. Figure 3-5 shows time on two algorithms NPR and NFSPA. Each represents computational time of NPR and NFSPA for delta values 0.01, 0.015 and 0.001.

Three Representative Entropy Measures

For efficient attribute reduction, rough set methods developed many attribute reduction algorithm (Largeron, Moulin, & Géry, 2011). To make it more efficient we have focus on three representative entropy measures of reduction.

Table 2. Time and feature selection of the algorithms NPR and improved NFSPA with $\delta = 0.01$

Dataset	Features	NPR		NFSPA	
		Features	Time (s)	Features	Time (s)
Reuters- 21578	5677	465	74.00	465	60.00
Classic 04	1411	101	40.00	101	25.00
Newsgroup 20	976	76	25.00	76	15.00

Table 3. Time and feature selection of the algorithms NPR and improved NFSPA with $\delta = 0.015$

Dataset	Features	NPR		NFSPA	
		Features	Time (s)	Features	Time (s)
Reuters- 21578	5677	448	60.00	448	55.00
Classic 04	1411	92	30.00	92	22.00
Newsgroup 20	976	71	20.00	71	10.00

Table 4. Time and feature selection of the algorithms NPR and improved NFSPA with $\delta = 0.001$

Dataset	Features	NPR		NFSPA	
		Features	Time (s)	Features	Time (s)
Reuters- 21578	5677	441	50.00	441	45.00
Classic 04	1411	86	25.00	86	20.00
Newsgroup 20	976	65	15.00	65	08.00

Figure 3. Comparison of computational time on Reuters -21578

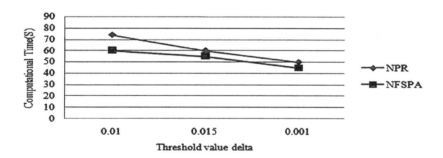

Figure 4. Comparison of computational time on Classic 04

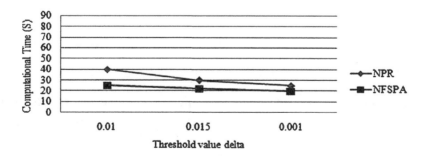

Figure 5. Comparison of computational time on Newsgroup 20

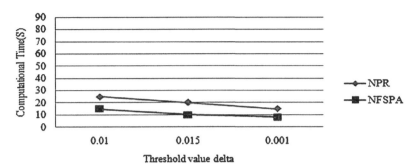

Decision table $IS = \left(U, C \cup D\right)$, obtain condition partition as $U\!/_{C} = \left\{X_{1}, X_{2}, \ldots, X_{m}\right\}$ and decision partition as $U\!/_{D} = \left\{Y_{1}, Y_{2}, \ldots, Y_{n}\right\}$. Considering these notations we introduce three types of entropy measures which define the significance measure.

Definition 10: Decision table $= \left(U, C \cup D\right)$, $B \subseteq C$ and $\forall_{a} \in B$. Significance measure of a in B is define as:

$$Sig_{1}^{inner}\left(a, B, D\right) = \gamma_{B}\left(D\right) - \gamma_{B-\{a\}}\left(D\right),$$

where

$$\gamma_{B}\left(D\right) = \frac{\left|POS_{B}\left(D\right)\right|}{\left|U\right|}.$$

Definition 11: Decision table $IS = \left(U, C \cup D\right)$, $B \subseteq C$ and $\forall_{a} \in C - B$. The significance measure of a in B is define as:

$$Sig_{1}^{outer}\left(a, B, D\right) = \gamma_{B \cup \{a\}}\left(D\right) - \gamma_{B}\left(D\right)$$

Classical model initiate Shannon's information entropy to explore reducts. Conditional entropy work out relative attributes reduction of a decision information system. Reduction remains unchanged the conditional entropy of target decision, it is denoted as SCE:

$$H\left(D \mid B\right) = -\sum_{i=1}^{m} p\left(X_{i}\right) \sum_{j=1}^{n} p\left(Y_{j} \mid X_{i}\right) \log\left(p\left(Y_{j} \mid X_{i}\right)\right)$$

where

$$p\left(X_i\right) = \frac{|X_i|}{|U|}$$

and

$$p\left(Y_i \mid X_i\right) = \frac{|X_i \cap Y_j|}{|X_i|}$$

Considering the Shannon's information conditional entropy, the significance measures expressed as:

Definition 12: Decision table $IS = \left(U, C \cup D\right)$, $B \subseteq C$ and $\forall_a \in B$. The significance measure of a in B is defined as:

$$Sig_1^{inner}\left(a, B, D\right) = H\left(D \mid B - \{a\}\right) - H\left(D \mid B\right)$$

Definition 13: Decision table $IS = \left(U, C \cup D\right)$, $B \subseteq C$ and $\forall_a \in C - B$. The significance measure of a in B is defined as:

$$Sig_1^{outer}\left(a, B, D\right) = H\left(D \mid B\right) - H\left(D \mid BU\{a\}\right)$$

Liang defines information and conditional entropy to measure uncertainty of information system. Shannon's entropy doesn't measure the fuzziness of decision in rough set. The entropy reduces redundant features proposed by Liang. This reduction method preserves the conditional entropy of a given decision table denoted as LCE. Conditional entropy is defined as:

$$E\left(D \mid C\right) = \sum_{i=1}^{m}\sum_{j=1}^{n} \frac{|Y_j \cap X_i|}{|U|} \frac{|Y_j^c \cap X_i^c|}{|U|}$$

The corresponding significance measures are:

Definition 14: Decision table $IS = \left(U, C \cup D\right)$ $B \subseteq C$ and $\forall_a \in B$. The significance measure of a in B is defined as:

$$Sig_3^{inner}\left(a, B, D\right) = E\left(D \mid B - \{a\}\right) - E\left(D \mid B\right)$$

Definition 15: Decision table $IS = (U, C \cup D)$ $B \subseteq C$ and $\forall_a \in C - B$. The significance measure of a in B is defined as:

$$Sig_3^{outer}(a, B, D) = E(D \mid B) - E(D \mid B \cup \{a\})$$

Uncertainty of information system measure and obtains feature subset conditional entropy (CCE) has been proposed. Hence CCE is expressed as:

$$CE(D \mid C) = \sum_{i=1}^{m} \left(\frac{|X_i|}{|U|} \frac{C_{|X_i|}^2}{C_{|U|}^2} - \sum_{j=1}^{n} \frac{|X_i \cap Y_j|}{|U|} \frac{C_{|X_i \cap Y_j|}^2}{C_{|U|}^2} \right)$$

where

$$C_{|X_i|}^2 = \frac{|X_i|_x (|X_i| - 1)}{2}$$

denotes pair of objects in the equivalence class X_i^2.

The conditional entropy constructs the significance measures of attribute decision tables.

Definition 16: Decision table $IS = (U, C \cup D)$ $B \subseteq C$ and $\forall_a \in B$. The significance measure of a in B is defined as:

$$Sig_4^{inner}(a, B, D) = CE(D \mid B - \{a\}) - CE(D \mid B)$$

Definition 17: Decision table $IS = (U, C \cup D)$ $B \subseteq C$ and $\forall_a \in C - B$. The significance measure of a in B is defined as:

$$Sig_4^{outer}(a, B, D) = CE(D \mid B) - CE(D \mid B \cup \{a\})$$

In following experiment, we compare LCE, SCE and CCE with NFSPA-LCE, NFSPA-SCE and NFSPA-CCE on three data sets shown in Tables 5, 6, and 7. The comparison of time and features with the original algorithm LCE,SCE and CCE and accelerate algorithm NFSPA-LCE, NFSPA-SCE and NFSPA-CCE on three UCI datasets is exposed in Tables 5, 6, and 7. From the Tables 5, 6, and 7, the modified algorithm is constantly work closer than the original counteract. While Figure 6-14 gives detailed change leaning line of two algorithms with data size become rising and shows the computational time. The feature subsets obtained are same as the original algorithm. These benefits significance measures of attributes of neighborhood feature selection positive approximation. The differences further are intensely superior as dataset increases. Hence, attribute reduction based found to be better solution on accelerator.

Table 5. Feature and Time of LCE and NFSPA-LCE

Dataset	Features	Threshold Value	LCE		NFSPA-LCE	
			Features	Time	Features	Time
Reuters- 21578	5677	0.01	465	55.00	455	55.00
		0.015	450	70.00	445	65.00
		0.001	435	60.00	430	55.00
Classic 04	1411	0.01	120	50.00	110	50.00
		0.015	100	50.00	100	40.00
		0.001	95	40.00	90	30.00
Newsgroup 20	976	0.01	76	30.00	74	25.00
		0.015	71	30.00	70	30.00
		0.001	65	20.00	65	20.00

Table 6. Feature and Time of SCE and NFSPA-SCE

Dataset	Features	Threshold Value	SCE		NFSPA-SCE	
			Features	Time	Features	Time
Reuters- 21578	5677	0.01	475	55.00	455	55.00
		0.015	460	70.00	455	60.00
		0.001	450	50.00	430	55.00
Classic 04	1411	0.01	140	50.00	130	50.00
		0.015	120	50.00	110	40.00
		0.001	95	40.00	90	30.00
Newsgroup 20	976	0.01	76	30.00	74	25.00
		0.015	71	30.00	70	30.00
		0.001	65	20.00	65	20.00

Table 7. Feature and Time of CCE and NFSPA-CCE

Dataset	Features	Threshold Value	CCE		NFSPA-CCE	
			Features	Time	Features	Time
Reuters- 21578	5677	0.01	465	55.00	455	55.00
		0.015	450	70.00	445	65.00
		0.001	435	60.00	430	55.00
Classic 04	1411	0.01	120	50.00	110	50.00
		0.015	100	50.00	100	40.00
		0.001	95	40.00	90	30.00
Newsgroup 20	976	0.01	76	30.00	74	25.00
		0.015	71	30.00	70	30.00
		0.001	65	20.00	65	20.00

Figure 6. Computational time of LCE and NFSPA-LCE versus threshold on Reuters-21578

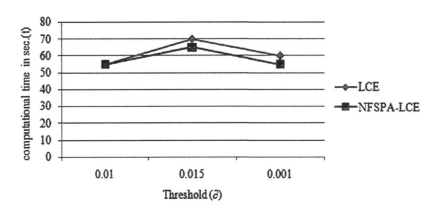

Figure 7. Computational time of LCE and NFSPA-LCE versus threshold on Classic 04

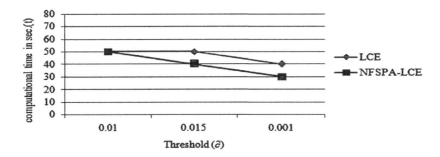

Figure 8. Computational time of LCE and NFSPA-LCE versus threshold on Newsgroup 20

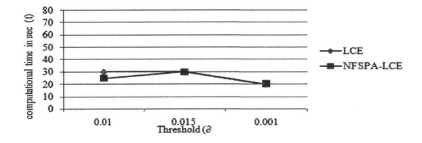

Stability Analysis

Information grows rapidly in size and difficulty arises in managing the data. To manage or classify data manually becomes infeasible. Redundant features decline the accurateness of the classifier. Less redundant features increases the accuracy else decreases. Hence to maintain the stability of classifier and to estimate the correctness precision, recall and f-measure parameter are considered. Experimental analysis is performed on two classifications KNN and Naïve Bayes.

Figure 9. Computational time of SCE and NFSPA-SCE versus threshold on Reuters-21578

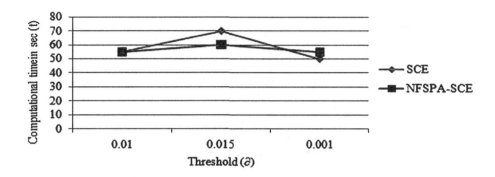

Figure 10. Computational time of SCE and NFSPA-SCE versus threshold on Classic 04

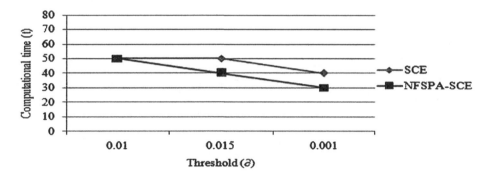

Figure 11. Computational time of SCE and NFSPA-SCE versus threshold on Newsgroup 20

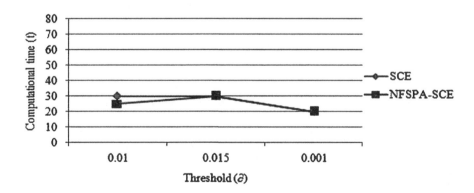

Results are summarized in Table 8 and Table 9. Graphical representation is shown in Figures 15-17.

CONCLUSION

This chapter has introduced the basic concepts of Rough set theory for feature selection and different types of attribute reduction methods. A brief review of existing feature selection strategies has been

Figure 12. Computational time of CCE and NFSPA-CCE versus threshold on Reuters 21578

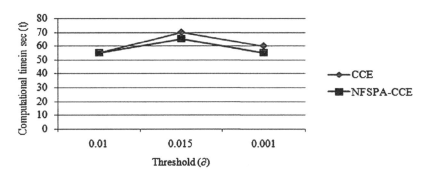

Figure 13. Computational time of CCE and NFSPA-CCE versus threshold on Classic 04

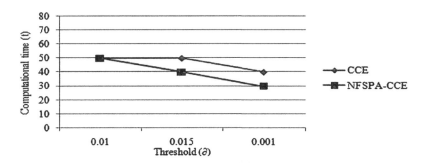

Figure 14. Computational time of CCE and NFSPA-CCE versus threshold on Newsgroup 20

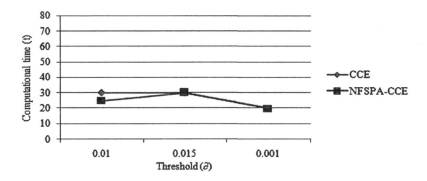

presented bringing out their shortcomings. Existing Rough set attribute reduction algorithm has been studied and a new approach for attribute reduction and selecting relevant features using rough set has been described in detail. Next we elaborate the implementation and testing details of the proposed neighborhood feature selection positive approximation scheme and other reduction techniques. The idea behind using this approach is to optimize the number of feature and improves the computational time. It has been demonstrated that the proposed scheme outperforms the high dimensionality of data.

Table 8. Stability Analysis on datasets using KNN and Naive Bayes

Dataset	No. of Features	KNN			Naive Bayes		
		Precision	Recall	F-Measure	Precision	Recall	F-Measure
Reuters-21578	5677	82.79	93.45	87.79	79.78	83.90	81.78
Classic 04	1411	84.67	89.76	87.14	78.89	83.45	81.10
Newsgroup 20	976	81.98	91.89	86.64	80.97	87.56	84.13

Figure 15. F-measure of KNN and NB on three data sets

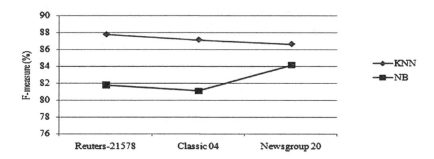

Table 9. Stability analysis with NFSPA using KNN and Naive Bayes

Dataset	No. of Features	KNN			Naive Bayes		
		Precision	Recall	F-Measure	Precision	Recall	F-Measure
Reuters-21578	497	90.67	94.55	92.56	87.67	88.78	88.22
Classic 04	112	90.86	92.67	91.75	89.56	93.67	89.56
Newsgroup 20	43	88.97	96.78	92.71	81.78	92.76	86.92

Figure 16. Features selection by NFSPA on three data sets

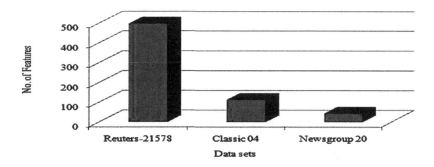

Figure 17. F-measure of KNN and NB on three data sets of NFSPA

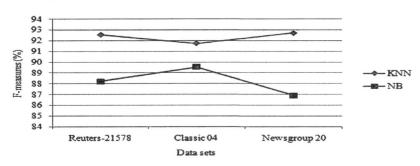

Hence achieves the curse of dimensionality. The proposed system implements for attribute reduction and finds the relevant features. An experimental result shows that the proposed neighborhood positive approximation provides the improvement in computational time and reduces the number of feature. Feature selection and computational time on three data sets is carried out with three to four different techniques. To evaluate the performance of the proposed approach rigorous experimentation has been carried out and the results are presented.

It is concluded that the proposed mechanism is suitable for further clustering task.

REFERENCES

Chen, D., Zhao, S., Zhang, L., Yang, Y., & Zhang, X. (2012, November). Sample Pair Selection for Attribute Reduction with Rough Set. *IEEE Transactions on Knowledge and Data Engineering*, *24*(11), 2080–2093. doi:10.1109/TKDE.2011.89

Hu, Q., Liu, J., & Yu, D. (2008). Mixed feature selection based on granulation and approximation. *Knowledge-Based Systems*, *21*(4), 294–304. doi:10.1016/j.knosys.2007.07.001

Hu, Q., Yu, D., Liu, J., & Wu, C. (2008). Neighborhood rough set based heterogeneous feature subset selection. *Information Sciences*, *178*(18), 3577–3594. doi:10.1016/j.ins.2008.05.024

Jensen, R., & Shen, Q. (2004). Semantics-preserving dimensionality reduction: Rough and fuzzy-rough-based approaches. *IEEE Transactions on Knowledge and Data Engineering*, *16*(12), 1457–1471. doi:10.1109/TKDE.2004.96

Largeron, C., Moulin, C., & Géry, M. (2011). Entropy based feature selection for text categorization. *ACM Symposium on Applied Computing*. 10.1145/1982185.1982389

Liang, J., Wang, F., Dang, C., & Qian, Y. (2012, July). A Group Incremental approach to feature Selection Applying Rough Set Technique. *IEEE Transactions on Knowledge and Data Engineering*, 9.

Lingras, P., & Peters, G. (2012). *Applying Rough Set Concepts to Clustering*. Springer-Verlag London Limited. doi:10.1007/978-1-4471-2760-4_2

Liu, H., & Yu, L. (2005, April). Toward Integrating Feature Selection Algorithms for Classification and Clustering. *IEEE Transactions on Knowledge and Data Engineering*, *17*(4), ●●●.

Miao, D., Duan, Q., Zhang, H., & Jiao, N. (2009). Rough set based hybrid algorithm for text classification. *Expert Systems with Applications*, *36*(5), 9168–9174. doi:10.1016/j.eswa.2008.12.026

Patil, L. H., & Atique, M. (2014). A Multistage Feature Selection Model for Document Classification Using Information Gain and Rough Set. *International Journal of Advanced Research in Artificial Intelligence*, *3*(11). Retrieved from www.ijarai.thesai.org

Patil, L. H., & Atique, M. (2015). An Improved feature selection based on neighborhood positive approximation rough set in document classification. *International Journal of Soft Computing and Software Engineering*, *5*(1), 13–30. doi:10.7321/jscse.v5.n1.2

Patil, L. H., & Atique, M. (2015). *A Novel Feature Selection and Attribute Reduction Based on Hybrid IG-RS Approach*. *Springer International Publishing Switzerland*. Doi:10.1007/978-3-319-13731-5_59

Pawlak, Z. (1991). *Rough set: Theoretical Aspects of Reasoning about Data*. Kluwer Academic Publishers. doi:10.1007/978-94-011-3534-4

Qian, Y., Liang, J., Pedrycz, W., & Dang, C. (2011). An efficient accelerator for attribute reduction from incomplete data in rough set framework. *Pattern Recognition*, *4*(8), 1658–1670. doi:10.1016/j.patcog.2011.02.020

Shen, Y., & Wang, F. (2011). Variable precision rough set model over two universes and its properties. *Soft Computing*, *15*(3), 557–567. doi:10.100700500-010-0562-6

Shieh, H.-L. (2012). A Hybrid Clustering Algorithm Based on Rough Set and Shared Nearest Neighbors. In *Applied Mechanics and Materials* (Vol. 145, pp. 189–193). Trans Tech Publications.

Uguz, H. (2011). A two-stage feature selection method for text categorization by using information gain, principal component analysis and genetic algorithm. *Knowledge-Based Systems*, *24*(7), 1024–1032. doi:10.1016/j.knosys.2011.04.014

Wang, F., Liang, J., & Qian, Y. (2013). Attribute reduction: A dimension incremental strategy. *Knowledge-Based Systems*, *39*, 95–1. doi:10.1016/j.knosys.2012.10.010

Wang, H. (2006, June). Nearest Neighbors by Neighborhood Counting. *IEEE Transactions on Pattern Analysis and Machine Intelligence*, *28*(6). PMID:16724588

Yao & Zhao. (2008). Attribute Reduction in Decision-Theoretic Rough Set Models. *Information Sciences*, *178*(17), 3356-3373.

Zhang, H. Y., Leung, Y., & Zhou, L. (2013). Variable-precision-dominance-based rough set approach to interval-valued information systems. *Information Sciences*, *244*, 75–91. doi:10.1016/j.ins.2013.04.031

Chapter 6
Clustering Techniques for Content-Based Feature Extraction From Image

Madan U. Kharat
MET Institute of Engineering, India

Ranjana P. Dahake
MET Institute of Engineering, India

Kalpana V. Metre
MET Institute of Engineering, India

ABSTRACT

Image retrieval is gaining significant attention in areas such as surveillance, access control, etc. The content-based feature extraction plays a very crucial role in image retrieval. For the characterization of a specific image, mainly three features (i.e., color, texture, and shape) are used. Multimedia can store text, image, audio, and video which can be processed and retrieved. The various techniques are used for image retrieval such as textual annotations, content-based image retrieval in many application areas like medical imaging, satellite imaging, etc. However, most of these techniques were designed for specific domains and universally accepted method is yet to be designed; hence, CBIR is a field of active research. Similar output images indicate efficiency of search and retrieval process. In this chapter, the authors have discussed various image feature extraction techniques and clustering approaches for content-based feature extraction from image and specifically focused on color based CBIR techniques.

INTRODUCTION

In past few decades limitations in the metadata-based system resulted into more research in content-based image retrieval as the usage of digital images increased in huge amount. In CBIR the two major processes are feature extraction and similarity measurement. CBIR clearly defines use of visual content of image like color, texture, shape etc. The contents of any image are explored by the visual feature.

DOI: 10.4018/978-1-5225-5775-3.ch006

These visual features/contents are retrieved from the images and are described by multidimensional vectors. The distance/ similarity between the feature vectors of data images is calculated and relevant images are retrieved. Image feature representation, extraction and indexing are the fundamental bases of content-based image retrieval. Mainly three features are used to characterize a specific image: color, texture and shape. Wide ranges of algorithms were developed to handle image retrieval based on these factors. Feature extraction is one of the essential requirements in image retrieval process. The color feature is one of the most popular visual features.

The simplest approach for content-based image retrieval is pixel to pixel comparison and the color difference between images is computed. The images need to resize to fixed dimension before comparison. Generally, color feature is represented using the color histogram. The approach based on global color histogram depicting the number of pixels belonging to each of specific set of colors. This approach does not consider the similarity of colors in neighborhood pixels. In the local histogram-based method, an image is partitioned into different rectangular cells and histograms for each cell are computed separately and the color difference between images is computed. A color signature-based method partitions an image and the color signature is calculated for each partition. The difference between the color signatures of the images decides the similarity of the images (Parekh, 2006).

To increase the accuracy of CBIR system, focus of research is shifting from designing sophisticated low-level feature extraction algorithms to reduce the 'semantic gap' between the visual features and the richness of human semantics.

The clustering groups the set of similar objects. Various clustering approaches are used to group, identify and reduce the content-based image features. Accuracy of clustering is based upon the algorithm, which is selected, and the use of parameters like distance function, density threshold and required number of clusters. General cluster models which are used includes: Connectivity models, Centroid models, Distribution models, Density models, and Graph-based models. In color clustering large patches of color in comparison with small scattered spots leads to clustering-based feature extraction. Two images appear to be similar if they contain large similar color patches roughly at the similar locations. This cluster-based approach isolates single color clusters in an image instead of image partitioning. A color space is mathematical representation of a set of color. There are several color spaces for specific area of applications. Different Color spaces like RGB, CMYK, CIE Lab, HSV emphasis three color variants that characterize color: hue, saturation, intensity. Lighting and shading are related to intensity and variation of this factor can affect the performance. Clustering of other attributes with color for feature extraction is essential for content-based image retrieval.

Clustering of color pixels in the image plays an important role in segmentation process. Various clusters can be created considering the color difference between them. The concept of connected component is utilized to form a specific color cluster. Decision can be taken based on dominant cluster and overlapping of them (Solomon, & Breckon, 2011). Feature extraction based on clustering provides more efficiency without any need to have the prior knowledge regarding the colors present in application. This approach can be combined with knowledge-based interpretation technique resulting in accuracy of content-based image retrieval system. The other features of image like texture as well as shape are also important for retrieval of similar query images from database. Various hybrid techniques of feature extraction and clustering are also required to get the accurate retrieval of images.

Further in various sections we have discussed about multimedia database, Image low and high-level features, different techniques of feature extraction, selection and clustering methods for image in CBIR system, last section provides applications of CBIR in various field.

BACKGROUND

With increased use of information and communication technology in various applications, the importance of content-based or concept-based system is playing an important role. With increasing processing power of computing the cost of hardware and software is decreasing. The term, multimedia, is a means of communication using multiple media such as text, image, graphics, animation, sound etc. We can utilize multimedia to its full extent with the help of knowledge of its internal content. The various content Based Image Retrieval related applications are serving best Industries, Education, Security, Research, Entertainment etc.

In the last two decades, the non-textual form has gained more significance. Recently Content Based Image Retrieval is a field of research and to retrieve the images from the repository images color, shape and texture play an important role. It is essential to study and use techniques for extracting these features and finally to get the more relevant search content. As the dimension of image features mostly larger so feature selection and clustering techniques are useful for particular image retrieval. However number of related literature is available but still limited due to fact that the multimedia deals with various media and a large number of concepts are put together as per the content in it.

The objective is to meet the requirement of providing fundamental concepts for Clustering techniques, feature extraction for Content-Based Image Retrieval. With the expectation that those seeking basic information about detail view on image feature, feature extraction techniques, clustering methods can be benefited. The focus is to introduce the reader to some key aspect of Content-based Image Retrieval and concepts and techniques in modern image processing.

MULTIMEDIA DATABASES

A Multimedia database can be defined as the collection of related multimedia data. It includes different primary media data types for example text, images, drawings audio clip and video. Multimedia Database Management System (MDMS) is a framework for management of these data basically represented using various formats on a wide array of media sources. MDMS provides support for various operations on these data types. Different operation on data include creation, access, storage, query processing etc.

Common multimedia data types are given below (Adjeroh, & Nwosu, 1997):

- Text document
- Graphics: sketches, drawing etc.
- Images: paintings, photos, maps etc.
- Animated images
- Video
- Audio
- A combination of two or more data types specified above

Continuous media and discrete media are two types in which media are categorized. In continuous media, the media changes along with the audio and video. The Media which is independent of time is categorized as discrete media category. Multimedia Database requires managing different additional information that is given as following.

- **Media Data:** The actual data representing an object such as images, graphics audio, video etc.
- **Media Format Data:** Details of the format of the media data.
- **Keyword Data:** The keyword descriptions which relate to generating media data.
- **Feature Data:** It contains color, shapes and texture descriptor information of media.

Multimedia databases should be able to uniformly process query data which is in various formats. It must have ability to query different media sources in parallel manner and also to support the different databases operations across them. They should retrieve media objects from storage accurately. Here in this chapter we have focused on Image retrieval from multimedia database.

Multimedia Database Characteristics

A multimedia database contains text, images, audio, video etc. Multimedia data consists of a many media formats that include TIFF, BMP, JPEG, MPEG, AVI, WAV, GIF, EPS, PNG, etc. Format conversion becomes important as the use of data becomes limited when it is bound to some specific format.
Multimedia data has following characteristics (Yu, & Brandenburg, 2011):

- **Lack of Structure:** Multimedia data is unstructured data and hence, standard indexing for CBIR may not be available.
- **Temporality:** As mentioned earlier different multimedia data types falls into two categories such as continuous and discrete. Continuous media are having temporal requirement such as video, audio, and animation sequences. Continuous media has implications on their storage, manipulation and presentation requirements. Discrete media like images, graphics have the spatial constraints when the content of media is concerned.
- **Massive Volume:** Size of multimedia data is huge as it takes a large amount of space when it is stored on the device.
- **Logistics:** As multimedia consists of multiple objects which make processing of it more complex one as multimedia database applications require use of compression algorithms to deal with objects such as images, audio and video.

In Figure 1, Multimedia Database Architecture is shown. Various components of it are meta-Data, Multimedia data. Depending upon the application using their various metadata and the query image or other data objects are processed and retrieved.

Figure 1. Multimedia database architecture

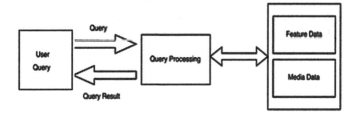

Image Searching

Nowadays information and communication technology is used in every field resulting more automation so more multimedia information becomes available. This large amount of data can be handled by making efficient browsing, searching, and retrieving of information. Content of media data are represented using three approaches such as keyword dependent, feature-dependent and concept dependent (Parekh, 2006).

- **Keyword-Based Approach/Text Based Annotation:** The previous search engines were using the keyword-based image retrieval approaches. In this technique, text annotations are used for describing the multimedia content. This approach is also known as Text Based Annotation which only uses well-defined queries. As it describes their contents with words it is a time-consuming process. Manual annotation is required and hence there can be many limitations as digital images may be annotated using inaccurate keywords. The significance of digital images is depending upon the friendliness as well as accuracy of retrieving relevant objects by the users. Advanced search and retrieval tools become essential in various image retrieval applications (Parekh, 2006).
- **Feature-Based Approach:** In this method set of features are used to represent and retrieval of the data. In various multimedia databases user can put the query by providing specific keywords and/or related image characteristics. The low-level features such as general information like color, texture, shape, speed, position are very useful for retrieving similar images from multimedia database. Particularly in the applications like face recognition, fingerprint recognition medical images use color, shape and texture for better retrieval (Parekh, 2006).
- **Concept-Based Approach:** In this approach concepts are used for the purpose of interpretation of the content of the image in order to retrieve the related similar images. This approach is specific for the particular domain. Here understanding the semantics of media content is important and accordingly interpretation based feature retrieval takes place. Meaning related to media content is identified in form of their association with real-world objects or concepts for example grass, road, sky, tree, water etc.

User provides query with specification using example. An object can be extracted by providing shape, color or the color distribution in image. The Content-Based Retrieval from multimedia database is, however, specifically based on above types of searches (Parekh, 2006).

CONTENT-BASED IMAGE RETRIEVAL

CBIR is one of the important alternatives to deal with the challenges come across various image retrieval techniques. Digital images, which are retrieved with help of CBIR system, are represented via a set of visual features. As shown in Figure 2 typical CBIR system concentrates to extract and store visual features from the image database. Query image is used as input to start the retrieval process. Set of relevant images are returned by CBIR based upon the user query (Yoshitaka, & Ichikawa, 1999; Ismail, 2017).

Figure 2. Overview of typical CBIR system

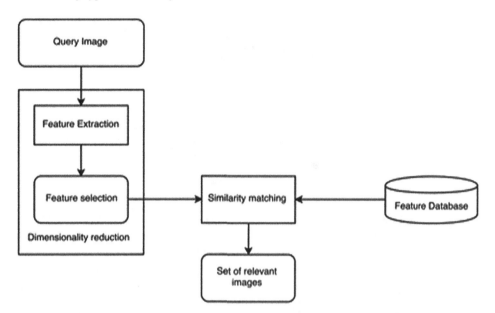

Image Features

The feature is one of the important part of information which is useful to solve the computational tasks in relevant applications. Features can be in a form of points, edges or objects. Features are retrieved from the operations such as feature detection or general neighborhood operation applied to the image. As it is very general concept in image retrieval domain, the selection of feature is directly related to specific problem. A Particular feature of an image can be represented in many ways, for example, Boolean variables are used for representing presence or absence of an edge.

Image Color Features

Color features extraction methods are classified into two types, global methods and local methods. In global methods the complete image is considered for feature extraction process. Whereas in local method only specific part of the image is considered, including local color histogram, color correlogram, color difference histogram, etc. Color feature is most popular and highly preferred low-level descriptor in CBIR system. There are various color spaces like RGB, CMYK, HSV etc. (Hughes, Van Dam, Mcguire, Sklar, Foley, Feiner, & Akeley, 2014).

Color Models

1. **RGB:** RGB uses additive color mixing. It specifies which kind of *light* needs to be *emitted* for producing a required color. Red, blue and green are the primary colors in RGB color model. The combination of red and green results to produce yellow, blue and green produce cyan, red and blue produces magenta. Blender of Red, green and blue results into producing white. Figure 3 shows RGB Color Model.

Figure 3. RGB color model

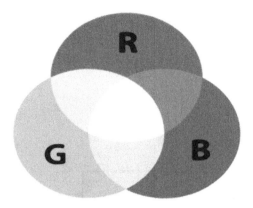

For a more accurate representation see the electronic version.

2.   **CMYK:** Printing process uses CMYK color model which is based on subtractive color mixing principal as it specifies which kind of ink need to be used to produce required color. CMYK color model stores ink values of cyan, magenta, yellow and black. As shown in Figure 4, CMYK color model has four primary colors such as cyan, magenta, yellow and black. When we mix all these four primary colors of CMYK model gray color is produced.

3.   **HSV:** Hue, saturation and value are building blocks for this model. Hue and saturation are the most important components as they define the way in which human eye perceive the color. Value component indicates the intensity of color. Many variation like HSL where with Hue and Saturation the their component is Lightness.

Histograms

A histogram is an accurate representation of the distribution of numerical data. The distribution of colors in an image is represented as color histogram. The color histogram can be produced for color spaces such as RGB or HSV.

Figure 4. CMYK color model

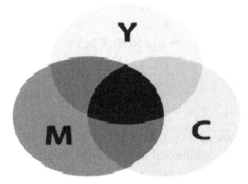

For a more accurate representation see the electronic version.

As shown in Figure 5 histogram has a region between two brightness values one is brighter and other is darker, such as eye's iris. The brighter part relates mainly to the skin on face. In darker image histogram can be concentrated towards black and in brighter image with lower contrast, histogram can be thinner and concentrated near the whiter brightness levels (Nixon, & Aguado, 2008).

Due to change in brightness of the original image, there might be changes in intensity level which may result in noise. Elimination of noise improve the appearance of the image and can help for better feature extraction techniques.

Image Shape Features

High-level feature extraction is concerned about finding shapes in stored images. If images are more complex then they needs to be decomposed into a structure of simple shapes. For example, in face image detection and recognition, we expect that eyes will be above the nose and the eye will be below the eyebrow. Invariance properties play important role in feature extraction process (Nixon, & Aguado, 2008). Different invariants are Illumination level, Position Invariance and Scale Invariance.

Image Texture Features

The image texture consists of a set of metrics generated in image processing to quantify the perceived texture of an image. It provides details related to the spatial location of color or intensities in the image. It may consist of artificial or natural texture. These textures are useful in segmentation or classification of images for image retrieval process (Sklansky, 1978).

Texture feature indicates the real-world image contents, for example clouds, skin, trees, fabric, etc. These texture feature reduces the gap present in image content and their high-level semantic for retrieval of images in CBIR systems. However, some texture features can directly affect the shape of the image region. These features can handle rectangular regions better rather than arbitrary region. One of the important alternatives to extract texture feature from non-regular regions is convex sets. The edge histogram

Figure 5. Histogram of eye image

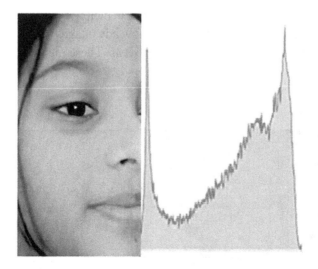

descriptor encodes the spatial distribution of images edges. This has set of local edge histograms which are retrieved from sub-images. These are grouped into horizontal, vertical, diagonal, anti-diagonal and neutral edges; however this method is sensitive to the specific scene and object distortions (Hubpages, 2017).

An example of natural texture of image is given in Figure 6 which is of different grass such, as real textures in farming area. If the image is captured from remote camera in Geographical Imaging System then other texture of land area can be visualized and these textures are labeled accordingly.

For analyzing texture pattern structural, statistical and combination approaches are used. Texture description is used for deriving some measurements which further are useful for classification.

Invariance is one of the important requirements for feature extraction, which consists of invariance to position, scale and rotation, which can apply equally to texture extraction. Position invariance has the measurements which describes that a texture must not change the position of the analyzed part changes. We also need rotation invariance (Nixon, & Aguado, 2008).

IMAGE FEATURE EXTRACTION

Feature extraction is used to construct combinations of the variables. It describes the data with sufficient amount of accuracy. Feature extraction helps in the reduction of resources in order to produce a description of large amount of data. In analysis of complex data, one major problem is the variables involved, which requires a huge amount of memory and computation power. For resolving this problem we need to have a subset involving initial features known as feature selection. The selected features must have the relevant details present in input image

In CBIR system feature extraction plays very important role, specifically for facial image recognition. There are a number of feature extraction methods. Holistic features and Local feature approaches are the two important categories for feature extraction. Holistic features divide the algorithm into various linear projection methods like principal component analysis, Two-Dimensional PCA, linear discriminate analysis and Independent Component Analysis. If illumination condition varies or image has occlusion in large amount these method can provide false results. The main reason is that image patterns present on a complex nonlinear and non-convex manifold in the high-dimensional space. For handling these kinds of cases, non-linear category approaches like kernel Principal Component Analysis etc. are used.

In the next category, local appearance features have few advantages in comparison with holistic features. There are various techniques like Local binary patterns. These methods can be found more stable

Figure 6. Example texture

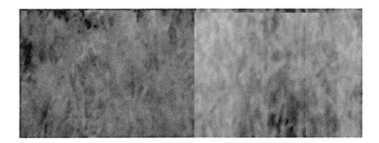

for local changes like occlusion and misalignment. They are simple representative methods for providing effective information about changes around the central pixel. Accurate feature extraction is an essential phase. It affects the overall system performance. Different clustering approaches are available such as K-means used for clustering. In case of few images, classification can be useful. Various samples are stored in the database by comparing that top most match relevant image is retrieved.

Lower level image features are color, shape, and texture, these features can be extracted and compared for retrieving the more relevant images. In the following section, different techniques are discussed for each of the feature extraction.

Color Feature Extraction

In CBIR, color is most important visual features. Color space, color quantization and similarity function selection to provide a huge impact in the process of feature extraction.

Color Histogram

A color histogram is generated with number of pixel which belongs to particular set of color. In this method color histogram feature is divided into global and local color extraction. The comparison and retrieval process of image is carried out by using distance present in between two images. A certain threshold is pre-decided and according to the value of distance the image is less or more similar to each other.

Local color histogram provides spatial details of image. Local color histogram also gives the details relevant to the color distribution of particular section of image. For using local histogram method the first important step is to divide the image into different regions afterward we can obtain a color histogram for individual block finally image is represented by these histograms. When we need to compare two images, we calculate the distance, using their histograms. Different distance measures can be used such as Euclidean, cosine distance. Region wise distance is calculated in both of the images. Figure 7 shows Global and local histogram-based approach. Clustering the similar images for retrieval is very essential steps for generation of expected results to the users query (Parekh, 2006).

Color Signature-Based Approach

This approach divides an image and the color signature is calculated for each partition. A representative color is defined for each partition whose percentage is greater than the predefined threshold value, for example color signature can be represented in stream of ones and zeros. Difference between the color signatures of the images decides the similarity of the images. This method is simple and computation efficient. This method provides features using representation of the color-spatial information of an image as a set of compact *signatures*. For the image retrieval process, the signatures of the query image are required to obtain which can be used to match with the various images from the database (Parekh, 2006). Some other methods for getting color feature are discussed here (Shukla, & Vania, 2014).

1. **Geometric Moments:** An image moment is the particular weighted average of the image pixels' intensities.
2. **Color Moments:** They are statistical moments of the probability distributions of colors.

Figure 7. a) Global histogram based approach; b) Local histogram based approach

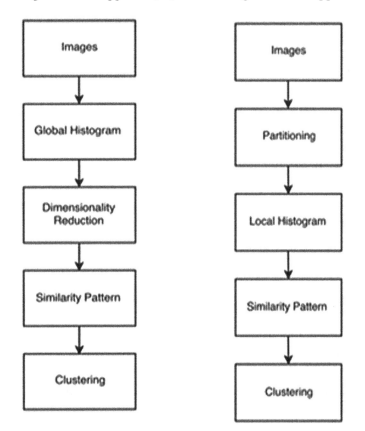

3. **Color Correlogram:** The color Correlogram includes the spatial correlation of colors, which is used to describe the global distribution of local spatial correlation of colors.
4. **Color Coherence Vector:** Then separate histograms can be generated for these two categories i.e. coherent & incoherent pixels thereby including some spatial information.
5. **Average RGB:** Different RGB components average can be taken a wide range of Red, Green, Blue color components are available to use.

Texture Feature Extraction

Homogeneity is used to explore the feature of texture with the help of visual patterns. It consists of the significant information regarding the structural arrangement of a surface such as bricks. It's easy to relate the relation of the surface within and around the environment. We can say that this feature expresses the distinct physical formation of a surface (Sklansky, 1978). One of the important examples of statistical representations of texture is: Co-occurrence Matrix.

There are three ways by which texture analysis can be described a namely spectral approach, structural approach and statistical approach. The frequency domain is used to handle the spectral approach of texture feature extraction.

Shape Feature Extraction

The characteristic configuration of an object is known as the feature of shape. Object can be differentiated from its surroundings with the help of outline. The shape feature plays a very crucial role in classification and retrieval of images as its one of the promising and proven way to describe the object (Hubpages, 2017). In comparison with color and texture feature shape feature is more effective to characterize the contents of an image. Shape descriptor does further get classified into contour-based shape descriptor and region-based shape descriptor. Various descriptors are to be used for illustration some of them are discussed here (Shukla, & Vania, 2014).

- **Fourier Descriptors:** These are generated by applying Fourier transform on the boundary of the shape. The coefficients generated by this process are known as the Fourier descriptors (Hall, Kruger, Dwyer, Hall, Mclaren, & Lodwick, 1971).
- **Curvature Scale Space Descriptors:** These are important for local shape features. Locations, as well as the degree of concavities, are detected with the help of scale space (Shukla, & Vania, 2014; Yoshitaka, & Ichikawa, 1999).
- **Zernike Moments:** Zernike moments descriptor does not require the boundary information. These results are to suitable for representation of the most complex shapes (Shukla, & Vania, 2014).

FEATURE SELECTION

Feature selection is the process of subset selection. These subsets are selected based upon the relevant features to make their use in the construction of a model (Bouaguel, 2015). Feature selection process is shown in Figure 8.

Following are the important reasons to use the feature selection techniques.

Figure 8. Feature selection process

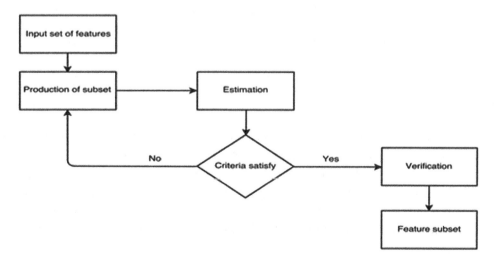

- Simple models make the interpretation easier for the user.
- Training time required is minimal.
- Enhanced generalization by reducing over fitting.

While using the feature selection techniques redundant and irrelevant features can be removed without much loss of information. Basically, a feature selection algorithm is a combination of various search technique to provide new feature subsets.

Procedure for Feature Selection:

- **Subset Production:** Candidate subset is generated from original feature set.
- **Estimation:** Estimation of the generated subset.
- **Calculation:** Comparing with user-defined threshold value.
- **Verification:** Test the validity of subset.

Feature selection is divided mainly into three categories: wrappers, filters and embedded methods (Bouaguel, 2015).

- **Wrapper Methods:** These methods use a predictive model to form subsets of features. Every new subset is used in the process of model training, which is then tested upon hold-out set. Recording the number of mistakes made on that hold-out set provides the score of the subset. Wrapper methods need more computational power as every new subset is trained, but these are the methods which provide the good and promising results.
- **Filter Methods:** The proxy measure is a criterion to score a feature subset in this kind of methods. This provides the faster computation while providing the meaningful feature set. Common measures required like the mutual information, Pearson product-moment correlation coefficient, inter/intra class distance or the scores of significance tests for each class/feature combinations. Filter methods require less computational power in comparison with wrapper methods.
- **Embedded Methods:** These methods perform feature selection as a part of the model construction phenomenon. Recursive Feature Elimination algorithm is one of important approach used with the help of Support Vector Machines to recursively construct a model and remove features having the low amount of weights. The computational power required for these methods is in between the power required to wrapper and filter methods.

CLUSTERING

Clustering is a technique of grouping a set of similar objects/entities together considering the degree of association between objects and groups. Cluster analysis is always used to create clusters of images for improving the efficiency and accuracy of image retrieval. Various clustering approaches are used to group, identify and reduce the content-based image features. It is expected in clustering process that there should be less inter-cluster similarity and more intra-cluster similarity. The accuracy of the result of content-based image retrieval depends on: 1) selection of the attributes on which objects are to be clustered; 2) clustering algorithm selection; 3) choosing similarity measure from the available; 4) creating the clusters or cluster hierarchies, which can be expensive in terms of computational resources, and; 5) assessing the validity of the clustering output.

For grouping the objects in a cluster, the value of degree of association between them is calculated. The association measure may be a distance measure, or a measure of homogeneity or heterogeneity. Some clustering techniques have a theoretical prerequisite for use of a specific measure (Euclidean distance etc.), but the measure to be used is decided by the researcher depending upon the application where clustering is used. There are various numbers of homogeneity measures available, and the selection of homogeneity measure affects the accuracy of the results of clustering process. The commonly used measures used in information retrieval applications are discussed in the subsequent section. Figure 9 shows image retrieval using clustering.

Clustering techniques can be used to cluster color, texture, shape features of images.

Types of Clustering

Categorization of the clustering techniques is done based on the type of cluster structure produced. The clustering methods can be classified mainly into two types i.e. hierarchical and the nonhierarchical techniques. The hierarchical technique groups a data set of N objects into M clusters, and the nonhierarchical methods require lesser computations than the hierarchical techniques. The simple nonhierarchical technique partitions the data set of N entities into M clusters where overlap is prohibited. Each item belonging to the cluster is most homogeneous than the other clusters and the cluster may be represented by a centroid or cluster representative that reveals the characteristics of the objects grouped in that cluster. In hierarchical methods, each data object belongs to separate clusters and a nested data set is produced by linking pairs of items or clusters successively until every object in the data set is linked. The hierarchical techniques use two approaches i.e. agglomerative, starting from un-clustered set of data objects and joining N - 1 pair wise objects or divisive, initially keeping all the entities in a single cluster and dividing bigger cluster through N - 1 partitions of some cluster into a smaller cluster. Both the algorithms are exactly reverse of each other.

Figure 9. Image retrieval using clustering

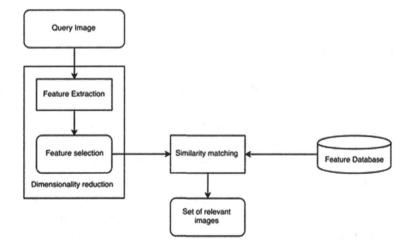

Nonhierarchical Methods

In the nonhierarchical methods, a priori decisions about the count of clusters, criterion for cluster membership, cluster size, and form of cluster representation are necessary. Since a large number of possible partitions of N items into M clusters makes an optimal solution impractical, the nonhierarchical techniques try to find an approximation and partition the data set in some way and then reassigns items/objects until some criterion is satisfied. The time complexity O(NM) is much lower than for the hierarchical techniques if M<<N so that large data sets can be partitioned. The nonhierarchical techniques were used for most of the early approaches in image and document clustering when computational resources were scarce (Irani, Pise, & Phatak, 2016).

A non-hierarchical method partitions a dataset producing a set of generally non-overlapping groups and there are no hierarchical relationships between them. Non-hierarchical methods generally require much less computational resources than the hierarchic methods. Three of the main types of non-hierarchical method are single-pass, relocation and nearest neighbor. Single-pass methods generate clusters depending upon the order of processing the data objects. Relocation methods allocate the data objects to the initial used defined clusters and then repetitively reassign data objects for the optimal results. It results in local optimization rather than global optimization.

In k-nearest neighbor method, it simply separates the data based on the assumed similarities between various data objects. Thus, the classes can be differentiated from one another by searching for similarities between the data provided. The data object is assigned to the same cluster as of their nearest neighbors. User-defined parameters will determine the number of nearest neighbors level of similarity between nearest neighbor lists.

Hierarchical Methods

Due to substantial work on clustering and availability of software for clustering purpose, and improved algorithms, nowadays the clustering approach is focused on the hierarchical agglomerative clustering methods. A hierarchical clustering is a set of nested clusters that are organized as a tree in the form of dendrograms. The order of pair wise grouping of the most similar entities in the data set and the value of the association/homogeneity function is important. The dendrogram is a useful representation when considering retrieval from a clustered set of objects since it indicates the paths that the retrieval process may follow.

Association/Similarity Measures

Similarity or association measures play a vital role in algorithms performance for clustering problems. The measures of performances include execution time, threshold value selection, classification accuracy etc. The clustering algorithm used is a two-step unsupervised method. A homogeneity measure can be defined as the distance between various data objects. As the distance increases, similarity decreases and vice-a-versa. While, homogeneity is an indicator of the strength of association between two data objects whereas heterogeneity deals with the measurement of separation between two data objects. In fact, the efficiency of many algorithms depends upon selection of a good association measure/function over the input data set. Here, a brief overview of association/homogeneity measure functions commonly used for clustering is described in the following subsections:

Euclidean Distance

Euclidean distance is always considered as the standard measure for geometrical problems. It is the distance or dissimilarity between two data objects represented as it points in different dimensions. Euclidean distance is useful for the data set having multidimensional data, including the images. Euclidean distance measure is used with the K-means algorithm. The Euclidean distance determines the square root of square of differences between the coordinates of a pair of objects represented by d-dimensions as shown in Equation (1) given below (Xu, & Wunsch Ii, 2005).

$$D(X,Y) = \sqrt{\sum_{i=1}^{d} (X_i - Y_i)^2} \tag{1}$$

where vector X={ x_1, x_2, x_3, ..., x_d} represents d-features of a query image and Y=(y_1, y_2, y_3, ... y_d) represents same d-features of the image in the database.

Cosine Distance

Cosine similarity is a measure of homogeneity between two non-zero vectors of n-dimensional space that measures the cosine of the angle between them. Cosine similarity is most commonly used in high-dimensional positive spaces. Cosine similarity gives a useful measure of how similar two objects are grouped together by considering the internal homogeneity and the external separation. Here θ gives the angle between two objects and A, B are d-dimensional vectors (Irani, Pise, & Phatak, 2016).

$$\cos(\theta) = A \cap B / |A|.|B| \tag{2}$$

Here, the angle between two objects is given by and A, B are d-dimensional vectors. The cosine similarity of two objects will range from 0 to 1.

Jaccard Distance

The Jaccard index/distance computes the similarity of the two data objects as the intersection divided by the union of the data items as shown in Equation (3) given below. The Jaccard similarity coefficient is used for comparing the similarity and diversity of data objects. It is defined as the size of the intersection divided by the size of the union of the data items (Irani, Pise, & Phatak, 2016).

$$J(A,B) = \frac{|A \cap B|}{|A \cup B|} \tag{3}$$

where A, B are d-dimensional vectors representing data items such as images. If *A* and *B* are both empty, we define *J(A,B)* = 1. Jaccard similarity of two objects will range from 0 to 1.

Manhattan Distance

Manhattan distance is a distance measure that is used to compute the absolute differences between coordinates/features of pair of data objects as shown in equation given below (Irani, Pise, & Phatak, 2016).

$$\text{Dist}(X, Y) = |X_{ik} - X_{jk}| \tag{4}$$

where X, Y are d-dimensional vectors representing data items such as images. Manhattan distance calculates the absolute differences between coordinates of pair of objects represented as points in d-dimensional space.

Chebyshev Distance

Chebyshev distance metric is also called the maximum value distance. It is a distance measure which calculates the absolute values of the differences between the coordinate of a pair of data objects represented as points in multidimensional space as given in Equation (5) given below (Irani, Pise, & Phatak, 2016).

$$\text{Dist}(X, Y) = \max_k |X_{ik} - X_{jk}| \tag{5}$$

where X, Y are d-dimensional vectors representing data objects.

Minkowski Distance

Minkowski Distance is referred as the generalized distance metric. As shown in Equation (6) given below. When p=2, the measure is same the Euclidean distance. Chebyshev distance metric is a variant of Minkowski distance metric where p=∞ (taking a limit). This distance can be used for variables that are both ordinal and quantitative in nature (Rui Xu, & Donald Wunsch Ii, 2005).

$$D\left(X, Y\right) = \left(\sum_{k=1}^{d} \left|X_{ik} - X_{jk}\right|^{\frac{1}{p}}\right)^{p} \tag{6}$$

where X, Y are d-dimensional vectors representing data objects.

CLUSTERING ALGORITHMS

Clustering algorithms can be categorized broadly into the following categories:

1. Density-Based Clustering
2. Partitional Clustering
3. Hierarchical Clustering

A distinction among different types of clustering is whether the set of clusters is nested or un- nested (Irani, Pise, & Phatak, 2016).

Density-Based Clustering

Density Based Clustering combines the data objects represented as points in n-dimensional space that are closely packed together and the data objects in low-density regions. DBSCAN is one of the most commonly used clustering algorithms. Figure 10 shows Density-based Clustering.

A cluster is defined as an optimum set of density connected data objects. Clusters are dense regions in the data space, separated by regions of lower object density. It generates clusters of arbitrary shape. A cluster is considered as a region in which the density of data objects exceeds a particular threshold value. DBSCAN algorithm is a generally used example of Density-based clustering approach.

The some of the terms related to Density-based clustering are as follows:

1. **ε-Neighborhood:** It is a set object which are within a radius of ε an object.
2. **High Density:** High density of the cluster is defined as a number of ε-Neighborhood of an object contains at least MinPts of objects. MinPts are defined.

Partitional Clustering

Partitional clustering is widely used clustering algorithm. A partitional clustering is simply a division of the set of data objects into non-overlapping clusters such that each data object is in exactly one cluster. Partitional clustering algorithm partitions the data objects into "k" groups, where each partition/group represents a cluster. The clustering is done based on an association measure/objective function. The data objects within a cluster are similar and the data objects in different clusters are dissimilar. It means intra-cluster similarity is more than the inter-cluster similarity. Partitional clustering methods are useful in applications where the number of clusters required is static and the dataset is not changing. K-means is an example of the partitioning clustering algorithms (Irani, Pise, & Phatak, 2016).

Figure 10. Density-based clustering

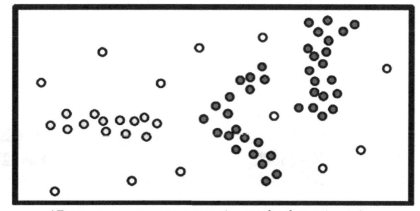

For a more accurate representation see the electronic version.

Hierarchical Clustering

In comparison with k-means clustering algorithm, hierarchical clustering does not require the assumption of any k value. A collection or sequence of partitions which are nested with each other is generated in this approach. These nested partitions categorized into two types such as agglomerative and divisive. In the first one, clustering starts using a single data object present in the single cluster and this object starts clustering using closest pair until all the available objects form a single cluster. Unlike first, in second approach clustering starts by putting all the data objects in the single cluster, and larger clusters are split into smaller ones until only one object left in each cluster.

COLOR CLUSTERING APPROACH

To extract clusters from an image three steps model is used. In the first step, a set of dominant colors are extracted. These colors have the highest number of pixel counts in the image. In next stage, a set of cluster is formed for every dominant color selected. The connected component approach searches all the connected components in an image and provides a unique label for all the points present in same component. Each cluster is represented by the minimum bounding rectangle. Finally, a large set of single-colored clusters can be derived in the second step. In the third step, these clusters are ranked in decreasing order of their sizes. Dominant clusters are found based on their sizes. The similarity in two clusters calculated using the overlap area (Parekh, 2006).

Connected Components Labeling

In this approach scanning of an image is taken place in a pixel-by-pixel manner from top to bottom and left to right. This scanning identifies connected pixel regions and then we require to have a grouping of these pixels into components on the basis of connectivity present in pixels. Most of the time, intensity values match for the pixels which are present in connected components.

After completion of this process, the equivalent label pairs are arranged in sorted order of their equivalent classes and then unique label is provided to different classes. Afterward we determine all groups and each pixel is labeled with a gray level or a color as per component it was assigned. Extraction, labeling and disjoint of connected component are very important for image analysis applications. In the last step, a second scan is made using the image, in which each label is expected to replace by the label assigned to its equivalence classes.

Figure 11. Color clustering example

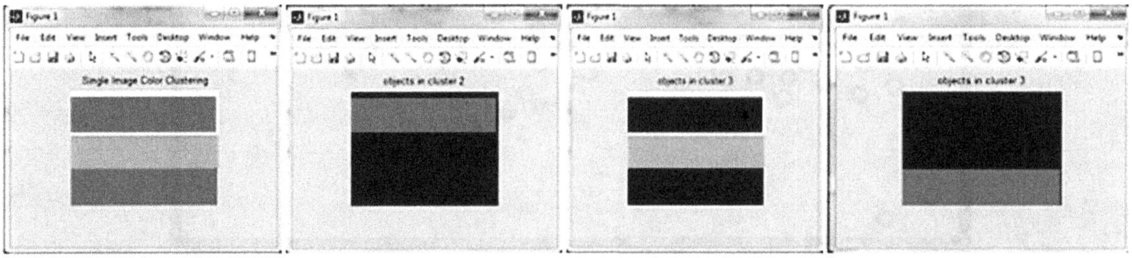

For a more accurate representation see the electronic version.

Color, shape, textures are most important attribute which are widely used for analysis and processing of images as discussed earlier. Object present in the image can be identified using these attributes. If number of objects present in the image then relationship between them can be found. Considering the simplicity and obviousness of color attribute, color feature is discussed in detail. The color is chosen due to the importance given by humans to this attribute. In this chapter, we have done analysis of the image color attribute. Various color spaces can be used such as RGB, YCrCb, HSV etc.

A sample color clustering with the use of RGB color space and k- means is shown in Figure 9. The original image is in RGB space and there are three clusters, they are Red, Green, Blue. Every advantage or weakness can be exposed, so it can be known what color spaces are the right choice which depend upon particular aspect and application. Among different clustering approaches particular can be chosen to get the cluster of specific color to extract the various features in the images depending on the desired objective in the image retrieval. Depending upon the distance\similarity measure relevant images can be retrieved form multimedia database. As illumination changes color, the feature becomes affected. Considering the same different hybrid techniques are proposed which use multiple image features with proper selection of clustering techniques.

As the various image features are considered in CBIR techniques, but image retrieval using texture and shape features suffers from some drawbacks. There are various numbers of shapes and sometimes the shapes are overlapping in the images. Due to variety of shapes and their sizes, the time complexity of extracting the shapes from the image increases. It affects the accuracy of the result also. While considering the texture as a feature in content-based image retrieval, there is varied number of textures and the texture should be extracted at finer levels. The color is chosen due to the importance given by humans as important attribute in CBIR, though it is affected by the variation in illumination. Color Chrominance is a potential feature for clustering and subsequent retrieval. Blending of multiple image features like color, shape, texture, size can serve better approaches for CBIR. Hybrid approach can be used for better image retrieval in CBIR where combination of clustering techniques and image contents like shapes, color are considered and evaluated (Kumar, & Kumar Shukla, 2017).

EVALUATION AND VALIDATION

The accuracy of the various clustering methods is verified by considering two aspects: 1) Suitability of a particular clustering method for a particular data set with specific application, and; 2) accuracy of the result of clustering process by determining whether the results of a clustering method truly represent the data (Dobb, 1999).

Evaluation

Many comparative and evaluative analysis have tried to elect the "best" clustering technique by implementing a range of clustering techniques to various test data sets and comparing the accuracy and quality of the results. It is crucial to evaluate clustering techniques because each technique has its own pros and cons. It is not possible to suggest a single best method. It is prudent to apply more than one clustering technique and use some validation technique to check the fidelity and accuracy of the results (Dobb, 1999).

Validation

Cluster validity procedures are used to justify whether the data structure generated by the clustering technique can be used to yield statistical evidence of the phenomenon under study.

APPLICATIONS OF CBIR

A wide range of applications for CBIR technology are as follows:

- **Digital Forensics:** Fingerprint matching and analysis of security systems crime detection.
- **Shapes Recognition:** Identification of parts, defect and fault inspection in industrial automation.
- **Medical Diagnosis:** Tumors detection, medical imaging measurement of internal organs.
- Journalism, Fashion, graphic design, advertising.
- **Remote Sensing:** Weather forecast, geographical information systems, monitoring of satellite images.
- An image search on the Internet.
- **Radar Engineering:** Guidance of aircraft and missiles, detection, and identification of targets.
- **Robotics:** Recognition of objects in a scene, motion control through visual feedback.

CONCLUSION

Content-Based Image Retrieval defines use of the visual contents of image like color, texture, shape etc. The visual feature of an image describes the contents of the image. We have discussed various feature extraction and clustering approaches which are essentially used in Content Based Image Retrieval. Among these approaches, color-based techniques are more focused in the chapter. The content-based feature extraction and selection play a vital role in image retrieval. Various hybrid techniques of feature extraction and clustering are used for the accuracy of the retrieval of images. The caveat of Content-Based Image Retrieval is that due to the semantic gap between the higher-level meaning and the low-level visual features of the image, the accuracy of the result may be compromised. Use of more than one image attribute like color and shape etc. and the selection of an appropriate clustering algorithm and parameter settings such as the distance function, similarity measure, a density threshold and the number of expected clusters improve the accuracy of results.

REFERENCES

Adjeroh, D. A., & Nwosu, K. C. (1997). Multimedia DatabaseManagement—Requirements and Issues. *IEEE MultiMedia*, *4*(3), 24–33. doi:10.1109/93.621580

Ben Ismail. (2017). A Survey on Content-based Image Retrieval. *International Journal of Advanced Computer Science and Applications*.

Bouaguel, W. (2015). *On Feature Selection for Credit Scoring*. Retrieved September 30, 2017 From https://www.researchgate.net

Dr. Dobb's Essential Books On Algorithms And Data Structures, Book 5. (1999). Miller Freeman, Incorporated.

Hall, E. L., Kruger, R. P., Dwyer, S. J., Hall, D. L., Mclaren, R. W., & Lodwick, G. S. (1971). A Survey of Preprocessing and Feature Extraction Techniques for Radiographic Images. *IEEE Transactions on Computers*. Retrieved from https://hubpages.com/technology/Image-Retrieval-Color-Coherence-Vector retrieved on 25/09/2017

Hughes, J. F., Van Dam, A., Mcguire, M., Sklar, D. F., Foley, J. D., Feiner, S. K., & Akeley, K. (2014). *Computer Graphics Principles and Practice*. Pearson Education.

Irani, Pise, & Phatak. (2016). Clustering Techniques And The Similarity Measures Used In Clustering: A Survey. *International Journal of Computer Applications, 134*.

Kumar & Shukla. (2017). Design and Analysis of CBIR System using Hybrid PSO and K-Mean Clustering Methods. *International Journal of Current Engineering and Technology*.

Nixon, M. S., & Aguado, A. S. (2008). *Feature Extraction and Image Processing*. Elsevier.

Parekh, R. (2006). *Principals of Multimedia* (2nd ed.). Mc Graw Hill.

Rui, X. A. D. W. I. (2005). Survey Of Clustering Algorithms. *IEEE Transactions on Neural Networks, 16*(3). PMID:15940994

Shukla & Vania. (2014). A Survey on CBIR Features Extraction Techniques. *International Journal of Engineering and Computer Science, 3*(12).

Sklansky, J. (1978). Image Segmentation And Feature Extraction. *IEEE Transactions on Systems, Man, and Cybernetics, 8*(4), 237–247. doi:10.1109/TSMC.1978.4309944

Solomon & Breckon. (n.d.). *Fundamentals of Digital Image Processing*. John & Sons Wiley. *Ltd.*

Yoshitaka, A., & Ichikawa, T. (1999). A survey on content-based retrieval for multimedia databases. *IEEE Transactions on Knowledge and Data Engineering, 11*(1), 81–93. doi:10.1109/69.755617

Yu & Brandenburg. (2011). Multimedia Database Applications: Issues And Concerns For Classroom Teaching. *The International Journal of Multimedia & Its Applications, 3*.

Chapter 7

Machine–Learning–Based External Plagiarism Detecting Methodology From Monolingual Documents:
A Comparative Study

Saugata Bose
University of Liberal Arts Bangladesh, Bangladesh

Ritambhra Korpal
Savitribai Phule Pune University, India

ABSTRACT

In this chapter, an initiative is proposed where natural language processing (NLP) techniques and supervised machine learning algorithms have been combined to detect external plagiarism. The major emphasis is on to construct a framework to detect plagiarism from monolingual texts by implementing n-gram frequency comparison approach. The framework is based on 120 characteristics which have been extracted during pre-processing steps using simple NLP approach. Afterward, filter metrics has been applied to select most relevant features and supervised classification learning algorithm has been used later to classify the documents in four levels of plagiarism. Then, confusion matrix was built to estimate the false positives and false negatives. Finally, the authors have shown C4.5 decision tree-based classifier's suitability on calculating accuracy over naive Bayes. The framework achieved 89% accuracy with low false positive and false negative rate and it shows higher precision and recall value comparing to passage similarities method, sentence similarity method, and search space reduction method.

DOI: 10.4018/978-1-5225-5775-3.ch007

INTRODUCTION

In this present Internet era, academics, as well as researchers are deeply concerned with plagiarism issue.

Plagiarism refers to copying from someone else's document without providing proper acknowledgements (Cosma & Joy, 2008). According to the Merriam-Webster online dictionary, plagiarism means stealing and passing off (the ideas or words of another) as one's own, using (another's production) without crediting the source, committing literary theft or presenting as new and original an idea or product derived from an existing source.

Plagiarism can be of many forms as shown in Figure 1. Either it can be an exact copy of the source document or some form of modified (addition, deletion, substitution in word level or in phrase level) version of source document, without properly acknowledging the source.

The severity of this copying can be understood by a finding (McCabe, 2002) where it is identified that 10% of American college students have been involved in partial copying their assignments whereas in high schools 52% of students have been involved in some form of plagiarism. To counter this problem, a study was conducted on why students are involved in plagiarism and it was found that 'means and opportunity' are their motivation (Bennett, 2005). Manually detecting plagiarized document is a humongous task, as well as a drain of academicians' precious time. As a result, academicians look for tools which can detect plagiarisms automatically. In recent years, many commercial detection tools have been developed such as Turnitin (iParadigms, 2010) and CopyCatch (CFL software, 2010) or MOSS (Aiken, 1994) for detecting plagiarism in computer programming source code (Chong, Specia, & Mitkov, 2010). In this paper, we concentrate on checking plagiarism in written text documents because there is

Figure 1. Forms of plagiarism
Reddy, 2013.

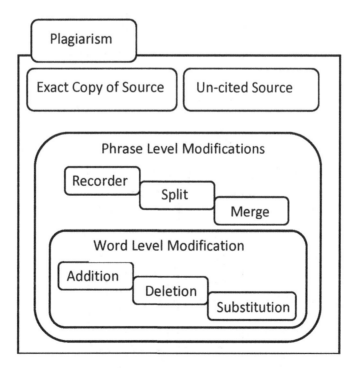

a 'challenge of distinguishing true cases of plagiarism from mere coincidental similarity of wording' (Buruiana, Scoica, Rebedea, & Rughinis, 2013).

For developing a detection tool, one cannot simply rely on 'exact-word or phrase matching' (Reddy, 2013). Paraphrasing or rearranging words of a sentence makes the task even more complex. Furthermore, academicians categorize plagiarism in two sections: external plagiarism where suspicious documents are compared with original ones and intrinsicplagiarism where one tries to find plagiarized passages within a document without accessing potential original documents.

As shown in Figure 2, the plagiarism detection methods are classified in three categories: fingerprinting, term occurrences and style analysis (Eissen, Stein, & Kulig, 2006). Among these, "term occurrence" is the familiar style, developers follow. According to Reddy, 'Plagiarism detection is a process of finding similar documents for a doubtful document by extracting different features like structural, semantic, syntactic and lexical features, from that document and analyzing those features'(Reddy, 2013).

In this paper, we have applied very simple NLP techniques for extracting different characteristics of documents while building the framework for detecting external plagiarism in a monolingual document.

Figure 2. Classification of plagiarism detection methods

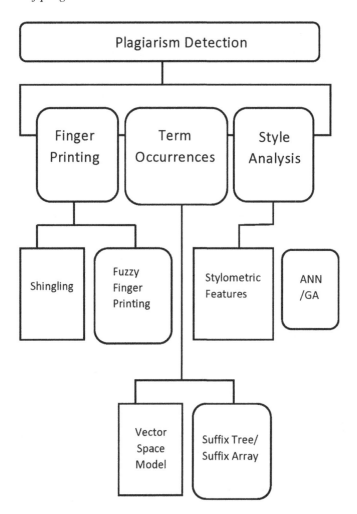

In our framework, the focus is on using "term occurrence" method. Later, we have discussed the suitability of our proposed framework comparing with four other plagiarism detection algorithms (*Sentence Similarity Based on Source Retrieval*, 2017; *Sentence Similarity Based on Text Alignment*, 2017; *Search Space Reduction*, 2011; *Passage Similarities*, 2010).

The rest of the paper is organized as follows: in Section 2, related works on plagiarism detection are discussed; in Section 3 proposed framework is presented. Following this in Section 4, we discuss the methodologies implemented to construct the framework and in Section 5 we present our findings using the proposed methodology. Section 6 evaluates out algorithm with 4 algorithms and finally, we draw our conclusion in Section 7.

PREVIOUS WORKS

In this section, the existing plagiarism detection approaches are discussed and our standing on the methodologies chosen.

Ceska has figured out few strategies which are used by current plagiarism detection tools. Those include "Relative frequency models", "Dotplot visualization", "Similarity measures", "Document fingerprinting" and "Word pairs metric" (Ceska, 2009) and all of these methods are non NLP based (Chong, Specia, & Mitkov, 2010). But these methods fail to detect plagiarism extensively because the algorithms of these methods try to compare suspect and original document at string level which in turn find out a number of overlapping words (Bull, Collins, Coughlin, & Sharp, 2001; Badge, & Scott, 2009). As a result, the accuracy score is not satisfactory using these methods (Lyon, Barrett, & Malcolm, 2003). Yet, few researchers had prophesized that a high accuracy in plagiarism detection can be achieved by using NLP techniques (Ceska, 2009; Clough, 2003; Androutsopoulos, & Malakasiotis, 2010) which have not been explored properly. However, earlier some researchers have discussed few techniques for detecting duplicate records using NLP (Chong, Specia, & Mitkov, 2010; Runeson, Alexandersson, & Nyholm, 2007) where they have implemented shallow as well as deep NLP techniques.

In a very simple way, plagiarism detection is found out the similarity among documents. As Barrón and Rosso have pointed out, 'If two (original and suspicious) text fragments are close enough, it can be assumed that they are a potential plagiarism case that needs to be investigated deeper' (Barrón-Cedeño, & Rosso, 2009).

A very simple proposal has emerged to find out how much close those documents are, which is, plagiarism can be detected after splitting original and suspicious documents in trigrams and counting the number of common chunks (Lyon, Barrett, & Malcolm, 2004). The same concept was discussed by (Papineni, Roukos, Ward, & Zhu, 2002) to categorize the texts. If comparing the earlier string matching algorithms this word n-gram methodology surely improves the accuracy score and it is very simple to implement.

Yet, a problem remains in implementing word n-gram methodology. Synonyms can be used in a plagiarized text to give an impression to the faculty or academician that, the writing is authentic but it is not. Word n-gram methodology fails to detect this synonym technique. To counter this, Wordnet tactic was proposed by (Mihalcea & Corley, 2006), and (Mohler & Mihalcea, 2009) which provides information about a similarity between word meanings.

Meuschke has proposed a mixed approach using citations, semantic argument structure of the documents and similarity among words along with character-based methods to detect plagiarism in academic documents with sufficiently high success rate (Meuschke, & Gipp, 2014).

Vani and Gupta investigate the effect of combining different similarity metrics on extrinsic plagiarism detection. They also compare and highlight the importance of combined multiple similarity metrics versus generally used single similarity metric. The combination of different metrics namely Cosine similarity, Dice coefficient, Match coefficient and Fuzzy-Semantic measure is explored along with and without Part of Speech tag information (Vani, & Gupta, 2015).

In this paper, a simpler framework is presented to detect the plagiarism in monolingual documents. Given a set of documents, original and suspicious, a 'simpler' framework can be developed, using lexical matching techniques (Papineni, Roukos, Ward, & Zhu, 2002; Baeza-Yates, & Ribeiro-Neto, 1999), word n-gram methodology, and shallow NLP approaches for pre-processing the suspicious and original documents. Using this framework and applying word metric approach to compare the similarity between documents can detect the plagiarized documents with a high degree of accuracy.

PROPOSED FRAMEWORK

This section elaborates the structure (Figure 3) of the proposed for plagiarism detection framework.

Figure 3. Proposed framework

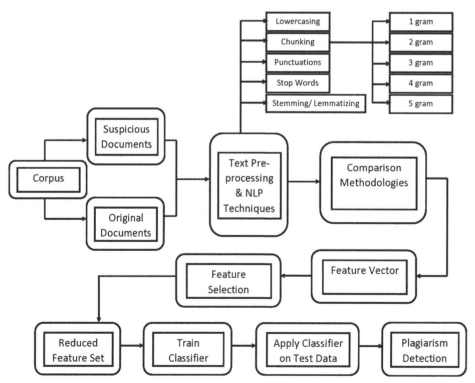

Corpus

Our research follows corpus-based evaluation approach to assessing proposed plagiarism detection system. As the goal is to detect external plagiarism from 'monolingual' documents, we decided to test the proposed plagiarism detection model on a corpus of "English" language. The corpus created by Dr. Paul Clough and Dr. Mark Stevenson of University of Sheffield (Clough, & Stevenson, 2011) was chosen for this purpose. This corpus contains a set of original texts and a set of plagiarized texts.

The chosen corpus was created manually by computer science students by rewriting five computer science-related short notes from Wikipedia. The students were instructed to rewrite the texts following four levels of plagiarism: near copy (verbatim), light revision (shallow paraphrasing), heavy revision (deep structural changes and paraphrasing) and non-plagiarized version (based on student's own idea) (Chong, Specia, & Mitkov, 2010).

The train corpus consists of 95 short answers that are between 200 and 300 words long and 60% of those are plagiarized. The classification of the corpus is depicted in Figure 4.

- **Total Corpus Size:** 285 samples were used to evaluate our proposed external plagiarism detection framework.
- **Train Data:** Train data comprises 94 instances with 120 features prepared by Clough and Stevenson.
- **Test Data:** We developed a test corpus by ourselves containing 191 instances rewriting those 5 original texts. Here, 115 M.Sc. first semester students of Savitribai Phule Pune University have helped us to re write those 5 original texts.

Figure 4. Classification of corpus

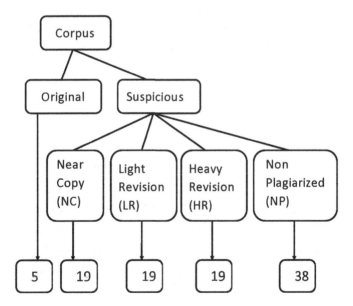

Text Pre-Processing

The input text, including both suspicious and source documents, are collected, for subsequent stages. The text is pre-processed using shallow NLP techniques like removing the blank spaces and converting the whole set of texts to either lower case or upper case. This is done for an obvious reason to exclude any possibility of match/mismatch due to the presence of extra/fewer spaces or tabs etc. So at this stage the text is prepared for further processing.

Similarity Scores

The preprocessed text is divided into various categories with different combinations of pre-processing performed. For example, 1-gram chunks with no stop words, no punctuation, no lower casing, 1-gram chunks with stop words, no punctuation, no-lower casing etc. Similarly, 2-gram and 3-gram chunks with different pre-processing combinations were generated for both original and suspicious documents. In this way, we calculate similarity scores up to 5 chunks. These 'chunked' texts of original and suspicious documents were then compared and similarity scores were generated.

Feature Vector Generation

The similarity scores generated for each suspicious document with original documents under each combination of the level of pre-processing forms the feature vector- 120 features were formed this way. Figure 5 illustrates those 120 features:

Feature Selection and Classification Model

A classification model was trained on the feature vector built in the previous stage. The classifiers built were used to classify the documents into four classes: Non-Plagiarized (NP), Highly Revised (HR), Lightly Revised (LR) and No Change (NC). Different classifiers were tried and different combinations

Figure 5. Unfiltered feature set

Stop Words/Punctuation1(L)
(No Stop Words/Punctuation)1(L)
No Stop Words1(L)
No Punctuations1(L)
Stop Words/Punctuations/Stemming1(L)
(No Stop Words/Punctuations)/Stemming1(L)
No Stop Words/Stemming1(L)
No Punctuations/Stemming1(L)
Stop Words/Punctuations/Lammetizing1(L)
(No Stop Words/Punctuations)/Lammetizing1(L)
No Stop Words/Lammetizing1(L)
No Punctuations/Lammetizing1(L)
Stop Words/Punctuation1(NC)
(No Stop Words/Punctuation)1(NC)
No Stop Words1(NC)
No Punctuations1(NC)

Stop Words/Punctuations/Lammetizing3(L)
Stop Words/Punctuations/Stemming3(NC)
(No Stop Words/Punctuations)/Stemming3(NC)
No Stop Words/Stemming3(NC)
No Punctuations3(NC)
Stop Words/Punctuations/Lammetizing3(NC)
(No Stop Words/Punctuations)/Lammetizing3(NC)
No Stop Words/Lammetizing3(NC)
No Punctuations/Lammetizing3(NC)
Stop Words/Punctuation4(L)
(No Stop Words/Punctuation)4(L)
No Stop Words4(L)
No Punctuations4(L)
Stop Words/Punctuations/Stemming4(L)
(No Stop Words/Punctuations)/Stemming4(L)
No Stop Words/Stemming4(L)
No Punctuations/Stemming4(L)

Stop Words/Punctuations/Stemming1(NC)
(No Stop Words/Punctuations)/Stemming1(NC)
No Stop Words/Stemming1(NC)
No Punctuations/Stemming1(NC)
Stop Words/Punctuations/Lammetizing1(NC)
(No Stop Words/Punctuations)/Lammetizing1(NC)
No Stop Words/Lammetizing1(NC)
No Punctuations/Lammetizing1(NC)
Stop Words/Punctuation2(L)
(No Stop Words/Punctuation)2(L)
No Stop Words2(L)
No Punctuations2(L)
Stop Words/Punctuations/Stemming2(L)
(No Stop Words/Punctuations)/Stemming2(L)
No Stop Words/Stemming2(L)
No Punctuations/Stemming2(L)

(No Stop Words/Punctuations)/Lammetizing4(L)
No Stop Words/Lammetizing4(L)
No Punctuations/Lammetizing4(L)
Stop Words/Punctuation4(NC)
(No Stop Words/Punctuation)4(NC)
No Stop Words4(NC)
No Punctuations4(NC)
Stop Words/Punctuations/Stemming4(NC)
(No Stop Words/Punctuations)/Stemming4(NC)
No Stop Words/Stemming4(NC)
No Punctuations/Stemming4(NC)
Stop Words/Punctuations/Lammetizing4(NC)
(No Stop Words/Punctuations)/Lammetizing4(NC)
No Stop Words/Lammetizing4(NC)
No Punctuations/Lammetizing4(NC)
Stop Words/Punctuation5(L)

Stop Words/Punctuations/Lammetizing2(L)
(No Stop Words/Punctuations)/Lammetizing2(L)
No Stop Words/Lammetizing2(L)
No Punctuations/Lammetizing2(L)
Stop Words/Punctuation2(NC)
(No Stop Words/Punctuation)2(NC)
No Stop Words2(NC)
No Punctuations2(NC)
Stop Words/Punctuations/Stemming2(NC)
(No Stop Words/Punctuations)/Stemming2(NC)
No Stop Words/Stemming2(NC)
No Punctuations/Stemming2(NC)
Stop Words/Punctuations/Lammetizing2(NC)
(No Stop Words/Punctuations)/Lammetizing2(NC)
No Stop Words/Lammetizing2(NC)
No Punctuations/Lammetizing2(NC)

(No Stop Words/Punctuations)/Stemming5(L)
No Stop Words5(L)
No Punctuations5(L)
Stop Words/Punctuations/Stemming5(L)
(No Stop Words/Punctuations)/Stemming5(L)
No Stop Words/Stemming5(L)
No Punctuations/Stemming5(L)
Stop Words/Punctuations/Lammetizing5(L)
(No Stop Words/Punctuations)/Lammetizing5(L)
No Stop Words/Lammetizing5(L)
No Punctuations/Lammetizing5(L)
Stop Words/Punctuation5(NC)
(No Stop Words/Punctuation)5(NC)
No Stop Words5(NC)
No Punctuations5(NC)
Stop Words/Punctuations/Stemming5(NC)
(No Stop Words/Punctuations)/Stemming5(NC)

Stop Words/Punctuation3(L)
(No Stop Words/Punctuation)3(L)
No Stop Words3(L)
No Punctuations3(L)
Stop Words/Punctuations/Stemming3(L)
(No Stop Words/Punctuations)/Stemming3(L)
No Stop Words/Stemming3(L)
No Punctuations/Stemming3(L)
Stop Words/Punctuations/Lammetizing3(L)
(No Stop Words/Punctuations)/Lammetizing3(L)
No Stop Words/Lammetizing3(L)
No Punctuations/Lammetizing3(L)
Stop Words/Punctuation3(NC)
(No Stop Words/Punctuation)3(NC)
No Stop Words3(NC)
No Punctuations3(NC)

No Stop Words/Stemming5(NC)
No Punctuations/Stemming5(NC)
Stop Words/Punctuations/Lammetizing5(NC)
(No Stop Words/Punctuations)/Lammetizing5(NC)
No Stop Words/Lammetizing5(NC)
No Punctuations/Lammetizing5(NC)

Stop Words/Punctuations/Stemming3(NC)
(No Stop Words/Punctuations)/Stemming3(NC)
No Stop Words/Stemming3(NC)
No Punctuations/Stemming3(NC)
Stop Words/Punctuations/Lammetizing3(NC)
(No Stop Words/Punctuations)/Lammetizing3(NC)
No Punctuations/Lammetizing3(NC)
Stop Words/Punctuation4(L)
(No Stop Words/Punctuation)4(L)
No Stop Words4(L)
No Punctuations4(L)
Stop Words/Punctuations/Stemming4(L)
(No Stop Words/Punctuations)/Stemming4(L)
No Stop Words/Stemming4(L)
No Punctuations/Stemming4(L)

of training data. Confusion Matrix was built for each classifier and number of false positives and false negatives were compared.

Once the acceptable level of accuracy was achieved it was decided to select that model as the final plagiarism detection model.

We decided to go a step further, to see if any of the features (out of 120) could be removed while still retaining the accuracy achieved. For this purpose, a correlation coefficient of each attribute with class attribute is calculated. Attributes having high correlation coefficient indicate a strong correlation between the class and that attribute/feature. For this purpose any correlation coefficient can be used without compromising the generality. We have chosen to implement Pearson Correlation Coefficient (PCC) as PCC computes linear relationship between 2 quantitative features. Here, we compute linear relationship of each of 120 features with Class attribute. Class attributes are evaluated as 0 for NP, 1 for HR, 2 for LR and 3 for NC. From 120 PCC values we chose 27 values which are the largest ones showing linear relationship. Figure 6 depicts filtered feature set from train data after calculating PCC values.

METHODOLOGY

This part explains the methodology; which is followed to implement the framework.

Input

Our program receives a text file as an input which contains short notes.

Pre-Processing

Before sending the input further for investigations to see if there are any plagiarized documents in the set, different preprocessing techniques applied to the input corpus.

- **Sentence Segmentation:** By doing this, we identify each sentence from any passage by dividing the text into sentences. For example, [To be or not to be– that is the question: whether 'tis nobler in the mind to suffer the slings and arrows of outrageous fortune. To die, to sleep no more – and by a sleep to say we end the heartache] becomes [[To be or not to be– that is the question: whether 'tis nobler in the mind to suffer the slings and arrows of outrageous fortune.][To die, to sleep no more – and by a sleep to say we end the heartache]].
- **Tokenization:** By applying tokenization, we identify each word, punctuation, symbols from each sentence, such as "To be or not to be– that is the question:" transfers to [To] [be] [or] [not] [to] [be] [–] [that] [is] [the] [question] [:].

After applying segmentation and tokenization, we decide to apply two fundamental operations (Figure 7) to our corpus, i.e. either convert the whole corpus into lowercase or uppercase.

- **With Stop Words:** By following this, we keep each and every stop words (Determiners, Coordinating conjunctions, Prepositions) in our sentence, such as "To be or not to be– that is the question:" remains as "To be or not to be– that is the question:"

Figure 6. Filtered feature set
Generated by Weka.

```
=== Run information ===

Scheme:    weka.classifiers.trees.J48 −C 0,25 −M 2
Relation:          filtered_train
Instances:         94
Attributes:        27
                   Stop Words/Punctuation1(L)
                   Stop Words/Punctuations/Stemming1(L)
                   Stop Words/Punctuations/Lammetizing1(L)
                   Stop Words/Punctuation1(NC)
                   Stop Words/Punctuations/Stemming1(NC)
                   Stop Words/Punctuations/Lammetizing1(NC)
                   (No Stop Words/Punctuation)1(L)
                   (No Stop Words/Punctuations)/Stemming1(L)
                   (No Stop Words/Punctuations)/Lammetizing1(L)
                   (No Stop Words/Punctuation)1(NC)
                   (No Stop Words/Punctuations)/Stemming1(NC)
                   (No Stop Words/Punctuations)/Lammetizing1(NC)
                   (No Stop Words/Punctuation)2(L)
                   (No Stop Words/Punctuations)/Stemming2(L)
                   (No Stop Words/Punctuations)/Lammetizing2(L)
                   (No Stop Words/Punctuations)/Stemming2(NC)
                   (No Stop Words/Punctuations)/Lammetizing2(NC)
                   No Stop Words1(L)
                   No Stop Words/Stemming1(L)
                   No Stop Words/Lammetizing1(L)
                   No Stop Words1(NC)
                   No Stop Words/Stemming1(NC)
                   No Stop Words/Lammetizing1(NC)
                   No Punctuations/Stemming1(L)
                   No Punctuations/Lammetizing1(L)
                   No Punctuations/Lammetizing1(NC)
                   Class
Test mode: evaluate on training data
```

- **Without Stop Words:** By applying this, we keep punctuations (Apostrophe, Brackets, Colon and semicolon, Comma, Dash and hyphen, Ellipsis, Exclamation mark, Full stop or Period, Guillemets, Question marks, Slash) in our corpus, such as "To be or not to be– that is the question:" remains as "To be or not to be– that is the question:"
- **With Punctuations:** By applying this, we keep punctuations (Apostrophe, Brackets, Colon and semicolon, Comma, Dash and hyphen, Ellipsis, Exclamation mark, Full stop or Period, Guillemets, Question marks, Slash) in our corpus, such as "To be or not to be– that is the question:" remains as "To be or not to be– that is the question:"

Figure 7. Preprocessing techniques after lowercasing/uppercasing

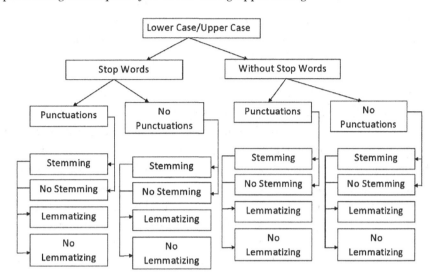

- **Without Punctuations:** This step removes all punctuations from our corpus, such as "To be or not to be– that is the question:" transforms as "To be or not to be that is the question".
- **With Stemming:** Applying stemming process converts all the words of our corpus to a common base form, such as if the word is Produced or Product or Produce or production it converts to "Produc".
- **Without Stemming:** The corpus remains as it is; stemming is not applied to the corpus.
- **With Lemmatizing:** Lemmatizing transforms words of our corpus into their dictionary base forms, such as a word Produced/ Product/ Production converts to "Produce".
- **Without Lemmatizing:** Following this approach, the words of our corpus remain as it without changing into dictionary base forms.

COMPARISON METHODOLOGY

Using various combinations of pre-processing techniques, different sets of corpus were built. Each set of corpus gave us 120 different similarity scores of the suspicious documents with the original documents. The major difference from earlier studies with ours one is that following these pre-processing techniques generates 120 dimensions of our corpus. Using these 120 features, we train classifiers with different combinations of instances.

To check whether the suspicious documents are similar to the original one, we propose a simple approach: *N-gram Frequency based similarity measure*. After applying NLP based pre-processing techniques, we divide the original document and suspicious documents in n-gram chunks. Then we compare n gram chunk of an original document with the n-gram chunk of a suspicious document to find out how many chunks are common between two and ultimately figure out the percentage of common chunks in total n-gram chunks. Finally we evaluate our methodology using C4.5 algorithm and using Naive Bayes algorithm.

We have chosen Naive Bayes algorithm as it is the simplest one which needs less training data. We did not depend our analysis upon one classifier. For this, J4.5 classifier was utilized as it is fastest to train the data and easily interpretable. Moreover, for overcoming data limitation, we utilize 10 fold cross validation where train data is partitioned into 10 equal size samples.

In the current research, the corpus was preprocessed into 1-gram, 2-gram, 3-gram, 4-gram and 5-gram chunk sizes to capture the best similarity scores.

Similarities between documents were compared based on those attributes which have highly linear relationship with Class attribute. If we consider the original text is [The girl is standing outside of PUCSD and talking with her friend] and the suspicious document is [The boy is talking with his friend outside of Symbiosis] and if the corpus is going to have "no (stop words and punctuations)" as well as "stemming, lemmatizing and lower casing" features which have the most relation with Class attribute then, the 1 gram representation of the original document is [[girl] [stand] [outside] [PUCSD] [talk] [her] [friend]]. The comparison technique detects suspicious document is 50% similar to the original one as there are 3 words were found (talk, friend and outside) as common within [boy],[talk],[his],[friend],[outside] and [Symbiosis] chunks. So the similarity is measured as (3 Common Chunks/ 6 1-gram chunks) x100= 50% similarity.

EXPERIMENTS

All the experiments were performed in Windows as well as in Linux environment on a machine equipped with a Pentium(R) Dual-Core Processor of 2.5 GHz speed. Besides, the program was tested on a machine with Intel® Atom™ processor N2600. Both machines have contained 2 GB RAM.

All the programs were written using Python 3.0 platform and its NLTK package. Furthermore, Weka data mining tool was used to train and build the classifiers.

We started our experiment with a corpus of 100 documents which has 5 original documents and 95 suspicious documents. As is explained earlier, the 95 suspicious documents were built from 5 original documents with different forms for plagiarism. After applying preprocessing techniques on our corpus, we find 120 dimensions to analyze the corpus for 95 instances.

Different classifiers, more specifically, Decision Tree based (C4.5) and Naive Bayes were built. The confusion matrices for these were generated and compared. It was also suspected that all attributes may not be needed to classify the documents with sufficiently high accuracy. Hence, it was decided to find and retain only the relevant features and this was investigated by calculating the Pearson's correlation coefficient of each attribute to the class attribute.

FINDINGS

Choice of Train Model

After implementing 10-fold cross validation, the training error of different classifiers models, namely Decision Tree (C4.5) and Naive Bayes-based was respectively 6.3% and 28%. It can be seen that C4.5 decision tree based classifier showed the lowest training error. Further Table 1 and Table 2 show the confusion matrix for each of these classifiers.

It was found that using a C4.5 classifier model correctly classifies 88 items among 94 ones (accuracy is over 93%) and the relevancy report shows that 88% correctly identified HR documents, 93% correctly identified LR documents, 92% correctly identified NC documents and all NP documents were identified correctly. The report has been depicted in Table 3.

Different classifiers were also compared on false positive rate (FPR) defined as false positive/ (false positive + true negative) and false negative rate (FNR) defined as false negative/ (false negative + true positive).

From Table 1, FPR for classifier C4.5 calculated, for HR, LR, NC and NP is 0.043, 0.013, 0.029 and 0 and FNR for HR, LR, NC and NP is 0.083, 0.17, 0.041 and 0 respectively. From Table 2, FPR and FNR for Naive Bayes classifiers of HR, LR, NC and NP are 0.171, 0.092, 0.1, 0.015 and 0.208, 0.67, 0.385, 0.036. It becomes obvious from the above facts that FPR and FNR of C4.5 are low whereas these are high for Naïve Bayes.

Table 1. Confusion matrix for C4.5

Class	Decision Tree Based (C4.5)			
Classified→ Actual ↓	HR	LR	NC	NP
HR	22	1	1	0
LR	2	15	1	0
NC	1	0	23	0
NP	0	0	0	28

Table 2. Confusion matrix for Naive Bayes

Class	Naive Bayes			
Classified→ Actual ↓	HR	LR	NC	NP
HR	19	3	1	1
LR	6	6	6	0
NC	5	4	15	0
NP	1	0	0	27

Table 3. Report on train data (weighted avg.)

Detailed Accuracy by Class						
TP Rate	FP Rate	Precision	Recall	F-Measure	ROC Area	Class
0.917	0.043	0.88	0.917	0.898	0.977	HR
0.833	0.013	0.938	0.833	0.882	0.98	LR
0.958	0.029	0.92	0.958	0.939	0.99	NC
1	0	1	1	1	1	NP
0.936	0.021	0.937	0.936	0.936	0.988	

Generated by Weka.

Naive Bayes classifier calculates probabilities based on the training data available, so classification accuracy changed with change in distribution of different plagiarized documents in the training data. This makes the model overfitted to the training data and cannot be generalized to any training data. High FPR and FNR coupled with the fact that model tends to be overfitted to the data, Naive Bayes was rejected.

As the percentage of incorrectly classified instance is very low (6.383%), with low FPR and FNR, we consider C4.5 model as a train model for future use. The values of ROC Area above 0.5 (0.997, 0.98, 0.99, 1) also justifies our decision to select this model as the final model.

Test Model Implementation

This model was then applied on a test data set of 191 instances and accuracy of over 89% (170 instances were correctly classified) could be achieved which was sufficiently high with low false positive and false negative rates.

Further investigations involved reducing the feature set. Pearson Correlation Coefficient (PCC) was calculated for each attribute to the class attribute. Table 4 shows PCC of top 10 attributes.

Furthermore, it can be noted from Table 5 as well as from Table 6 that the FPR for HR, LR, NC, and NP is 0.079, 0.021, 0.045 and 0 whereas the FNR scores are for HR is 0.125, for LR is 0.17, for NC is 0 and for NP is only 0.145.

The model also display 16.2889% relative absolute error and 53.7651% root relative squared error.

Low FPR and FNR further support the choice of the classifier. Low FPR and Low FNR are important to show that cost, if any, of misclassification, will be within acceptable limits. While accuracy tells us how many instances can be correctly classified, low FPR and FNR reiterate the fact especially when misclassifying has a lot at stake.

COMPARISON WITH OTHER METHODS

The research has been initiated having a goal to detect external plagiarism from monolingual documents. Later we have expanded the research to evaluate our proposed algorithm with other available detection algorithms.

Table 4. Top 10 attributes

Attributes	PCC
(No Stop Words/Punctuation)2(L)	0.86
No Punctuations/Stemming 1(L)	0.86
(No Stop Words/Punctuations)/Lammetizing1(L)	0.86
(No Stop Words/Punctuations)/Stemming1(L)	0.86
Stop Words/Punctuations1 (NC)	0.86
Stop Words/Punctuation1(L)	0.86
No Stopwords1(L)	0.85
No Punctuations/Lammetizing1(NC)	0.85
(Stop Words/Punctuations)/Stemming1(NC)	0.85
No Stopwords1(NC)	0.84

Table 5. Report on test data (weighted avg.)

Detailed Accuracy by Class						
TP Rate	**FP Rate**	**Precision**	**Recall**	**F-Measure**	**ROC Area**	**Class**
0.857	0.082	0.286	0.857	0.429	0.897	HR
0.833	0.005	0.833	0.833	0.833	0.905	LR
1	0.027	0.615	1	0.762	0.996	NC
0.888	0	1	0.888	0.941	0.944	NP
0.89	0.004	0.952	0.89	0.911	0.943	

Generated by Weka.

Table 6. Confusion matrix for test data

Class	C4.5 on test data of 191 instances			
Classified→ Actual ↓	**HR**	**LR**	**NC**	**NP**
HR	7	1	0	0
LR	0	5	1	0
NC	0	0	8	0
NP	26	6	14	271

In this case, we compare our "N-gram Frequency based similarity measure" algorithm with Passage Similarities proposed by (Vania, & Adriani, 2010), Sentence similarity proposed by (Zubarev, & Sochenkov, 2017), Search space reduction method carried on PAN'11 proposed by (Oberreuter, Lhuillier, Ros, & Velsquez, 2011) and the results are enlisted in Table 7.

Comparing to other methods, our proposed external plagiarism detection approach correctly identifies 95.2% times, only 5% times the decision turns to be incorrect. Moreover, our approach successfully detects 89% plagiarism cases.

Table 7. Evaluation of algorithm on test data

Algorithms	Precision	Recall
N-gram Frequency based similarity measure using simple NLP approach,2017	0.952	0.89
Sentence similarity based on Source Retrieval,2017	0.608	0.83
Sentence similarity based on Text Alignment,2017	0.885	0.382
Search space reduction,2011	0.9116530	0.2257937
Passage Similarities,2010	0.9114	0.2620

FUTURE RESEARCH OPPORTUNITY

Based on our result, we need to apply this proposed framework on large dataset (as we have trained our methodology on 95 size corpus and test our methodology on 191 size corpus) to find out how does it affect in large scale. Besides, there remains a possibility to explore our proposed methodology on multilingual documents.

CONCLUSION

The research has been initiated having a goal to detect external plagiarism from a monolingual text by implementing NLP techniques. For this purpose, a simple frequency comparison technique has been used where the original document and suspicious document have been divided in n-gram word chunks and the similarity scores have been figured out after comparing those chunks. As a result, for over 89% cases, our model correctly identifies classes of the documents.

Additionally, NLP techniques can be combined with the similarity matrices to detect plagiarism and it also unveils a very high accuracy which will be discussed in our next paper.

However, there are other challenges which have not been considered in present research such as plagiarism detection from multilingual documents, integrating Wordnet with the current framework to capture the semantics and paraphrasing context. Yet, it can be concluded that plagiarism detection tools can be developed using simple Natural Language Processing approaches which ultimately yields high accuracy.

REFERENCES

Androutsopoulos, I., & Malakasiotis, P. (2010). A Survey of Paraphrasing and Textual Entailment Methods. *Journal of Artificial Intelligence Research, 38*(2010), 135-187. Retrieved from https://www.jair.org/media/2985/live-2985-5001-jair.pdf

Badge, J., & Scott, J. (2009). *Dealing with plagiarism in the digital age*. University of Leicester. Retrieved from http://evidencenet.pbworks.com/w/page/19383480/Dealing%20with%20plagiarism%20in%20the%20digital%20age

Baeza-Yates, R., & Ribeiro-Neto, B. (Eds.). (1999). *Modern Information Retrieval*. Addison Wesley Longman Limited. Retrieved from http://people.ischool.berkeley.edu/~hearst/irbook/print/chap10.pdf

Barrón-Cedeño, A., & Rosso, P. (2009). On Automatic Plagiarism Detection Based on n-Grams Comparison. *Advances in Information Retrieval*, 696-700. Retrieved from http://www.cs.upc.edu/~albarron/publications/2009/BarronNgramsECIR.pdf

Bennett, R. (2005). Factors associated with student plagiarism in a post-1992 University. *Journal of Assessment and Evaluation in Higher Education, 30*(2), 137-162. Retrieved from https://www.scribd.com/document/309860125/Bennett-2005-Factors-Associated-With-Student-Plagiarism-in-a-Post-1992-University

Bull, J., Collins, C., Coughlin, E., & Sharp, D. (2001). *Technical review of plagiarism detection software report*. Luton: Computer Assisted Assessment Centre. Retrieved from https://www.researchgate.net/publication/247703683_Technical_Review_of_Plagiarism_Detection_Software_Report

Buruiana, F., Scoica, A., Rebedea, T., & Rughinis, R. (2013). Automatic Plagiarism Detection System for Specialized Corpora. *Proceedings of the 19th International Conference on Control Systems and Computer Science (CSCS)*, 77-82. Retrieved from https://www.researchgate.net/publication/251899410_Automatic_Plagiarism_Detection_System_for_Specialized_Corpora

Ceska, Z. (2009). *Automatic Plagiarism Detection Based on Latent Semantic Analysis* (Unpublished Ph.D Thesis). University of West Bohemia.

Chong, M., Specia, L., & Mitkov, R. (2010). Using Natural Language Processing for Automatic Plagiarism Detection. *Proceedings of the 4th International Plagiarism Conference*. Retrieved from http://www.academia.edu/326444/Using_Natural_Language_Processing_for_Automatic_Detection_of_Plagiarism

Clough, P. (Ed.). (2003). *Old and new challenges in automatic plagiarism detection*. National UK Plagiarism Advisory Service. Retrieved from http://ir.shef.ac.uk/cloughie/papers/pas_plagiarism.pdf

Clough, P., & Stevenson, M. (2011). Developing a corpus of plagiarised short answers. *Language Resources and Evaluation*, *45*(1), 5-24. Retrieved from https://www.researchgate.net/publication/220147549_Developing_a_corpus_of_plagiarised_short_answers

Cosma, G., & Joy, M. (2008). Towards a definition of source-code plagiarism. *IEEE Transactions on Education*, *51*(2), 195-200. Retrieved from https://www.researchgate.net/publication/3052950_Towards_a_Definition_of_Source-Code_Plagiarism

Eissen, S. M. Z., Stein, B., & Kulig, M. (2006). Plagiarism Detection without Reference Collections. *Proceedings of the 30th Annual Conference of the Gesellschaft für Klassifikatione. V.*, 359-366. Retrieved from http://www.uni-weimar.de/medien/webis/publications/papers/stein_2007a.pdf

Lyon, C., Barrett, R., & Malcolm, J. (2003). *Experiments in Electronic Plagiarism Detection*. Computer Science Department, University of Hertfordshire. Retrived from http://homepages.herts.ac.uk/~comqcml/TR5.3.5.doc

Lyon, C., Barrett, R., & Malcolm, J. (2004). A Theoretical Basis to the Automated Detection of Copying Between Texts, and its Practical Implementation in the Ferret Plagiarism and Collusion Detector. *Proceedings of the Plagiarism: Prevention, Practice and Policies Conference*. Retrieved from http://homepages.herts.ac.uk/~comqcml/LyonPaperFerretx.pdf

McCabe, D. (2002). Cheating: Why Students Do It and How We Can Help Them Stop. *American Educator*. Retrieved from http://www.aft.org/periodical/american-educator/winter-2001/cheating

Meuschke, N., & Gipp, B. (2014). Reducing computation effort for plagiarism detection by using citation characteristics to limit retrieval space. In *Proceedings of the 14th ACM/IEEE Conference on Digital Libraries* (pp. 567–575). Retrieved from http://www.academia.edu/28340526/Reducing_Computational_Effort_for_Plagiarism_Detection_by_using_Citation_Characteristics_to_Limit_Retrieval_Space

Mihalcea, R., & Corley, C. (2006). Corpus-based and knowledge-based measures of text semantic similarity. *Proceedings of the Twenty-first National Conference on Artificial Intelligence (AAAI-06)*, 775–780. Retrieved from https://www.aaai.org/Papers/AAAI/2006/AAAI06-123.pdf

Mohler, M., & Mihalcea, R. (2009). Text-to-text semantic similarity for automatic short answer grading. *Proceedings of the 12th Conference of the European Chapter of the ACL (EACL 2009)*, 567–575. Retrived from http://www.aclweb.org/anthology/E09-1065

Oberreuter, G., Lhuillier, G., Ros, S. A., & Velsquez, J. D. (2011). Approaches for intrinsic and external plagiarism detection - notebook for pan at clef 2011. *Proceedings of the Conference on Multilingual and Multimodal Information Access Evaluation (CLEF 2011) Labs and Workshop.* Retrieved from http://ceur-ws.org/Vol-1177/CLEF2011wn-PAN-OberreuterEt2011.pdf

Papineni, K., Roukos, S., Ward, T., & Zhu, W. (2002). Bleu: a method for automatic evaluation of machine translation. *Proceedings of the 40th Annual Meeting on Association for Computational Linguistics*, 311-318. Retrieved from http://www.aclweb.org/anthology/P02-1040.pdf

Reddy, K. D. (2013). *Plagiarism Detection using Enhanced Relative Frequency Model* (Unpublished M.Sc Thesis). Department of Computer Science and Engineering, National Institute of Technology Rourkela, India. Retrieved from http://ethesis.nitrkl.ac.in/5401/1/211CS3297.pdf

Runeson, P., Alexandersson, M., & Nyholm, O. (2007). Detection of Duplicate Defect Reports Using Natural Language Processing. *Proceedings of the 29th International Conference on Software Engineering, ICSE'07*, 499-510. Retrieved from https://www.semanticscholar.org/paper/Detection-of-Duplicate-Defect-Reports-Using-Natura-Runeson-Alexandersson/0d459e3be20f7f529bc0d92d42fa63e60fc1e1ba

Vani, K., & Gupta, D. (2015). Investigating the impact of combined similarity metrics and POS tagging in extrinsic text plagiarism detection system. *Proceedings of the 4th International Conference on Advances in Computing, Communications and Informatics (ICACCI)*, 1578-1584. Retrieved from https://www.deepdyve.com/lp/institute-of-electrical-and-electronics-engineers/investigating-the-impact-of-combined-similarity-metrics-and-pos-Z29pbXpVIw

Vania, C., & Adriani, M. (2010). Automatic external plagiarism detection using passage similarities. *Proceedings of the Conference on Multilingual and Multimodal Information Access Evaluation (CLEF 2010).* Retrieved from http://ceur-ws.org/Vol-1176/CLEF2010wn-PAN-VaniaEt2010.pdf

Zubarev, D. V., & Sochenkov, I. V. (2017). Paraphrased plagiarism detection using sentence similarity. *Proceedings of the International Conference on Computational Linguistics and Intellectual Technologies: Dialogue 2017.* Retrieved from http://www.dialog-21.ru/media/3965/zubarevdvsochenkoviv.pdf

KEY TERMS AND DEFINITIONS

Classifier: An algorithm that identifies which of the set of categories an observation belongs on the basis of a training data set whose categories are known.

Confusion Matrix: Confusion matrix is a standard construct to find the true positives, true negatives, false positive and false negatives and helps to calculate the accuracy of a classifier from these values obtained.

J48 Classifier: It is a C4.5 algorithm based decision tree used for classification purposes. At each node of the decision tree, the algorithm chooses the attribute of the data that splits the dataset into subsets. The splitting criterion is the normalized information gain (difference in entropy). The attribute with the highest normalized information gain is chosen to make the decision. The C4.5 algorithm then recurs on the smaller sublists.

Naive Bayes Classifier: The classifier is based upon Bayesian theorem. Bayesian theorem works upon conditional probability. It can be expressed as: $P(y \mid x) = \dfrac{P(X \mid y) P(y)}{P(X)}$, where P(y) is prior probability, P(y | X) is posterior probability.

Supervised Machine Learning: Algorithm which learns from the training dataset. In this chapter, we have implemented classification-based supervised machine learning algorithm to categorize output variable.

Ten-Fold Cross Validation: After randomizing the dataset, it is divided into 10 equal-sized partitions where 10th dataset partition is used for testing and nine partitions are used for training the classifier. In this program, we apply 10-fold cross validation upon training data to create a validation set and the best parameters.

Test Data: A dataset-independent of the training data. This dataset is used to assess the machine learning classifier which was used by train data to learn.

Train Data: A dataset which is used to learn the machine learning classifier.

Chapter 8
Segmentation of Multiple Touching Hand Written Devnagari Compound Characters:
Image Segmentation for Feature Extraction

Prashant Madhukar Yawalkar
MET Institute of Engineering, India

Madan Uttamrao Kharat
MET Institute of Engineering, India

Shyamrao V. Gumaste
MET Institute of Engineering, India

ABSTRACT

One of the most widely used steps in the process of reducing images to information is segmentation, which divides the image into regions that hopefully correspond to structural units in the scene or distinguish objects of interest. Segmentation is often described by analogy to visual processes as a foreground/background separation, implying that the selection procedure concentrates on a single kind of feature and discards the rest. Machine-printed or hand-drawn scripts can have various font types or writing styles. The writing styles can be roughly categorized into discrete style (handprint or boxed style), continuous style (cursive style), and mixed style. We can see that the ambiguity of character segmentation has three major sources: (1) variability of character size and inter character space; (2) confusion between inter character and within-character space; and (3) touching between characters.

DOI: 10.4018/978-1-5225-5775-3.ch008

INTRODUCTION

One of the most widely used steps in the process of reducing images to information is segmentation which divides the image into regions that hopefully correspond to structural units in the scene or distinguish objects of interest. The segmentation of connected handwritten characters or digits is a main bottleneck in the Hand Written Character Recognition system. There are two major categories of touching strings, single touching and multiple-touching strings and they are divided into five subtypes of touching, as shown in Figure 1. Many algorithms have been proposed in the past years which can be classified into three categories based on the segmentation approaches: foreground-based, background-based, and recognition-based (Chen & Jhing-Fa, 2000). The methods working on foreground pixels (black pixels in a binary image) are categorized to the foreground-based approach. There are several possible techniques, such as contour tracing, stroke analysis, etc., in this category (Tang, Tu, Liu, Lee, Lin, & Shyu, 1998). They tend to become much more unstable in trying to accommodate for multiple-touching numeral strings or single-touching strings with long touching part. Most of the connected numeral strings of type 1 and type 2 in Figure 1 can be successfully segmented with foreground-based methods, but they may fail or could not get precise results in separating the connected numeral strings of type 3 (no obvious segmentation point), type 4 (containing useless stroke), or type 5 (multiple-touching). The sample for single-touching and multiple-touching handwritten devnagari compound characters is shown in Figure 2. The methods working on background pixels (white pixels in a binary image) are categorized to the background-based approach. The background-based methods first locate the feature points on the background regions (such as face-up valley, face-down valley, loop region...) or the feature points on the background skeletons (such as upper segment, lower segment, hole segment...). Then, the algorithm connects these feature points to get the segmentation path. The background-based methods still fail to separate the single-touching strings with long touching part and the multiple-touching strings especially when there are more than two touching points. It is similar to the foreground-based approach in that most of the connected numeral strings of type 1 and type 2 in Figure 1 are successfully segmented, but they usually fail or cannot get precise results in segmenting the connected numeral strings of type 3, type 4, or type 5 (Chen & Jhing-Fa, 2000). The methods applying a recognizer to separate the connected numeral strings are categorized to the recognition-based approach. In the recognition-based approach, the correct rate of segmentation depends too much on the robustness of recognizer and it is time consuming. The approach usually fails to separate the connected strings with overlap between the left and the right character or digit. Besides, they might fail in segmenting the connected numeral strings of type 4. This is because that the useless strokes of type 4 may cause the failure of a recognizer. The Chapter starts with introduction, then giving the basics of Image Processing, further discussion on various segmentation techniques followed by various techniques for feature extraction. Finally a detail discussion on segmentation of single and multiple touching hand written character or numeral strings which can help in improvising the accuracy of character recognition system has been done.

IMAGE PROCESSING ESSENTIALS

An image may be defined as a two-dimensional function, $f(x, y)$ where x and y are *spatial* (plane) coordinates, and the amplitude of f at any pair of coordinates (x, y) is called the *intensity* or *gray level* of the image at that point. When x, y, and the intensity values of f are all finite, discrete quantities, we call

Figure 1. Types of connected strings

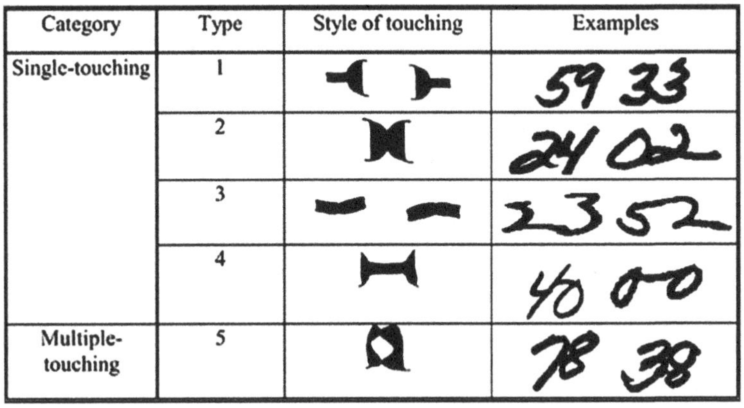

Category	Type	Style of touching	Examples
Single-touching	1	◄ ►	*59 33*
	2	⋈	*24 02*
	3	▬ ▬	*2352*
	4	⋈	*40 00*
Multiple-touching	5	⊘	*78 38*

Figure 2. Sample of single touching and multiple touching characters

the image a *digital image*. The field of digital image processing refers to processing digital images by means of a digital computer. Normally a digital image is composed of finite elements called Pixel that has a specific location and value (Gonzalez and Woods). The Basic fundamental steps in digital image processing are: Image acquisition, Image enhancement, Image restoration, Color image processing, Wavelets, Compression, Morphological processing, Segmentation, Representation and description, feature selection, Recognition, etc.

SEGMENTATION

It is often the critical step in image analysis, the point at which we move from considering each pixel as a unit of observation to working with *objects* (or parts of objects) in the image, composed of many pixels. If segmentation is done well then all other stages in image analysis are made simpler. All Text image segmentation can be achieved at three levels, as we move at different levels of text segmentation hierarchy, we obtain specifically finer details. Although use of all the three levels is not compulsory, Segmentation at any of these levels directly depends on the nature of the application. More the details required for the image, the more is the level of segmentation. Line segmentation is the primary step for text based image segmentation. It includes horizontal scanning of the image, pixel-row by pixel-row from left to right and top to bottom. At each pixel the intensity is tested. Depending on the values of the pixels we group pixels into multiple regions from the entire image. The different region indicates different content in the image file. Subsequently the desired content can be extracted. Word segmentation is the next level of segmentation. It includes vertical scanning of the image, pixel-row by pixel-row from left to right and top to bottom. At each pixel the intensity is tested. Depending on the values of the pixels we group pixels into multiple regions from the entire image. The different region indicates different content in the image file. Subsequently the desired content can be extracted. Character segmentation is the final level for text based image segmentation. Pixel counting approach is a simple technique to implement, but it cannot be used in situations when the text line in the document has a higher degree of skew, when the characters overlap, or when there is irregular spacing between the text lines. The Histogram approach is a method to automatically identify and segment the text line regions of a handwritten document. In the smearing method the consecutive black pixels along the horizontal direction are smeared consequently; the white space between the black pixels is filled with black pixels. Stochastic method is based on probabilistic algorithm, which accomplishes nonlinear paths between overlapping text lines. These lines are extracted through hidden Markov modeling (HMM). The water flow algorithm assumes hypothetical water flows under a few angles of the document image from left to right and top to bottom (Dave, 2015).

There are five general approaches to segmentation are thresholding, edge-based, region-based, fuzzy theory-based, ANN-based, clustering techniques and matching. In thresholding, pixels are allocated to categories according to the range of values in which a pixel lies. Pixels with values less than 128 are placed in one category, and the rest are placed in the other category. In edge-based segmentation, an edge filter is applied to the image, pixels are classified as *edge* or *non-edge* depending on the filter output, and pixels which are not separated by an edge are allocated to the same category. Region-based segmentation algorithms operate iteratively by grouping together pixels which are neighbors and have similar values and splitting groups of pixels which are dissimilar in value. Fuzzy Theory-Based Segmentation uses Fuzzification function to remove noise from image and transform a gray-scale image into a fuzzy image. In ANN-Based Segmentation every neuron corresponds to the pixel of an image and the Image is mapped to the neural network, which is further trained using training samples and finally connection between neurons is found. Then the new images are segmented from the trained image. In Clustering techniques an attempt to group together patterns that are similar in some sense is done. Finally in Matching, when we know what an object we wish to identify in an image (approximately) looks like, we use this knowledge to locate the object in an image. Let us discuss these techniques in detail one by one.

Thresholding Based Segmentation

The most frequently used technique to segment an image is Thresholding which is a grey value remapping operation g defined as in Equation (1) :

$$g(v) = \begin{cases} 0 & if \ v < t \\ 1 & if \ v \geq t \end{cases} \tag{1}$$

where v represents a grey value and t is the threshold value. Thresholding maps a grey-valued image to a binary image. After the thresholding operation, the image has been segmented into two segments, identified by the pixel values 0 and 1 respectively. If we have an image which contains bright objects on a dark background, thresholding can be used to segment the image. Since in many types of images the grey values of objects are very different from the background value, thresholding is often a well-suited method to segment an image into objects and background. If the objects are not overlapping, then we can create a separate segment from each object by running a labeling algorithm on the thresholded binary image, thus assigning a unique pixel value to each object.

Many methods exist to select a suitable threshold value for a segmentation task. Perhaps the most common method is to set the threshold value interactively; the user manipulating the value and reviewing the thresholding result until a satisfying segmentation has been obtained. The histogram is often acts as a valuable tool in establishing a suitable threshold value. When several desired segments in an image can be distinguished by their grey values, threshold segmentation can be extended to use multiple thresholds to segment an image into more than two segments: all pixels with a value smaller than the first threshold are assigned to segment 0, all pixels with values between the first and second threshold are assigned to segment 1 *etc*. If n thresholds $(t_1, t_2, \ldots, t_n)$ are used as in Equation (2):

$$g(v) = \begin{cases} 0 & if \ v < t_1 \\ 1 & if \ t_1 \leq v < t_2 \\ 2 & if \ t_2 \leq v < t_3 \\ \vdots & \vdots \\ n & if \ t_n \leq v \end{cases} \tag{2}$$

After thresholding, the image has been segmented into $n+1$ segments identified by the grey values 0 to n respectively (Khan, 2013).

Edge Based Segmentation

Since a (binary) object is fully represented by its edges, the segmentation of an image into separate objects can be achieved by finding the edges of those objects. A typical approach to segmentation using edges is:

- Compute an edge image, containing all possible edges of an original image.
- Process the edge image so that only closed object boundaries remain.
- Transform the result to an ordinary segmented image by filling in the object boundaries.

The first and third step of computing an edge image and filling of boundaries, are simple steps. The difficulty often lies in the middle step where transforming an edge image to closed boundaries often requires the removal of edges that are caused by noise or other artifacts, the bridging of gaps at locations where no edge was detected (but there should logically be one) and intelligent decisions to connect those edge parts that make up a single object. Watershed segmentation and active contours deal with methods that avoid having to link edge parts by manipulating like a rubber band contours that are always closed until they best fit an edge image. In some of the rare cases where an edge image already shows perfect closed object boundaries, edge-based segmentation can be achieved by techniques like: Edge linking, Hough transform, Neighborhood search etc.

Region Based Segmentation

Finding an object by locating its boundary and finding it by establishing the region it covers will give you exactly the same object; the boundary and the region are just different representations of the same object. In practice, however, taking an edge-based approach to segmentation may give radically different results than taking a region based approach. The reason for this is that we are bound to using imperfect images and imperfect methods; hence the practical result of locating an object boundary may be different from locating its region. Region based segmentation methods have only two basic operations: *splitting* and *merging*, and many methods even feature only one of these. The basic approach to image segmentation using merging is:

- Obtain an initial (over)segmentation of the image
- Merge those adjacent segments that are similar in some respect to form single segments
- Repeat step 2 until there are no more segments to be merged.

The initial segmentation may simply be all pixels, *i.e.,* each pixel is a segment by itself. The heart of the merging approach is the similarity criterion used to decide whether or not two segments should be merged. This criterion may be based on grey value similarity (such as the difference in average grey value, or the maximum or minimum grey value difference between segments), the edge strength of the boundary between the segments, the texture of the segments, or one of many other possibilities. The basic form of image segmentation using splitting is:

- Obtain an initial segmentation of the image
- Split each segment that is inhomogeneous in some respect (*i.e.,* each segment that is unlikely to *really* be a single segment).
- Repeat step 2 until all segments are homogeneous.

The initial segmentation may be no segmentation at all, *i.e.,* there is only a single segment, which is the entire image. The criterion for in homogeneity of a segment may be the variance of its grey values, the variance of its texture, the occurrence of strong internal edges, or various other criteria. The basic merging and splitting methods seem to be the top-down and bottom-up approach to the same method of segmentation, but there is an intrinsic difference: the merging of two segments is straightforward, but the splitting of a segment requires establishing suitable sub-segments the segments can be split into. In essence, we still have the segmentation problem we started with, except it is now defined on a more local level. To avoid this problem, the basic splitting approach is often enhanced to a combined *split and merge* approach, where inhomogeneous segments are split into simple geometric forms (usually into four squares) recursively. This of course creates arbitrary segment boundaries (that may not be correlated to realistic boundaries), and merge steps are included into the process to remove incorrect boundaries.

Fuzzy Theory Based Segmentation

Fuzzy set theory is used in order to analyze images, and provide accurate information from any image. Fuzzification function can be used to remove noise from image. A gray-scale image can be easily transformed into a fuzzy image by using a fuzzification function. Different morphological operations can be combined with fuzzy method to get better results. Fuzzy k-Means and Fuzzy C-means (FCM) are widely used methods in image processing. A fuzzy rule-based image segmentation technique which can integrate the spatial relationship of the pixels. A Membership function for Region pixel distribution, to measure the closeness of the region, and to find the spatial relationship among pixels. There is no need to define parameters in their technique, like FCM algorithm. Fuzzy rules use membership functions and fuzzy IF-THEN rule structure to perform segmentation of an image.

A new image segmentation technique based on fuzzy connectedness using dynamic weights was introduced. It was found that traditional segmentation schemes can't solve the problems of fuzzy medical images so DyW algorithm was introduced which dynamically adjusts the linear weights in fuzzy connectedness. The seed DyW algorithm is applied successfully to the images of different modalities, whereas multiple seed is applied to infrared face segmentation. Later A new fuzzy color image segmentation algorithm based on feature divergence and fuzzy dissimilarity that claimed to improve segmentation quality was introduced. This algorithm extracts sub-images feature Eigen-vector using watershed technique. Firstly, color image is transform into gray level image, histogram is created in order to form clusters for applying FCM to each cluster. Further erosion, dilation, and region growing operations are applied on the resultant image. Finally the segmented region image is produced and the image is taken with complex background, i.e., photographic image.

ANN Based Segmentation

In Artificial Neural Network, every neuron is corresponding to the pixel of an image. Image is mapped to the neural network. Image in the form of neural network is trained using training samples, and then connection between neurons, i.e., pixels is found. Then the new images are segmented from the trained image. Some of the mostly used neural networks for image segmentation are Hopfield, Back Propagation, Feed Forward, Multi-Layer Feed Forward, Multi-Layer Perceptron, etc. Segmentation of image using neural network is perform in two steps, i.e., pixel classification and edge detection. A new Fast Learning Artificial Neural Network (FLANN) based color image segmentation approach for R-G-B-S-V (i.e., RGB and HSV) cluster space was introduced (Marinai, Gori, & Soda, 2005). In first step, noise is removed using 3*3 averaging filter to reduce the disparity in color distribution. In second step, pixels are converted to RGBSV space using HSV conversions. FLANN clustering is performed to produce a cluster result of image in which pixels with same color are separated and segment number is assigned to each segment of image. Effect of tolerance and neighborhood size is observed in order to produce perfect segments for colors in the image. A fast C-means based training of Fuzzy Hopfield Neural network was introduced in order to apply it into image segmentation. Initially clusters are formed from given data, then perform normalization, i.e. grey level images, calculate centroids, then compute distances, find new centroids, and compute new membership function value using fuzzy C-means. An objective function is used based on 2-f Fuzzy Hopfield Neural Network to find the average distance between image pixels and cluster's centroids. Fuzzy HNN provides better segmentation as compare to other methods.

Clustering Techniques

Clustering techniques is the collective name for methods that attempt to group together measurements points ('patterns'). The objective of clustering techniques is to identify clusters in data. Clustering techniques are often formulated for data of arbitrary dimension that can readily be applied to two or three-dimensional images. The images best suited for applying clustering techniques are those which are similar in appearance or of a very sparse nature, the dark pixels forming quasi-coherent clouds etc. If we wish to apply clustering to a binary image, we use a similar representation: each pixel with value one is included in a data list of coordinate pairs. For grey-valued images there may not be a natural conversion to a list of data points. For some types of grey-valued images, it is possible to consider the grey value as the number of data points measured at a certain location (Khan, 2013).

Matching

If we want to locate an object in an image, and we have available an example of what it should look like (a *template*), we can find this object by matching the template to various image locations until we have found the object. The most straightforward way of determining whether a template 'fits' would be to place the template at a certain image location, and see whether the grey values of the template and the underlying image grey values all match (Cheung, Yeung, & Chin, 2002). However, because there will generally be some differences between the image and template values because of noise and other artifacts, this is not a very practical method. More useful is a quantitative measure of fit such as in Equation (3):

$$M_1(p,q) = \sum_{x=0}^{M-1}\sum_{y=0}^{N-1}\left(g(x,y) - f(x+p,y+q)\right)^2 \tag{3}$$

where f is the image, g the $M \times N$ template, and the variables p and q determine the location of the template in the image. This measure will be small if the template is similar to the part of the image under investigation; then all grey value differences $g(x, y)-f(x+p, y+q)$ are small and the sum M_1 will be small. The location of optimal template fit is found by minimizing M_1 to p and q.

Besides the squared form M_1, another often used measure is M_2, which uses the actual grey value differences instead of their squares as in Equation (4):

$$M_2(p,q) = \sum_{x=0}^{M-1}\sum_{y=0}^{N-1}\left|g(x,y) - f(x+p,y+q)\right| \tag{4}$$

M_2 puts less weight on relatively large grey value differences than M_1. But perhaps the most commonly used measure is the *cross correlation M_3*, which is defined by Equation (5):

$$M_3(p,q) = \sum_{x=0}^{M-1}\sum_{y=0}^{N-1}g(x,y)f(x+p,y+q) \tag{5}$$

The maximum of M_3 with respect to p and q is assumed to indicate the location in the image where the template fits best. There is a strong relation between the measures M_1 and M_3, which is most obvious if we extend the sums in the measure M_1 to the entire image f (and pad the template g with zeros); then the measure M_3 appears literally between constants if we expand the square using Equation (6):

$$M_1^*\left(p,q\right) = \sum_{x=0}^{d_x-1}\sum_{y=0}^{d_y-1}\left(f\left(x,y\right) - g\left(x-p,y-q\right)\right)^2$$
$$= \underbrace{\sum\sum f^2\left(x,y\right)}_{constant} - 2\underbrace{\sum\sum f\left(x,y\right)g\left(x-p,y-q\right)}_{=M_3} + \underbrace{\sum\sum g^2\left(x-p,y-q\right)}_{constant} \tag{6}$$

where dx and dy are the dimensions of the image f.

FEATURE EXTRACTION

Feature extraction is one of the most important fields in artificial intelligence. It consists to extract the most relevant features of an image and assign it into a label. In image classification, the crucial step is to analyze the properties of image features and to organize the numerical features into classes. There are various techniques for extracting features: Color Features, Texture Features and Shape Features. In Color Features the color histogram represents the most common method to extract color feature. It is regarded as the distribution of the color in the image. The efficiency of the color feature resides in the fact that is independent and insensitive to size, rotation and the zoom of the image. In Texture Features texture is a group of pixel that has certain characteristic which is classified into two categories: spatial texture feature extraction and spectral texture feature extraction. Finally Shape Features are very useful in object recognition and shape description and are further classified as: region based and contour based.

Harris Corner Detection

Harris corner detector is a well-known interest key point detector due to its invariance to rotation, It is based on local auto-correlation function of a signal where local auto-correlation function measures the local changes of the signal with patches shifted by a small amount in different directions. Harris promotes a formula that can be calculated out the change of the pixel values in any direction, rather than fixed in the 8 directions. Let the grey of pixel (x, y) be g(x,y), then the grey variation of pixel (x, y) with a shift (p, q) can be described as in Equation (7):

$$Z_{\left(p,q\right)}\left(x,y\right) = \sum_{p,y}W_{\left(p,q\right)}\left(f\left(x+p,y+q\right) - f\left(x,y\right)\right) \tag{7}$$

In equation (7), the gray variation can be define using differential operation as in Equation (8):

$$Z_{\left(p,q\right)}\left(x,y\right) = \sum_{p,y}W_{\left(p,q\right)}\left(\left(pf_x + qf_y\right) + o\left(p^2 + q^2\right)\right)^2 \tag{8}$$

f_x, f_y is the first-order gray gradient, and u, v is Gaussian operator. Calculate the auto-correlation matrix as in Equation (9):

$$M = \begin{bmatrix} f_x^2 & f_x f_y \\ f_x f_y & f_y^2 \end{bmatrix}$$

(9)

To extract the corner, Harris constructed the formula as in Equation (10):

$$R = \det(M) - k(t_M)$$

(10)

$\det(M)$ is the determinant of M and t_M is the trace of M, where k is the parameter greater than zero. The feature points that are the pixel value corresponding with the local maximum interest point are taken into consideration with Harris method (Bhenda, Joshi, Vikram, & Agrawal, 2014).

SUSAN

Smallest Univalue Segment Assimilating Nucleus (SUSAN) places a circular mask or called window over the pixel to be tested. The region of the mask is pixel in mask represented by m. The nucleus is at m_0. The brightness of pixel with in mask is compared with that of the nucleus. Every pixel is compared to the nucleus using function given by Equation (11):

$$c\left(\vec{m}\right) = e^{-\left(\frac{I(\vec{m}) - I(\vec{m_0})}{t}\right)^6}$$

(11)

here t represent radius, power of exponent is determined empirically. The area of SUSAN is given by Equation (12),

$$n\left(M\right) = \sum_{\vec{m} \in M} c\left(\vec{m}\right)$$

(12)

If c is rectangular function, then n is the number of pixels in the mask which are within t of the nucleus. The response of the SUSAN operator is given by Equation (13):

$$R\left(M\right) = \begin{cases} g - n\left(M\right) & if \ n\left(M\right) < g \\ 0 & otherwise \end{cases}$$

(13)

Then after, first, the centroid of the SUSAN is found. A proper corner will have the centroid far from the nucleus. The second is that all points on the line from the nucleus through the centroid out to the edge of the mask are in the SUSAN (Bhenda, Joshi, Vikram, & Agrawal, 2014).

FAST

The detection of corner was prioritized over edges in FAST as corners were found to be the good features to be matched because it shows a two-dimensional intensity change, and thus well distinguished from the neighboring points. Generally the corner detector should satisfy the following criteria.

- The detected positions should be consistent, insensitive to the variation of noise, and they should not move when multiple images are acquired of the same scene.
- **Accuracy:** Corners should be detected as close as possible to the correct positions.
- **Speed:** The corner detector should be fast enough.

FAST incremented the computational speed required in the detection of corners. This corner detector uses a corner response function (CRF) that gives a numerical value for the corner strength based on the image intensities in the local neighborhood. CRF was computed over the image and corners which were treated as local maxima of the CRF. A multigrid technique is used to improve the computational speed of the algorithm and also for the suppression of false corners being detected. FAST is an accurate and fast algorithm that yields good localization (positional accuracy) and high point reliability specifically proposed for identifying interest points in a image. An interest point in an image is a pixel which has a well-defined position and can be robustly detected. Interest points have high local information content and they should be ideally repeatable between different images. Interest point detection has applications in image matching, object recognition, tracking etc (Piotr Dollar & Lawrence, 2015). There are several well-established algorithms like: Moravec corner detection algorithm, Harris and Stephens corner detection algorithm, SUSAN corner detector, etc. The reason behind the work of the FAST algorithm was to develop an interest point detector for use in real time frame rate applications like SLAM on a mobile robot, which have limited computational resources.

SURF

SURF (Speed Up Robust Features) algorithm, is base on multi-scale space theory and the feature detector is based on Hessian matrix. Since Hessian matrix has good performance and accuracy. A basic second order Hessian matrix approximation is used for feature point detection. The approximation with box filters is pushed to take place of second-order Gaussian filter and a very low computational cost is obtained by using integral images. The Hessian-matrix approximation lends itself to the use of integral images, which is a very useful technique that drastically reduces computation time. In the construction of scale image pyramid in SURF algorithm, the scale space is divided into octaves, and there are 4 scale levels in each octave. Each octave represents a series of filter response maps obtained by convolving the same input image with a filter of increasing size. The minimum scale difference between subsequent scales depends on the length of the positive or negative lobes of the partial second order derivative in the direction of derivation. Non-maximum suppression in a 3x3x3 neighborhood is performed to get the steady feature points and the scale of values. In order to be invariant to image rotation, the Haar wavelet responses are calculated in x and y direction within a circular neighborhood of radius 6s around the feature point, s is the scale at which the feature point was detected. The Haar wavelet responses are represented as vectors, then sum of all the vector of x and y direction of the Haar wavelet responses within a sliding orientation window covering an angle of size π/3 around the feature point is done (Panchal & Shah, 2013). The two-summed response yield a new vector and the longest vector is the dominant orientation of the feature point.

For extraction of the descriptor, construct a square region with a size of 20s and split the interest region up into 4x4 square sub-regions with 5x5 regularly spaced sample points inside. Compute the Haar wavelet response x-direction d_x and the Haar wavelet response y-direction d_y. Weight the response with a Gaussian kernel centered at the interest point. Sum the response over each sub-region for d_x and d_y separately. In order to bring in information about the polarity of the intensity changes, extract the sum of absolute value of the responses (Bhenda, Joshi, Vikram, & Agrawal, 2014). Therefore, each sub-region is formed a 4-dimensional vector as in Equation (14):

$$Vec\left(\sum d_x, \sum d_y, \sum |d_x|, \sum |d_y|\right) \hspace{4cm} (14)$$

Finally, normalize the vector into unit length for invariance to contrast.

SIFT

Matching features across different images is a common problem in computer vision. When all images are similar in nature (same scale, orientation, etc) simple corner detectors can work. But when you have images of different scales and rotations, you need to use the Scale Invariant Feature Transform. Scale Invariant Feature Transform (SIFT) isn't just scale invariant and so one can change Scale, Rotation, Illumination, or Viewpoint and still get good results (Panchal & Shah, 2013). It basically consists of four stages as below:

- **Scale-Space Extrema Detection:** The first stage of computation searches over all scales and image locations. It is implemented efficiently by using a difference-of-Gaussian function to identify potential interest points that are invariant to scale and orientation.
- **Keypoint Localization:** At each candidate location, a detailed model is fit to determine location and scale. Key points are selected based on measures of their stability.
- **Orientation Assignment:** One or more orientations are assigned to each keypoint location based on local image gradient directions. All future operations are performed on image data that has been transformed relative to the assigned orientation, scale, and location for each feature, thereby providing invariance to these transformations.
- **Keypoint Descriptor:** The local image gradients are measured at the selected scale in the region around each keypoint. These are transformed into a representation that allows for significant levels of local shape distortion and change in illumination.

The first stage used difference of Gaussian (DOG) function to identify potential interest points, which were invariant to scale and orientation. DOG was used instead of Gaussian to improve the computation speed (Bhenda, Joshi, Vikram, & Agrawal, 2014). In order to reduce the confusion in understanding of these steps let us split the entire algorithm in to multiple steps as follows:

Constructing a Scale Space

Real world objects are meaningful only at a certain scale. You might see a sugar cube perfectly on a table. But if looking at the entire milky way, then it simply does not exist. This multi-scale nature of objects is quite common in nature. And a scale space attempts to replicate this concept on digital images. Do you want to look at a leaf or the entire tree? If it's a tree, get rid of some detail from the image (like the leaves, twigs, etc) intentionally. While getting rid of these details, you must ensure that you do not introduce new false details. The only way to do that is with the Gaussian Blur (it was proved mathematically, under several reasonable assumptions). So to create a scale space, you take the original image and generate progressively blurred out images. SIFT takes scale spaces to the next level. You take the original image, and generate progressively blurred out images. Then, you resize the original image to half size and you generate blurred out images again by repeating this step.

- **Octaves and Scales:** The number of octaves and scale depends on the size of the original image. While programming in SIFT, you'll have to decide for yourself how many octaves and scales you want. However, the creator of SIFT suggests that 4 octaves and 5 blur levels are ideal for the algorithm.
- **The First Octave:** If the original image is doubled in size and anti aliased a bit (by blurring it) then the algorithm produces more four times more key points. The more the key points, the better!
- **Blurring:** Mathematically, "blurring" is referred to as the convolution of the gaussian operator and the image. Gaussian blur has a particular expression or "operator" that is applied to each pixel. What results is the blurred image given by Equation (15):

$$L\left(x,y,\sigma\right) = G\left(x,y,\sigma\right) * I\left(x,y\right) \qquad (15)$$

The symbols:

- L is a blurred image
- G is the Gaussian Blur operator
- I is an image
- x,y are the location coordinates
- σ is the "scale" parameter. Think of it as the amount of blur. Greater the value, greater the blur.
- The * is the convolution operation in x and y. It "applies" gaussian blur G onto the image I as in Equation (16):

$$G\left(x,y,\sigma\right) = \frac{1}{2\pi\sigma^2} e^{-\left(x^2+y^2\right)/2\sigma^2} \qquad (16)$$

This is the actual Gaussian Blur operator.

- **Amount of Blurring:** The amount of blurring in each image is important. It goes like this. Assume the amount of blur in a particular image is σ. Then, the amount of blur in the next image will be k*σ. Here k is whatever constant you choose. In the first step of SIFT, you generate several octaves of the original image. Each octave's image size is half the previous one. Within an octave, images are progressively blurred using the Gaussian Blur operator. In the next step, we'll use all these octaves to generate Difference of Gaussian images.

LoG Approximations

In the previous step, we created the scale space of the image. The idea was to blur an image progressively, shrink it, blur the small image progressively and so on. Now we use those blurred images to generate another set of images, the Difference of Gaussians (DoG). These DoG images are a great for finding out interesting key points in the image.

- **Laplacian of Gaussian:** The Laplacian of Gaussian (LoG) operation goes like this. You take an image, and blur it a little. And then, you calculate second order derivatives on it (or, the "laplacian"). This locates edges and corners on the image. These edges and corners are good for finding keypoints. But the second order derivative is extremely sensitive to noise. The blur smoothes it out the noise and stabilizes the second order derivative.The problem is, calculating all those second order derivatives is computationally intensive. So we cheat a bit.
- **The Con:** To generate Laplacian of Guassian images quickly, we use the scale space. We calculate the difference between two consecutive scales or, the Difference of Gaussians. These Difference of Gaussian images are approximately equivalent to the Laplacian of Gaussian. And we've replaced a computationally intensive process with a simple subtraction (fast and efficient). These DoG images comes with another little goodie. These approximations are also "scale invariant".
- **The Benefits:** Just the Laplacian of Gaussian images aren't great. They are not scale invariant. That is, they depend on the amount of blur you do. This is because of the Gaussian expression given by Equation (17).

$$G\left(x,y,\sigma\right) = \frac{1}{2\pi\sigma^2} e^{-\left(x^2+y^2\right)/2\sigma^2} \tag{17}$$

See the σ^2 in the demonimator? That's the scale. If we somehow get rid of it, we'll have true scale independence. So, if the laplacian of a gaussian is represented as in Equation (18):

$$\nabla^2 G \tag{18}$$

Then the scale invariant laplacian of gaussian would look like Equation (19):

$$\sigma^2 \nabla^2 G \tag{19}$$

But all these complexities are taken care of by the Difference of Gaussian operation. The resultant images after the DoG operation are already multiplied by the σ^2. Thus it has also been proved that this scale invariant thingy produces much better trackable points.

- **Side Effects:** You know the DoG result is multiplied with σ^2. But it's also multiplied by another number. That number is (k-1). This is the k we discussed in the previous step. But we'll just be looking for the *location* of the maximums and minimums in the images. We'll never check the actual values at those locations. So, this additional factor won't be a problem to us. (Even if you multiply throughout by some constant, the maxima and minima stay at the same location) Two consecutive images in an octave are picked and one is subtracted from the other. Then the next consecutive pair is taken, and the process repeats. This is done for all octaves. The resulting images are an approximation of scale invariant laplacian of gaussian (which is good for detecting keypoints). There are a few "drawbacks" due to the approximation, but they won't affect the algorithm.

Finding Key Points

Up till now, we have generated a scale space and used the scale space to calculate the Difference of Gaussians. These are further used to calculate a Laplacian of Gaussian approximation that is scale invariant. Finding key points is a two part process:

- **Locate Maxima/Minima in DoG Images:** The first step is to roughly locate the maxima and minima. For each pixel all its neighbors are checked. The check is done within the current image, and also the one above and below it. X which represents the current pixel, is marked as a "key point" if it is the greatest or least of all 26 neighbors. Usually, a non-maxima or non-minima position won't have to go through all 26 checks since a few initial checks are usually sufficient to discard it. Note that keypoints are not detected in the lowermost and topmost scales since there are not enough neighbors for comparison. So we simply skip them and the marked points are the approximate maxima and minima. They are "approximate" because the maxima/minima almost never lie exactly on a pixel. It lies somewhere between the pixel. But we simply cannot access data "between" pixels. So, we must mathematically locate the sub pixel location.
- **Find Sub Pixel Maxima/Minima:** Using the available pixel data, subpixel values are generated. This is done by the Taylor expansion of the image around the approximate key point. Mathematically, it's like Equation (20):

$$D\left(x\right) = D + \frac{\partial D^T}{\partial x} x + \frac{1}{2} x^T \frac{\partial^2 D}{\partial x^2} x \tag{20}$$

We can easily find the extreme points of this equation (differentiate and equate to zero). On solving, we'll get sub pixel key point locations. These sub pixel values increase chances of matching and stability of the algorithm. Here, we detected the maxima and minima in the DoG images generated in the previous step. This is done by comparing neighboring pixels in the current scale, the scale "above" and the scale "below". Next, we'll reject some keypoints detected here. This is because they either don't have enough contrast or they lie on an edge.

Getting Rid of Low Contrast Key Points

A lot of key points are generated some of them lie along an edge, or they don't have enough contrast. In both cases, they are not useful as features. So we need to get rid of them. The approach is similar to the one used in the Harris Corner Detector for removing edge features. For low contrast features, we simply check their intensities.

- **Removing Low Contrast Features:** If the magnitude of the intensity at the current pixel in the DoG image (that is being checked for minima/maxima) is less than a certain value, it is rejected. Because we have sub pixel keypoints (we used the Taylor expansion to refine key points), we again need to use the taylor expansion to get the intensity value at sub pixel locations. If its magnitude is less than a certain value, we reject the key point.
- **Removing Edges:** The idea is to calculate two gradients at the key point. Both perpendiculars to each other. Based on the image around the key point, three possibilities exist. The image around the key point can be a flat region, an edge, or a corner. Here, both gradients will be big. Corners are great key points which we want. If both gradients are big enough, we let it pass as a key point. Otherwise, it is rejected. Mathematically, this is achieved by the Hessian Matrix. Using this matrix, you can easily check if a point is a corner or not. Both extreme images go through the two tests: the contrast test and the edge test. They reject a few key points (sometimes a lot) and thus, we're left with a lower number of key points to deal with.

In this step, the number of key points is reduced. This helps increase efficiency and also the robustness of the algorithm. Key points are rejected if they had a low contrast or if they are located on an edge.

Key Point Orientations

After step 4, we have legitimate key points. They've been tested to be stable. We already know the scale at which the key point was detected (it's the same as the scale of the blurred image). So we have scale invariance. The next thing is to assign an orientation to each key point. This orientation provides rotation invariance. The more invariance you have the better it is. The idea is to collect gradient directions and magnitudes around each key point. Then we figure out the most prominent orientation(s) in that region. And we assign this orientation(s) to the key point. Any later calculations are done relative to this orientation. This ensures rotation invariance. The size of the "orientation collection region" around the key point depends on its scale. The bigger the scale, the bigger is the collection region. Gradient magnitudes and orientations are calculated using Equations (21) and (22) given below:

$$m\left(x,y\right)=\sqrt{\left(L\left(x+1,y\right)-L\left(x-1,y\right)\right)^{2}+\left(L\left(x,y+1\right)-L\left(x,y-1\right)\right)^{2}} \tag{21}$$

$$\theta\left(x,y\right)=\tan^{-1}\left|\frac{L\left(x,y+1\right)-L\left(x,y-1\right)}{L\left(x+1,y\right)-L\left(x-1,y\right)}\right| \tag{22}$$

The magnitude and orientation is calculated for all pixels around the key point. A histogram is created for this in which the 360 degrees of orientation are broken into 36 bins (each 10 degrees). Let's say the gradient direction at a certain point (in the "orientation collection region") is 18.759 degrees, then it will go into the 10-19 degree bin. And the "amount" that is added to the bin is proportional to the magnitude of gradient at that point. Once you've done this for all pixels around the key point, the histogram will have a peak at some point. Also, any peaks above 80% of the highest peak are converted into a new key point. This new key point has the same location and scale as the original. But it's orientation is equal to the other peak. So, orientation can split up one key point into multiple key points.

- **Magnitudes**: In SIFT, you need to blur it by an amount of 1.5*sigma.
- **Size of the Window:** The window size, or the "orientation collection region", is equal to the size of the kernel for Gaussian Blur of amount 1.5*sigma.
- To assign an orientation we use a histogram and a small region around it. Using the histogram, the most prominent gradient orientation(s) are identified. If there is only one peak, it is assigned to the key point. If there are multiple peaks above the 80% mark, they are all converted into a new key point (with their respective orientations).

Generating a Feature

Till now, we had scale and rotation invariance. Now we create a fingerprint for each key point, used as its identification. If an eye is a key point, then using this fingerprint, we'll be able to distinguish it from other key points, like ears, noses, fingers, etc. We need to generate a very unique fingerprint for the key point that should be easy to calculate and relatively lenient when it is being compared against other key points. Things are never EXACTLY same when comparing two different images. To do this, a 16x16 window around the key point is considered (as shown in Figure 3). This 16x16 window is broken into sixteen 4x4 windows. Within each 4x4 window, gradient magnitudes and orientations are calculated. These orientations are put into an 8 bin histogram. Orientation in the range 0-44 degrees add to the first bin. 45-89 add to the next bin and so on. The amount added to the bin depends on the magnitude of the gradient and the distance from the key point. Thus gradients that are far away from the key point will add smaller values to the histogram.

Figure 3. 16X16 Window with details of processing

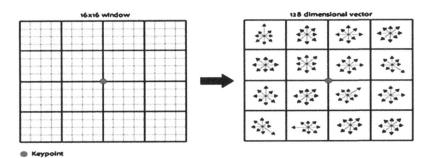

This is done using a "Gaussian weighting function". This function simply generates a gradient (it's like a 2D bell curve). You multiply it with the magnitude of orientations, and you get a weighted thing y. The farther the pixel, the lesser is the magnitude.

Doing this for all 16 pixels results in to 16 totally random orientations into 8 predetermined bins. We do this for all sixteen 4x4 regions as shown in Figure 4 ending up with 4x4x8 = 128 numbers which are further normalize to form the "feature vector". This key point is uniquely identified by this feature vector. The 16x16 window takes orientations and magnitudes of the image "in-between" pixels. So it is necessary to interpolate the image to generate orientation and magnitude data "in between" pixels.

Problems

The feature vector introduces a few complications. We need to get rid of them before finalizing the fingerprint.

1. **Rotation Dependence:** The feature vector uses gradient orientations. Clearly, if the image is rotated, everything changes. All gradient orientations also change. To achieve rotation independence, the key point's rotation is subtracted from each orientation. Thus each gradient orientation is relative to the key point's orientation.

2. **Illumination Dependence:** If we threshold numbers that are big, we can achieve illumination independence. So, any number (of the 128) greater than 0.2 is changed to 0.2. This resultant feature vector is normalized again to obtain an illumination independent feature vector.

Consider a 16x16 window of "in-between" pixels around the key point. Split that window into sixteen 4x4 windows. From each 4x4 window you generate a histogram of 8 bins. Each bin corresponding to 0-44 degrees, 45-89 degrees, etc. Gradient orientations from the 4x4 are put into these bins. This is done for all 4x4 blocks. Finally, normalize the 128 values. To solve a few problems, subtract the key point's orientation and also threshold the value of each element of the feature vector to 0.2 (and normalize again)as in Equation (23).

$$D\left(x,y,\sigma\right) = \left(G\left(x,y,k\sigma\right)G\left(x,y,\sigma\right)\right) * I\left(x,y\right)$$
$$= L\left(x,y,k\sigma\right)L\left(x,y,\sigma\right)$$

(23)

Figure 4. A 4 X 4 circular window with pixel details

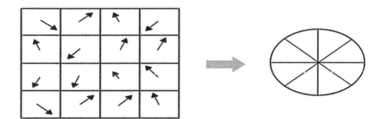

where * is the convolution operator, $G(x, y, \sigma)$ is a variable scale Gaussian, $I(x, y)$ is the input image $D(x, y, \sigma)$ is Difference of Gaussians with scale k times. In the key point localization step, they are rejected the low contrast points and eliminated the edge response. Hessian matrix is used to compute the principal curvatures and eliminate the key points that have a ratio between the principal curvatures greater than the ratio. An orientation histogram is formed from the gradient orientations of sample points within a region around the key point in order to get an orientation assignment.

- **PCA-SIFT:** Principal Component Analysis (PCA) is a standard technique for dimensionality reduction and has been applied to a broad class of computer vision problems, including feature selection. PCA-SIFT can be summarized in the following steps:
  - Pre-compute an eigen space to express the gradient images of local patches.
  - Given a patch, compute its local image gradient.
  - Project the gradient image vector using the eigen space to derive a compact feature vector.

The input vector is created by concatenating the horizontal and vertical gradient maps for the 41x41 patch centered at the key point. Thus, the input vector has 2x39x39=3042 elements. Then normalize this vector to unit magnitude to minimize the impact of variations in illumination. Projecting the gradient patch onto the low-dimensional space appears to retain the identity related variation while discarding the distortions induced by other effects. Eigen space can be build by running the first three stages of the SIFT algorithm on a diverse collection of images and collect patches. Each patch is processed as described above to create a element vector, and PCA is applied to the covariance matrix of these vectors. The matrix consisting of the top n eigenvectors is stored and used as the projection matrix for PCA-SIFT (Bhenda, Joshi, Vikram, & Agrawal, 2014). The images used in building the eigen space are discarded and not used in any of the matching experiments. Apart from the above specified techniques there are many more like: zoning, Support Vector Machine, Background Directional Distribution (BDD), Distance Profile, and Projection Histogram (Zhou, Wang, Tian, & Liu, 2013) etc. which are not discussed here.

SEGMENTATION OF MULTIPLE TOUCHING HAND WRITTEN DEVNAGARI COMPOUND CHARACTERS

A segmentation algorithm to segment the single- or multiple-touching hand-written characters and numeral strings is discussed. This algorithm links the feature points on the foreground and background alternately to get the possible segmentation path. Then, the mixture Gaussian probability function of size M is used to rank all of the possible segmentation paths. The most favorable path should appear in the front of the list. If the Gaussian probability of the most favorable path is greater than a confidence value, then it is regarded as the best segmentation path. Otherwise, it is rejected. Besides, useless strokes are removed from the connected numeral strings. The extraction of feature points is discussed, and the construction of possible segmentation paths for single and multiple-touching characters is shown.

Extraction of Feature Points

For finding all of the feature points on the foreground and background of the image, the thinning algorithm is first applied to foreground and background regions, respectively. The definitions of different segments on the foreground and background skeletons are adapted and are given as follows:

- **Top-Segment:** The segment generated from the upper part of the background region.
- **Bottom-Segment:** The segment generated from the lower part of the background region.
- **Stroke-Segment:** The segment generated from the foreground region.
- **Hole-Segment:** The segment generated from the hole-region of the background.

The feature points used in are the fork points, end points, and corner points on top-segment, bottom-segment, and hole-segment. Only fork points and corner points are extracted on the stroke-segment because a segmentation path never contains any end point on a stroke-segment from our observation. The different kinds of feature points are defined as follows:

- **Fork Point:** The point on a segment which has more than two connected branches.
- **End Point:** The point on a segment that has only one neighbor.
- **Corner Point:** The point on a segment where the curvature of the segment changes sharply.

A 9X9 window centered at a point on the segment (as shown in Figure 5) to decide whether it is a corner point. If the angle of the point is greater than 20 degrees, we regard the point as a corner point.

Construction of Possible Segmentation Paths

After locating all of the feature points on the foreground and background skeletons, respectively, construction of possible segmentation path is done. The reason is that we don't know the touching style of the strings during constructing all of the possible segmentation paths; we simultaneously apply two different stages single touching stage and a multiple-touching stage. To construct all of the possible

Figure 5. A 9X9 Window for computing a corner point

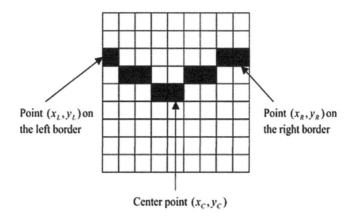

Point (x_L, y_L) on the left border

Point (x_R, y_R) on the right border

Center point (x_C, y_C)

segmentation paths on the connected strings, all of the possible segmentations are recorded for processing later. Sometimes there is no matched feature point on the stroke-segment or bottom-segment and a vertical searching path is constructed downward until it touches the bottom-segment. Besides, an upward searching is proceeded in the same way to construct possible segmentation paths from bottom-segment to top-segment. As we construct a segmentation path of single-touching stage (use the progress of downward searching as an example), the following constraints must be satisfied:

The coordinates (x,y) of a feature point on stroke segment or bottom-segment to be matched must satisfy:

$$\left(xpres - xbound\right) < x < \left(xpres + xbound\right)$$

and

$$\left(ypres - yupper - bound\right) < y < \left(ypres + ylower - yupper\right))$$

where x_{pres} and y_{pres} are the coordinates of the present feature point, and $x_{bound,}$ $y_{upper-bound}$ and $y_{lower-bound}$, are the parameters used to restrict the searching region. There must be no stroke-segment between two matched feature points. There exists only one foreground-background or background-foreground transition on the straight line connecting the current feature point to the matched point. The ratio between the count of foreground pixels and the count of background pixels on the segmentation path must be smaller than a threshold (Chen & Jhing-Fa, 2000).

Constructing Possible Segmentation Paths with Multiple-Touching Stage If the segmentation path separates the multiple-touching character or numeral string; the segmentation path must contain one or more hole-regions. Though, we must alternately connect several feature points on the background and foreground segments. The searching of possible segmentation paths of multiple-touching stage consists of both downward and upward searching. In downward searching, the possible segmentation path starts from a feature point on top-segment, passes a matched feature point on stroke-segments, matches a feature point on hole-segment, reaches a feature point on stroke-segment, and matches a feature point on hole-segment or bottom-segment. If the feature point is on bottom-segment, the path ends. If the next feature point is on hole-segment, we continue to find the following matched feature point on stroke-segment until the next matched feature point is found on bottom segment. Sometimes, we can't find any matched feature point on the bottom-segment and a vertical searching path is constructed downward until it touches the bottom-segment. In the same manner, an upward searching is proceeded to construct possible segmentation paths from bottom-segment to top-segment. As we construct the possible segmentation paths of multiple-touching stage by using the progress of downward searching so as to satisfy the constraints of matching the (x,y) coordinates of a feature point on stroke segment or bottom-segment given by:

$$\left(xpres - xbound\right) < x < \left(xpres + xbound\right)$$

and

$$\left(ypres - yupper - bound\right) < y < \left(ypres + ylower - bound\right)$$

where x_{pres} and y_{pres} are the coordinates of the present feature point, and x_{bound}, $y_{upper\text{-}bound}$ and $y_{lower\text{-}bound}$, are the parameters used to restrict the searching region The criterion is the same as processing path of single-touching numeral strings. The coordinates (x,y) of a feature point on hole segment to be matched must satisfy:

$$\left(xpres - xbound\right) < x < \left(xpres + xbound\right)$$

and

$$\left(ypres + yupper - zone\right) < y < \left(ypres + ylower - zone\right)$$

where x_{pres} and y_{pres} are the coordinates of the present feature point, and x_{bound}, $y_{upper\text{-}zone}$ and $y_{lower\text{-}zone}$, are the parameters used to restrict the searching region.

- There must be no stroke-segment between two matched feature points.
- There exists only one foreground-background or background-foreground transition on the straight line connecting the current feature point to the matched point.
- The ratio between the count of foreground pixels and the count of background pixels on the segmentation path must be smaller than a threshold of 0.6.

All the parameters used in constructing the possible segmentation paths should be set according to the size of the image. We set x_{bound} = third of image width, $y_{upper\text{-}bound}$ = fifth of image height, $y_{lower\text{-}bound}$ = half of image height, $y_{upper\text{-}zone}$ = one-tenth of image height, and $y_{lower\text{-}zone}$ = quarter of image height. After simultaneously applying both of the single-touching stage and multiple touching stage to the connected characters or numeral strings, all of the possible segmentation paths are found and recorded for further processing.

Removing Useless Strokes

For getting more precise results of segmentation, we find all possible segmentation paths by matching feature points on foreground and background segments alternatively. Besides, the connected character and numeral strings of type 4 in Table 1 contain useless strokes and we try to remove it. Consequently, the regions between two segmentation paths of the same start point and ending point are searched for removing useless stroke on the image after finding all of the possible segmentation paths. If all of the following constraints are satisfied, the stroke is regarded as a useless stroke and is removed.

- The stroke is inside the region between two possible segmentation paths of the same start point and ending point.
- The horizontal length of the stroke is greater than $T_{stroke\text{-}length}$, where $T_{stroke\text{-}length}$ is fifth of image width.

- The angle between the stroke and the horizontal line is not greater than ±30.
- There must be at least one hole-segment in both of the left and right part of connected numeral string separated by the two segmentation paths.

Based on the observation, most of the useless strokes have a certain length (the second constraint) and the skew of most useless strokes is between +30 degrees and -30degrees (the third constraint). If the stroke is useless and removed in this stage, the two possible segmentation paths are regarded as a single one (Chen & Jhing-Fa, 2000).

Deciding the Best Segmentation Path

After finding all of the possible segmentation paths, we use the mixture Gaussian probability to decide which one is the best segmentation path or reject it. First, a connected character or numeral string is split into separated parts by a segmentation path. Some geometric parameters adapted from are used to determine mixture Gaussian probability function and are listed as follows:

G1: Ratio between the widths of the two separated parts.
G2: Ratio between the heights of the two separated parts.
G3: Ratio between the counts of black pixels of the two separated parts.
G4, G5: Ratio between the widths to the height of the two separated parts respectively.
G6: Ratio between the horizontal length of any overlap of the two separated parts and the smaller of the widths of the two separated parts.
G7: Normalized horizontal distance between the center of segmentation path and the center of image.
G8: Ratio between the counts of black pixels on the segmentation path and the height of the image.

The eight parameters are collected to give a feature vector of a segmentation path. Then, we pick the best segmentation path from this. Segmenting the Devnagri compound characters using this technique during the preprocessing phase can help in improving the performance of the recognition system.

CONCLUSION

Various techniques are available for segmentation which helps in improvising the accuracy of various recognition systems. The Segmentation technique used for hand written multiple touching characters shall definitely help in improvisation of recognition accuracy. It can also be helpful in dealing with confusing characters. At primary level our implemented system has shown satisfactory results for handwritten Devanagari compound characters, numeric digits as well as English numeric digits and letters when trained and tested separately.

REFERENCES

Almazan, J., Gordo, A., Fornes, A., & Valveny, E. (2014, December). Word Spotting and Recognition with Embedded Attributes. *IEEE Transactions on Pattern Analysis and Machine Intelligence, 36*(12), 2552–2566. doi:10.1109/TPAMI.2014.2339814 PMID:26353157

Bheda, Joshi, & Agrawal. (2014). A Study on Features Extraction Techniques for Image Mosaicing. *International Journal of Innovative Research in Computer and Communication Engineering, 2*(3).

Chen, Y.-K., & Wang, J.-F. (2000, November). Segmentation of Single- or Multiple-Touching Handwritten Numeral String Using Background and Foreground Analysis. *IEEE Transactions on Pattern Analysis and Machine Intelligence, 22*(11).

Cheung, K.-W., Yeung, D.-Y., & Chin, R. T. (2002, August). Bidirectional Deformable Matching with Application to Handwritten Character Extraction. *IEEE Transactions on Pattern Analysis and Machine Intelligence, 24*(8).

Dave, N. (2015). Segmentation Methods for Hand Written Character Recognition, International Journal of Signal Processing. *Image Processing and Pattern Recognition, 8*(4), 155–164. doi:10.14257/ijsip.2015.8.4.14

Dollar, P., & Lawrence Zitnick, C. (2015). Fast Edge Detection Using Structured Forests. *IEEE Transactions on Pattern Analysis and Machine Intelligence, 37*(8), 1558–1570. doi:10.1109/TPAMI.2014.2377715 PMID:26352995

Gonzalez & Woods. (n.d.). *Digital Image Processing* (3rd ed.). Pearson Publication.

Khan (2013). Image Segmentation Techniques: A Survey. *Journal of Image and Graphics, 1*(4).

Marinai, S., Gori, M., & Soda, G. (2005, January). Artificial Neural Networks for Document Analysis and Recognition. *IEEE Transactions on Pattern Analysis and Machine Intelligence, 27*(1), 23–35. doi:10.1109/TPAMI.2005.4 PMID:15628266

Panchal, Panchal, & Shah. (2013). A Comparison of SIFT and SURF. *International Journal of Innovative Research in Computer and Communication Engineering, 1*(2).

Tang, Y. Y., Tu, L.-T., Liu, J., Lee, S.-W., Lin, W.-W., & Shyu, I.-S. (1998, May). Offline Recognition of Chinese Handwriting by Multifeature and Multilevel Classification. *IEEE Transactions on Pattern Analysis and Machine Intelligence, 20*(5).

Zhou, X.-D., Wang, D.-H., Tian, F., & Liu, C.-L. (2013, October). Handwritten Chinese/Japanese Text Recognition Using Semi-Markov Conditional Random Fields. *IEEE Transactions on Pattern Analysis and Machine Intelligence, 35*(10), 2413–2426. doi:10.1109/TPAMI.2013.49 PMID:23969386

Chapter 9
Logo Matching and Recognition Based on Context

Tapan Kumar Das
VIT University, India

ABSTRACT

Logos are graphic productions that recall some real-world objects or emphasize a name, simply display some abstract signs that have strong perceptual appeal. Color may have some relevance to assess the logo identity. Different logos may have a similar layout with slightly different spatial disposition of the graphic elements, localized differences in the orientation, size and shape, or differ by the presence/absence of one or few traits. In this chapter, the author uses ensemble-based framework to choose the best combination of preprocessing methods and candidate extractors. The proposed system has reference logos and test logos which are verified depending on some features like regions, pre-processing, key points. These features are extracted by using gray scale image by scale-invariant feature transform (SIFT) and Affine-SIFT (ASIFT) descriptor method. Pre-processing phase employs four different filters. Key points extraction is carried by SIFT and ASIFT algorithm. Key points are matched to recognize fake logo.

INTRODUCTION

The logo design began in early 1800s. The earliest logos are nothing more than a distinctive mark, symbol or literal brand to mark who the maker of the product. The ancestors of the modern logo were born on early 1900s, and it is during this time that you start to see logos and corporate identities being trademarked for the first time. Present day of logos is simple, flexible, and adaptable to any kind of media and truly built to last for their brand until the next step evolution comes. In the early to mid-2000s counterfeit products became popular in all over countries because of the impact of economic development. Growing over 10,000% in the last two decades, counterfeit products exist in virtually every area, including food, beverages, clothes, shoes, pharmaceuticals, electronics, auto parts, toys, and currency. The spread of counterfeit goods is worldwide, and in 2008 a study by the international chamber of commerce (ICC) estimated the global value of all counterfeit goods reached $650 billion every year, doubling the estimated annual profit made from the sale of illegal drugs worldwide. The same study projected that in 2015 the upper bound of the global value of counterfeit and pirated goods could be $1.77 trillion.

DOI: 10.4018/978-1-5225-5775-3.ch009

Logo Images are now one of the key enables of user's connectivity. When consumers think of counterfeit goods, immediately a notion of fake handbags, fake groceries and fake beauty products comes to mind. However, many citizens do not realize the harmful effects that counterfeit products have on Indian businesses. Others realize that most consumers do not care if the goods they buy are counterfeit and just wish to purchase inexpensive products. Especially in cosmetic products the toxic levels of mercury, lead and arsenic are high, in many of these fake formulations have led to serious illness, severe allergic reactions and long-term health problems. In light of these fake logos users will buy those products because of inexpensive cost and the need of tools to help users control access of buying these products.

Every organizations or companies have their own logos which is a legal symbol for the identification of their products. However, some other organizations or individuals used the duplicate logos that have small variations from the original ones in order to deceive customers. Logos has the essential role to recall in the customer the expectations associated with a particular product or service (Das, Acharjya & Patra, 2014). This economical relevance has motivated the active involvement of companies in soliciting smart image analysis solutions to scan logo archives to find evidence of similar already existing logos, discover either improper or non-authorized use of their logo, unveil the malicious use of logos that have small variations with respect to the originals so to deceive and discovery of an image analysis system in order to reveal the non-authorized used of logos.

RELATED WORK

Early work on logo detection and recognition was concerned with providing some automatic support to the logo registration process. The system must check whether other registered logos in archives of millions, exist that have similar appearance to the new coming logo image, in order to ensure that it is sufficiently distinctive and avoid confusion. Kato's system was among the earliest ones. It mapped a normalized logo image to a 64 pixel grid, and calculated a global feature vector from the frequency distributions of Edge pixels.

A method was proposed by Lowe (2004) for extracting invariant features from images that can be used to perform reliable matching between different views of an object. The recognition was done by matching individual features to a database of features from known objects using a fast nearest-neighbor algorithm (Das & Chowdhury, 2017) which was followed by a hough transform to identify clusters belonging to a single object. In another embodiment, Ballan et al proposed trademark detection and recognition system while advertising trademark in a sports videos (Ballan, Bertini & Jain, 2008). It is a semi-automatic system for detecting and retrieving trade-mark appearances in a sports videos. A human annotator supervises the results of the automatic annotation through an interface that shows the time and the position of the detected trademarks.

Smeulders et al. (2000) discuss about the working conditions of content-based retrieval: patterns of use, types of pictures, the role of semantics, and the sensory gap (Smeulders, Worring, Santini, Gupta & Jain, 2000). Subsequent sections discuss computational steps for image retrieval systems. Step one of the review is image processing for retrieval sorted by color, texture, and local geometry. Features for retrieval are discussed next, sorted by: accumulative and global features, salient points, object and shape features, signs, and structural combinations thereof. Similarity of pictures and objects in pictures is reviewed for each of the feature types, in close connection to the types and means of feedback the user of the systems is capable of giving by interaction (Chandrasekhar & Das, 2011).

Jing and Baluja (2008) studied the image-ranking problem into the task of identifying "authority" nodes on an inferred visual similarity graph and proposes an algorithm to analyze the visual link structure that can be created among a group of images. Through an iterative procedure based on the PageRank computation, a numerical weight is assigned to each image; this measures its relative importance to the other images being considered.

A procedure describing a compact representation of trademarks and video frame content based on SIFT feature points is discussed by Bagdanov, Ballan, Bertini, and Bimbo (2007). Classification of trademarks is performed by matching a set of SIFT feature descriptors for each trademark instance against the set of SIFT features detected in each frame of the video. Localization is performed through robust clustering of matched feature points in the video frame. A key step for the effective use of local image features (i.e., highly distinctive and robust features) for recognition or image matching is the appropriate grouping of feature matches (Carneiro & Jepson, 2004). Spatial constraints are important in this grouping because, during a recognition process, they allow for the reduction of the number of hypotheses that must be verified and also reduce the number of false positives present in each of these hypotheses. A common choice for this grouping task is to use the Hough transform on the global spatial transformation parameters of the hypothesized matches.

A research on scalable logo recognition approach that extends the common bag-of-words model and incorporates local geometry in the indexing process is reported (Kalantidis, Pueyo, Trevisiol, Zwol & Avrithis, 2011). Given a query image and a large logo database, the goal is to recognize the logo contained in the query, if any. Features are grouped in triples using multi-scale delaunay triangulation and represent triangles by signatures capturing both visual appearance and local geometry. A trademark image retrieval (TIR) system is proposed by Wei, Li, Chau and Li (2009) that use Canny edge detector for extraction of edge.

SIFT

The scale invariant feature transform, SIFT (Lowe, 2004), extracts a set of descriptors from an image. The extracted descriptors are invariant to image translation, rotation and scaling. SIFT descriptors have also proved to be robust to a wide family of image transformations, such as slight changes of viewpoint, noise, blur, contrast changes, scene deformation, while remaining discriminative enough for matching purposes. The SIFT algorithm consists of two successive and independent operations: the detection of interesting points (i.e. key points) and the extraction of a descriptor associated to each of them. These descriptors are usually used for matching pairs of images.

SIFT was introduced in 1999 (Lowe, 1999). It set off a series of competitors; SURF (Bay, Tuytelaars & Gool, 2006), MOPS (Brown, Szeliski & Winder 2005), ASIFT(Yu & Morel, 2011) and SFOP (Forstner, Dickscheid & Schindler. 2009). In addition to these, variant methods using binary descriptors; BRISK (Leutenegger, Chli & Siegwart, 2011) and ORB (Rublee, Rabaud, Konolige & Bradski, 2011) are reported.

The algorithm principle (Rey-Otero & Delbracio, 2014).

SIFT detects a series of key points from a multi-scale image representation. This multi-scale representation consists of a family of increasingly blurred images. Each key point is a blob-like structure whose center position (x, y) and characteristic scale σ are accurately located. SIFT computes the dominant orientation θ over a region surrounding each one of these key points. For each key point, the quadruple (x, y, σ, θ) defines the center, size and orientation of a normalized patch where the SIFT descriptor is computed. As a result of this normalization, SIFT key point descriptors are in theory invariant to any translation, rotation and scale change. The algorithm has following steps:

- Compute the Gaussian scale-space
- Compute the Difference of Gaussians (DoG)
- Find candidate key points
- Refine candidate key points location
- Filter unstable key points due to noise
- Filter unstable key points laying on edges
- Assign a reference orientation to each keypoint
- Build the key points descriptor

Following the tremendous popularity of SIFT, researchers proposed variants of SIFT ; PCA-SIFT (Ke & Sukthankar, 2004), CSIFT (Abdel-Hakim & Farag, 2006), GSIFT (Mortensen, Deng & Shapiro, 2005) for better performance. The performance of SIFT and its variants in different situations is studied and the result is presented in Table 1.

The results are rated in the scale of 1 to 4; 1 (common), 2 (good), 3 (better), 4 (best).

PROPOSED SYSTEM

The author presents a novel solution for logo detection and recognition, which is based on the definition of a context- dependent similarity (CDS) that directly incorporates the spatial context of local features (Eakins, Boardman & Graham, 1998). The proposed method has pre-processing steps, which is accomplished by using four filters. Context is considered with respect to each single SIFT and ASIFT key point formally, the CDS function is defined as the fixed points of three terms. This method is not limited to any derivable arrangement model means it is model free. It mainly deals with the spatial context of local features. At first, two logos; reference logo and test logo are considered. Then the logos are resized and matched by considering a list of interest points. SIFT descriptor is used for matching purpose (Mortensen, Dengand & Shapiro, 2005). Each single SIFT key point represented as context. Finally average precision is computed. This context criterion considers pair of interest points of reference and test logos with high alignment score. The limitation of existing system is it can't give accuracy result in blur images so that

Table 1. Performance of SIFT and its variants

Algorithm	Scale and Rotation	Blur	Illumination	Affine	Time Cost
SIFT	4	2	3	2	3
ASIFT	2	1	1	4	1
PCA-SIFT	3	3	3	2	3
GSIFT	2	4	4	2	3
CSIFT	4	3	2	3	2

Wu, Cui, Sheng, Zhao, Su & Gong, 2013.

partial logos cannot be detected as fake or original. To overcome this drawback, the author move on to advanced context dependent similarity algorithm which includes all the steps in the existing algorithm with additional pre-processing matching module which is used to detect the partial logo.

Let SX, SY be respectively the list of key points taken from a reference logo and a test image (the value of n, m may vary with SX, SY). We borrow the definition of context and similarity design in order to introduce a new matching procedure applied to logo detection. High level architecture of proposed SIFT and ASIFT method is represented in Figure 1.

SYSTEM ARCHITECTURE

The detailed architecture of the proposed system is shown in Figure 2.

The detailed process from a customer perspective is shown in Figure 3.

METHODOLOGY

The experiment consists of the following five steps:

Step 1: Pre-Processing

The advanced context dependent similarity algorithm is matching the reference and test image logo with the adjacency matrices. The output from this matrix model is subjected to the preprocessing module which will detect the partial logo. Under this process the author has added four filters. They are median filter, average filter, Gaussian filter, Wiener filter. Input images are reference and test logo images and the output is gray scale images.

Figure 1. High level architecture

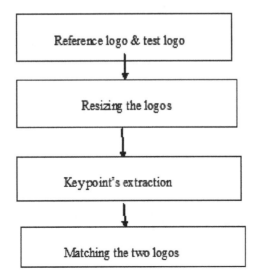

Figure 2. Detailed architecture

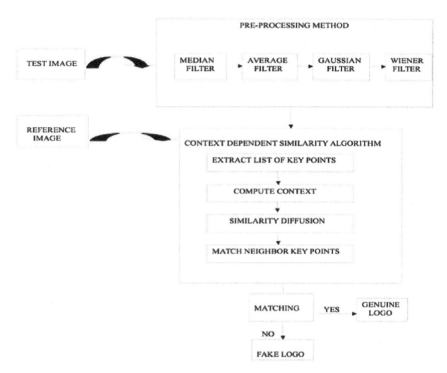

Figure 3. Retailers process

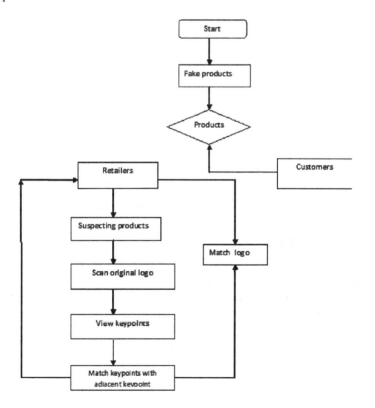

Median Filter

The median filter is a nonlinear digital filtering technique, often used to remove noise. Such noise reduction is a typical pre-processing step to improve the results of later processing (for example, edge detection on an image). Median filtering is very widely used in digital image processing because, under certain conditions, it preserves edges while removing noise.

Average Filter

Mean filter, or average filter is filter of linear class, that soothes signal (image). The filter works as low-pass one. The basic idea behind filter is for any element of the signal (image) take an average across its neighborhood. To understand how that is made in practice.

Gaussian Filter

Gaussian filters have the properties of having no overshoot to a step function input while minimizing the rise and fall time. This behavior is closely connected to the fact that the Gaussian filter has the minimum possible group delay. It is considered the ideal time domain filter, the ideal frequency domain filter. These properties are important in areas such as oscilloscopes and digital telecommunication systems. Mathematically, a Gaussian filter modifies the input signal by convolution with a Gaussian function.

Wiener Filter

The Wiener filter is a filter used to produce an estimate of a desired or target random process by linear time-invariant filtering of an observed noisy process, assuming known stationary signal and noise spectra, and additive noise. The Wiener filter minimizes the mean square error between the estimated random process and the desired process.

Step 2: Key Points Extraction

Interest point detection is a recent terminology in computer vision that refers to the detection of interest points for subsequent processing. An interest point is a point in the image it has a well-defined position in image space (Bay, Ess, Tuytelaars & Gool, 2008). The interest points are extracted using histogram method. Input images are reference and test logo images and the output is key point's extracted images.

Step 3: Context Computation

The context is defined by the local spatial configuration of interest points. Context is used to find interest point correspondences between two images in order to tackle logo detection. Input image is interest point's extracted images and output is extraction of context.

Step 4: Similarity Diffusion Process

Resulting from the definition of context, similarity between interest points is recursively detected. The adjacency matrices related to a reference logo and a test image logo is formed respectively, each of which collects the values of the logo. Input is context image and the output is extraction of similarity between the reference and test image.

Step 5: Matching Process

The final stage of advance context dependent similarity algorithm is matching the reference and test image logo with the adjacency key points with matching key points and it show whether it is fake or original.

Context -Dependent Similarity Algorithm

Context

The context is defined by the local spatial configuration of interest points in both SX and SY. Formally, in order to take into account spatial information, an interest point $x_i \in SX$ is defined as:

$$x_i = \left(\psi_g(x_i), \psi_f(x_i), \psi_o(x_i), \psi_s(x_i), w(x_i) \right)$$

where the symbol $\psi_g(x_i) \in R2$ stands for the 2D coordinates of x_i while $\psi f(x_i) \in Rc$ corresponds to the feature of x_i .

Let

$$d(x_i, y_j) = \left\| \psi f(x_i) - \psi f(y_j) \right\|^2$$

measure the dissimilarity between two interest point features. The context of x_i is defined as in the following:

$$N^{\theta,\rho}(x_i) = \left\{ x_j : w(x_j) = w(x_i), x_j \neq x_i \right\}$$

such that following two equations hold

$$\frac{\rho - 1}{N_r} \in_p \le \left\| \psi_g(x_i) - \psi_g(x_j) \right\|_2 \le \frac{\rho}{N_r} \in_p$$

$$\frac{\theta - 1}{N_\alpha} \pi \le \angle \left(\psi_0(x_i), \psi_g(x_j) - \psi_g(x_i) \right) \le \frac{\theta}{N_\alpha} \pi$$

where $\left(\psi_g(x_j) - \psi_g(x_i) \right)$ is the vector between the two point coordinates $\psi_g(x_j)$ and $\psi_g(x_i)$.

Similarity Design

We define k as a function which, given two interest points $(x, y) \in SX \times SY$, provides a similarity measure between them. For a finite collection of interest points, the sets *SX, SY* are finite. Provided that we put some (arbitrary) order on *SX, SY*, we can view function k as a matrix K, let

$$D(x, y) = d(x, y) = \|\psi f(x) - \psi f(y)\|_2$$

Using this notation, the similarity K between the two objects *SX, SY* is obtained by solving the following minimization problem:

$$\min_K Tr(KD') + \beta Tr(K \log K') - \alpha \Sigma_{\theta,\rho} Tr(KQ_{\theta,\rho}K'P'_{\theta,\rho})$$

such that $K \geq 0$ and $\|K\|_1 = 1$.

Here $\alpha, \beta \geq 0$ and the operations log (natural), $\geq$ are applied individually to every entry of the matrix.

Solution

Let's consider the adjacency matrices $\left\{ (P_{\theta,\rho})_{\theta,\rho}, (Q_{\theta,\rho})_{\theta,\rho} \right\}$ related to a reference logo *SX* and a test image *SY* respectively:

$$\xi = \frac{\alpha}{\beta} \sum_{\theta,\rho} \left\| P_{\theta,\rho} u Q'_{\theta,\rho} + P'_{\theta,\rho} u Q_{\theta,\rho} \right\|_\infty$$

where $\|,\|_\infty \cdot_\infty$ is the entry wise L_∞ norm.

Algorithm:

Input: Reference logo image: I_x, Test image: I_y, CDS parameters: *Na, Nr, α, β, τ.*
Output: A Boolean value determining whether the reference logo in I_x is detected in I_y.

Extract SIFT from I_x, I_y and let $S_x := \{x_1 \ldots x_n\}$, $S_y := \{y_1, \ldots, y_m\}$ be respectively the list of interest points taken from both images;

```
for i=1:n
        Compute the context of xi, given Na, Nr;
end
for j =1: m
        Compute the context of y j, given Na, Nr;
end
 t =1, max =30;
```

```
if (convergence == 0 || t>max)
        for i=1:n
                for j=1:m
                Compute CDS matrix entry K(t)xi, y j, given α, β;
                end
        end
end
K = K(t);
for i=1:n
        for j =1:m
        Kyⱼ|xᵢ = Kxᵢ,yⱼ / sum of (for s=1:m   compute Kxᵢ,yₛ);
        if (Kyⱼ|xᵢ >= sum of (for s~=j:m compute Kyₛ|xᵢ)
        A match between xᵢ and yⱼ is declared.
        end
end
if number of matches in Sᵧ > τ|Sₓ |
return true;                      // logo detection
else
return false;
end
```

RESULTS AND DISCUSSION

Ensemble-based framework to improve micro aneurysm detection. Unlike the well-known approach of considering the output of multiple classifiers, we propose a combination of internal components of micro aneurysm detectors, namely pre-processing methods and candidate extractors. We have evaluated our approach for micro aneurysm detection in an online competition. The central aim is to implement optimal combination of preprocessing and candidate extractor method.

Subsequently, four different filters are employed in preprocessing phase.

The values of mean square error and peak signal-to-noise ratio of all the filters used are being represented in Table 1. It is clear that Weiner filter has high PSNR value.

The numerical value of the result of matching by SIFT and ASIFT procedure are represented in Table 2. It is imperative from the result that ASIFT has a slightly edge over SIFT.

Subsequently, the system is being tested for other two logos (Levis and CocaCola). The test result is being represented in Table 3 and Table 4 respectively.

Table 2. Values of filters

Filters	Median	Average	Gaussian	Weiner
MSE	6.0216e-04	0.0044	4.235e-04	1.7843e-04
PSNR	80.333	71.697	81.217	83.125

Table 3. Starbucks logo

Algorithm	Key Point for Matching Reference Image	Key Point Matching for Test Image	Time Taken	Matching Percentage	Matches Identified
SIFT	1975	1966	2 seconds	1.5%	31
ASIFT	3841	4123	2 seconds	1.9%	783

Table 4. Levi's logo

Algorithm	Key Point for Matching Reference Image	Key Point Matching for Test Image	Time Taken	Matching Percentage	Matches Identified
SIFT	1300	613	0 seconds	10%	65
ASIFT	2253	3024	0 seconds	6%	175

Table 5. Coca Cola logo

Algorithm	Key Point for Matching Reference Image	Key Point Matching for Test Image	Time Taken	Matching Percentage	Matches Identified
SIFT	854	887	0 seconds	9%	82
ASIFT	7825	8031	0 seconds	28%	2307

CONCLUSION

This chapter elucidates a novel logo detection and localization approach based on similarities which is referred as context dependent. The merit of the method settles in several aspects: (1) the inclusion of the information about the spatial configuration in similarity design as well as visual features; (2) the ability to control the influence of the context and the regularization of the solution via our energy function; (3) the tolerance to different aspects including partial occlusion, makes it suitable to detect both near-duplicate logos as well as logos with some variability in their appearance, and; (4) the theoretical soundness of the matching framework which shows that under the hypothesis of existence of a reference logo into a test image, the probability of success of matching and detection is high. In extension of this work, real time logos as test image for matching and recognition process can be included. Furthermore, the application of this method can be extended to logo retrieval in videos.

REFERENCES

Abdel-Hakim, A. E., & Farag, A. A. (2006). CSIFT: A SIFT Descriptor with Color Invariant Characteristics. *Proceedings - IEEE Computer Society Conference on Computer Vision and Pattern Recognition, 2,* 1978–1983.

Bagdanov, A. D., Ballan, L., Bertini, M., & Bimbo, A. D. (2007). Trademark matching and retrieval in sports video databases. *Proc. ACM Int. Workshop Multimedia Inf. Retr.*, 79–86. 10.1145/1290082.1290096

Ballan, L., Bertini, M., & Jain, A. (2008). A system for automatic detection and recognition of advertising trademarks in sports videos. *Proc. ACM Multimedia*, 991–992. 10.1145/1459359.1459544

Bay, H., Tuytelaars, T., & Gool, L. V. (2006). SURF: Speeded Up Robust Features, *Proceedings of European Conference on Computer Vision*, 404-417.

Bay, H., Ess, A., Tuytelaars, T., & Gool, L. V. (2008). Speeded-up robust features (SURF). *Computer Vision and Image Understanding*, *110*(3), 346–359. doi:10.1016/j.cviu.2007.09.014

Brown, M., Szeliski, R., & Winder, S. (2005). Multi-image matching using multi-scale oriented patches. *Proceedings of IEEE Conference on Computer Vision and Pattern Recognition*.

Carneiro, G., & Jepson, A. (2004). Flexible spatial models for grouping local image features. *Proc. Conf. Comput. Vis. Pattern Recognit.*, 2, 747–754. 10.1109/CVPR.2004.1315239

Chandrasekhar, U., & Das, T.K. (2011). A Survey of Techniques for Background Subtraction and Traffic Analysis on Surveillance Video. *Universal Journal of Applied Computer Science and Technology*, *1*(3), 107-113.

Das, T. K., & Chowdhury, C. L. (2017). Implementation of Morphological Image Processing Algorithm using Mammograms. *Journal of Chemical and Pharmaceutical Sciences*, *10*(1), 439–441.

Das, T. K., Acharjya, D. P., & Patra, M. R. (2014). Business Intelligence from Online Product Review - A Rough Set Based Rule Induction Approach. Proceedings of International Conference on Contemporary Computing and Informatics (IC3I- 2014), 800-803.

Eakins, J. P., Boardman, J. M., & Graham, M. E. (1998). Similarity retrieval of trademark images. *IEEE MultiMedia*, *5*(2), 53–63.

Forstner, W., Dickscheid, T., & Schindler, F. (2009). Detecting interpretable and accurate scale-invariant keypoints. *Proceedings of IEEE 12th International Conference on Computer Vision*, 2256-2263.

Jing, Y., & Baluja, S. (2008). Pagerank for product image search. *Proc. WWW*, 307–316.

Kalantidis, Y., Pueyo, L. G., Trevisiol, M., Zwol, R. V., & Avrithis, Y. (2011). Scalable Triangulation-based Logo Recognition. *Proceedings of the 1st International Conference on Multimedia Retrieval*, 20:1-20:7.

Kayaken. (2017). *Simple Taylor Swift Red Wallpaper Hd Burger King and Starbucks Join forces Against Mcdonald S*. Retrieved from: http://big5kayakchallenge.com/taylor-swift-red-wallpaper-hd/simple-taylor-swift-red-wallpaper-hd-burger-king-and-starbucks-join-forces-against-mcdonald-s/

Ke, Y., & Sukthankar, R. (2004). PCA-SIFT: A More Distinctive Representation for Local Image Descriptors. Computer Vision and Pattern Recognition (CVPR-2004), 2, 506-513.

Leutcncgger, S., Chli, M., & Siegwart, R. Y. (2011). BRISK: Binary Robust Invariant Scalable Keypoints. *Proceedings of IEEE International Conference on Computer Vision*, 2548-2555.

Lowe, D. G. (1999). Object recognition from local scale-invariant features. *Proceedings of Seventh IEEE International Conference on Computer Vision*, 2, 1150-1157. 10.1109/ICCV.1999.790410

Lowe, D. G. (2004). Distinctive image features from scale-invariant keypoints. *International Journal of Computer Vision*, *60*(2), 91–110. doi:10.1023/B:VISI.0000029664.99615.94

Mortensen, E. N., Deng, H., & Shapiro, L. (2005). A SIFT descriptor with global context. *Proceedings of IEEE Computer Society Conference on Computer Vision and Pattern Recognition (CVPR 2005)*, 1, 184-190. 10.1109/CVPR.2005.45

Rey-Otero, I., & Delbracio, M. (2014). Anatomy of the SIFT Method, *Image Processing. Online (Bergheim)*, *4*, 370–396.

Rublee, E., Rabaud, V., Konolige, K., & Bradski, G. (2011). ORB: An efficient alternative to SIFT or SURF. *Proceedings of IEEE International Conference on Computer Vision*, 2564–2571.

Smeulders, A., Worring, M., Santini, S., Gupta, A., & Jain, R. (2000). Content based image retrieval at the end of the early years. *IEEE Transactions on Pattern Analysis and Machine Intelligence*, *22*(12), 1349–1380. doi:10.1109/34.895972

Wei, C. H., Li, Y., Chau, W. U., & Li, C. T. (2009). Trademark image retrieval using synthetic features for describing global shape and interior structure. *Pattern Recognition*, *42*(3), 386–394. doi:10.1016/j.patcog.2008.08.019

Wu, J., Cui, Z., Sheng, V. S., Zhao, P., Su, D., & Gong, S. (2013). A Comparative Study of SIFT and its Variants. *Measurement Science Review*, *13*(3), 122–131. doi:10.2478/msr-2013-0021

Yu, G., & Morel, J.-M. (2011). ASIFT: An Algorithm for Fully Affine Invariant Comparison, *Image Processing. Online (Bergheim)*, *1*, 11–38.

Chapter 10
Detecting and Tracking Segmentation of Moving Objects Using Graph Cut Algorithm

Raviraj Pandian
GSSS Institute of Engineering and Technology for Women, India

Ramya A.
KalaignarKarunanidhi Institute of Technology, India

ABSTRACT

Real-time moving object detection, classification, and tracking capabilities are presented with system operates on both color and gray-scale video imagery from a stationary camera. It can handle object detection in indoor and outdoor environments and under changing illumination conditions. Object detection in a video is usually performed by object detectors or background subtraction techniques. The proposed method determines the threshold automatically and dynamically depending on the intensities of the pixels in the current frame. In this method, it updates the background model with learning rate depending on the differences of the pixels in the background model of the previous frame. The graph cut segmentation-based region merging algorithm approaches achieve both segmentation and optical flow computation accurately and they can work in the presence of large camera motion. The algorithm makes use of the shape of the detected objects and temporal tracking results to successfully categorize objects into pre-defined classes like human, human group, and vehicle.

INTRODUCTION

Automated video analysis is important for many vision applications, such as surveillance, traffic monitoring, augmented reality, vehicle navigation, etc. (Yilmaz, Javed, & Shah, 2006; Moeslund, Hilton, & Kruger, 2006). As pointed out in (Yilmaz, Javed, & Shah, 2006), there are three key steps for automated video analysis: object detection, object tracking, and behavior recognition. As the first step, object detec-

DOI: 10.4018/978-1-5225-5775-3.ch010

tion aims to locate and segment interesting objects in a video. Then, such objects can be tracked from frame to frame, and the tracks can be analyzed to recognize object behavior. Thus, object detection plays a critical role in practical applications.

Object detection is usually achieved by object detectors or background subtraction (Yilmaz, Javed, & Shah, 2006). An object detector is often a classifier that scans the image by a sliding window and labels each sub image defined by the window as either object or background. Generally, the classifier is built by offline learning on separate datasets (Papageorgiou, Oren, & Poggio, 1998; Viola, Jones, & Snow, 2005) or by online learning initialized with a manually labeled frame at the start of a video (Grabner & Bischof, 2006; Babenko, Yang, & Belongie, 2011). Alternatively, background subtraction (Piccardi, 2004) compares images with a background model and detects the changes as objects. It usually assumes that no object appears in images when building the background model (Toyama, Krumm, Brumitt, & Meyers, 1999; Moeslund, Hilton, & Kruger, 2006). Such requirements of training examples for object or background modeling actually limit the applicability of above-mentioned methods in automated video analysis.

Another category of object detection methods that can avoid training phases are motion-based methods (Yilmaz, Javed, & Shah, 2006; Moeslund, Hilton, & Kruger, 2006), which only use motion information to separate objects from the background. The problem can be rephrased as follows: Given a sequence of images in which foreground objects are present and moving differently from the background, can we separate the objects from the background automatically? Figure 1(a) shows a walking lady is always present and recorded by a handheld camera. Figure 1(b) shows such an example, where the surveillance video at the airport. The goal is to take the image sequence as input and directly output a mask sequence of the walking lady. The example is consolidated in Figure 1.

The most natural way for motion-based object detection is to classify pixels according to motion patterns, which is usually named motion segmentation (Vidal & Ma, 2004; Cremers & Soatto, 2005; Tsai, Yang, & Black, 2016). These approaches achieve both segmentation and optical flow computation accurately and they can work in the presence of large camera motion. However, they assume rigid motion (Vidal & Ma, 2004) or smooth motion (Vidal & Ma, 2004) (Jiang, & Song, 2016) in respective regions, which is not generally true in practice. In practice, the foreground motion can be very complicated with non-rigid shape changes. Also, the background may be complex, including illumination changes and varying textures such as waving trees and sea waves. Figure 1 shows such a challenging example. The video includes an operating escalator, but it should be regarded as background for human tracking purpose. An alternative motion-based approach is background estimation (Gutchess, Trajkovics, Cohen-Solal, Lyons, & Jain, 2001; Nair & Clark, 2004). Different from background subtraction, it estimates a background model directly from the testing sequence. Generally, it tries to seek temporal intervals inside which the pixel intensity is unchanged and uses image data from such intervals for background estimation. However, this approach also relies on the assumption of static background. Hence, it is difficult to handle the scenarios with complex background or moving cameras. The algorithm for moving object detection which falls into the category of motion based methods. It solves the challenges mentioned above in a unified framework named Detecting Contiguous Outliers in the LOw-rank Representation (DECOLOR). It assumes that the underlying background images are linearly correlated. Thus, the matrix composed of vectorized video frames can be approximated by a low-rank matrix, and the moving objects can be detected as outliers in this low-rank representation.

In the previous study (Ramya, & Raviraj, 2013; Ramya, & Raviraj, 2014), the authors have performed an incremental literature review and analysis to understand the cause of the variations in moving object

Figure 1. (a) A sequence of 40 frames, where a walking lady is recorded by a handheld camera. From left to right are the first, 20th, and 40th frames. (b) A sequence of 48 frames clipped from a surveillance video at the airport.

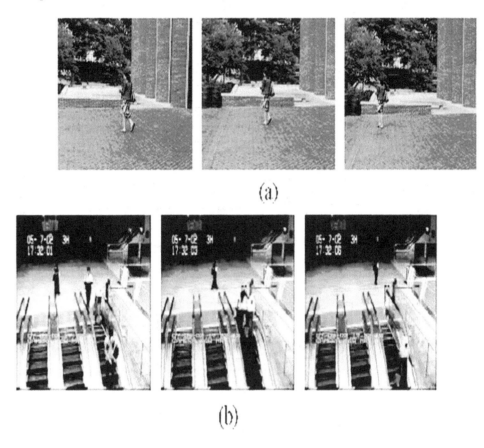

detection and segmentation techniques. The proposed research efforts are mainly focused on video analysis at the object level, i.e., object detection and segmentation.

ARCHITECTURE DESIGN OF THE PROPOSED METHODOLOGY

The architecture design of the proposed idea is given in the Figure 2.

The proposed work has been explained as below with the inclusion of different modules such as Region Merging Object Detection Approach, Graph Cut Algorithm, Moving Background Detection, Graph Cut Region Merging Motion Segmentation, Region Merging.

Region Merging Object Detection Approach

Distinguishing foreground objects from the stationary background is both a significant and difficult research problem. Almost the visual surveillance systems' entire first step is detecting foreground objects. This both creates a focus of attention for higher processing levels such as tracking, classification

Figure 2. Architecture design of proposed work

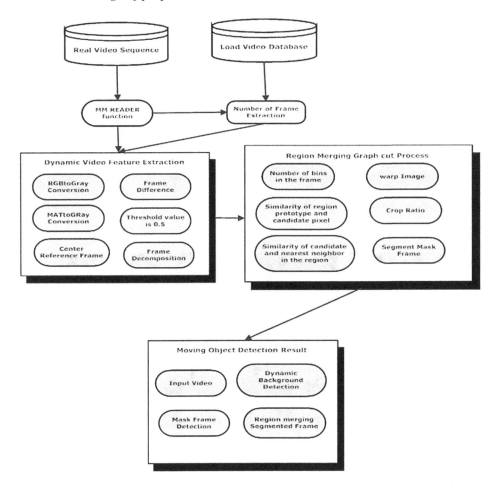

and behavior understanding and reduces computation time considerably since only pixels belonging to foreground objects need to be dealt with. Short and long term dynamic scene changes such as repetitive motions (e. g. waiving tree leaves), light reflectance, shadows, camera noise and sudden illumination variations make reliable and fast object detection difficult. Hence, it is important to pay necessary attention to object detection step to have reliable, robust and fast visual surveillance system. Our method depends on a six stage process to extract objects with their features in video imagery.

The first step is the background scene initialization. There are various techniques used to model the background scene in the literature. In order to evaluate the quality of different background scene models for object detection and to compare run-time performance, we implemented three of these models which are adaptive background subtraction, temporal frame differencing and adaptive online Gaussian mixture model. The background scene related parts of the system is isolated and its coupling with other modules is kept minimum to let the whole detection system to work flexibly with any one of the background models.

Temporal differencing makes use of the pixel-wise difference between two or three consecutive frames in video imagery to extract moving regions. It is a highly adaptive approach to dynamic scene changes; however, it fails in extracting all relevant pixels of a foreground object especially when the object has uniform texture or moves slowly. When a foreground object stops moving, temporal differencing method fails in detecting a change between consecutive frames and loses the object. Special supportive algorithms are required to detect stopped objects.

Graph Cut Algorithm

Graph Cut looks for a set of optimum segment boundary lines that separate interior and exterior markers. In a Graph Cut algorithm the image is treated as a graph with a set of vertices and edges. In the graph structure, vertices correspond to image pixels and edges represent the links between vertices in four directions. The objective is to minimize a function (energy function) who is modeling the boundary of the object.

When the camera is in a static position and the scene in the video does not almost change it is common to use a background subtraction algorithm where the background is modeled using probabilistic methods. When the camera moves freely these kinds of methods do not have good performance. It is proposed a block based iterative appearance modeling technique that uses temporal model propagation and spatial model composition. The algorithm also employs Graph Cut to generate the final segmentation mask where the inputs of Graph Cut are the likelihood maps from the temporal and spatial models. The algorithm is implemented in real time and the camera moves freely. Precision, recall and f-measure results demonstrate the good performance of the algorithm. A temporal propagation model is also used. It presents an interactive approach where a video cutout1 system automatically propagates the segmentation results frame by frame based on the optical flow. In the final phase a Region merging algorithm is implemented to refine the propagated segmentation results.

A dynamic object segmentation algorithm using a combination of a background subtraction model (bgs) and a matting algorithm. Initially, the dynamic object is detected with the bgs model; next, a heuristic algorithm defines the pixels seeds localization of background, foreground and unknown regions (unknown regions is the limit between the background and foreground where is not clear where one region ends and the other begins). Then, an energy minimization algorithm is implemented to identify the improved foreground region. The complete algorithm achieves a speed of 5 fps at the resolution of 320x240 pixels.

This model takes the binary mask of the initial frame as an opacity map and propagates this information to the current frame by minimizing a cost function. The algorithm was tested in a variety of video sequences and compared with probability maps generated by precision Estimation, Weighted Kernel Density Estimation, and Local Classifiers showing improvements with respect to these methods. Results demonstrate that this method can handle abrupt illumination changes.

Image segmentation can be broadly classified into two types:

1. Local segmentation
2. Global segmentation

Global segmentation is concerned with segmenting a whole image. Global segmentation deals mostly with segments consisting of relatively large number of pixels. This makes estimated parameter values for global segments most robust. Image segmentation can be approach from three different philosophical perspectives. They are as region approach, boundary approach and edge approach as illustrated in Figure 3.

Figure 3. Image segmentation approach

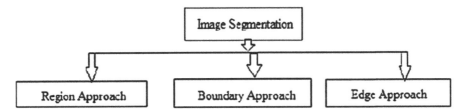

If the pixel belongs to object, it has value one, otherwise it is zero. Segmentation is the operating at the threshold between low-level image processing and image analysis. After the complete procedure of segmentation, the pixel belongs to the object.

Moving Background Detection

The video training frames must be repeated for each scene where the algorithms are deployed, but training information may not always available, and the background parameters may need to be continuously updated if the scene is dynamic. For instance, it is often assumed that the foreground moves in a consistent direction (temporal persistence), with faster appearance changes than the background. Such assumptions are not always valid, and are particularly questionable when there is ego motion (e.g. a camera that tracks a moving object). To address these limitations, we propose a novel paradigm for background subtraction. This paradigm is inspired by biological vision, where background subtraction is inherent to the task of deploying visual attention. This can be done in multiple ways but frequently relies on motion saliency mechanisms, which identify regions of the visual field where objects move differently from the background. The dynamic background subtraction is formulated as the complement of saliency detection algorithm.

The major contributions of this module is,

- To calculate center frame in the video frame sequences.
- To find the similarity value of the each frame is with help of center frame.
- To set wrapping threshold value is 0.5.

Graph Cut Region Merging Motion Segmentation

A robust and novel approach to automatically extract a set of projective transformations induced by these frame regions, detect the occlusion pixels over multiple consecutive frames, and segment the scene into several motion layers. First, after determining a number of seed regions using correspondences in two frames, to expand the seed regions and reject the outliers employing the graph cuts region merging method integrated with salient motion representation. Next, these initial regions are merged into several initial layers according to the motion similarity. Third, an occlusion order constraint on multiple frames is explored, which enforces that the occlusion area increases with the temporal order in a short period and effectively maintains segmentation consistency over multiple consecutive frames.

Split and merge technique is the opposite of the region growing. This technique works on the whole image. Region splitting is a top-down approach. It begins with a whole image and divides it up such that the segregated parts are more homogenous than the whole. Splitting alone is insufficient for reasonable segmentation as it severely limits the shapes of segments. Hence, a merging phase after the splitting is always desirable, which is termed as the split-and-merge algorithm. Any region can be split into sub regions, and the appropriate regions can be merged into a region. Rather than choosing seed points, user can divide an image into a set of arbitrary unconnected regions and then merge the regions in an attempt to satisfy the conditions of reasonable image segmentation. Region splitting and merging is usually implemented with theory based on quad tree data.

Region Merging

A region merging process, based on graph-cuts that takes into account dissimilarities between regions. Many energy functions are related to measures on regions, for instance, length of the region boundaries, histograms, areas, volumes, etc. The aim of this section is to define arc capacities of the adjacency graph so that a cut merges regions of similar characteristics. In this section we will consider the gray levels of an image and the watershed transform of its gradient image. An object/background masking, it is still a challenging problem to extract accurately the object contour from the background because only a small portion of the object/background features are indicated by the user. Object and background provide some key features of object and background, respectively. Similar to graph cut and marker based watershed, where the mask is the seed and starting point of the algorithm, the proposed region merging method also starts from the initial mask regions and all the non-mask regions will be gradually labeled as either object region or background region. The lazy snapping cutout method proposed, which combines graph cut with watershed based initial segmentation, is actually a region merging method. It is controlled by a max-flow algorithm. We present an adaptive similarity based region merging mechanism to identify all the non-mask regions under the guidance of object and background region.

The mask regions cover only a small part of the object and back- ground. Those object regions that are not marked by the user. Since they are from the same object, the non- mask object regions will usually have higher similarity with the mask object regions than the background regions. Therefore, in the automatic region merging process, the non-marker object regions will have high probabilities to be identified as object.

SOFTWARE OVERVIEW

Matlab is software which is user friendly and allows even the fresher to understand the software efficiently. It is very flexible. It can be used in various fields such as digital image processing, digital signal processing, medical fields, mathematical operations, simulations, system designing etc…

The main advantages of choosing this software is that it is user friendly, simple codes, easy to design, platform independent, predefined functions, easy to plot etc…

MATLAB

MATLAB desktop is the main window which contains five sub windows: the command window, the workspace browser, the current directory window, the command history window, and figure window.

Command Window: Is where the user types MATLAB commands and expressions at the prompt (>>) and where the outputs of those command are displayed.

- **Workspace Browser:** Shows the variables and some information about it.
- **Current Directory:** The current directory tab above the workspace tab shows the contents of the current directory window, whose path is shown in the current directory.
- **Command History Window:** Contains the record of the command a user has entered in command window, including both current and previous.

ALGORITHMATIC IMPLEMENTATION OF THE PROPOSED IDEA

The proposed idea has been implemented as per the flowchart given below. The algorithm of the same has been explained as follows.

Figure 4. Implementation procedure of the proposed idea

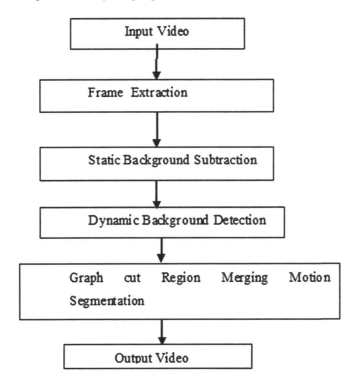

Input Design

As the proposed work is concentrated fully matching the template over the input image which are considered for the Gray scale image processing so that the input parameters are considered.

Gray Scale Image

A grayscale (or gray level) image is nothing bust the colors are only the shades of gray. The reason for differentiating such images from any other sort of color image is that less information is required for each pixel. In fact a 'gray' color is one in which the red, green and blue components all have equal intensity in RGB space, and so that it is only necessary to specify a single intensity value for each pixel, as opposed to the three intensities needed to specify each pixel in a full color image.

Often, the grayscale intensity is stored as an 8-bit integer giving 256 possible different shades of gray from black to white. If the levels are evenly spaced then the difference between successive gray levels is significantly better than the gray level resolving power of the human eye.

Algorithm for Frame Extraction

The frame feature extraction algorithm design as follows:

Step 1: The mmreader () function supports more number of video format if go for avireader() it allows only avi files.

Step 2: The cdata argument contains the read the actual image information from the video file.

Step 3: Using imwrite () we are actually writing the image on the hard disk. Image name=strcat (int2str (i), '.jpeg'); Here I'm appending the i.jpg ex: 2.jpg if you want to have in the other formats you can simply write .bmp or .jpg or .png instead of jpeg in the above file.

Step 4: Source (:,:,:,i); written the video frames.

Algorithm for Static Background Subtraction

Step 1: Read colored or grayscale video file in matlab using mmreader function.

Step 2: Extract frames in some structure (i.e., color or grayscale and reshape the frame array with same dimensions).

Step 3: Convert frames to grayscale using rgb2gray matlab function.

Step 4: Calculate the difference between the current frame and reference frame.

Step 5: Estimate the background for time t.

Step 6: Subtract the estimated background from the input frame.

Step 7: Apply the threshold value to get the absolute difference to get the foreground mask.

Step 8: Frame difference | framei – framei-1| > Threshold.

Step 9: If the threshold value is greater than the frame difference then foreground part is marked as "1"else background part is "0".

Algorithm for Dynamic Background Detection

Step 1: Convert input video using mmreader function.
Step 2: Calculate the number of frames in the given input video.
Step 3: Get the center frame as reference frame.
Step 4: Calculate the similarity function of number of frames with reference frame.
Step 5: Convert frame as MATtoGRAY function.
Step 6: Get the Frame decomposition with help svd function.
Step 7: Get the Background part in the input video.

Algorithm for Graph Cut Region Merging Motion Segmentation

Step 1: Select seed pixels within the image;
Step 2: From each seed pixel grow a region:
Step 3: Set the region prototype to be seed pixel;
Step 4: Calculate the similarity between the region prototype and the candidate pixel;
Step 5: Calculate the similarity between the candidate and its nearest neighbor in the region;
Step 6: Include the candidate pixel if both similarity measures are higher than experiment all set thresholds;
Step 7: Update the region prototype by calculating the new principal component;
Step 8: Go to the next pixel to be examined.

Output Design

Output design generally refers to the results and information that are generated by the system. This system shows the result for the users to view the output in an efficient manner.

EXPERIMENTAL RESULTS

The performance of the proposed video segmentation algorithm is tested with many video sequences. Both the Precision and Recall and F-Measure quality evaluations are applied on our algorithm. For quantitative evaluation, we measure the accuracy of outlier detection by comparing a foreground occlusion with support S_0 with S_1 energy. We regard it as a classification problem and evaluate the results using precision and recall, which are defined as:

$$precision = \frac{TP}{TP + FP} \tag{1}$$

$$recall = \frac{TP}{TP + FN} \tag{2}$$

where TP, FP, TN, and FN mean the numbers of true positives, false positives, true negatives, and false negatives, respectively. Precision and recall are widely used when the class distribution is skewed. A quantitative evaluation of using the sequences from the Berkeley Motion Segmentation Dataset and Real sequence is shown in Table 1.

The higher the F-measure is, the better the detection accuracy is. A quantitative evaluation of F Measure is given in Table 2.

Quatitative evaluation of F-Measure is given in Figure 5.

Few Experimental Screen Shots

Some experimental screenshots are provided in Figure 6, Figure 7, Figure 8, Figure 9 and Figure 10 respectively.

CONCLUSION AND FUTURE WORK

A new algorithm has been proposed that segments foreground objects from dynamic moving backgrounds. To achieve this, robust region merging Graph cut algorithm is derived. The experiments showed that the algorithm can successfully segment the foreground objects, even if they share a similar grayscale distribution with the background. Furthermore, segmentation results could be further improved via the customary post-processing via morphological operations on the foreground mask.

Table 1. Quantitative evaluation using the sequences from the Berkeley motion segmentation dataset and real sequence

Sequence	Proposed		DECOLOR (DEtecting Contiguous Outliers in the LOw-rank Representation)		GRASTA (Grassmannian Robust Adaptive Subspace Tracking Algorithm	
	Precision	**Recall**	**Precision**	**Recall**	**Pecision**	**Recall**
People_1.avi	94.3%	94.8%	93.6%	93.3%	92.1%	92.7%
People_1.avi	95.2%	98.3%	92.5%	96.5%	90.4%	91%
MOV02049.avi	86.2%	89.9%	83.7%	85.1%	82.3%	83.1%
MOV02048.avi	80.75	88.3%	72.6%	88.4%	70%	78.6%

Table 2. Quantitative evaluation (F-measure) on the sequences

Sequence	Proposed Algorithm	DECOLOR	GRASTA
People_1.avi	0.95	0.93	0.92
People_1.avi	0.91	0.82	0.79
MOV02049.avi	0.88	0.81	0.73
MOV02048.avi	0.82	0.83	0.77

Figure 5. Quantitative evaluation (F-measure)

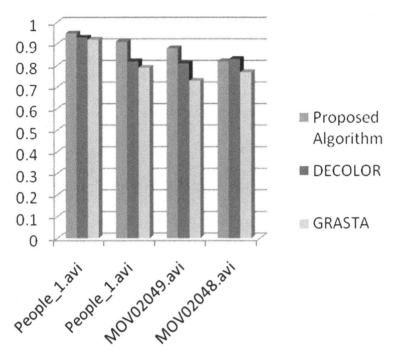

Figure 6. Input video file

Figure 7. Frame extraction

Figure 8. Static background difference frame

A technique is used to detect and segment moving objects in complex dynamic scenes shot by possibly moving cameras. The proposed idea only works on a sub grid of pixels, and do not model the background. Moreover, this method is not computationally and memory expensive. The use of spatial, dynamic and region features allows the extraction of moving foreground objects even in presence of illumination changes and fast variations in the background.

The proposed algorithm is efficient in working with real time video under illuminous condition, occlusion etc. Further practical applications will be investigated in our future work with different real time sequence. In future we to add temporal consistency either on a frame-to-frame basis or within a tracker whose (re)initialization would rely on detection maps.

Figure 9. Dynamic Background Detection

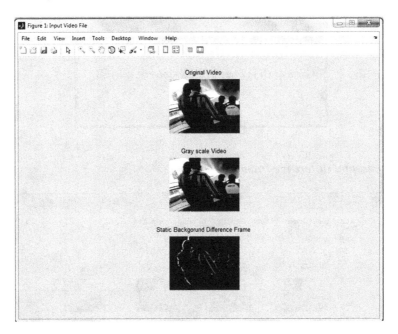

Figure 10. Graph Cut Region Merging Segmentation

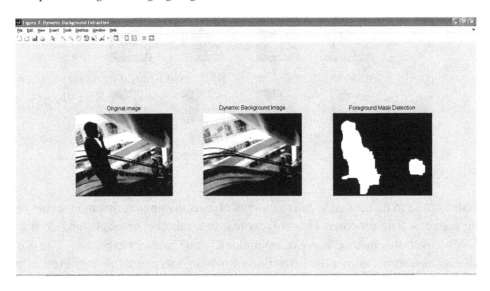

REFERENCES

Babenko, B., Yang, M. H., & Belongie, S. (2011). Robust object tracking with online multiple instance learning. *IEEE Transactions on Pattern Analysis and Machine Intelligence, 33*(8), 1619–1632. doi:10.1109/TPAMI.2010.226 PMID:21173445

Cremers, D., & Soatto, S. (2005). Motion competition: A variational approach to piecewise parametric motion segmentation. *International Journal of Computer Vision, 62*(3), 249–265. doi:10.100711263-005-4882-4

Grabner, H., & Bischof, H. (2006, June). On-line boosting and vision. In *Computer Vision and Pattern Recognition, 2006 IEEE Computer Society Conference on* (Vol. 1, pp. 260-267). IEEE. 10.1109/CVPR.2006.215

Gutchess, D., Trajkovics, M., Cohen-Solal, E., Lyons, D., & Jain, A. K. (2001). A background model initialization algorithm for video surveillance. In *Computer Vision, 2001. ICCV 2001. Proceedings. Eighth IEEE International Conference on* (Vol. 1, pp. 733-740). IEEE. 10.1109/ICCV.2001.937598

Jiang, J., & Song, X. (2016). An Optimized Higher Order CRF for Automated Labeling and Segmentation of Video Objects. *IEEE Transactions on Circuits and Systems for Video Technology, 26*(3), 506–516. doi:10.1109/TCSVT.2015.2416557

Moeslund, T. B., Hilton, A., & Krüger, V. (2006). A survey of advances in vision-based human motion capture and analysis. *Computer Vision and Image Understanding, 104*(2-3), 90–126. doi:10.1016/j.cviu.2006.08.002

Nair, V., & Clark, J. J. (2004, June). An unsupervised, online learning framework for moving object detection. In *Computer Vision and Pattern Recognition, 2004. CVPR 2004. Proceedings of the 2004 IEEE Computer Society Conference on* (*Vol. 2*, pp. II-II). IEEE. 10.1109/CVPR.2004.1315181

Papageorgiou, C. P., Oren, M., & Poggio, T. (1998, January). A general framework for object detection. In *Computer vision, 1998. sixth international conference on* (pp. 555-562). IEEE. 10.1109/ICCV.1998.710772

Piccardi, M. (2004, October). Background subtraction techniques: a review. In *Systems, man and cybernetics, 2004 IEEE international conference on* (Vol. 4, pp. 3099–3104). IEEE.

Ramya, A., & Raviraj, P. (2013). A Survey and Comparative Analysis of Moving Object Detection and Tracking. *International Journal of Engineering Research and Technology, 2*, 147–176.

Ramya, A., & Raviraj, P. (2014, March). Performance evaluation of detecting moving objects using graph cut segmentation. In *Green Computing Communication and Electrical Engineering (ICGCCEE), 2014 International Conference on* (pp. 1-6). IEEE. 10.1109/ICGCCEE.2014.6921413

Toyama, K., Krumm, J., Brumitt, B., & Meyers, B. (1999). Wallflower: Principles and practice of background maintenance. In *Computer Vision, 1999. The Proceedings of the Seventh IEEE International Conference on* (Vol. 1, pp. 255-261). IEEE.

Tsai, Y. H., Yang, M. H., & Black, M. J. (2016). Video segmentation via object flow. *Proceedings of the IEEE Conference on Computer Vision and Pattern Recognition*, 3899-3908.

Vidal, R., & Ma, Y. (2004, May). A unified algebraic approach to 2-D and 3-D motion segmentation. In *European Conference on Computer Vision* (pp. 1-15). Springer. 10.1007/978-3-540-24670-1_1

Viola, P., Jones, M. J., & Snow, D. (2003, October). Detecting pedestrians using patterns of motion and appearance. In *Null* (p. 734). IEEE.

Yilmaz, A., Javed, O., & Shah, M. (2006). Object tracking: A survey. *ACM Computing Surveys, 38*(4), 13.

Chapter 11
Deep–Learning–Based Classification and Diagnosis of Alzheimer's Disease

Rekh Ram Janghel
NIT Raipur, India

ABSTRACT

Alzheimer's is the most common form of dementia in India and it is one of the leading causes of death in the world. Currently it is diagnosed by calculating the MSME score and by manual study of MRI scan. In this chapter, the authors develop and compare different methods to diagnose and predict Alzheimer's disease by processing structural magnetic resonance image scans (MRI scans) with deep learning neural networks. The authors implement one model of deep-learning networks which are convolution neural network (CNN). They use four different architectures of CNN, namely Lenet-5, AlexNet, ZFNet, and R-CNN architecture. The best accuracies for 75-25 cross validation and 90-10 cross validation are 97.68% and 98.75%, respectively, and achieved by ZFNet architecture of convolution neural network. This research will help in further studies on improving the accuracy of Alzheimer's diagnosis and prediction using neural networks.

INTRODUCTION

Convolution Neural Network (CNN) is a deep learning algorithm which helps in classification to extract low to high-level features. In this paper, various different architectures of Convolution Neural Network have been used to classify Alzheimer's Disease. This kind of medical data is classified to potentially develop a model which can predict or system that can recognize the type disease from normal subjects or to estimate the stage of the disease. Classification of Alzheimer's disease has always been a challenging task and most difficult task has been to select the most different features. CNN helps to extract low to high level features automatically by learning features

DOI: 10.4018/978-1-5225-5775-3.ch011

Alzheimer's Disease

Alzheimer's Disease(AD) is the most common type of dementia in 65 years and older, in which the mental ability of persons gradually declines and reaches a stage where it becomes difficult for them to lead a normal life. With the disease progressing gradually, patients find themselves more dependent on their immediate family member for survival. Its expectation is 1 in 85 people will be affected by 2050 and the number of affected people is double in the next 20 years. Alzheimer's disease was named after the German psychiatrist and pathologist Alois Alzheimer after he examined a female patient (post mortem) in 1906 that had died at age 51 after having severe memory problems, confusion, and difficulty understanding questions (Grady, McIntosh, Beig, Keightley, Burian, & Black, 2013). Alzheimer report two common abnormalities in the brain of this patient, "1. Dense layers of protein deposited outside and between the nerve cells. 2. Areas of damaged nerve fibres, inside the nerve cells, which instead of being directly had become tangled". Moreover, these plaques and tangles have been used to help diagnose AD.

There are 3 phases of AD: normal case, mild cognitive impairment(MCI), and dementia. MCI includes "mild changes in memory. Dementia means severity of the disease. The symptoms of AD different between patients. The following are common Symptoms of Alzheimer's:

- Memory loss that disrupts daily life.
- Challenges in planning or solving problems.
- Problem understanding visual images and spatial relationships.
- Decreased or poor judgment.
- Withdrawal from work or social activities.

The current state-of-the-art clinical diagnosis of AD requires a specialty clinic and includes a medical examination, neuropsychological testing, neuro imaging, cerebrospinal fluid (CSF) analysis and blood examination. This process is neither time nor cost-effective. Additionally, given the quickly aging global population with an expected striking increase of AD cases, there are insufficient numbers of specialty

Figure 1. Alzheimer's effect over age groups in India
Laske, Sohrabi, Frost, López-de-Ipiña, Garrard, Buscema... O'Bryant, 2015.

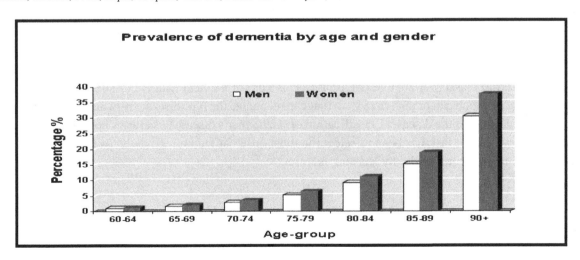

clinics to meet the growing needs (Grady, McIntosh, Beig, Keightley, Burian & Black, 2003). While CSF and neuro imaging markers are gold standards for the in vivo assessment of the patients, they are incursive and expensive and, therefore, have limited utility as frontline screening and diagnostic tools. In addition, prior work has shown that non-specialist clinicians are inaccurate at identifying early AD and mild cognitive impairment (MCI). Which is a major impetus to the search for clinically useful screening and diagnostic tools (Laske, Sohrabi, Frost, López-de-Ipiña, Garrard, Buscema... O'Bryant, 2015).

Dementia affects every person in a different way. Its impact can depend on what the person was like before the disease; his/her personality, life-style, significant relationships and physical health. The problems linked to dementia can be best understood in three stages. The duration of each stage is given as a guideline; sometimes people can deteriorate quicker, and at other times more slowly.

It is estimated that over 3.7 million people are affected by dementia in India. This is expected to double by 2030. It is estimated that the cost of taking care of a person with dementia is about 43,000 annually; much of which is met by the families. The financial burden will only increase in the coming years (Vemuri, Prashanthi, Jones, & Clifford, 2012). The challenge posed by dementia as a health and social issue is of a scale we can no longer ignore. Despite the magnitude, there is gross ignorance, neglect and scarce services for people with dementia and their families. We know that dementia is not part of aging and is caused by a variety of diseases. We now have a range of options to treat the symptoms of dementia and offer practical help to those affected. Alzheimer's and Related Disorders Society of India (ARDSI) the national voluntary organization dedicated to the care, support and research of dementia has been in the forefront to improve the situation since 1992. ARDSI is committed to developing a society which is dementia friendly and literate. This could only happen if we have the political commitment at all levels to provide a range of solutions that deliver a life with dignity and honour for people with dementia.

Diagnosing Alzheimer's disease requires very careful medical assessment, including patient history, a mini mental state examination (MMSE), physical and neurobiological exams. (Warsi, & Mohammed, 2012) In addition to these evaluations, structural magnetic resonance imaging and resting state functional magnetic resonance imaging (rs-fMRI) offer non-invasive methods of studying the structure of the brain, functional brain activity, and changes in the brain. During scanning using both structural (anatomical) and rs-fMRI techniques, patients remain prone on the MRI table and do not perform any tasks. This allows data acquisition to occur without any effects from a particular task on functional activity in the brain (Grady, McIntosh, Beig, Keightley, Burian & Black, 2003). Alzheimer's disease causes shrinkage of the hippo campus and cerebral cortex and enlargement of ventricles in the brain. The level of these effects is dependent upon the stage of disease progression. In the advanced stage of AD, severe shrinkage of the hippocampus and cerebral cortex, as well as significantly enlarged ventricles, can easily be recognized in MR images. This damage affects those brain regions and networks related to thinking, remembering (especially short-term memory), planning and judgment. Since brain cells in the damaged regions have degenerated, MR image (or signal) intensities are low in both MRI and rs-fMRI techniques (Tripoliti, Fotiadis, & Argyropoulou, 2012). However, some of the signs found in the AD imaging data are also identified in normal aging imaging data. Identifying the visual distinction between AD data and images of older subjects with normal aging effects requires extensive knowledge and experience (Sarraf, & Tofighi, 2016), which must then be combined with additional clinical results in order to accurately classify the data (i.e., MMSE) (Mareeswari, & Wiselin Jij, 2015). Development of an assistive tool or algorithm to classify MR-based imaging data, such as structural MRI and rs-fMRI data, and, more importantly, to distinguish brain disorder data from healthy subjects, has always been of interest to clinicians (Wyman, 2013). A robust machine learning algorithm such as Deep Learning, which is able to classify Alzheimer's disease, will assist scientists and clinicians in diagnosing this brain disorder and will also aid in the accurate and timely diagnosis of Alzheimer's patients (Sarraf, & Tofighi, 2016).

Deep Learning

Deep learning is a branch of machine learning based on a set of algorithms that attempt to model high level abstractions in data. In a simple case, you could have two sets of neurons: ones that receive an input signal and ones that send an output signal. When the input layer receives an input it passes on a modified version of the input to the next layer. In a deep network, there are many layers between the input and output, allowing the algorithm to use multiple processing layers, composed of multiple linear and non-linear transformations.

Deep learning is part of a broader family of machine learning methods based on learning representations of data. An observation (e.g., an image) can be represented in many ways such as a vector of intensity values per pixel, or in a more abstract way as a set of edges, regions of particular shape, etc. Some representations are better than others at simplifying the learning task. One of the promises of deep learning is replacing handcrafted features with efficient algorithms for unsupervised or semi-supervised feature learning and hierarchical feature extraction

Various deep learning architectures such as deep neural networks, convolution deep neural networks, deep belief networks and recurrent neural networks have been applied to fields like computer vision, automatic speech recognition, natural language processing, audio recognition and bioinformatics where they have been shown to produce state-of-the-art results on various tasks.

There are several types of Deep Learning Networks:

1. **Convolution Neural Network:** It is a type of feed-forward artificial neural network in which the connectivity pattern between its neurons is inspired by the organization of the animal visual cortex. Individual cortical neurons respond to stimuli in a restricted region of space known as the receptive filed. The receptive fields of different neurons partially overlap such that they tile the visual field.
2. **Deep Belief Network:** In machine learning, a deep belief network is a generative graphical model, or alternatively a type of deep neural network, composed of multiple layers of latent variables, hidden units, with connections between the layers but not between units within each layer.
3. **Recurrent Neural Network:** A recurrent neural network is a class of artificial neural network where connections between units form a directed cycle. This creates an internal state of the network which allows it to exhibit dynamic temporal behavior. Unlike feed forward neural networks, RNNs can use their internal memory to process arbitrary sequences of inputs. This makes them applicable to tasks such as un segmented connected handwriting recognition or speech recognition.

Data Acquisition

For this study, Data was acquired from Alzheimer's Disease Neurological Initiative (ADNI). ADNI is a global research effort that actively supports the investigation and development of treatments that slow or stop the progression of AD. This multisite, longitudinal study assesses clinical, imaging, genetic and bio specimen biomarkers through the process of normal aging to early mild cognitive impairment (EMCI), to late mild cognitive impairment (LMCI), to dementia or AD. With established, standardized methods for imaging and biomarker collection and analysis, ADNI facilitates a way for scientists to conduct cohesive research and share compatible data with other researchers around the world.

The Dataset consists of 54 Images present in NIFTI Format and is acquired through the standard protocol present in the ADNI Site. It consists of 27 males out of which 18 are classified as suffering from Alzheimer's Disease with average MMSE score of 42.26. Rest are females out of which 9 are suffering from Alzheimer's Disease with average MMSE score of 41.2. The images acquired are structural MRI scans with weighting T1 and slice thickness as 1mm. Scanning was performed on three different Tesla scanners, General Electric (GE) Healthcare, Philips Medical Systems, and Siemens Medical Solutions, and was based on identical scanning parameters. Anatomical scans were acquired with a 3D MPRAGE sequence (TR=2s, TE=2.63 ms, FOV=25.6 cm, 256×256 matrix, 160 slices of 1mm thickness). Table 1 presents a summary of data acquired.

Table 1 presents the demographic information for both subsets, including mini mental state examination (MMSE) scores

The introduction part provides wide information about the background of work and about all major deep learning-based models.

BACKGROUND

Deep Learning is one of the emerging fields in machine learning. It has various application which extend upon fields such as Medical Imaging, Network Classification, Sentiment Analysis, Game Playing, Prediction of weather etc. Some of the common deep learning networks are Convolution Network, Deep Spiking Neural Network and Stacked Encoders.

In recent times, different algorithms for classification of Alzheimer's Disease have emerged. (Sarraf & Tofigi, 2016) devised an algorithm to classify Alzheimer's Disease using Deep Learning. Initially Structural MRI Scans and Functional MRI Scans were acquired from Alzheimer's Disease Neurological Initiative using a standard protocol (Liu, Cai,, Pujol, Kikinis, & Feng, 2014). After acquisition digital image processing techniques were applied to the raw MRI Scans. First, Brain was extracted using brain extraction tool present in FSL library provided by oxford. Then the images were segmented into three parts: Grey Matter, White Matter, Cerebral Fluid using the FSL Library. After Segmentation, Images were normalized using Gaussian kernel with Sigma value equal to 2, 3, and 4 and then linearly registered. Next, Convolution neural network was applied to the image dataset to classify Alzheimer's Disease Patient from a normal human. The Accuracy of classification for FMRI Scans for LeNet Architecture was 99.42% and for googleNet architecture was 99.49%. The accuracy of classification of Structural MRI Scans using spatial smoothing was 98.51%.

Table 1. Demographic information for both subsets, including mental state examination (MMSE) score

Modality	Total Subject	Group	Subject	Female	Mean of Age	SD	Male	Mean of Age	SD	MMSE SD
MRI	52	Alzheimer	27	9	79.42	15.16	18	80.54	15.98	27.90
		Normal	25	16	80.15	12.36	9	81.75	27.43	28.20

(Sarraf & Tofighi, 2016) also devised an algorithm to compare classification result for smoothed dataset and unsmoothed dataset. Using LeNet Architecture, the classification accuracy achieved was 98.789% for the unsmoothed dataset and 99.21% for the smoothed dataset and using the GoogleNet architecture the classification accuracy achieved was 98.824% for unsmoothed Dataset and 99.46% for smoothed dataset. The methodology applied was the same as mentioned in previous literature (Sørensen, Igel, Hansen, Osler, Lauritzen, Rostrup, & Nielsen, 2015).

Another framework which used stacked auto encoder was proposed by S Lui, it improved upon the accuracy given by Support Vector Machine by being 97% accurate in classification whereas classification using SVM was 74% accurate (Liu, Cai,, Pujol, Kikinis, & Feng, 2014).

Detection of MRI disease using MRI Hippocampal texture using a logistic regression model was achieved by L Sensen by extracting Hippocampal texture features and applying a Logistic Regression model to the features. The accuracy achieved was 74% for AD vs NL classification. In addition to AD vs NL classification, the accuracy for AD vs MCI vs NL classification was 71% (Li, Tran, Thung, Ji, Shen, & Li, 2015).

(Li, Tran, Thung, Ji, Shen, & Li, 2015) developed a robust algorithm for classification of Alzheimer Disease and improved the accuracy result by 6.3% over classical neural network. Utilizing the dropout technique to improve classical deep learning by preventing weight co-adaptation, this is a typical cause of over-fitting in deep learning. In addition, they incorporated stability selection, an adaptive learning factor and a multi-task learning strategy into the deep learning framework.

The literature review contains recent papers of renowned sources, and focuses each and every aspects of related problem.

Table 2. Literature review summarized part 1. It summarizes the previous work done in this particular research field.

Title	Keywords	Author	Methods and Performance	Year	Publication
Classification of Alzheimer's Disease Structural MRI Data by Deep Learning Convolutional Neural Networks	CNN, ADNI, FSL, Alzheimer's, Classification, Structural MRI Scans, Deep Learning	S Sarraf and G Tofighi	Convolution neural networks lenet architecture & 94.14%	2016	Future Technologies Conference 2016, At San Francisco
DeepAD: Alzheimer's Disease Classification via Deep Convolutional Neural Networks using MRI and fMRI	CNN, ADNI, FSL, Alzheimers, Classification, fMRI Scans, Structural MRI Scans, Deep Learning	S Sarraf and G Tofighi	Convolution neural Networks, Lenel and GoogleNet Architecture & 94.79%, 98.84%	2016	Future Technologies Conference 2016, At San Francisco
Deep Learning-Based Feature Representation for AD/MCI Classification	Stacked Auto Encoder, Classification, Alzheimer's, Deep Learning	H Suk and D Shen	Stacked Auto Encoder & 94.9%, 85.0%, and 75.8%	2013	Med ImageComputhttps://www.ncbi.nlm.nih.gov/pubmed/24579188ComputAssistInterv. 2013;16(Pt 2):583-90.
Early diagnosis of alzheimer's disease with deep learning	Stacked Auto Encoder, Softmax Refression, Classification, Deep Learning, Alzheimers's	Siqi Liu	Stacked Auto Encoder, Softmax Regression & 87.76%	2013	2014 IEEE 11th International Symposium on Biomedical Imaging (ISBI
Early detection of Alzheimer's disease using MRI hippocampal texture	classification; early diagnosis; hippocampus; image analysis; machine learning	Lauge Sørensen	Image Analysis of Hippocampal texture & 83%	2015	Hum Brain Mapp. 2016 Mar;37(3):1148-61. doi: 10.1002/hbm.23091. Epub 2015 Dec 21.

Table 3. Literature review summarized. It contains the summary of Alzheimer's and soft computing.

Title	Keywords	Author	Methods	Year	Publication
A hybrid manifold learning algorithm for the diagnosis and prognostication of Alzheimer's disease	PCA, ADNI,MDL, Alzheimer's, Classification, Structural MRI Scans, Deep Learning	P Dai and F. Gawdry	Support Vector machine	2015	AMIA Annu Symp Proc. 2015; 2015: 475–483.
2015 Alzheimer's disease facts and figures	Alzheimer's, AD, MD, NH	Alzheimer's Association.	Facts And Figures	2015	Alzheimer's Dement. 2015 Mar;11(3):332-84.
Decision Support System for the Intelligient Identification of Alzheimer using Neuro Fuzzy logic	Neural Network, Fuzzy logic, Neuro Fuzzy System & Alzeimer	Obi J.C . And Imainvan A. .	Fuzzy Logic	2011	International Journal on Soft Computing (IJSC), Vol.2, No.2, May 2011
Machine Learning, Wearable Computing and Alzheimer's Disease	Alzheimer's, Machine Learning	Jun Jie Ng Yanrong Li	Machine Learning	2016	Technical Report No. UCB/EECS-2016-108
Recent trends in disease diagnosis using soft computing techniques: a review	Disease Diagnosis, Fuzzy Expert System, Genetic Algorithm, Particle Swarm Optimization, Soft Computing	Bishnupriya Mukherjee	Genetic Algorithm	2016	3rd International Conference on Recent Innovations and Technology, 2016.

METHODOLOGY

Classification of Alzheimer's disease images and normal, healthy images required several steps, from pre-processing to recognition, which resulted in the development of an end-to-end pipeline. Three major modules formed this recognition pipeline: a) pre-processing; b)data conversion; and c) classification, respectively. After the pre-processing steps, the data were converted from medical image data to a Portable Network Graphics (PNG) format to input into the deep learning-based classifier. Finally, the various CNN architecture receiving images in their input layer were trained and tested (validated) using 75% and 25% of the dataset and 90% and 10% of the dataset, respectively. Figure 2 depicts the End to End recognition based on deep learning architectures is composed of Pre-processing, Image conversion and Classification. The structural MRI images are pre-processed using FSL Library which are then converted into 2D images along Z axis.

Structural MRI Data Pre-Processing

MRI Data was pre-processed using Functional Magnetic Resonance Image Brain (FMRIB) Software Library (Commonly known as FSL) developed by oxford, it is a widely-used library for MRI images pre-processing.

Non-Brain Tissue Extraction

High Resolution MR Image or known as structural MRI Image contain considerable amount of non-brain tissue such as eyeball, skin, fat, muscle etc. BET is carried out to improve the registration robustness

Figure 2. Flowchart of proposed methodology

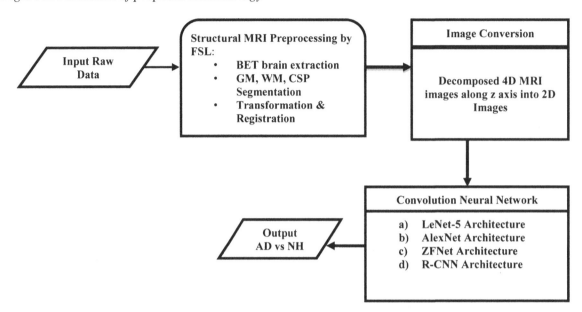

by removing these non-brain tissue pre-registrations. Image Registration is defined as the process of transforming different sets of data into one coordinate system. These sets could be multiple images, data from different time or depth etc. Algorithm for Brain Extraction tool is given below. First the histogram of intensity is calculated using which the low and high intensity threshold are identified. Next the image is temporarily binarized using the threshold to identify the Center of Gravity and equivalent radius is calculated by counting all voxels above a particular threshold. Tessellated surface is initialized, it is updated by iteration, final tessellated image is formed. If it is intersecting, then new tessellated image is initialized. Else, we get a brain extracted image (Nipy.org, 2016).

Grey Matter, White Matter, Cerebral Spinal Fluid Segmentation

Next, using Hidden Markov Random Field Generation and estimation maximization, the brain images are further segmented into grey matter, white matter and cerebral-fluid images based on voxel intensity. It is also done to improve the robustness for image registration process. GM images were selected and registered to the GM ICBM-152 standard template using linear affine transformation. The registered images were concatenated and averaged and were then flipped along the x-axis, and the two mirror images were then re- averaged to obtain a first-pass, study-specific affine GM template (Nipy.org, 2016).

Image Registration

Second, the GM images were re-registered to this affineGM template using non-linear registration, concatenated into a 4D image which was then averaged and flipped along the x-axis. Both mirror images were then averaged to create the final symmetric, study-specific non1linear GM template at 2x2x2 mm3 resolution in standard space. Following this, all concatenated and averaged 3D GM images (one 3D image per subject) were concatenated into a stack (4D image = 3D images across subjects). Additionally,

Algorithm: Brain Extraction Tool

Input: MRI Scan as MRI_SCAN

Output: MRI Scan with non-brain tissue removed.

Begin

Step 1: Compute Histogram of Intensity for MRI_Scan

Step 2: Compute the threshold Intensity t1 and t2

Step 3: Compute Brain_Image ←Binarise(MRI_SCAN, t1, t2)

Step 4: Compute Center of Image of Brain_Image

Step 5: Initialize the tessellated surface.

Step 6: Update the tessellated surface through iteration.

Step 7: Compute the final tessellated surface.

Step 8: If tessellated surface is self-intersecting, then

Step 9: Update t1 and t2 locally.

Step 10: Go to step 5

Step 11: End if.

End.

Figure 3. Raw structural MRI scan

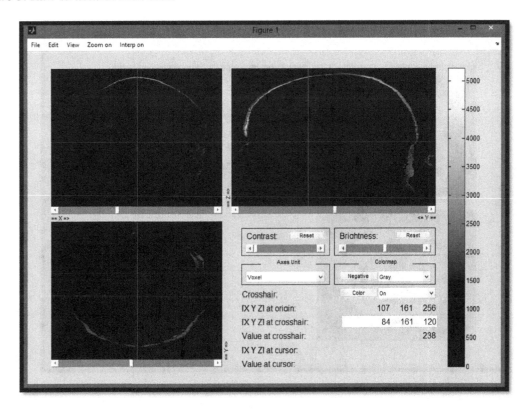

Figure 4. Brain extraction tool applied

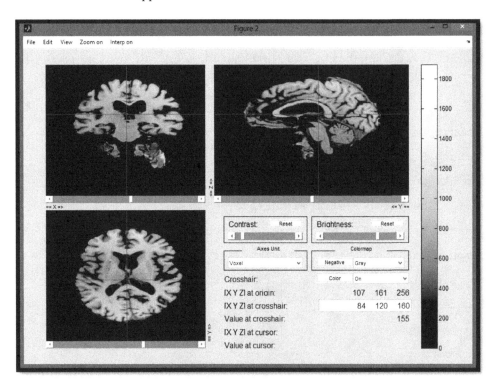

Figure 5. Grey matter extracted image

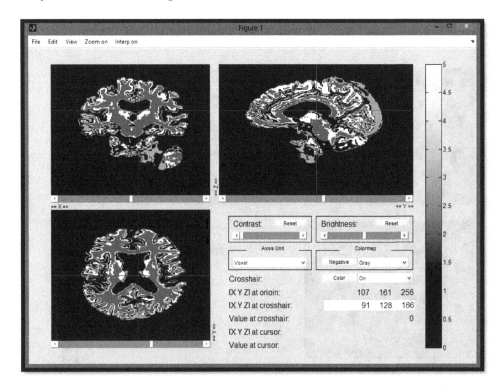

Figure 6. Linear affine registration

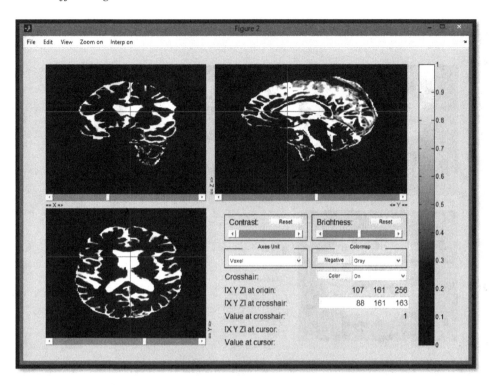

Figure 7. Flipped linear affine registration

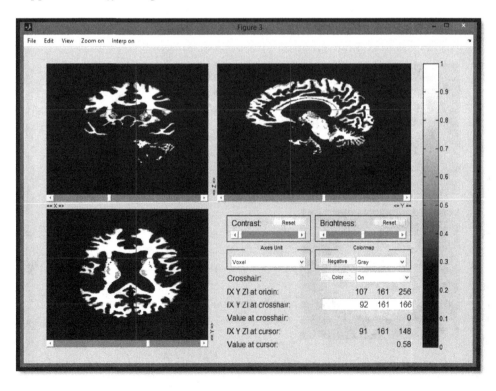

Figure 8. Averaged linear affine registration

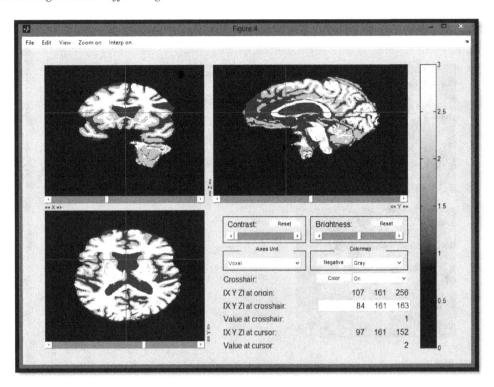

Figure 9. Smoothed linear affine registration

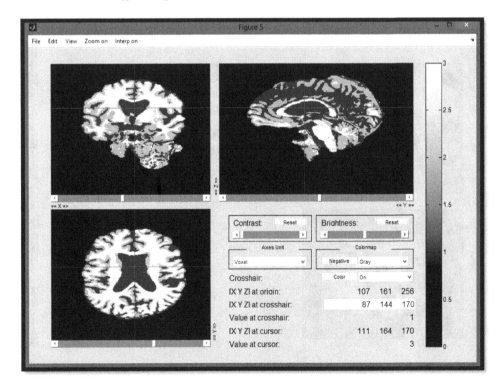

Figure 10. Non linear affine registration

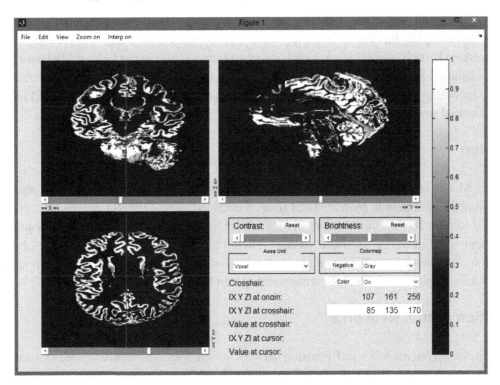

Figure 11. Averaged non-linear affine registration

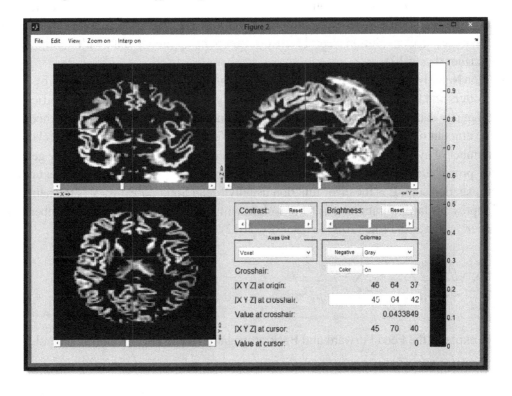

the FSL-VBM protocol introduced a compensation or modulation for the contraction/enlargement due to the non-linear component of the transformation, where each voxel of each registered grey matter image was multiplied by the Jacobian of the warp field. The modulated 4D image was then smoothed by a range of Gaussian kernels, sigma = 2, 3, 4 mm (standard sigma values in the field of MRI data analysis), which approximately resulted in full width at half maximums (FWHM) of 4.6, 7 and 9.3 mm. The various spatial smoothing kernels enabled us to explore whether classification accuracy would improve by varying the spatial smoothing kernels.

Conversion

All the Grey Matter Images were converted from 3D images to 2D images using Nibabel and OpenCv which are libraries available in python. Total images obtained were 4765 2D images after conversion. Then first 10 and last 10 slices were removed for each 3D image as they showed no significant information and mean voxel intensity was equal to zero. Therefore, a total of 3682 Images were obtained for classification of Alzheimer's. 1982 images were those belonging to Alzheimer's Class and rest belonged to Normal Class. Algorithm for image conversion is given below.

Convolution Neural Networks

Convolution Neural Network is a self-learning network which does not require feature extraction. Convolution neural network are based on a paradigm called Graph Transformer Networks. It allows training all the modules to optimize a global performance criterion. Traditional classification algorithm consists of two parts: a) Feature Extractor, and; b) Trainable Classifier. Most of the work goes into devising algorithms for feature extraction. Convolution neural network can be applied to many different fields such as Image Classification, Object Recognition, Sound Wave Recognition, Light Wave Recognition and Text Classification. Convolution Neural Network cannot be applied to data with multiple attributes as of now (Krizhevsky, 2012).

Convolution Neural network incorporate knowledge about the in variances of 2D shapes by using local connection patters and by imposing constraints on the weight. It has been designed specifically on the assumption that raw data is only of two dimension which enable certain properties to be encoded. Also, it reduces the amount of hyper parameters. Convolution Neural Network utilize spatial relationship to reduce the number of hyper parameter which must be learned, thereby improving upon the general feedforward back propagation network. Equation one demonstrates the calculation of gradient component in a back propagation step. E is the error function usually Mean Squared Error, Y is the neuron, $N_{ij}x$ is the input, l represents layer numbers, w is filter weight with a and b indices, N is the number of neuron in a given layer, and m is the filter size (Krizhevsky, 2012).

$$\frac{\partial E}{\partial \omega_{ab}} = \sum_{i=0}^{N-m}\sum_{i=0}^{N-m} \frac{\partial E}{\partial x_{ij}^l} \frac{\partial x_{ij}^l}{\partial \omega_{ab}} = \sum_{i=0}^{N-m}\sum_{i=0}^{N-m} \frac{\partial E}{\partial x_{ij}^l} \frac{\partial x_{ij}^l}{\partial \omega_{ab}} y_{(i+a)(i+b)}^{l-1} \qquad (1)$$

Figure 14 explains the Feed Forward and Back propagation steps in Convolution Neural Network.

Figure 12. Smoothed non-linear affine registration

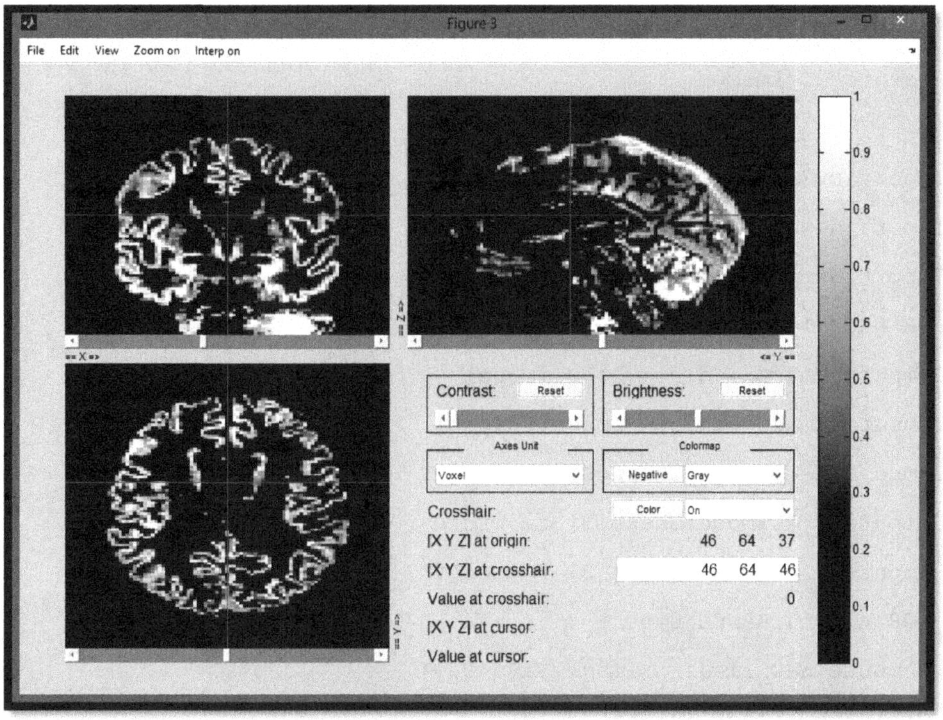

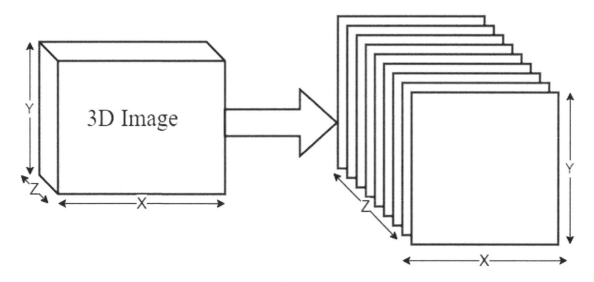

Figure 13. Three dimensional to two-dimensional conversion

Algorithm Image Conversion

```
Input: List of 3D Images
Output: List of 2D Images
Begin
Step 1: Import cv2 // to read and write images
Step 2: Import dicom // to read nifty images
Step 3: Import Numpy // to modify numpy array
Step 4: FOR EACH Image in 3D Images
Step 5: Compute Image ← dicom.load(image)
Step 6: Compute Image_Shape ← Image.shape()
Step 7: Compute x ← Image_Shape[0] // Height
Step 8: Compute y ← Image_Shape[1] // Width
Step 9: Compute z ← Image_Shape[2] // Length
Step 10: FOR num in RANGE 0 to z
Step 11: Compute new_image ← Image.Save(x,y)
Step 12: Write new_image in .png file
Step 13: Save new_image as Image_num // where num is a number for 0 to z
Step 14: End FOR loop
Step 15: End FOR EACH Loop
end
```

Figure 14. Basic Architecture of Convolution Neural Network

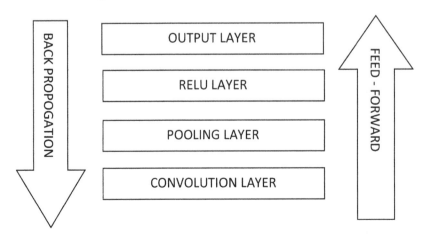

The features are learned through gradient based training. In Equation 2 'y' is the probability that an image belongs to a particular class. W is the network parameters such as weights and bias and x is an image of size MxM.

$$y = f\left(x, w\right) \tag{2}$$

In gradient based learning the goal is to minimize the error E (see Equation 3) to learn parameters W. For the same iterative gradient descent is used (refer to Equation 4):

$$E\left(f\left(x0, w\right), y0\right) = -\log\left(f\left(x0, w\right) - y0\right) \tag{3}$$

$$w\left(t\right) = w\left(t - 1\right) - \lambda * \left(-\partial E / \partial w\left(t\right)\right) \tag{4}$$

It contains of five basic layer: 1) Input Layer; 2) Convolution Layer; 3) Rectified Linear Unit; 4) Pooling layer, and; 5) Fully Connected Layer.

Input Layer

Input Layer contains the raw pixel value of the Image in the RBG or Grayscale format. The size of input layer determines the size of convolution neural network architecture.

Convolution Layer

It computes the output of n local neurons that are connected to local regions in the input, each of the neuron computes a dot product between their weights and a small region with which they are connected to the input volume. The output depth will depend upon the number of filters we decide to learn. Convolutions layer's parameter consist of a group of learnable filters. The filters are small spatially but extend through the full depth of the input volume. Each filter is slided across the width and height of image and dot product is computed between the entries of the filter and the input at any position producing a 2-dimensional activation map which gives response of a particular file at every spatial position. The network learns filter which are activated when they happen upon a feature such as edge or a blotch. Each filter will produce a two-dimensional activation map which will be stacked along the depth dimension to produce the output volume (Krizhevsky, 2012).

Pooling Layer

It is quite common to introduce a pooling layer to progressively reduce the spatial size of the representation. By reducing the spatial size of representation, we can reduce the number of parameters and computation the network, thereby controlling over fitting. It operates independently on every image and resizes it spatially using the MAX operation. Pooling layers of various sizes are applied and are either pooled with strides such that there is no overlapping or with strides such that overlapping is present. A 2X2 Pooling discards 75% of the activation (Krizhevsky, 2012).

Fully-Connected Layer

They have full connections to all the activations present in the previous layer same as normal neural network. Therefore, the activations are computed with a matrix multiplication followed by a bias offset (Krizhevsky, 2012).

Different architectures of Convolution Neural Network are used in this study. They are mentioned below.

1.   LeNet-5 Architecture
2.   AlexNet Architecture
3.   ZFNet Architecture
4.   R-CNN Architecture

LeNet-5 Architecture

LeNet-5 was first designed by Y. LeCun. This architecture successfully classified digits and was applied to hand-written check numbers. The application of this fundamental but deep network architecture expanded into more complicated problems by adjusting the network hyper parameters. LeNet-5 architecture, which extracts low-to mid-level features, includes two convolution layers, two pooling layers, and two fully connected layers and one last output layer consisting of two output neurons. It was the first Convolution neural network architecture to be developed (Zeiler, Matthew, & Fergus, 2014).

Layer 1 is a convolution layer which convolves the 32*32 image in a 28*28*6 with 6 representing the depth field or number of parameters learned in the first layer. They are stacked upon each other to create the depth. Layer 2 is a pooling layer which performs a down sampling operation to reduce the size of image to 14*14 and produces an output of 14*14*6. Layer 3 is a convolution layer which performs a convolution operation. It contains 16 feature maps of 10*10 image. Layer 4 is a pooling layer that down samples the size of image to 5*5 with 16 feature map. Layer 5 is a fully connected layer containing 120 neurons which are all feature maps of 1*1 instead of 5*5. Layer 6 is a fully connected layer and then layer 7 is the output layer (Zeiler, Matthew, & Fergus, 2014).

Figure 15. LeNetArchitecture
Zeiler, Matthew, & Fergus, 2014.

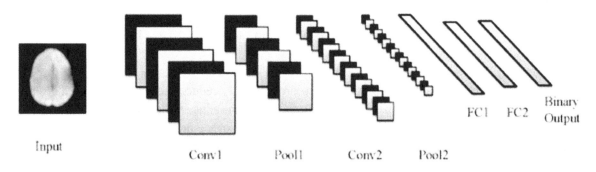

Algorithm: LeNet Architecture

```
Input: List of Images, List of Image Label

Output: Classification of Images based on Weights learned in training period.

Step 1: For each Image in Images.

Step 2: Compute I(X,Y) ← Image.load() // Load image as matrix of size (x,y).

Step 3: For map in Feature_Maps // All maps are learned and none is pre-defined2.

Step 4: Compute I_map(X,Y)← I(X,Y) x map // Map ← (5,5) Feature map.

Step 5: Combine all the I_map into I_conv_result (X, Y, Number of Feature Map).

Step 6: Compute I_pool1_result← Max of all pixes (I_conv_result x kernel(M,N) with stride K for each feature map in conv_result).

Step 7: Compute I_conv2_result using step 3&4 with different feature maps.

Step 8: Compute I_pool2_result using step 6.

Step 9: Compute I_fully1-connected← I_pool2_result by applying step 3 but with Map ← (1,1) and feature map number increasing.

Step 10: Compute I_fully2-connected by fully connecting it with fully connected layer 1 and calculating the activation function.

Step 11: Classify the image.
```

AlexNet Architecture

It was introduced by a team of scientists at annual ImageNet LSVRC competition. It is the pioneer in introducing Convolution neural network into existence once more. It consists of 8 layers in total in which 5 are convolution layer and 3 are fully connected layer. Tradtionally, it was run with 2 GPU but in this experiment the same has been done with only one GPU due to computational constraints. This increases the training time and also the error rate (Zeiler, Matthew, & Fergus, 2014). The first convolution layer which filters the 224x224x3 with 96 kernels using 11x11x3 matrix size with a stride of 4. The second convolution layer takes as input the (response-normalized and pooled) output of the first convolution layer and filters it with 256 kernels of size 5x5x48. The third, fourth, and fifth convolution layers are connected to one another without any intervening pooling or normalization layers. The third convolution layer has 384 kernels of size 3x3x256 connected to the (normalized, pooled) outputs of the second convolution layer. The fourth convolution layer has 384 kernels of size 3x3x192, and the fifth convolution layer has 256 kernels of size 3x3x192. The fully-connected layers have 4096 neurons each. But the output layer only has 2 neuron for binary classification (Zeiler, Matthew, & Fergus, 2014).

ZFNet Architecture

It is an improvement upon AlexNet by tweaking the hyper parameters and expanding the middle layer of AlexNet architecture. Architecture of our 8 layer convnet model. A 224 by 224 crop of an image (with 3 color planes) is presented as the input. This is convolved with 96 different 1st layer filters (red),

Figure 16. Architecture of AlexNet

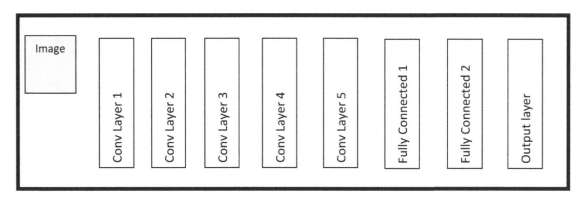

each of size 7 by 7, using a stride of 2 in both x and y. The resulting feature maps are then: (1) passed through a rectified linear function (not shown); (2) pooled (max within 3x3 regions, using stride 2) and; (3) contrast normalized across feature maps to give 96 different 55 by 55 element feature maps. Similar operations are repeated in layers 2, 3, 4, and 5. The last two layers are fully connected, taking features from the top convolution layer as input in vector form $(6 \cdot 6 \cdot 256 = 9216$ dimensions). The final layer is a C-way softmax function, C being the number of classes. All filters and feature maps are square in shape (Ren, Shaoqing, He, Girshick, & Sun, 2015).

R-CNN

Here, a new training algorithm that fixes the disadvantages of CNN and SPPnet is applied, while improving on their speed and accuracy. We call this method R-CNN because it's comparatively fast to train and test (Ren S. et.al., 2015). The R-CNN method has several advantages:

1. Higher detection quality (mAP) than CNN, SPPnet
2. Training is single-stage, using a multi-task loss
3. Training can update all network layers
4. No disk storage is required for feature caching

Figure 17. ZFNet architecture
Ren, Shaoqing, He, Girshick, & Sun, 2015.

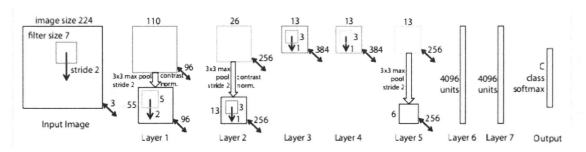

R-CNN Architecture

A R-CNN network takes as input an entire image and a set of object proposals. The network first processes the whole image with several convolutional (conv) and max pooling layers to produce a conv feature map. Then, for each object proposal a region of interest (RoI) pooling layer extracts a fixed-length feature vector from the feature map. Each feature vector is fed into a sequence of fully connected (fc) layers that finally branch into two sibling output layers: one that produces softmax probability estimates over K object classes plus a catch-all "background" class and another layer that outputs four real-valued numbers for each of the K object classes. Each set of 4 values encodes refined bounding-box positions for one of the K classes (Ren, Shaoqing, He, Girshick, & Sun, 2015).

The RoI pooling layer uses max pooling to convert the features inside any valid region of interest into a small feature map with a fixed spatial extent of H × W (e.g., 7 × 7), where H and W are layer hyperparameters that are independent of any particular RoI. In this paper, an RoI is a rectangular window into a conv feature map. Each RoI is defined by a four-tuple (r, c, h, w) that specifies its top-left corner (r, c) and its height and width (h, w).

RoI max pooling works by dividing the h × w RoI window into an H × W grid of sub-windows of approximate size h/H × w/W and then max-pooling the values in each sub-window into the corresponding output grid cell. Pooling is applied independently to each feature map channel, as in standard max pooling. The RoI layer is simply the special-case of the spatial pyramid pooling layer used in SPPnets in which there is only one pyramid level. We use the pooling sub-window calculation given in (Ren, Shaoqing, He, Girshick, & Sun, 2015).

RESULTS

The different neural network models were initially set with hyper parameters such as Stochastic Gradient Descent with a gamma = 0.1, amomentum = 0.9, abaselearningrate = 0.01, aweight decay = 0.0005, and a step learning rate policy dropping the learning rate in steps by a factor of gamma every step size iteration. Next, the models were trained and tested by 75% and 25% of the data. The comparative results are shown in the table below along with architectures used for Convolution Neural Network.

From the Tables 4 and 5 it is evident that ZFNet is performing the best among all the architectures in consideration. ZFNet has the highest accuracy of 97.68% whereas LeNet has an accuracy of 93.47% for 75% to 25% validation. The accuracy is calculated with the help of confusion matrix as shown in table 3 and 5. Similarly precision, sensitivity and specificity are also calculated. Accuracy is defined as the ratio of True positive plus true negative by total number of specimens. Precision is defined as the ratio of true positive by actual positive. Sensitivity is defined as the ratio of true negative by actual negative. Specificity is defined as the ratio of true positive by true negative.

Table 6 and 7 shows the accuracy of proposed work and different works done for the same problem but cannot establish any comparison between the previous work done in the same fields as they work with different methodologies and work with different sets of data from the same source. We also find that when we decrease the test data size the accuracy increases. This may suggest that at different test data size we may get less accuracy from the proposed methodology. Also, R-CNN gives the worst accuracy of all which is due to the reason that it is mainly used to classify objects in an image and our MRI scan

Figure 18. R-CNN architecture

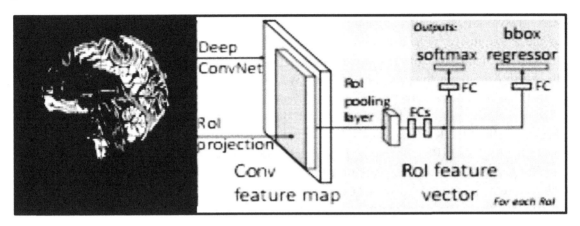

Table 4. Result with 75 - 25 cross validation

Architecture Name			Predicted Value			Accuracy
			AD	NL		
LeNet-5 Architecture	Actual Value	AD	452	35	487	93.47%
		NL	27	436	463	
			479	471		
AlexNet Architecture	Actual Value	AD	459	28	487	94.42%
		NL	25	438	463	
			484	466		
ZFNet Architecture	Actual Value	AD	477	10	487	**97.68%**
		NL	12	451	463	
			489	461		
R-CNN Architecture	Actual Value	AD	363	124	487	77.57%
		NL	89	374	463	
			452	498		

Table 5. Comparison of sensitivity, specificity, precision, and accuracy

CNN Architecture	Accuracy	Precision	Sensitivity	Specificity
Lenet-5	93.47%	92.56%	94.16%	92.81%
AlexNet	94.42%	93.99%	94.60%	94.25%
ZFNet	**97.68%**	**97.83%**	**97.40%**	**97.94%**
R-CNN	77.57%	75.10%	80.77%	74.53%

Table 6. Result with 90-10 cross validation

Architecture Name			Predicted Value			Accuracy
			AD	NL		
LeNet-5 Architecture	Actual Value	AD	457	35	487	94.67%
		NL	27	443	463	
			479	471		
AlexNet Architecture	Actual Value	AD	459	28	487	96.22%
		NL	25	438	463	
			484	466		
ZFNet Architecture	Actual Value	AD	477	10	487	**98.78%**
		NL	12	451	463	
			489	461		
R-CNN Architecture	Actual Value	AD	363	124	487	79.57%
		NL	89	374	463	
			452	498		

Table 7. Comparison for 90-10 cross validation

CNN Architecture	Accuracy	Precision	Sensitivity	Specificity
Lenet-5	94.67%	93.36%	95.66%	93.85%
AlexNet	96.22%	94.29%	96.90%	96.45%
ZFNet	**98.78%**	**98.34%**	**97.80%**	**98.44%**
R-CNN	79.83%	76.30%	81.74%	76.63%

Table 8. Comparison with related work done in the field

Reference	Modality	Method	Accuracy
Sarraf et al.	MRI+fMRI	Using LeNet-5 architecture (CNN)	96.86%
Proposed Work	MRI	Using LeNet-5 architecture (CNN 75% -25% cross validation)	93.47%
Proposed Work	MRI	Using ZFNet architecture(CNN 75% -25% cross validation)	94.42%
Proposed Work	MRI	Using AlexNet architecture (CNN 75% -25% cross validation)	97.68%
Proposed Work	MRI	Using Region based Convolution Neural Network (75%-25% cross validation)	77.57%
Suk et al.	MRI	Using Stacked Auto Encoder	94.90%
Zhang et al.	MRI	Using Support Vector Machine	93.20%
Sorenson et al.	MRI	Using Feature extraction of MRI Hippocamical texture	87.76%
Sarraf et al.	MRI + fMRI	Using GoogleNet Architecture	99.90%
Proposed Work	MRI	Using LeNet-5 architecture (CNN 90% -10% cross validation)	94.67%
Proposed Work	MRI	Using ZFNet architecture(CNN 90% -10% cross validation)	96.22%
Proposed Work	MRI	Using AlexNet architecture (CNN 90% -10% cross validation)	98.78%
Proposed Work	MRI	Using Region based Convolution Neural Network (90% - 10% cross validation)	79.83%

is just a single object in an image. The training and testing time of algorithms increased in the order of complexity of the different architectures.

This cutting-edge deep learning-based framework points to a number of applications in classifying brain disorders in both clinical trials and large-scale research studies. This study also demonstrated that the developed pipelines served as fruitful algorithms in characterizing multimodal MRI biomarkers. Table 8 shows the comparison of method with existing methods

CONCLUSION

The proposed methods demonstrate strong potential for predicting the stages of the progression of Alzheimer's disease and classifying the effects of aging in the normal brain. The proposed methodology could be extended to include algorithms such as Evolutionary Algorithms, Hybrid Algorithms, and Nature Algorithms. Comparison of various different algorithms will provide a clear perception about the performance of neural networks for Alzheimer Classification and will lead to development of algorithm which could be commercialized and used widely.

REFERENCES

Douaud, G., Smith, S., Jenkinson, M., Behrens, T., Johansen-Berg, H., Vickers, J., ... James, A. (2007). Anatomically related grey and white matter abnormalities in adolescent-onset schizophrenia. *Brain*, *130*(9), 2375–2386. doi:10.1093/brain/awm184 PMID:17698497

Grady, McIntosh, Beig, Keightley, Burian, & Black. (2013). Evidence from functional neuroimaging of a compensatory prefrontal network in Alzheimer's disease. *The Journal of Neuroscience*, *23*(3), 986–993. PMID:12574428

Grady, Furey, Pietrini, Horwitz, & Rapoport. (2001). Altered brain functional connectivity and impaired short-term memory in Alzheimer's disease. *Brain*, *124*(4), 739–756. doi:10.1093/brain/124.4.739 PMID:11287374

Krizhevsky, A., Sutskever, I., & Hinton, G. E. (2012). Imagenet classification with deep convolutional neural networks. *Advances in Neural Information Processing Systems*, 1097–1105.

Laske, C., Sohrabi, H. R., Frost, S. M., López-de-Ipiña, K., Garrard, P., Buscema, M., ... O'Bryant, S. E. (2015). Innovative diagnostic tools for early detaction of Alzheimer's disease by chrishtophLaske. *NCBI, 5*.

LeCun, Y., Bottou, L., Bengio, Y., & Haffner, P. (1998). Gradient-based learning applied to document recognition. *Proceedings of the IEEE*, *86*(11), 2278–2323. doi:10.1109/5.726791

Li, F., Tran, L., Thung, K. H., Ji, S., Shen, D., & Li, J. (2015). A Robust Deep Model for Improved Classification of AD/MCI Patients. *IEEE Journal of Biomedical and Health Informatics*, *19*(5), 1610–1616. doi:10.1109/JBHI.2015.2429556 PMID:25955998

Liu, S., Cai, W., Liu, S., & Zhang, F. (2015). Multimodal Neuroimaging & Depression. Springer.

Liu, S. S., Cai, W., Pujol, S., Kikinis, R., & Feng, D. (2014). Early Diagnosis of Alzheimer's Disease With Deep Learning. University of Sydney.

Mareeswari, S., & Dr, G. (2015). A survey: Early Detection of Alzheimer's Disease using Different Techniques. *International Journal on Computational Sciences & Applications*, *5*(1), 27–37. doi:10.5121/ijcsa.2015.5103

Ren, S., He, K., Girshick, R., & Sun, J. (2015). Faster R-cnn: Towards Real-time Object Detection with Region Proposal Networks. *Advances in Neural Information Processing Systems*, 91–99.

Sarraf, S., & Golestani, A. M. (2016). A robust and adaptive decision-making algorithm for detecting brain networks using functional mri within the spatial and frequency domain. *IEEE International Conference on Biomedical and Health Informatics (BHI)*, 1–6. 10.1109/BHI.2016.7455833

Sarraf, S., & Tofighi, G. (2016). Classification of Alzheimer's Disease Structural MRI Data by Deep Learning Convolutional Neural Networks. *arXiv*, 1–14.

Sørensen, L., Igel, C., Liv Hansen, N., Osler, M., Lauritzen, M., Rostrup, E., & Nielsen, M. (2015). Early detection of Alzheimer's disease using MRI hippocampal texture. *Human Brain Mapping, Alzheimer's DiseaseNeuroimaging Initiative*, *37*(3), 1148–1161. doi:10.1002/hbm.23091 PMID:26686837

Townsend, J. T. (1971). Theoretical analysis of an alphabetic confusion matrix. *Attention, Perception & Psychophysics*, *9*(1), 40–50. doi:10.3758/BF03213026

Tripoliti, E. E., Fotiadis, D. I., & Argyropoulou, M. (2008). A supervised method to assist the diagnosis and classification of the status of alzheimer's disease using data from an fmri experiment. *30th Annual International Conference of the IEEE*, 4419–4422. 10.1109/IEMBS.2008.4650191

Tripoliti, Fotiadis, & Argyropoulou. (2012). A supervised method to assist the diagnois and classification of the status of Alzheimer's disease using data from an FMRI experiment. *Brain*.

Vemuri, P., Jones, D. T., & Jack, C. R. (2012). Resting state functional MRI in Alzheimer's Disease. *Alzheimer's Research & Therapy*, *4*(1). PMID:22236691

Warsi, M. A. (2012). The Fractal Nature and Functional Connectivity of Brain Function as Measured by BOLD MRI in Alzheimer's Disease. *Magnetic Resonance Materials in Physics, Biology and Medicine*, *25*(5), 335–344. doi:10.100710334-012-0312-0

Wyman, B. T., Harvey, D. J., Crawford, K., Bernstein, M. A., Carmichael, O., Cole, P. E., & Jack, C. R. (2013). Standardization of analysis sets for reporting results from ADNI MRI data. *Alzheimer's & Dementia*, *9*(3), 332–337. doi:10.1016/j.jalz.2012.06.004 PMID:23110865

Zeiler, M. D., & Fergus, R. (2014). Visualizing and understanding convolutional networks. In *European conference on computer vision*. Springer International Publishing.

Chapter 12
Application of Object Recognition With Shape-Index Identification and 2D Scale Invariant Feature Transform for Key-Point Detection

Chiranji Lal Chowdhary
VIT University, India

ABSTRACT

Humans make object recognition look inconsequential. In this chapter, scale-invariant feature extraction and shape-index depiction are used on a range of images for identifying objects. The shape-index is attained and used as a local descriptor or key-point descriptor. First surface properties for shape index identification and second as 2D scale invariant feature transformed for key-point detection and feature extraction. The object recognition classification is compared results with shape-index identification and 2D scale-invariant feature transform for key-point detection with SIFT and SURF. The authors are using images from the ImageNet dataset, and with use of shift-index + SIFT descriptors, they are finding better accuracy at the classification stage.

1. INTRODUCTION

Object recognition is an inspiring task because of its unpredictable features for diverse objects. This application is implemented by taking an image as an input and from that an object is identified using the dataset which encompasses trained images. Different algorithms are proposed by some researchers (Lowe, 2004; Chowdhary, 2011; Chowdhary, Muatjitjeja & Jat, 2015) to make this recognition easy. In contemporary surveillance classification, scanning an item/object from an apprehended image from a camera became a very tricky job for all the surveillance professionals. Those professional want an expert system to recognize the objects. Recognizing objects from a rotated, scale invariant and occluded

DOI: 10.4018/978-1-5225-5775-3.ch012

images is a challenging task and hard to identify an object from 2D and 3D view images. But the issue is the results from those expert systems is not that much exact as we are predicting. So, such a system is required which produces more precise results. Identifying object from an image with more noise and occlusion is also a confusing task.

The standing methodologies recognize an object by its size, structure and position. Such systems may be failed to find an object which is in upside down or a slight change in its position. This failure causes due to the reason that it is compared with its default position. It is required to develop such an expert system to recognize and understand the 3D-structure of an object. After adopting 3D-structures of an object for object recognition, the results are not failed in the cases where the system tends to detect the object in every position. High-definition (HD) cameras are like human eyes in recent days. HD cameras are highly trending technology in present world because they capture images with more accurate pixels, 3D sensing and displaying. If the cameras are auspicious to capture accurate pixels and equally important 2D, 3D sensing, capturing and displaying then it is possible to identify and recognize the objects which has been captured by those high-definition cameras. It is found difficult to recognize or identify the objects on the surveillance system with normal cameras so the high-definition cameras are good option to capture 2D and 3D view images which lead to design a system to identify and recognize an object which may assist surveillance experts. Usual surveillance systems available in airports, temples, malls and different public places are using object recognition with low accurate results so it is needed to to develop an expert system with more accurate results to identify and recognize an object.

In most of the object recognition system find it difficult in recognition when the object is occluded by another object. Some object is taken and segmented, then stored as dataset which is mainly used in map. Using this dataset the scanned image is identified. The identified object is depending on the feature generated from the scanned image and that feature point is mapped onto the object using the dataset. Objects in a captured or sensed image had been identified and recognized by the expert system. Even now also there are numerous expert systems helping for surveillance experts for security purposes but the issue is how accurate the expert system is producing the results. In order to increase the accuracy, we are proposing an expert system which includes two mechanisms to recognize an object from a captured image. This mechanism can be applied to any range image where an image is with scale invariant, rotation and occluded images.

The shape-index is defined as a single valued measure of local curvature which is derived from the eigenvalues of the Hessian. The shape-index can be castoff to invention erections constructed on their apparent local shape. The shape index maps to values from -1 to 1 which signify diverse type of shapes (Koenderink & van Doorn, 1992). A shape index is actually of spatial measurement. This measurement marks the numerical connection among mathematical modelling and empirical study (Prasad, Gupta & Biswas, 2001).

Among collective glitches in pattern recognition and image processing approach, feature matching between diverse images in main. In cases of same scales or similar orientations of an image, results can be achieved by detecting corners. This will not be easy for such images which are having unlike scales and rotations. Scale Invariant Feature Transform (SIFT) is used in such cases (Lowe, 2004). SIFT is fairly a convoluted algorithm. SIFT is having manifold portions in entire algorithm. The working order of SIFT is having these important steps: construct a scale space, LoG Approximation, outcome key points, dispose of unscrupulous key points, allocate an orientation to the key points and produce SIFT features.

The mechanisms which we are using in this chapter are the shape-index for key-point detection and scale invariant feature transformed (SIFT) for feature detection and identification. Shape-index method is used for key-point description and also for key-point detection, which has been grown from the feature and which will be used for matching those key-points with the input image and scale invariant feature transformed (SIFT) is the method used for feature detection, and those detected features had been matched with those key-points detected by the shape index method and after matching results generated, which are more accurate than other already existing expert systems for object recognition and/or identification.

The objective behind this chapter is to hybridize shape-index method and SIFT mechanisms for object recognition which is applicable to all range images with 2D and 3D view images. More accurate results can be achieved by both the methods shape-index and scale invariant feature transformed (SIFT) so object recognition system is more efficient than others existing approaches. The rest of this chapter is folded as follows: Section 2 is covering literature survey/background and Section 3 is for proposed framework/system architecture and its steps. Experimental Evaluation and result analysis is covered in Section 4 and Section 5, respectively. Section 6 and Section 7 are having experimental evaluation followed by conclusion and future work.

2. LITERATURE REVIEW/BACKGROUND

Shape-identification by feature-based method includes local features, global features, feature distribution and spatial method (Bayramoglu & Alatan, 2010). There features need normalization and partial matching is not supported by such feature-based shape-identification. The local feature method is only option to identify a shape partially. Graph-based approach is also relevant for shape-identification. Some of the graph-based methods are a model graph which is suitable to solid models and skeletal graph. Graph methods are applicable to volume models including human and animal shapes. The graph-based approach is less robust than the feature-based approach (Tangelder & Veltkamp, 2008). The proposed method of shape-index combined with 2D scale invariant feature transform for key-point detection will provide scope to overcome these limitations.

Some distinctive points for the three-dimensional object are there and after that matching it with the object available in the database. Object matching follows some steps as: (1) they are getting a three-dimensional object and; (2) constructing regions. Once such region is constructed after they are getting shape descriptors by methods like Harmonic shape descriptor and later they are measuring distinction regions. If the region is distinctive then they are assigning 1 else 0. Once the distinctive region is measured they are mapping to vertices, subsequently the mapped three-dimension surfaces are matched with the database and the results are generated. Calculating the most important regions on a surface is useful for shape matching but this require peculiar regions based on performing a shape-based search for each region as a query against a database. Individual regions of a surface have the shape consistent with objects of the same type and different from objects of other types. Shape-matching and shape- index help for demonstration to detect distinctive regions and mesh visualization, icon generation and mesh simplification (Bustos, Keim, Saupe, Schreck & Vranic, 2005).

Shilane and Funkhouser (2007) are getting a three-dimensional object, next partitioning that object into parts and finding analogous parts in that object. It will search for similar parts and after that find similarities between those objects in spite of different shape. Part analogy in sets of objects is a very simple searching and retrieval application, and the partitioning three-dimensional object is done by shape-diameter function (SDF) and uses it to find corresponding parts in other objects. Here automatically analogies are found among set of objects. The method first partitions the objects to create a parts hierarchy, and then defines a signature for each part and these signatures are later used to find analogous parts among sets of objects. They have shown that such analogies can support part search queries in a shape retrieval application. A stronger approach would try to analyse or partition the object in various ways depending on the query context. Moreover, since both objects partitioning and parts signatures are based on the SDF, the method is suitable for certain types of objects. For every type of images even for that images in the data set, and for the input images also parts will be separated in order to match and recognize an object. The parts are body, torso, head, front leg, back legs, tail these are level zero parts by this the parts level go until level 5. By matching the similar parts the object will be recognized. As a result, they have presented a method that automatically finds analogies among set of objects. The method first partitions the objects to create a parts hierarchy, and then defines a signature for each part and these signatures are later used to find analogous parts among sets of objects. The drawback to this approach is it is apposite only for animals and for human beings, and it is not applicable for objects. They have shown that such analogies can support part search queries in a shape retrieval application. A stronger approach would try to analyse or partition the object in various ways depending upon the query context. Moreover, since both objects partitioning and parts signatures are based on the SDF, the method is suitable for certain types of objects (Shalom, Shapira, Shamir & Cohenor, 2008).

Tangelder and Veltkamp (2008) used a view-based approach to identify shapes with rotation invariant. Here a view-based approach is explored to recognize free-form objects in range images. A set of local features is used to calculate and it is robust to partial occlusions. By combining those features in a multidimensional histogram, a highly discriminant classifiers are obtained without the need for segmentation. Recognition is performed using either histogram matching or a probabilistic recognition algorithm. Graph-based approach is also apt for shape identification and some of the graph-based methods are the model graphs which are applicable to solid models and skeletal graph and free graph methods are applicable to volume models (Tangelder & Veltkamp, 2008; Hetzel, Leibe, Levi & Schiele, 2001).

Lowe (2004) explained that extracting distinctive invariant features from images that are used for matching and object identification. Features in that object are scale invariant and rotation. Those features are highly distinctive. These features are extracted for object identification/recognition. Object recognition proceeds by matching those individual distinctive features extracted. Scale space extrema detection is the method used to search and identify interest points from scale invariant object. From those identified interest points, the key-points are selected to be used for matching and recognizing an object. The local image gradients are measured at each key point. This approach has been named the scale invariant feature transform (SIFT) because it transforms image data into scale-invariant coordinates relative to local features (Blum, Springenberg, Wulfing & Riedmiller, 2012). By adding the shape-index descriptor in feature extracting approach may give more attractive results.

Chen and Bhanu (2007) integrating local surface descriptor for surface representation and object recognition. Local surface descriptors are calculated for all the 3D surface points. They are calculated for feature points that are in areas with large shape variation. They are representing hash table for local surface patches to speed up the retrieval of the surface descriptors. In feature point extraction, feature points are defined in areas with large shape variation measured by shape index. They are defining a local surface patches with its feature points and neighbours for object identification. Those local surface patches are used to build hash table. In the object recognition process, they are comparing those local surface patches and then grouping corresponding pairs of local surface patches. Once those pairs of local surface patches are grouped then verification process will be initiated, and object will be recognized (Johnson & Hebert, 1999).

Blum, Springenberg, Wulfing and Riedmiller (2012) are approaching better than the other way of feature extraction evaluation. They are evaluated using RGB-D dataset. As RGB-D images gave RGB and depth information about the image using those and this leads to recognize the object easily. Feature extraction stands as a basic and main step in object recognition. RGB-D dataset will be good because other datasets do not allow high resolution data. The feature descriptors in RGB-Dataset are tried using different object recognition approaches. Interest points are taken before feature extraction. The procedure starts with detecting interest points in the input image. This continues with cropping of exactly 16×16 *PX* area at each interest point is extracted. Image patch inside the area of 6×6 *PX* is taken and compared with the feature dictionary. The advantage is the SURF points are taken as interest points as they are fast and taking some image patches around the interest points and not exactly using the edges as a feature (Doan & Poulet, 2014). Speed-up robust feature (SURF) points are used for improving feature descriptors object recognition rate. Some researchers are found explaining about large-scale data sets. There is problem in using large-scale datasets to classify an image and many challenges rising using large-scale datasets. Histogram-of-Oriented-Gradients (HOG) and local binary patterns (LBP) are used as the feature descriptor (Chowdhary & Acharjya, 2016; 2017).

3. PROPOSED FRAMEWORK

3.1 Pre-Processing/Segmentation

Pre-processing/segmentation process includes image enhancement and segmentation of images by noise removal from an input image and histogram equalization/threshold. Any type of images like JPEG, TIF, PNG, PGM, etc., can be used. Pre-processing leads to improve the accuracy as the result. Though the input images are in the RGB coloured format and once it has been pre-processed it will be converted as gray-scale colour, and the final output image will be in the gray-scale format only. The system has been designed to take the input image from the capturing by webcam or from ImageNet dataset (Russakovsky, Deng, Su, Krause, Satheesh, Ma... & Fei-Fei, 2015). The images in the ImageNet dataset are pre-processed and trained by support vector machine (SVM) method to recognize the object (Chowdhary, 2016).

3.2 Shape Index

Shape Index is the approach used for identifying the unique key-points from the input image and the range image data. Three-dimensional coordinates (X, Y, Z) for each pixel will be calculated and then the quadratic surface coefficients for local patch will be calculated which is used for calculating the polynomial surface equation

$$ax^2 + by^2 + cxy + dx + f = z.$$

The polynomial surface equation is used to calculate the shape-index value

$$SIndex = 0.5 + \left(\arctan 2(K1 + K2) / (PI * (K1 - K2)) \right)$$

Figure 1. Proposed design

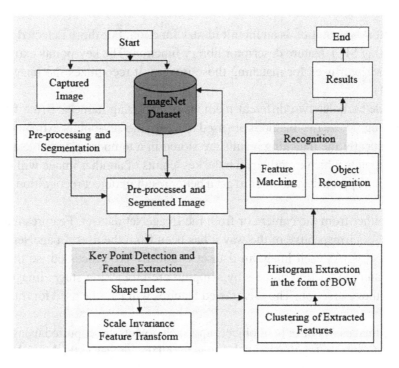

for each pixel on the range image.

The shape-index values are found for each pixel on the input image, and the coordinates (X, Y, Z) of each pixel has been encoded for each pixel on the input image. The coordinate values of the images in the ImageNet dataset has been encoded using the support vector machine (SVM) training approaches which are used for object recognition later. This shape-index value has been used as an input for the scale invariant feature transform (SIFT) approach in order to find the features for all the input images.

Each shape is characterized by a set of feature vectors where respectively feature vector encodes pairwise geometrical association amid a pair of breakthrough points on the shape. Each feature vector consists of inner distance, relative angles, contour distance, articulation invariant centre of mass and bag of features which are vigorous to unbending transformations and articulations.

3.3 Feature Extraction

Aimed at image matching and recognition, SIFT features are initially extracted after a customary of orientation images and stowed in a database. A novel image is co-ordinated by separately associating apiece feature from the novel image to this preceding database and outcome candidate matching features constructed on Euclidean distance of their feature vectors.

Scale invariant feature transformed (SIFT) is an approach used to identify the objects in an image even if the images are rotated, occluded and scale invariant. It has some sub-modules namely, feature detection, feature descriptor computation or matching. These sub-modules include some methods and finally matching with results. Feature detection can be done using some of the SIFT feature detector inbuilt or library function. Feature detector object detects features and then identify the key-points for an input image, and those detected key-points are marked and stored in a separate folder which is later used for matching.

Feature descriptor computation is an inbuilt library function. For those detected features key-points will be extracted using SIFT feature descriptor library function. The key-points extracted from the features by feature descriptor used for matching those images. It recognizes the image and identifies an object (Lowe, 2004).

Matching module includes two different methods of matching namely, Brute force matching and Flann-based matching. These two methods are used to match the key-points extracted from the detected features and subsequently the matching results are stored in a temporary variable and then the results are generated. Key-points which exactly match the key-points of another image will be drawn by a line. Flann-based matching approach is in order to get a better result in object recognition (Farhangi, Soryani & Fathy, 2012).

Input image is either from the camera or from the ImageNet dataset. Features have to be extracted for all the input images irrespective of the way it has been from the user. ImageNet dataset is used for this recognition process. As each image in dataset is already pre-processed, so this can directly use these images for feature extraction process by skipping pre-processing stage. Images in the ImageNet dataset undergo feature extraction. Those extracted features will later be used for training the images in the ImageNet dataset.

The dataset has images of house hold objects and such objects are captured using the 3D camera by placing it in a table. Feature extraction has to be done for all the images in the ImageNet dataset to recognize the object. Each image in the data set undergoes this approach to extract features for all the images. This key-point is used in the further process such as dataset training (Tangelder & Veltkamp, 2008).

3.4 Clustering of Extracted Features

Clustering is nothing but grouping the features from the images. K-means clustering is the approach used to group the feature which is similar and this is the type from vector quantization. K-means clustering is a type of vector quantization. This approach uses a simple and easy way to classify the given dataset (Chowdhary & Acharjya, 2017). The images in the ImageNet dataset are all having same features and they are extracted by the scale invariant feature transform (SIFT) approach for grouping. Those sorted/ clustered features are made as the single feature for all the images with a common feature. Those sorted features are called as the feature vector and used by the matchless-ID; this is called as cluster-ID in case of k-means clustering. Feature vectors are taken as code-word and they are assigned to the closest centroid which is used as cluster-ID. The rare ID for the grouped/clustered feature vectors are used for training the images in the ImageNet dataset (Chowdhary, 2016).

3.5 Extracting Histogram in the Form of Bag-of-Words

Bag-of-Words (BOW) is a visual descriptor of the extracted features and this is used for data classification. The process starts with selecting the set of images and extracted SIFT feature points from all those images and got SIFT descriptor for each extracted feature point. Next step is to cluster around those feature descriptors and to get the visual vocabulary. The Bag-of-Words (BOW) is using the cluster as the vocabulary to construct the histogram. By simply counting the number features from each image belonging to each cluster. Then the histogram is normalized by dividing into the number of features. Each image used from the dataset is represented by one histogram (Farhangi, Soryani & Fathy, 2012).

Histogram is nothing but a value for all the feature descriptors of the input image which has been extracted using scale invariant feature transform (SIFT) the input image reaches that particular value by grouping/clustering. Now histogram values are found for all the input images and store in an unrelated file which visible to us. The system adopts Bag-of-Words (BoW) method and the histogram values are like a codeword. The codeword are assigned for all the feature descriptors of each input image and the images with same codeword are grouped to store in a different file with .yml extension (Chowdhary, 2016).

The final step in the BoW model is to convert vector represented patches to "codeword" (analogy to words in text documents) and produces a "codebook" (analogy to a word dictionary). A codeword can be considered as a representative of several similar patches. One simple method is performing k-means clustering over all the vectors. Codewords are defined as the centres of the learned clusters. The number of the clusters is the codebook size (analogy to the size of the word dictionary). Each patch in an image is mapped to a certain codeword through the clustering process and the image represents the histogram of the codewords. With use of simple feature matching provides just local information. So, BOW model get global representation of each object. By taking a set of features and create a representation for that image in a simpler form to classify it (Lowe, 2004; Farhangi, Soryani & Fathy, 2012).

3.6 Dataset Training

Before recognizing an object from an image, the datasets need training to get more accurate results. We can adopt any training mechanism. For training the ImageNet dataset support vector machine (SVM). In kernel type of support vector machine (SVM) there are two different types as cumulative and non-linear support vector machine (SVM). We use additive support vector machine (SVM) for more accuracy in results. Support vector machine (SVM) is used to analyse data and recognize patterns for classification.

Support vector machine (SVM) model starts with setting up the training data. After setting it up, support vector machine (SVM) train function is called. Regions are classified using support vector machine (SVM) predicted function and the support vectors are found. The training data are sent. The labels of those images, two matrix values, some parameters with some default values and the output will be of Boolean type. Training the data to set is must for more accurate results. In MATLAB support vector machine (SVM) is a separate predefined/library function whereas in OpenCV implementation it is called as the support vector machine (SVM) wrapper.

3.7 Recognition

Object recognition is the important and final process. The clustered feature value for the input images in the dataset are matched with the values for the input images. Once the values are matched and now the objects are recognized. The key value which matches with the descriptor values in the dataset subsequently the object is recognized. The matching with the trained data from the dataset and the input images their descriptor values reaches the particular threshold value which lead to object recognition.

4. EXPERIMENTAL EVALUATION

4.1 Shape Index: Description

Shape-index is the process of key-point detection for the extracted features within an image. Shape-index takes an image and then it extracts the features from that image. In reality the features are different depending on the object taken. For that extracted features, the key-points are identified for all images and those key-points are used for matching the object. The shape-index functions took each pixel from that image to get the coordinates and then encode it for matching and recognition.

Shape-index implementation actually takes every single pixel from an input image and takes the three-dimensional coordinates (X, Y, Z) values and subsequently encoded it for later use. Shape-index is the approach used for identifying the unique key-points for the input image. For the range image data three-dimensional coordinates (X, Y, Z) for each pixel will be calculated and then the quadratic surface coefficients for local patch will be calculated. They are used for calculating the multinomial surface equation. The polynomial surface equation is used to calculate the shape index value at each pixel on the range image.

Variable names used in pseudo code are data coefficients (a, b, c, d, e), expressions (x,y) and pixels values are represented by K1, K2, HX, HXX, HXY, HY, HYY, H and K.

Pseudo Code for Shape Index Program

1. Declare Data Coefficients a, b, c, d, e
2. $HX = 2 \times a \times x + c \times y + d$
3. $HXX = 2 \times a$
4. $HY = 2 \times b \times y + c \times x + e$
5. $HYY = 2 \times b$
6. $HXY = c$
7. $H = 0.5 \times \left(+ \dfrac{(1 + HX \times HY) \times HYY - 2 \times HX \times HY \times HXY}{SQRT \left[\left(1 + HX \times HX + HY \times HY\right) \times \left(1 + HX \times HX + HY \times HY\right) \times \left(1 + HX \times HX + HX \times HX\right) \right]} \right)$
8. $K = \dfrac{(HXX \times HYY - HXY \times HXY)}{(1 + HX \times HX + HY \times HY) \times (1 + HX \times HX + HY \times HY)}$
9. $K1 = (H + SQRT(H \times H - K))$
10. $K2 = (H - SQRT(H \times H - K))$
11. $SIndex = 0.5 - \dfrac{1}{PI} \times a \tan 2(K1 + K2, K1 - K2)$

4.2 Feature Extraction: Code Description

Features for an image are extracted in many different approaches like scale invariant feature transform (SIFT) and speeded-up to robust feature (SURF). Scale invariant feature transformed (SIFT) are used for images with noise, occluded, rotated. In the implemented code, we are using an extractor from scale invariant feature transform (SIFT) method and for all the images in the dataset extracting features using the extractor object. By the looping conditions features are extracted for all the images in the dataset. Feature extraction is done for detecting the key-points which are used for matching and recognizing the object. There are numerous methods available for extracting features and detecting key-points. Features are not same for all types of objects it will differ depending on the object for considering.

4.3 Clustering of Features: Description

Clustering is the process of grouping and here scale invariant feature transform (SIFT) extracted features are grouped. Grouping is promising only if the objects have same set of features or the key-points are similar. The features are grouped using Bag-of-Words (BoW) a trainer. Once it is clustered/grouped then stores the grouped feature because it is possible by storing it in a dictionary which is a matrix by using the keyword set vocabulary. This can store the extracted feature.

4.4 Histogram Extraction in the Form of BOW: Description

Histogram extraction is the process of tabulating the common values. From the extracted feature, detect a key-point for all those extracted features. Using the Bag-of-Words (BoW) dictionary, compute a histogram values for every single image in the dataset. For the extracted histograms, store it with labels. Now, assign a label value for the images. The assigned label value extracts histogram values which are common. The stored label value are matched for the input objects which is matched with the images from the input folder and then the matching is be tested for recognizing the object.

4.5 Dataset Training: Description

Dataset training is important for object matching and detection. The dataset has to be trained in order to get accurate results in object matching and recognition. There are different training mechanisms are available in training the dataset images. Histogram extraction process is the pre-requisite for training the data sets. The descriptor values and the label values in the histogram are stored in matrix file. This descriptor value is used here for matching and recognizing objects within the input image.

4.6 Object Recognition: Description

Object recognition is the final process and the main theme throughout this work. Different approaches are used in algorithms form implementing the object matching and recognizing. Histogram approach is used for storing the descriptor values and the label values compute histogram for every image in the dataset. The histogram extraction is applicable for the images in the data set and also for the images in the input folder. This histogram extraction for the images in the dataset and for the images in the input folder is due to the values obtained during the histogram extraction process for the images.

5. RESULT ANALYSIS

Most object recognition research papers provide both algorithmic description and implementation results. In this Section, overall result analysis is summarized. Earliest, one should keep in intellect that the estimate and evaluation of matter-of-fact results is forever intricate by the piece of information that the computational environments can be extremely dissimilar from algorithm to algorithm. In addition to this, convinced papers initiate general information of common attention, while others algorithms offer very specific techniques.

Let us first introduce in Figure 8 for results by shape-index identification and 2D SIFT for key-point detection. In this, we compared among accuracy results of matching and recognition for recognizing objects. Evaluation is in the midst of SIFT, SURF and SIFT+Shaap-Index descriptors approaches. Dataset selected for evaluation is ImageNet (Russakovsky, Deng, Su, Krause, Satheesh, Ma... & Fei-Fei, 2015). Accuracy of 78%, 80% and 82% for SIFT, SURF and SIFT-Index + SIFT are achieved respectively (Figure 2 and Table 1).

Figure 2. Results by shape-index identification and 2D SIFT for key-point detection

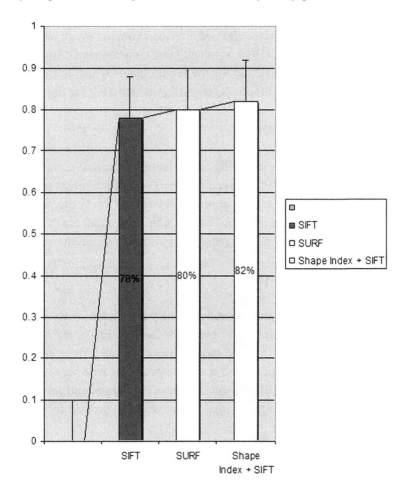

Table 1. Comparative accuracy of recognized objects

Key Point Detection and Feature Extraction	Accuracy in Matching and Recognizing Objects From an Image
SIFT	78%
SURF	80%
Shape Index + SIFT	82%

6. CONCLUSION

Object recognition is pertinent to all surveillance applications and supports in distinguishing objects while scanning a bag/luggage for scrutiny in temples, airports, malls and many public places. As the system is designed for object recognition it assistances the surveillance officers burden with more accuracy. In this image processing approach MATLAB and OpenCV tools are used. In this proposed framework image classification with ImageNet dataset are measured based on shift-index + SIFT descriptors and SIFT and SURF descriptors are compared. Accuracy of 78%, 80% and 82% for SIFT, SURF and Shift-Index + SIFT are achieved respectively. The key-points in the proposed method are fast feature extraction and support vector machine training.

7. FUTURE WORK

Future works for proposed object recognition system are as follows:

- Try with different datasets.
- The response time for the object recognition takes more than a minute and it better to have less than 10 seconds.
- Frequently recognizing objects had to be stored individually.
- Notification for harmful objects/newer objects.

REFERENCES

Bayramoglu, N., & Alatan, A. A. (2010, August). Shape index SIFT: Range image recognition using local features. In *Pattern Recognition (ICPR), 2010 20th International Conference on* (pp. 352-355). IEEE.

Blum, M., Springenberg, J. T., Wulfing, J., & Riedmiller, M. (2012). A Learned Feature Descriptor for Object Recognition in RGB-D Data. *IEEE International Conference on Robotics and Automation (ICRA)*, 1298-1303. 10.1109/ICRA.2012.6225188

Bustos, B., Keim, D., Saupe, D., Schreck, T., & Vranic, D. (2005). Feature-based Similarity Search in 3D Object Databases. *ACM Computing Surveys*, *37*(4), 345–387. doi:10.1145/1118890.1118893

Chen, H., & Bhanu, B. (2007). 3D Free-form Object Recognition in Range Images using Local Surface Patches. *Pattern Recognition Letters*, *28*(10), 1252–1262. doi:10.1016/j.patrec.2007.02.009

Chowdhary, C. L. (2011). Linear Feature Extraction Techniques for Object Recognition: Study of PCA and ICA. *Journal of the Serbian Society for Computational Mechanics*, *5*(1), 19–26.

Chowdhary, C. L. (2016). A Review of Feature Extraction Application Areas in Medical Imaging. *International Journal of Pharmacy and Technology*, *8*, 4501–4509.

Chowdhary, C. L., & Acharjya, D. P. (2016). Breast Cancer Detection using Intuitionistic Fuzzy Histogram Hyperbolization and Possibilitic Fuzzy c-mean Clustering algorithms with texture feature based Classification on Mammography Images. *AICTC'16 Proceedings of the International Conference on Advances in Information Communication Technology & Computing*. 10.1145/2979779.2979800

Chowdhary, C. L., & Acharjya, D. P. (2016). A Hybrid Scheme for Breast Cancer Detection Using Intuitionistic Fuzzy Rough Set Technique. *International Journal of Healthcare Information Systems and Informatics*, *11*(2), 38–61. doi:10.4018/IJHISI.2016040103

Chowdhary, C.L., & Acharjya, D.P. (2017). A Hybrid Scheme for Breast Cancer Detection Using Intuitionistic Fuzzy Rough Set Technique. *Biometrics: Concepts, Methodologies, Tools, and Applications*, 1195-1219.

Chowdhary, C. L., & Acharjya, D. P. (2017). Clustering Algorithm in Possibilistic Exponential Fuzzy C-mean Segmenting Medical Images. *Journal of Biomimetics, Biomaterials and Biomedical Engineering*, *30*, 12–23. doi:10.4028/www.scientific.net/JBBBE.30.12

Chowdhary, C. L., Muatjitjeja, K., & Jat, D. S. (2015). Three-dimensional object recognition based intelligence system for identification. *International Conference on Emerging Trends in Networks and Computer Communications (ETNCC)*, 162-166. 10.1109/ETNCC.2015.7184827

Doan, T.N., & Poulet, F. (2014). Large-scale Image Classification: Fast Feature Extraction and SVM Training. *Advances in Knowledge Discovery and Management*, 155-172.

Farhangi, M.M., Soryani, M. & Fathy, M. (2012). Improvement the Bag of Words Image Representation Using Spatial Information. *Advances in Computing and Information Technology*, 681-690.

Hetzel, G., Leibe, B., Levi, P., & Schiele, B. (2001). 3D Object Recognition from Range Images using Local Feature Histograms. *IEEE Computer Society Conference on Computer Vision and Pattern Recognition*, *2*, II-394-II-399.

Johnson, A. E., & Hebert, M. (1999). Using Spin Images for Efficient Object Recognition in Cluttered 3D Scenes. *IEEE Transactions on Pattern Analysis and Machine Intelligence*, *21*(5), 433–449. doi:10.1109/34.765655

Koenderink, J. J., & van Doorn, A. J. (1992). Surface Shape and Curvature Scales. *Image and Vision Computing*, *10*(8), 557–564. doi:10.1016/0262-8856(92)90076-F

Lowe, D. G. (2004). Distinctive Image Features from Scale-Invariant Keypoints. *International Journal of Computer Vision*, *60*(2), 91–110. doi:10.1023/B:VISI.0000029664.99615.94

Prasad, B. G., Gupta, S. K., & Biswas, K. K. (2001). Color and shape index for region-based image retrieval. *Visual Form*, *2001*, 716–725.

Russakovsky, O., Deng, J., Su, H., Krause, J., Satheesh, S., Ma, S., ... Fei-Fei, L. (2015). ImageNet Large Scale Visual Recognition Challenge. *International Journal of Computer Vision*, *115*(3), 211–252. doi:10.100711263-015-0816-y

Shalom, S., Shapira, L., Shamir, A., & Cohenor, D. (2008). Part Analogies in Sets of Objects. *1st Eurographics Conference on 3D Object Retrieva*, 33-40.

Shilane, P., & Funkhouser, T. (2007). Distinctive Regions of 3D Surfaces. *ACM Transactions on Graphics*, *26*(2), 7, es. doi:10.1145/1243980.1243981

Tangelder, J. W. H., & Veltkamp, R. C. (2008). A Survey of Content-based 3D Shape Retrieval Methods. *Multimedia Tools and Applications*, *39*(3), 441–471. doi:10.100711042-007-0181-0

Chapter 13

Image Segmentation for Feature Extraction:
A Study on Disease Diagnosis in Agricultural Plants

C. Deisy
Thiagarajar College of Engineering, India

Mercelin Francis
Thiagarajar College of Engineering, India

ABSTRACT

This chapter explores the prevailing segmentation methods to extract the target object features, in the field of plant pathology for disease diagnosis. The digital images of different plant leaves are taken for analysis as most of the disease symptoms are visible on leaves apart from other vital parts. Among the different phases of processing a digital image, the substantive focus of the study concentrates mainly on the methodology or algorithms deployed on image acquisition, preprocessing, segmentation, and feature extraction. The chapter collects the existing literature survey related to disease diagnosis methods in agricultural plants and prominently highlights the performance of each algorithm by comparing with its counterparts. The main aim is to provide an insight of creativeness to the researchers and experts to develop a less expensive, accurate, fast and an instant system for the timely detection of plant disease, so that appropriate remedial measures can be taken.

INTRODUCTION

Agriculture plays a major role in the existence of life. India is one of the largest producers in the world globe, depending mainly on agriculture of various crops. It is the second largest producer of rice, wheat, sugarcane, cotton, oilseeds, fruits & vegetables throughout the world. India holds the second largest agricultural land in the world, about 157.35 million hectares as of June 2017. Out of which a large area of the whole land is used for cultivating rice (Agriculture, 2017).

DOI: 10.4018/978-1-5225-5775-3.ch013

Different types of crops are produced in a land area based on the climate, soil, etc. crops can be categorized as Kharif (rice, maize, cotton, etc.), Rabi (wheat, potato, tomato, etc) and Zaid (cucumber, bitter gourd, etc.) based on the different seasons. Based on usage, crops can be categorized into 4 namely- Food crops (wheat, maize, rice, etc.), Cash crops (sugarcane, cotton, etc.), plantation crops (coconut, rubber, etc.) and Horticulture crops (fruits and vegetables). In India the highest producer of rice, wheat, cotton, coffee and spices is West Bengal, Uttar Pradesh, Gujarat, Karnataka, Kerala respectively. Major producers of different crops in Tamilnadu are rice, cotton, sugarcane, tea and coffee. In Tamilnadu, the per-hectare yield of sugarcane is high when compared to its other major producers (Crops in India, 2016).

The main stream of our population is farmers, who play a primary role in India's economic system. Poor farmers may possess small area of land for agriculture and they rely on other off-farm income for their survival. Current generation, after foreseeing the growing challenges in farming, the researchers and the practitioners together with the extension workers and farmers, were successful in incorporating Information and Communication Technology(ICT) tools for agriculture to improve its yield and thereby facilitating the future farming. ICT plays a vital role in exchange or sharing of knowledge between the extension workers and farmers in a more convenient way, with limited time, via Web portals, call centres (mobile or telephone), etc. TNAU AGRITECH portal is one of the ICT enabled agricultural initiative in Tamilnadu for agro-advisory services. Similarly, a large number of ICT projects are developed in national (Farmers Call centre, KVK, etc.) and international level (JavaRosa, CropLife, etc.) (Saravanan, 2012).

NEED FOR DISEASE DIAGNOSIS IN AGRICULTURAL PLANTS

Though, India has positioned one among the top countries in producing food cereals, farmers are still struggling for their livelihood. This may be due to several reasons like- less yield, unaware about the current market value, etc. Fewer yields may be due to many factors, in which, the most prominent one is the occurrence of disease in crops. Disease in crops reduces the products quality and quantity; thereby makes the farmers poorer and poor. Consequently, it affects our economy also.

Disease can be defined as any abnormality found in plants based on its appearance or function suspending its growth. Plant diseases can be categorized into 2- Biotic and Abiotic diseases. The causal agents are called pathogens. Disease affected plants are caused by pathogens namely fungi, bacteria and virus, depreciating the major functions of the plant viz. photosynthesis, transpiration, etc. A water-soaked tiny pale green spot which later gets enlarged and appear as dry dead spots can be identified as a symptom for bacterial infection. Symptoms found for viral diseases are wrinkling and curling up of the leaves followed with stop in growth. These diseases are difficult to diagnose as the same symptoms can be caused due to nutrient deficiencies and herbicide injury. Table 1 shows the various visual symptoms of occurrence various types of pathogens, its mode of transmission and lists some diseases caused by each pathogen. Amount of damage caused may vary depending on the type of pathogen and its combinations infected. The virulence of infection depends on the susceptibility of the variety, timing of infection, insects, and environmental conditions. Therefore early diagnosis of disease is necessary for increasing the productivity, quality of the food.

In recent decades wheat blast is one of the most fearsome and intractable wheat diseases caused by the fungus Magnaporthe oryzae. Recently, wheat blast menace entered India through Bengal-Bangladesh border. The fungus entered Asia, in 2016, for the first time creating havoc in Bangladesh where crops of over 20,000 hectares in six districts had to be burnt. Once infected there is no way to cure rather than burning crops. Rice Blast was first recorded in India during 1918. It is also known as rotten neck or rice fever. Expected loss if occurred to maximum is 70-80% (Bhattacharya & Pal, 2017). Timely measures like applying pesticides or fungicides can prevent or decrease the severity of attack due to such virulent pathogens (bacteria, fungi, virus, etc.) causing diseases. Hence easy, apt and quick diagnosis of plant disease and its remedies play a vital role in the betterment of agriculture.

Diseases found may vary depending on the type of the crop, soil, climate, etc. Several tools and techniques are adopted to detect the various symptoms, but this may vary depending on the target occurrence, pathogen involved and the favorable environmental conditions. Hence disease existence can be depicted in the form of a triangle called as disease triangle, first published by Stevens in 1960, as shown in Figure 1. (Stevens, 1960).

Major Paddy Crop Diseases and Its Severity Prediction

Rice is one of the most important food crops in the world. Farmers face economic losses, incurred due to some pathogens namely – fungi, bacteria and viruses. These losses can be overcome, if the disease symptoms are identified early and appropriate actions or remedial measures are taken accordingly. Figure 2 portrays the major rice producing countries in world and different states in India.

Table 1. Types of pathogens and their symptoms

	Fungi	**Bacteria**	**Viruses**
Visual Symptoms	Visual symptoms appear on the lower, older leaves. As disease matures it appears on both the sides. Water-soaked gray green spots darken to brown or yellow color and later white patches are found as fungal growth	Tiny pale green spots. Water soaked. Lesions enlarge and appear as dead spots.	Difficult to diagnosis. Can be caused due to nutrient deficiencies or herbicide injury
Mode of transmission	By air, rain or water, or less importantly on insects or seeds.	Mainly spread by insects.	Aphids, leafhoppers, whiteflies and cucumber beetle insects are the carriers of this disease
Examples	Late blight, Early blight, Downey mildew.	Bacterial leaf spot	Tomato Spotted Wilt Virus, Mosaic virus

Figure 1. Disease triangle
Source: First published by Stevens in 1960.

Host - crop

DISEASE

Pathogen – Fungi, Bacteria, Viruses, Nematodes, etc.

Favorable Environment – Air temperature, soil temperature, soil fertility, soil type, soil pH, soil moisture, rainfall, relative humidity

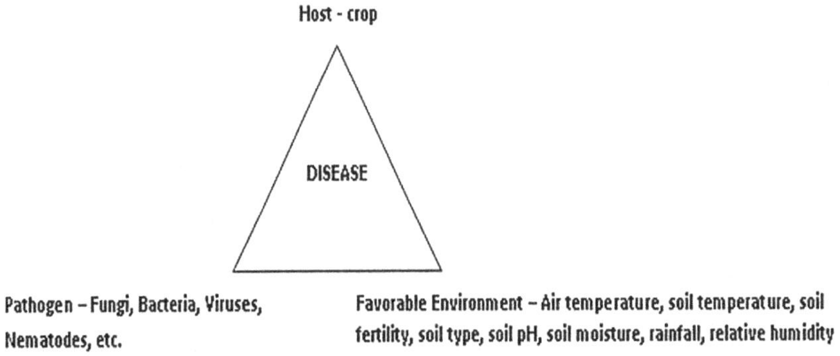

Figure 2. Major rice producing countries in the world and various rice producing states in India

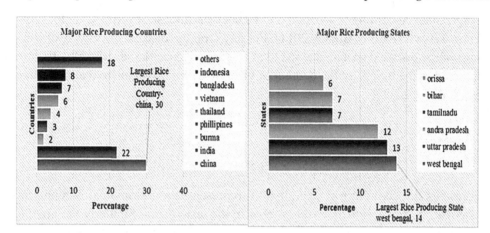

Figure 3. Pesticide consumption of different crops particularly rice, in India

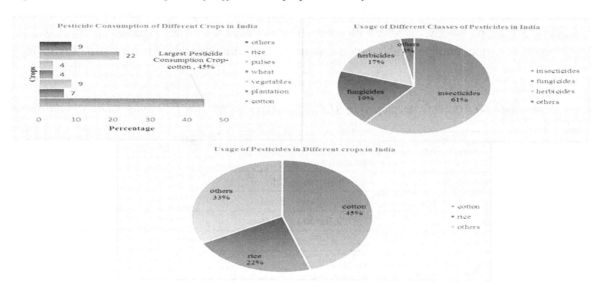

Some of the major paddy crop diseases found and requires attention are viz., Rice Blast, Rice Bacterial sheath blight, Rice Sheath blight. Initially it appears as spots around the infected areas. So detecting and predicting severity of the disease rely mainly on the spots and the total area in which the leaf is affected. Spots can be varied in their size and shape. More than one disease can show the symptom of similar spots which increases the complexity in identification. In such cases, additional factors like the rice variety and the local environmental conditions are also considered for prediction and for applying remedial measures in the form of pesticides. Figure 3 depicts the percentage of usage of different classes of pesticides particularly in rice, in India.

Disease infected plants vary based on the leaf spots and color. The leaf infected can be divided into 2 parts – infected part (lesion) and the non-infected portion. Image analysis can be done to quantify the affected area. Later determine the color, boundaries and area of the lesion to predict the occurrence and severity of the disease.

A disease severity scale is developed by Horsfall and Heuberger to assess the brown spot disease infected in sugarcane. According to Horsfall and Heuberger, disease severity scale for brown spot disease is given in Table 2 (Patil & Bodhe, 2011). For any crop the disease severity level is calculated as the percentage of the diseased spot area to the total leaf area. Hence the severity classification category can be represented as the ratio k, of the number of pixel in the lesion region to that in the normal region (Tian, Wang, & Zhou, 2011).

$$k = \frac{A_l}{A} = \frac{N_l}{N} \tag{1}$$

where A represents the diseased leaf total area, A_l represents the lesion area, N represents the pixel number in the leaf, N_l represents the pixel number in the lesion area. Similarly the grading standards for different crops is collected from different research papers and is listed in Table 3, which categorizes 6 levels of severity or damage.

The maximum accuracy and the reduced execution time and cost, for detecting a disease and predicting the severity level after classification, is improved by combining the computer vision and image processing in plant pathology, together with some efficient machine learning algorithms. This led to the development of various knowledgeable expert systems and Information and Communication Technology

Table 2. Disease severity scale developed by Horsfall and Heuberger for Brown Spot Disease detection

Category	Severity
0	Apparently infected
1	1-25% leaf area infected
2	26 – 50% leaf area infected
3	51 – 75% leaf area infected
4	>75% leaf area infected

Table 3. Crop disease classification standard

Level	0	1	2	3	4	5	Author
Cucumbers	0%	0.1%-5%	5.1%-10%	10.1%-25%	25.1%-50%	>50%	(Tian et. al, 2011, 431)
Corn	0%	0.1%-5%	5.1%-10%	10.1%-30%	30.1%-70%	>70%	(Tian et. al, 2011, 431)
Grape	0%	0.1%-5%	5.1%-30%	30.1%-50%	>50%		(Tian et. al, 2011, 431)
Sugarcane	0%	1-25%	26-50%	51-75%	>75%		(Patil et.al, 2011, 299)
Wheat leaf rust	<=15%	16-30%	31-45%	46-60%	>60%		(Xu et.al, 2017, 839)
Olive leaf spot	0%	1-33% (1-2 leaf spots)	34-66% (3-5 leaf spots)	>67% (>5 leaf spots)			(Mokhled et.al, 2013, 1210)

(ICT) based systems for agricultural plants performing different tasks namely plant crop management from the pre-sowing stage to post harvesting stage, weather and disease prediction, disease diagnosis and remedial measures, market price of the agricultural products, etc.

Most of the disease symptoms are visible on the leaves apart from the other vital parts of the plant namely root, stem, flower or fruits. Due to its vastness, the chapter is restricted to the different operations performed on a plant leaf for further analysis. The plant leaves play a vital role in sustaining life by generating oxygen for the humans to breathe. It also helps in preparing food for itself, for its own existence and well growth. Diseases if not detected timely, results in devastating loss of the entire crop affecting the human beings or the entire livelihood.

Therefore, for early detection of disease based on its symptoms found on the captured or acquired leaf image is processed via different phases namely – preprocessing, segmentation and feature extraction. The extracted features can be stored for further analysis viz. to detect diseases in plants. Through proper training using various machine learning algorithms, it identifies whether the leaf is diseased or healthy based on the features stored.

Earlier, preliminary diagnosis is done manually by farmers or experts after visualizing the symptoms occurred on leaves with a guess and preventive measures are taken accordingly. But this has some disadvantages such as:

- Accuracy is not guaranteed
- Late detection of infection
- Inappropriate use of pesticides
- Laborious
- High monitoring cost
- Challenging task for large areas
- Lack of sensitivity
- Requires specific and expensive equipment for diagnosis
- Requires expert personnel for advice
- Time consuming

Alternate expert diagnostic systems are developed to overcome these drawbacks resulting in early detection of diseases which leads to:

- Increased crop yield and quality
- Timely disease control
- Reduction in cost
- Appropriate use of pesticides type and quantity
- Increased sustainability

Earlier images as such is stored and processed, which takes much amount of memory and time for processing. Now-a-days unique features are extracted from the region of interest, segmented from the captured image. These features are stored for analysis and processing based on the application. Due to the advancements of image processing approach in various interdisciplinary fields, the chapter focuses on the different phases of image processing methods mainly the segmentation methods for feature extraction. The main objective is to enlighten the researchers to effectively use memory by reducing storage space and also to increase the processing speed and efficiency in predicting the results, by applying the appropriate methods based on performance evaluated and collected from the literature discussed in this chapter.

ROLE OF DIGITAL IMAGE PROCESSING IN DISEASE DIAGNOSIS OF AGRICULTURAL PLANTS

Now-a-days researchers concentrate on analyzing the different approaches for automatic detection of diseases in plants, which includes – image enhancement, image segmentation, feature extraction. Figure 4 shows the different fundamental steps in image processing which leads to disease diagnosis. Figure 5 portrays the substeps in image processing methods.

Image Acquisition

Traditionally farmers used to monitor the field manually and detect diseases found visually through experience, spotted by human eye on leaves. Now-a-days due to advancement in technology, image/video capturing sensors are used for continuous monitoring of the field and easier detection of diseases. This increases the efficiency by capturing images that is left un-noticed by the farmers. Figure 5(a) shows the different modes of image acquisition.

Whenever an image is captured, it is converted to a digitized form causing some form of degradation. An image is a two-dimensional array of pixels represented in the form of M x N matrix denoting

Figure 4. Image processing steps

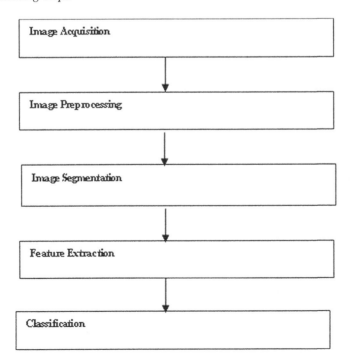

Figure 5. Different image processing steps (a) Image acquisition, (b) Image preprocessing (c) Target object extraction (d) Existing methods for image segmentation

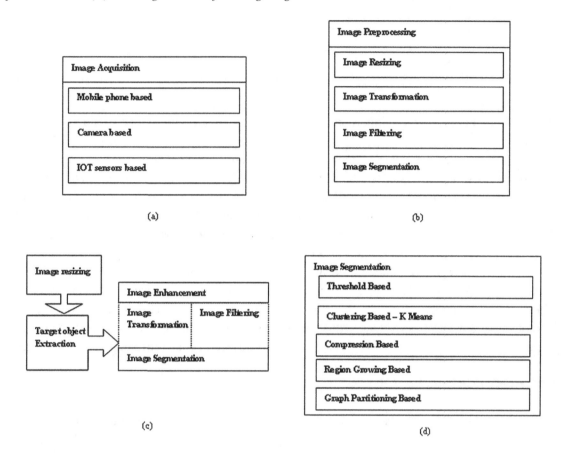

M rows and N columns. The value of each pixel is the intensity of the point from the scene in the form of brightness. Degradation can be modeled as a matrix vector notation,

$$g = Hf + \eta.$$ (2)

where g, f and η are MN dimensional vectors, and H is an (MN x MN) block-circulant matrix. Block circulant matrix consist of M x M blocks is represented as:

$$\begin{bmatrix} H_0 & H_{M-1} & H_{M-2} & \cdots & H_1 \\ H_1 & H_0 & H_{M-1} & \cdots & H_2 \\ H_2 & H_1 & H_0 & \cdots & H_3 \\ \vdots & \vdots & \vdots & \cdots & \vdots \\ H_{M-1} & H_{M-2} & H_{M-3} & \cdots & H_0 \end{bmatrix}$$

where each H_i is of N x N size is represented as:

$$\begin{bmatrix} h(i,0) & h(i,N-1) & h(i,N-2) & \cdots & h(i,1) \\ h(i,1) & h(i,0) & h(i,N-1) & \cdots & h(i,2) \\ h(i,2) & h(i,1) & h(i,0) & \cdots & h(i,3) \\ \vdots & \vdots & \vdots & \cdots & \vdots \\ h(i,N-1) & h(i,N-2) & h(i,N-3) & \cdots & h(i,0) \end{bmatrix}$$

Any form of degradation is found in this matrix. Hence matrix H can also be called as the degradation matrix.

Images of healthy and diseased samples are captured and uploaded from the farm using a digital camera, manually by the farmers (Al-Hiary, Bani-Ahmad, Reyalat, Braik, & AlRahamneh, 2011; Arivazhagan, Shebiah, Ananthi, & Varthini, 2013; Sannakki, Rajpurohit, Nargund, & Arunkumar, 2013) or with the aid of a mobile robot to which it is mounted (Ebrahimi, Khoshtaghaza, Minaei, & Jamshidi, 2017). Nowadays due to the boom of Internet-of-Things, many different types of spectroscopic and imaging sensors are used within a robot or an autonomous vehicle for acquiring the real-time images for instant diagnosis (Sankaran, Mishra, Ehsani, & Davis, 2010). Also frames can be extracted from the video, to monitor the unusual presence of objects on plant leaves (Ma, Li, Wen, Fu, & Zhang, 2015). In the above said cases target leaf need to be extracted from the complex background which is a complex and tedious task to achieve. So to reduce this complexity, farmers can capture an image placing a white sheet behind the leaf using their smart phone (Sanjaya, Vijesekara, Wickramasinghe, & Analraj, 2015).

Image Preprocessing

Preprocessing takes a digital image as input and produces the enhanced and segmented region for analysis. The major techniques of preprocessing include image enhancement and segmentation. It improves the degraded image by enhancing the appearance and features of the image by removing the noise or distortions present, if any. This can be resulted by increasing or decreasing the dominance of some features based on the specific application. This process is called as image enhancement. Later depending on the specific application the target region is extracted for further processing. This process is termed as image segmentation. Figure 5(b) shows the different steps in preprocessing.

Image Resizing

Image resizing can be either up sampling or down sampling to a fixed resolution, based on the increase or decrease in the resolution, required for any application. The main purpose is to improve the bandwidth reducing the storage space. Limitation is some information is lost during the process which may affect error in segmentation and feature extraction. Mostly used methods for interpolation are nearest neighborhood& bilinear interpolation methods.

Captured images are resized to a specified resolution either after or before preprocessing to utilize the storage space and to reduce the computational cost for later processing (Sannakki, Rajpurohit, Nargund, & Arunkumar, 2013; Al-Tarawneh, 2013; Zhang, Shang, & Wang, 2015).

Image Enhancement

A color is defined on its color space by its attributes like – brightness, hue, and its color. Color spaces can be device dependent and device independent. Device dependent color space includes- RGB, CMY(K). Device independent color space comprise of CIELab, CIELuv, HSI, HSV, HSL, etc. different color spaces are used based on the applications. Image processing on the RGB image directly may result in less processing speed and precision. Most of the algorithm simulations work effectively on binary and grayscale images rather than RGB. Therefore, transformations of image from RGB to various forms are made based on the task for analysis. In RGB model red green and blue channels are combined together forming various colors. The initial transformation can be done by decomposing the image into different color scheme. Compare the different image channel histograms with the original image. The image of leaf in G channel is the clearest for identifying the spots. Hence, G channel is chosen for further processing (Xu, Wu, Guo, Chen, Yang, & Zhang, 2017). Green pixels are masked based on a threshold value which distinguishes the healthy (green pixels) from the diseased (non green pixels) later the masked cells can be removed for detecting the diseased part alone, thereby reducing the processing time in classification (Arivazhagan, Shebiah, Ananthi, & Varthini, 2013; Zhang, Shang, & Wang, 2015).

Poor contrast is one defect found in the captured image. This may be due to some environmental factors like inadequate lighting or due to some of the physical characteristics of the camera. This can be enhanced by stretching or scaling the graylevel histogram of the image or by modifying the pixels values of the captured image which is converted to the fuzzy domain. The entire process is known as contrast intensification.

To reduce complexity and improving computational efficiency RGB color model is converted to HSI (Arivazhagan, Shebiah, Ananthi, & Varthini, 2013; Bai, Li, Fu, Ly, & Zhang, 2017; Majumdar, Kole, Chakraborty, & Majumder, 2015) or HSV(Sanjaya, Vijesekara, Wickramasinghe, & Analraj, 2015; Singh & Misra, 2016; Patil & Bodhe, 2011; Zhang, Shang, & Wang, 2015), or L*a*b* (Al-Tarawneh, 2013; Chitade & Katiyar, 2010; Zhang, Wu, You, & Zhang, 2017)before enhancing contrast for efficient feature extraction. Color transformation to L*a*b* is chosen as it determines the luminosity and chromaticity layers based on the human vision (Al-Tarawneh, 2013; Zhang, Wu, You, & Zhang, 2017). In HSI, Hue (H), Saturation(S) and Intensity (I) are color attributes referring to dominant color, perceived by the observer, amount of white light added to hue, amplitude of light respectively (Arivazhagan, Shebiah, Ananthi, & Varthini, 2013; Chaudhary, Chaudhari, Cheeran, & Godara, 2012).

To enhance the contrast of the image Gamma operator is applied (Gonzalez, 1992). Color space normalization and color vegetation indices are computed in (Bai, Li, Fu, Lv, & Zhang, 2017; Lavania & Matey, 2015) before performing segmentation. Plant canopy can be identified from the RGB image directly using Blob analysis.

Image filtering is done to remove noise if any present in the preprocessed image for further analysis. Binary filter is used for region growing and smoothing (Schor et.al, 2016, 356). Median filter is a non-linear higher order filter which replaces the value of the center pixel, by the median of the gray levels enclosed by the filter in the image area (Chaudhari et. al, 2012, 67). Improved vector median filtering (Al-Tarawneh, 2013) takes the average of all vectors X_i to the mean vector $\overline{X}$. The minimum value after computing the distances is taken as the vector median in the window, replacing the pixel vectors in the window center. Calculations can be computed using the following equations:

$$\bar{r} = \sum_{i=1}^{s} {r_i}\Big/{s} \tag{3}$$

$$\bar{g} = \sum_{i=1}^{s} {g_i}\Big/{s} \tag{4}$$

$$\bar{b} = \sum_{i=1}^{s} {b_i}\Big/{s} \tag{5}$$

$$S_i^{'} = x_i - \bar{x} \tag{6}$$

Hence the leaf images are enhanced by applying vector median filtering with better edge and small amount of calculations (Tian, Wang, & Zhou, 2011).

Gaussian filter is mostly best used for removal of noise (Sannakki, Rajpurohit, Nargund, & Arunkumar, 2013; Sanjaya, Vijesekara, Wickramasinghe, & Analraj, 2015). After segmentation some holes are formed in the image as noise. Such noise can be filled using morphological operations. Morphological open and close operations are also performed to remove blurs and petiole borders (Bai, Li, Fu, Lv, & Zhang, 2017) also can be used to recover the over segmented spots. Erosion and dilation operations can be represented using the following equations (Han, 2015; Ma, Li, Wen, Fu, & Zhang, 2015):

$$A \oplus B = \left\{ x : \hat{B}_x \cap A \neq \Phi \right\} \tag{7}$$

$$A \ominus B = \left\{ x : B_x \subseteq A \right\} \tag{8}$$

Use of preprocessing tools such as interaction between the user and the application through an input stroke, as well as the use of color distance maps improve the performance in recovering the over-segmented region (Grand-Brochier, Vacavant, Cerutti, Kurtz, Weber, & Tougne, 2015).

Segmentation

Different types of segmentation exist based on – Thresholding, Clustering, Compression, Region, and Graph Partitioning.

Thresholding based is a simple method using threshold value to turn gray scale to binary. The major steps include the following:

1. Initialize the threshold, T= (max value of image brightness+ minimum value of image brightness)/2

2. Group the image pixels into 2 set of pixels namely B & N, where B consist of pixels less than T and N comprise of pixels greater than T.
3. Compute the average of B & N separately as ub, un respectively.
4. Recompute the threshold value as, T=(ub+un)/2.
5. Repeat steps 2 to 4 until the required image is obtained.

Research is being done on choosing the threshold values. Threshold values can be found using maximum entropy, histograms of color intensities and Otsu method.

Thresholds can be chosen manually by observing the histograms of 3 color bands to segment diseased and non-diseased portion (Sanjaya, Vijesekara, Wickramasinghe, & Analraj, 2015). Histogram based segmentation is very efficient as it requires only one pass through the pixels. Clusters can be formed based on the peaks and valleys found on the histogram depending on the entire pixels of the image. Most of the authors choose Otsu method and its improved versions for choosing the threshold value (Bai, Li, Fu, Lv, & Zhang, 2017; Chaudhary, Chaudhari, Cheeran, & Godara, 2012; Ebrahimi, Khoshtaghaza, Minaei, & Jamshidi, 2017; Lavania & Matey, 2015; Schor, Bechar, Ignat, Dombrovsky, Elad, & Berman, 2016). It gives the exact binary image without noise. Limitation identified is its sensitivity to illumination which leads to loss of some descriptive ability of the image. Therefore optimal threshold need to be achieved, in which image is converted to fuzzy domain and maximum fuzzy correlation criterion is calculated (Gao & Wu, 2015).

Clustering based is an unsupervised method used for learning as well as for classification. Mainly 2 methods are existing – maxmin algorithm and K-means algorithm.

Maxmin algorithm determines the possible classes in which the data point belongs such that the inter class distance is maximized (Chanda & Majumdar). It proceeds by choosing a random value from the dataset as the first centroid c_1, and by setting the set C of centroids to $\{c_1\}$. During the ith iteration, c_i is chosen such that it maximizes the minimum Euclidean distance between c_i and observations in C.

K-means clustering is one of the simplest unsupervised clustering based segmentation method to find the best possible cluster by satisfying some criteria. It was developed by Macqueen (1967) and then by Hartigan and Wong (1979). The main goal is to partition the leaf image into k clusters based on the set of features with nearest mean obtained from the "center" or "centroid" of the n data points (Valliammal & Geethalakshmi, 2012; Zhang, Wu, You, & Zhang, 2017). The general algorithm for k-means algorithm is as follows:

1. Randomly pick k cluster centers either manually or by any heuristic approach.
2. Assign each pixel in image to a cluster with minimum distance.
3. Recompute the cluster centers by averaging all the pixels belonging to the specific cluster.
4. Repeat Steps 2 and 3 until there is no change in the pixel allocation to the clusters.

Distance can be computed as squared or absolute difference between a pixel and the corresponding cluster center, based on pixel color, intensity, texture, or a weighted combination of these factors. Euclidean distance, Mahalabonis or Manhattan distance measures are used to find the intra class distances. These distances metric can be used depending on the type of the data. Iteration is repeated to minimize the distances. Euclidean distances can be used to compare the images for similarity.

Euclidean Distance:

$$d\left(p,q\right) = \sqrt{\sum_{i=1}^{N}\left(q_i - p_i\right)^2} \tag{9}$$

Manhattan Distance or City Block Distance:

$$d\left(p,q\right) = \sum_{i=1}^{N}\left|q_i - p_i\right| \tag{10}$$

One or more clusters may contain diseases, where leaf is infected by more than one disease, therefore, according to Macqueen, Hartigan, and Wong, classification is done by minimizing the sum of the squares of the distance between the objects or pixels and the corresponding cluster or the class centroid.

Fuzzy C-means clustering allows a pixel point to belong to more than one clusters. This technique was first introduced by Professor Jim Bezdek in 1981 (Wikipedia). It partitions a finite collection of elements into a set of fuzzy clusters. It is mainly based on the minimization of the objective function. The objective function is defined as:

$$J_m = \sum_{i=1}^{N}\sum_{j=1}^{C} u_{ij}^m x_i - c_j^2 \tag{11}$$

where m is any real number called the Fuzziness component greater than 1, N is the number of pixel points, C is the number of clusters, u_{ij} is the degree of membership of x_i in the cluster j, x_i is the ith dimensional data, c_j is the cluster center and $\| * \|$ indicates the norm expressing the similarity between the measured data from the center. Steps to compute the FCM is as follows:

1. Choose 2 centroids randomly.
2. Compute membership matrix.

$$u_{ij} = \cfrac{1}{\sum_{k=1}^{C}\left(\cfrac{x_i - c_j}{x_i - c_k}\right)^{2/(m-1)}} \tag{12}$$

where, $x_i - c_j$ is the distance from point i to the cluster center j, and $x_i - c_k$ is the distance from the point i to the other cluster centers k.

3. Calculate the c cluster centers.

$$c_j = \cfrac{\sum_{i=1}^{N} u_{ij}^m . x_i}{\sum_{i=1}^{N} u_{ij}^m} \tag{13}$$

It gives best result for overlapped dataset and is better than k-means algorithm. Unlike k-means, the data point may belong to more than 1 clusters.

Hence Fuzzy C Means is a soft segmentation method which is used to find an optimal cluster center based on the similarity between the pixels and the cluster center. Fuzzy C Means clustering and its improved versions are frequently used for clustering based segmentation of diseased leaf from its complex background for further processing. If disease spots are found in any cluster formed after applying FCM, then its intensity will be high (Bai, Li, Fu, Lv, & Zhang, 2017; Majumdar, Kole, Chakraborty, & Majumder, 2015). Color based image segmentation, done by K-means algorithm, reduces the amount of error by increasing the value of k (Sannakki, Rajpurohit, Nargund, & Arunkumar, 2013; Chitade & Kativar, 2010).

From a HSI image, the gradient map of brightness, hue and saturation components – I, H, S respectively is segmented. Compared to the traditional segmentation methods watershed segmentation based on mathematical morphology performs well. This can be carried out by 3 runs of marked watershed algorithm on the different components (Bai, Li, Fu, Lv, & Zhang, 2017; Tang, Liu, Zhao, & Tao, 2009; Han, 2015).

Edge detection based helps in detecting border between 2 regions due to the abrupt changes in the image. A large number of image information can be gained by analyzing the edge. Common edge detection is mainly based on exploration and zero crossing.

Sobel operator edge detection is based on exploration, used to compute the horizontal and vertical derivatives. Sobel operator uses a 3x3 matrix filter represented using 2 kinds of matrix on a discrete image, A can be represented as:

$$M_x = \begin{bmatrix} -1 & 0 & +1 \\ -2 & 0 & +2 \\ -1 & 0 & +1 \end{bmatrix} * A \tag{14}$$

$$M_y = \begin{bmatrix} +1 & +2 & +1 \\ 0 & 0 & 0 \\ -1 & -2 & -1 \end{bmatrix} * A \tag{15}$$

(Valliammal & Geethalakshmi, 2012). The gradient value and its direction can be computed as:

$$G = \sqrt{M_x^2 + M_y^2} \tag{16}$$

$$\theta = arctan\left(\frac{M_y}{M_x}\right) \tag{17}$$

The brightness value can be got from the convolution of the images by the 2 operators. 2D xy-color histogram input can be given as an input to the SVM classifier for disease classification purpose based on pattern recognition and quantization of x, y pixels (Zhou, Kaneko, Tanaka, Kayamori, & Shimizu, 2014).

Polygon cropping is an alternate method which follows the edge contour of the entire image in its gray scale, to define a mask containing only the region of interest. The determined mask is convoluted with the filtered image, resulting in to a cropped or segmented image (Al-Tarawneh, 2013; Zhang, Shang, & Wang, 2015).

Figure 6 shows the sample output in its grayscale, the different stages in processing a paddy leaf image which is affected by the disease, Rice Blast. Here the region of interest (leaf) is segmented from the background by cropping the image through the end points. Later the diseased spot is segmented from the leaf using the k-means clustering algorithm. 4 clusters are formed in which 3rd cluster gives the appropriate region of interest (the diseased spot). This cluster is given as input to the feature extraction phase. Implementation is done using OpenCV and Python on Ubuntu Operating system.

Figure 6 shows the sample output in its grayscale, the different stages in processing a paddy leaf image which is affected by the disease, Rice Blast. Here the region of interest (leaf) is segmented from the background by cropping the image through the end points. Later the diseased spot is segmented from the leaf using the k-means clustering algorithm. Four clusters are formed in which 3rd cluster gives the appropriate region of interest (the diseased spot). This cluster is given as input to the feature extraction phase. Implementation is done using OpenCV and Python on Ubuntu Operating system.

Figure 6. Different stages in processing a paddy leaf image

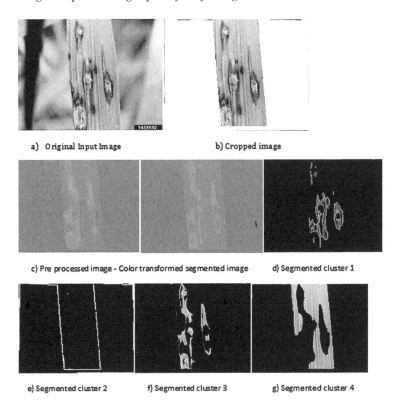

a) Original Input Image   b) Cropped image

c) Pre processed image - Color transformed segmented image   d) Segmented cluster 1

e) Segmented cluster 2   f) Segmented cluster 3   g) Segmented cluster 4

To test the accuracy and success of any segmentation algorithm, manually segmented image is compared with those segmented based on any algorithm. Testing the accuracy consist of 2 procedures that mathematically compared these two set of images taking manually segmented image as reference.

1. All pixels are analyzed in the image, is represented as:

$$z = \sum_{i=1}^{m}\sum_{j=1}^{n} I(i, j) \tag{18}$$

2. All pixels forming a part of diseased region is analyzed, is represented as:

$$d = \sum_{i=1}^{m}\sum_{j=1}^{n} I(i, j) == 1 \tag{19}$$

3. Perfect match in segmentation can be said when all the pixels in the diseased region is present in the image segmented based on any algorithm, is represented as

$$d_t = \sum_{i=1}^{m}\sum_{j=1}^{n} \left(\left(t(i, j) p(i, j) \right) == 1 \right) \tag{20}$$

4. Compare the differences between the 2 set of images pixel by pixel, to determine the percentage of misclassification, is represented as:

$$z_t = \frac{\left[\sum_{i=1}^{m}\sum_{j=1}^{n} \left(t(i, j) \neq p(i, j) \right) \right] * (m * n)}{100} \tag{21}$$

5. Difference value for the N set of images is represented as:

$$av = \left(\mu(d_t) - \mu(z_t) \right) \tag{22}$$

$$\mu(d_t) = \frac{\sum_{im=1}^{N} d_t(im)}{N} \tag{23}$$

$$\mu\left(z_t\right) = \frac{\sum_{im=1}^{N} z_t\left(im\right)}{N} \tag{24}$$

where 'z' represents all the pixels in the image, 'd' is the diseased regions within 'z', 't' is the label for automatically generated set, 'p' is the label for manually classified set, 'im' is the image set and 'μ' is the median (Camargo & Smith, 2009).

Feature Extraction

Feature extraction is related to dimensionality reduction. Binary representation obtained from segmented regions will be used here. Image features mainly relates to color shape and texture. It reduces the image data by measuring certain features like number of occurrences of zero as well as the number of connected components in the image, color& shape (Sanjaya, Vijesekara, Wickramasinghe, & Analraj, 2015), color & texture together with entropy (Sannakki, Rajpurohit, Nargund, & Arunkumar, 2013), median, mode, variance, standard deviation, number of peaks in the histogram and also the green density measured by fraction of pixels (Majumdar, Kole, Chakraborty, & Majumder, 2015).

Classification can be based on the texture, color, size and shape. Texture information is based on intensity of the pixel. Therefore RGB is converted to HSI. Color, size and shape features are based on the object.

Texture analysis is one of the most important techniques used in the analysis and classification of images. Textures are a pattern of non-uniform spatial distribution of image intensities differed from one pixel to another. Different properties of texture include uniformity, regularity, density, linearity, directionality, roughness, coarseness, phase and frequency (Gavhale & Gawande, 2014).

Texture based features can be obtained from the statistical models such as the spatial gray-level dependence matrix (SGDM) (Al-Bashish, Braik, & Bani-Ahmad, 2011) or Gray Level Co-occurrence Matrix (GLCM) or Color Co-occurrence Matrix (CCM). Later computations are done to identify the features namely- inertia, correlation, energy and homogeneity (Singh & Misra, 2016; Al-Bashish, Braik, & Bani-Ahmad, 2011) for the individual color space models for representing the images. A co-occurrence matrix represents the distribution of intensity values co-occurring at a given offset. It also represents the distance and angular spatial relationship over an image sub-region of specific size. GLCM is created from a gray-scale image. GLCM calculates how often a pixel with graylevel value i occurs either horizontally, vertically, or diagonally to adjacent pixels with the graylevel value j based on the resolution of the image. After creating the GLCMs, several statistics are calculated using various formulas (Pixia & Xiangdong, 2013).

Color co-occurrence method can be opted to extract the texture features of the image along with the color features resulting in a unique feature set. The extracted features obtained is given as an input to the classification phase, where using an appropriate machine learning algorithm, the classification of diseased and healthy plants is done, predicting the severity if diseased.

CCM method can be described in 3 major steps.

1. RGB images of leaves are converted to HSI color space representation, since it is based on human vision.
2. Generate a color co-occurrence matrix for Hue (H), Saturation (S) and Intensity (I) pixels.
3. Hue is based on wavelength of light, Intensity is the amplitude of light and Saturation measures the color in HSI space

The following equations are used to transform RGB to HSI.

$$\text{Intensity (I)} = \frac{R + G + B}{3} \tag{25}$$

$$\text{Saturation(S)} = 1 - \frac{3\min\left(R, G, B\right)}{R + G + B} \tag{26}$$

$$\text{Hue(H)} = \begin{cases} , & \text{if B} \leq \text{G} \\ 360 - , & \text{if B} > \text{G} \end{cases} \tag{27}$$

$$, = \cos^{-1}\left\{\frac{\frac{1}{2}[(R - G) + (R - B)]}{\sqrt{(R - G)^2 + (R - B)(G - B)}}\right\} \tag{28}$$

Color co-occurrence texture analysis was developed from the spatial Gray Level Dependency Matrix (SGDM). Both the matrices measure the number of occurrence of a particular pixel's gray level,i at any position p, from any other pixel's gray level j, resulting in a matrix P_{ij}. SGDM are represented by the function $P(i,j,d,\theta)$ where i represents the gray level value in the image $I(x,y)$ and j represents the gray level of the pixel at a distance d from the location (x,y) at an orientation angle of θ. GLCM function in matlab is used to create the gray-level co-occurrence matrix. The number of gray levels is set to 8 and the symmetric value is set to true and finally, offset is given a 0 value.

CCM matrices can be normalized using the following equations:

$$\text{Image attribute matrix, } p(i, j) = \frac{p\left(i, j, 1, 0\right)}{\sum_{i=0}^{L-1} \sum_{j=0}^{L-1} p(i, j, 1, 0)} \tag{29}$$

where p(i,j,1,0) is Intensity co-occurrence matrix, L is the total number of intensity levels,

Marginal probability matrix, $p_x(i) = \sum_{j=0}^{L-1} p(i,j)$ (30)

Sum and difference matrices, $p_{x+y}(k)$, $p_{x-y}(k)$ can be represented as:

$$p_{x+y}(k) = \sum_{i=0}^{L-1} \sum_{j-0}^{L-1} p(i,j)$$ (31)

where k=1+j; for k=0, 1, 2, …, 2(L-1)

$$p_{x-y}(k) = \sum_{i=0}^{L-1} \sum_{j-0}^{L-1} p(i,j)$$ (32)

where k=1-j; for k=0, 1, 2, …, 2(L-1) (Al-Bashish, Braik, & Bani-Ahmad, 2011)

Texture features can be identified based on the angular moment, mean intensity level, variation of image intensity, Correlation, contrast of the image, energy, entropy, the sum and difference of entropies, etc. significance of each and its computation is given below.

Angular moment is the measure of the image homogeneity, defined as:

$$I_1 = \sum_{i=0}^{L-1} \sum_{j=0}^{L-1} \left[p(i,j) \right]^2$$ (33)

The mean intensity level is the measure of image brightness.

$$I_2 = \sum_{i=0}^{L-1} i p(i)$$ (34)

Variation of image intensity, $I_4 = \dfrac{\sum_{i=0}^{L-1} \sum_{j-0}^{L-1} ij\ p(i,j) - I_2^{\ 2}}{I_3}$ (35)

The produce moment is analogous to the covariance of the intensity co-occurrence matrix computed as:

$$I_5 = \sum_{i=0}^{L-1} \sum_{j=0}^{L-1} \left(i - I_2\right)\left(j - I_2\right) P(i,j)$$ (36)

Contrast of an image is the inverse difference moment. This can be computed as:

$$I_6 = \sum_{i=0}^{L-1} \sum_{j=0}^{L-1} \frac{P(i,j)}{1 + (i-j)^2}$$ (37)

This can also be measured as the intensity contrast between a pixel and its neighbor over the whole image. This can be represented as:

$$= \sum_{i=0}^{L-1}\sum_{j=0}^{L-1} P(i,j)^2 \tag{38}$$

The entropy feature is the measure of the amount of order in an image. It is computed as:

$$I_7 = \sum_{i=0}^{L-1}\sum_{j=0}^{L-1} p(i,j) \ln P(i,j) \tag{39}$$

The sum and difference entropies can be computed as:

$$I_8 = \sum_{k=0}^{2(L-1)} P_{x+y}(k) \ln P_{x+y}(k) \tag{40}$$

$$I_9 = \sum_{k=0}^{L-1} P_{x-y}(k) \ln P_{x-y}(k) \tag{41}$$

The information measures of correlation is measured as:

$$I_{10} = \frac{I_7 HXY1}{HX} \ and \ I_{11} = \left[1 - e^{-2(HXY2-I_7)}\right]^{1/2} \tag{42}$$

where:

$$HX = -\sum_{i=0}^{L-1} Px(i) \ln P(i) \tag{43}$$

$$HXY1 = -\sum_{i=0}^{L-1}\sum_{j=0}^{L-1} P(I,j) \ln [Px(i) Px(j)] \tag{44}$$

$$HXY1 = -\sum_{i=0}^{L-1}\sum_{j=0}^{L-1} Px(i) Px(j) \ln [Px(i) Px(j)] \tag{45}$$

$$Energy, \ I_{12} = \sum_{i=0}^{L-1}\sum_{j=0}^{L-1} [P(i,j)]^2 \tag{46}$$

After feature extraction it results in 2 files namely training texture feature information and test texture feature information. Figure 7 shows a sample output of feature extraction while processing the rice blast infected image.

For instance, for any image feature extraction resulting in 192 rows indicates that, 32 samples are collected and processed for each 6 categories of leaves. Each row represents the number of features associated with each image. Hence features are considered as columns, for example 10. To the end of each row, consist of a number which represents the class to which the feature vector belongs. It can be numbered as 1, 2, 3, 4, 5, 6 depending on the category to which it need to be classified. In case of disease detection and classification application 1 denotes for Early scorch disease infected leaf, 2 for cottony mold disease, 3 represents ashen mold disease, 4 represents the late scorch disease, 5 as tiny whiteness disease and finally 6 indicates normal healthy leaf (Al-Bashish, Braik, & Bani-Ahmad, 2011). This final classification can be performed using Neural Network, Discriminant Analysis, Support Vector Machine (SVM), Self-Organizing Map (SOM).

From the existing literature taken for study it was found that the main task which needs attention is in the selection of the threshold for segmenting the region of interest, feature extraction and classification. Various methods are adopted to perform each task. Each has its own advantages and drawbacks. Segmentation of healthy and diseased is performed by means of thresholding, namely Otsu's thresholding and local entropy thresholding, in which the later gives the best result (Barbedo, 2013). Later shape and color features are extracted which forms a basis of set rule for detecting the presence of disease. In addition to the computation of various metrics for extracting texture features, it makes use of difference operators, Fourier transform and wavelet packet decomposition. Hence, Feature Extraction is an important phase with several advantages. Firstly, time and storage space can be reduced. Secondly, visualization of data can be made easier when reduced to very low dimensions – 2D or 3D. Final classification can be made by thresholding the feature using a weighted voting system (Barbedo, 2013).

EVALUATION AND PERFORMANCE ANALYSIS

Table 4 lists the performance of various segmentation methods, analyzing its role, their advantages and disadvantages.

According to the Albashish et.al (2011) the percentage classification accuracy results of the test data for various diseases after extracting the selected texture features is listed in the table given below. The classifier used is Neural Network with feed forward backpropagation principle. Al-Hiary et.al (2011) improved the classification accuracy rate to 94.3 from 92.7 obtained from the previous method, with a difference in the texture feature calculation. The comparison methods of various color feature models in classification is listed in Table 5. In which M1 model is evaluated to be the best. Here feature extracted is reduced using redundancy elimination of intensity features considering only the hue and saturation features. Hue and saturation are the robust features to variation of light.

Table 6 shows the different feature extraction methods & its accuracy when implemented along with a classifier for classification purposes.

Among the different methods implemented the best algorithm is chosen based on its simplicity, sensitivity, specificity and the accuracy in the performance. These are measured using various metrics depending on the task or application of the system. These statistical computations can be eliminated by adopting Fuzzy C-Means clustering (FCM), k-means clustering, etc. A good feature vector can be attained by reducing the dimensionality of the feature set improving its performance in identifying the object from the background with high reliability. This can be achieved by utilizing Principal Component Analysis (PCA) (Zhang, Wu, You, & Zhang, 2017).

Figure 7. Features extracted from the selected segmented clusters containing the region of interest for the Rice Blast infected paddy leaf image

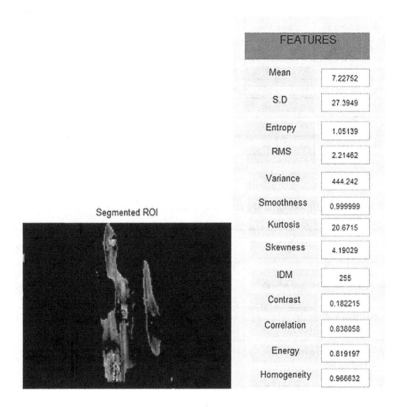

Table 4. Performance of various segmentation methods

Methods	Process	Purpose	Advantages	Disadvantages
Threshold	Segmentation	Masking the green pixels	Rapid, stable, good adaptability properties	Susceptible to noise, leading to misclassification
Otsu	Segmentation- thresholding	Leaf region is segmented	Simple and stable,	Hard segmentation as it leads to misclassification in case of dim target, homogeneous background, gray level overlaps between targets and background
Histogram based	Segmentation	image segmentation	Simple and efficient as it requires only one pass	Difficult in identifying the significant peaks and valleys from the image
K-means	Segmentation – clustering based	To partition the image into clusters - uses squared Euclidean distances	Simple and efficient	Difficult in predicting initial k
Fuzzy C- means	Target recognition and segmentation	Segmentation	Partition to more number of clusters such that a data point belong to more than 1 cluster	High dependence on initial clusters and local optimization. Fail to perform well in presence of noise

Table 5. Comparing the Analysis of Various combination of color model features for classification developed by Albashish et.al (2011) and Al-Hiary et.al (2011)

Model	Color Features	Early Scorch		Cottony Mold		Ashen Mold		Late Scorch		Tiny Whiteness		Normal		Overall Average	
		B	**H**	**B**	**H**	**B**	**H**	**B**	**H**	**B**	**H**	**B**	**H**	**B**	**H**
M1	HS	95	98	93	96	80	89	83	91	87	92	100	100	89.5	94.3
M2	H	89	90	86	92	69	86	79	89	83	93	98	98	84	91.3
M3	S	88	90	87	89	72	85	80	89	77	81	98	98	83.66	88.7
M4	I	89	92	88	89	79	84	81	88	83	86	97	99	86.16	89.7
M5	HSI	79	81	80	84	70	78	74	79	75	81	100	99	80.13	83.7

Table 6. Feature extraction methods and its accuracy in classification

Sl. no.	Paper	Accuracy	Feature Extraction Method
1	Detection and classification of leaf diseases using K-means based segmentation and neural-networks based classification	93%	Texture features (10) extracted using Color co-occurrence methodology. Color and texture combination results unique features
2	Fast and accurate detection and classification of plant diseases	94%	SGDM matrix generation for H and S using Color co-occurrence method
3	An empirical investigation of olive leaf spot disease using auto-cropping segmentation and fuzzy c-means classification	TAR-86% FAR-14%	Avoids image feature calculation by using fuzzy c-means fuzzy clustering classification
4	Detection of unhealthy region of plant leaves and classification of plant leaf diseases using texture features	95% using SVM classifier	Co-occurrence texture analysis method is developed. Textural features like contrast, energy, local homogeneity, shade and cluster prominence are derived from the co-occurrence matrix of H image
5	Leaf image based cucumber disease recognition using sparse representation	91.25%	Reshape to a vector of length 1024 from shape and color feature vector computed.
6	Vision based pest detection based on SVM classification	97%	H, S, I are extracted using equations
7	Plant disease recognition based on plant leaf image	90% using KNN classifier	Color, shape and texture features are extracted from the co-occurrence matrix of segmented and thresholded RGB image
8	Recognition of Greenhouse Cucumber Disease based on Image Processing Technology	96% using Minimum distance Criterion	Morphological, Color, Texture extracted from Gray Level Co-occurrence Matrix (GLCM)

CONCLUSION

The different methods of image segmentation, identifies the region of interest from the target area, equivalent to the human perspective for effective feature extraction. Different feature extraction methods help in identifying the unique or combination of features to detect the presence and severity of a particular disease on the target. Based on the features extracted, different classifiers are designed for specific classification purposes improving the performance, time and accuracy. Various applications to which the different methods can be applied are agricultural, medical, satellite imagery etc. Apart from disease diagnosis and management in agricultural field, different research is going on incorporating the various methods of image processing and computer vision techniques, together with the sensor technology. Some of the research areas include monitoring the growth and type of the crop based on the type of soil, moisture and the nutrient deficiency, differentiating one crop from the other, treatment and control of weeds, predicting the type of the grain produced based on the shape, size and color of the grain, sorting the grain types to various categories, etc.

REFERENCES

Agriculture. (2017, June). Retrieved from https://www.ibef.org/download/Agriculture-June-2017.pdf

Al-Bashish, D., Braik, M., & Bani-Ahmad, S. (2011). Detection and classification of leaf diseases usin K-means based segmentation and neural networks based classification. *Information Technology Journal, 10*(2), 267-275. doi: 10.3923/itj.2011.267.275

Al-Hiary, H., Bani-Ahmad, S., Reyalat, M., Braik, M., & AlRahamneh, Z. (2011). Fast and accurate detection and classification of plant diseases. *International Journal of Computers and Applications, 17*(1), 31–38. doi:10.5120/2183-2754

Al-Tarawneh, S. M. (2013). An empirical investigation of olive leave spot disease using auto-cropping segmentation and fuzzy C-means classification. *World Applied Sciences Journal, 23*(9), 1207–1211.

Arivazhagan, S., Shebiah, R. N., Ananthi, S., & Varthini, S. V. (2013). Detection of unhealthy region of plant leaves and classification of plant leaf diseases using texture features. *Agricultural Engineering International: CIGR Journal, 15*(1), 211–217.

Bai, X., Li, X., Fu, Z., Lv, X., & Zhang, L. (2017). A fuzzy clustering segmentation method based on neighborhood grayscale information for defining cucumber leaf spot disease images. *Computers and Electronics in Agriculture, 136*, 157–165. doi:10.1016/j.compag.2017.03.004

Barbedo, J. G. A. (2013). Digital image processing techniques for detecting, quantifying and classifying plant diseases. *SpringerPlus, 2*(660), 1–12. doi:10.1186/2193-1801-2-660 PMID:23419944

Bhattacharya, R., & Pal, S. (2017, March 5). Deadly wheat blast symptoms enters India through Bangladesh border, Bengal Govt. burning crops on war footing. *Hindustan Times*. Retrieved from http://www. hindustantimes.com/kolkata/deadly-wheat-blast-symptoms-enters-india-through-the-bangladesh-border-bengal-govt-burning-crops-on-war-footing/story-3zoWQ0H7sdMU4HxQyzWUsN.html

Camargo, A., & Smith, J. S. (2009). An image-processing based algorithm to automatically identify plant disease visual symptoms. *Biosystems Engineering, 102*(1), 9–21. doi:10.1016/j.biosystemseng.2008.09.030

Chanda, B., & Majumdar, D.D. (n.d.). *Digital Image Processing & Analysis*. New Delhi: Prentice Hall of India Pvt. Ltd.

Chaudhary, P., Chaudhari, A.K., Cheeran, A.N., & Godara, S. (2012). Color transform based approach for disease spot detection on plant leaf. *International Journal of Computer Science and Telecommunications, 3*(6), 65-70.

Chitade, A. Z., & Dr.Katiyar, S. K. (2010). Colour based image segmentation using K-means clustering. *International Journal of Engineering Science and Technology, 2*(10), 5319–5325.

Crops in India – GK notes in PDF. (2016). Retrieved from https://testbook.com/blog/crops-in-india-gk-notes-pdf/

Ebrahimi, M. A., Khoshtaghaza, M. H., Minaei, S., & Jamshidi, B. (2017). Vision-based pest detection based on SVM classification method. *Computers and Electronics in Agriculture, 137*, 52–58. doi:10.1016/j.compag.2017.03.016

Gao, R., & Wu, H. (2015). Agricultural image target segmentation based on fuzzy set. *Optik – International Journal for Light and Electron Optics*, 1-13. doi: 10.1016/j.ijleo.2015.09.006

Gavhale, K.R., & Gawande, U. (2014). An overview of the research on plant leaves disease detection using image processing techniques. *IOSR Journal of Computer Engineering, 16*(1), 10-16.

Grand-Brochier, M., Vacavant, A., Cerutti, G., Kurtz, C., Weber, J., & Tougne, L. (2015). Tree leaves extraction in natural images: Comparative study of preprocessing tools and segmentation methods. *IEEE Transactions on Image Processing, 24*(5), 1549–1560. doi:10.1109/TIP.2015.2400214 PMID:25667351

Gulhane, V.A., & Gurjar, A.A. (2011). Detection of diseases on cotton leaves and its possible diagnosis. *International Journal Image Processing, 5*(5), 590-598.

Han, B. (2015). Watershed segmentation algorithm based on morphological gradient reconstruction. *2nd International conference on information science and control engineering*. doi: 10.1109/ICISCE.2015.124

Lavania, S., & Matey, P.S. (2015). Novel method for weed classification in maize field using Otsu and PCA implementation. *IEEE international conference on computational intelligence & communication technology*, 534-537. doi: 10.1109/CICT.2015.71

Ma, J., Li, X., Wen, H., Fu, Z., & Zhang, L. (2015). A key frame extraction method for processing greenhouse vegetables production monitoring video. *Computers and Electronics in Agriculture, 111*, 92–102. doi:10.1016/j.compag.2014.12.007

Majumdar, D., Kole, D.K., Chakraborty, A., & Majumder, D.D. (2015). *An integrated digital image analysis system for detection, recognition and diagnosis of disease in wheat leaves*. doi: 10.1145/2791405.2791474

Patil, S. B., & Dr.Bodhe, S. K. (2011). Leaf disease severity measurement using image processing. *IACSIT International Journal of Engineering and Technology, 3*(5), 297–230.

Pixia, D., & Xiangdong, W. (2013). Recognition of greenhouse cucumber disease based on image processing technology. *Open Journal of Applied Science, 3*, 27-31.

Sanjaya, K.W.V., Vijesekara, H.M.S.S., Wickramasinghe, I.M.A.C., & Analraj, C.R.J. (2015). Orchid classification, disease identification and healthiness prediction system. *International Journal of Scientific and Technology Research, 4*(3), 215-220.

Sankaran, S., Mishra, A., Ehsani, R., & Davis, C. (2010). A review of advanced techniques for detecting plant diseases. *Computers and Electronics in Agriculture, 72*(1), 1–13. doi:10.1016/j.compag.2010.02.007

Sannakki, S. S., Rajpurohit, V. S., Nargund, V. B., & Arunkumar, R. (2013). Disease identification and grading of pomegranate leaves using image processing and fuzzy logic. *International Journal of Food Engineering*, *9*(4), 467–479. doi:10.1515/ijfe-2012-0241

Saravanan, R. (2012). ICTs for agricultural extension in India: Policy implications for developing countries. New India Publication Agency.

Schor, N., Bechar, A., Ignat, T., Dombrovsky, A., Elad, Y., & Berman, S. (2016). Robotic disease detection in greenhouses: combined detection of powdery mildew and tomato spotted wilt virus. *IEEE Robotics and Automation Letters, 1*(1), 354–360. doi: 10.1109/LRA.2016.2518214

Singh, V., & Misra, A. K. (in press). Detection of plant leaf disease using image segmentation and soft computing techniques. *Information Processing in Agriculture*. doi:10.1016/j.inpa.2016.10.005

Stevens, R. B. (1960). *Plant pathology, an advanced treatise* (vol. 3). New York: Academic Press. Retrieved from https://www.apsnet.org/edcenter/instcomm/TeachingArticles/Pages/DiseaseTriangle.aspx

Tang, X., Liu, M., Zhao, H., & Tao, W. (2009). *Leaf extraction from complicated background*. IEEE. doi:10.1109/CISP.2009.5304424

Tian, Y., Wang, L., & Zhou, Q. (2011). Grading method of crop disease based on image processing, Springer. *IFIP Advances in Information and Communication Technology, 369*, 427–433. doi:10.1007/978-3-642-27278-3_45

Valliammal, N., & Geethalakshmi, S.N. (2012). Plant leaf segmentation using non linear k-means clustering. *International Journal of Computer Science Issues, 9*(3), 212-218.

Xu, P., Wu, G., Guo, Y., Chen, X., Yang, H., & Zhang, R. (2017). Automatic wheat leaf rust detection and grading diagnosis via embedded image processing system. *Procedia Computer Science, 107*, 836–841. doi:10.1016/j.procs.2017.03.177

Zhang, S., Wu, X., You, Z., & Zhang, L. (2017). Leaf image based cucumber disease recognition using sparse representation classification. *Computers and Electronics in Agriculture, 134*, 135–141. doi:10.1016/j.compag.2017.01.014

Zhang, S. W., Shang, Y. J., & Wang, L. (n.d.). Plant disease recognition based on plant leaf image. *The journal of animal & plant sciences, 25*(3suppl.1), 42–45.

Zhou, R., Kaneko, S., Tanaka, F., Kayamori, M., & Shimizu, M. (2014). Disease detection of cercospora leaf spot in sugar beet by robust template matching. *Computers and Electronics in Agriculture, 108*, 58–70. doi:10.1016/j.compag.2014.07.004

Compilation of References

Abdel-Hakim, A. E., & Farag, A. A. (2006). CSIFT: A SIFT Descriptor with Color Invariant Characteristics. *Proceedings - IEEE Computer Society Conference on Computer Vision and Pattern Recognition, 2,* 1978–1983.

Aboulmagd, H., El-Gayar, N., & Onsi, H. (2009). A new approach in content-based image retrieval using fuzzy. *Telecommunication Systems, 40*(1), 55–66. doi:10.100711235-008-9142-9

Adjeroh, D. A., & Nwosu, K. C. (1997). Multimedia DatabaseManagement—Requirements and Issues. *IEEE MultiMedia, 4*(3), 24–33. doi:10.1109/93.621580

Agriculture. (2017, June). Retrieved from https://www.ibef.org/download/Agriculture-June-2017.pdf

Ahmadian, A., & Mostafa, A. (2003). An efficient texture classification algorithm using Gabor wavelet. In *Engineering in Medicine and Biology Society, 2003. Proceedings of the 25th Annual International Conference of the IEEE* (Vol. 1, pp. 930-933). IEEE. 10.1109/IEMBS.2003.1279918

Al-Bashish, D., Braik, M., & Bani-Ahmad, S. (2011). Detection and classification of leaf diseases usin K-means based segmentation and neural networks based classification. *Information Technology Journal, 10*(2), 267-275. doi: 10.3923/itj.2011.267.275

Al-Hiary, H., Bani-Ahmad, S., Reyalat, M., Braik, M., & AlRahamneh, Z. (2011). Fast and accurate detection and classification of plant diseases. *International Journal of Computers and Applications, 17*(1), 31–38. doi:10.5120/2183-2754

Almazan, J., Gordo, A., Fornes, A., & Valveny, E. (2014, December). Word Spotting and Recognition with Embedded Attributes. *IEEE Transactions on Pattern Analysis and Machine Intelligence, 36*(12), 2552–2566. doi:10.1109/TPAMI.2014.2339814 PMID:26353157

Al-Tarawneh, S. M. (2013). An empirical investigation of olive leave spot disease using auto-cropping segmentation and fuzzy C-means classification. *World Applied Sciences Journal, 23*(9), 1207–1211.

Androutsopoulos, I., & Malakasiotis, P. (2010). A Survey of Paraphrasing and Textual Entailment Methods. *Journal of Artificial Intelligence Research, 38*(2010), 135-187. Retrieved from https://www.jair.org/media/2985/live-2985-5001-jair.pdf

Arivazhagan, S., Shebiah, R. N., Ananthi, S., & Varthini, S. V. (2013). Detection of unhealthy region of plant leaves and classification of plant leaf diseases using texture features. *Agricultural Engineering International: CIGR Journal, 15*(1), 211–217.

Athanasiadis, T., Simou, N., Papadopoulos, G., Benmokhtar, R., Chandramouli, K., Tzouvaras, V., ... Huet, B. (2009). Integrating image segmentation and classification for fuzzy knowledge-based multimedia indexing. *Advances in Multimedia Modeling,* 263-274.

Babenko, B., Yang, M. H., & Belongie, S. (2011). Robust object tracking with online multiple instance learning. *IEEE Transactions on Pattern Analysis and Machine Intelligence*, *33*(8), 1619–1632. doi:10.1109/TPAMI.2010.226 PMID:21173445

Badge, J., & Scott, J. (2009). *Dealing with plagiarism in the digital age.* University of Leicester. Retrieved from http://evidencenet.pbworks.com/w/page/19383480/Dealing%20with%20plagiarism%20in%20the%20digital%20age

Baeza-Yates, R., & Ribeiro-Neto, B. (Eds.). (1999). *Modern Information Retrieval.* Addison Wesley Longman Limited. Retrieved from http://people.ischool.berkeley.edu/~hearst/irbook/print/chap10.pdf

Bagdanov, A. D., Ballan, L., Bertini, M., & Bimbo, A. D. (2007). Trademark matching and retrieval in sports video databases. *Proc. ACM Int. Workshop Multimedia Inf. Retr.*, 79–86. 10.1145/1290082.1290096

Bai, X., Li, X., Fu, Z., Lv, X., & Zhang, L. (2017). A fuzzy clustering segmentation method based on neighborhood grayscale information for defining cucumber leaf spot disease images. *Computers and Electronics in Agriculture*, *136*, 157–165. doi:10.1016/j.compag.2017.03.004

Ballan, L., Bertini, M., & Jain, A. (2008). A system for automatic detection and recognition of advertising trademarks in sports videos. *Proc. ACM Multimedia*, 991–992. 10.1145/1459359.1459544

Banerjee, M., Kundu, M. K., & Maji, P. (2009). Content-based image retrieval using visually significant point features. *Fuzzy Sets and Systems*, *160*(23), 3323–3341. doi:10.1016/j.fss.2009.02.024

Barbedo, J. G. A. (2013). Digital image processing techniques for detecting, quantifying and classifying plant diseases. *SpringerPlus*, *2*(660), 1–12. doi:10.1186/2193-1801-2-660 PMID:23419944

Barrón-Cedeño, A., & Rosso, P. (2009). On Automatic Plagiarism Detection Based on n-Grams Comparison. *Advances in Information Retrieval*, 696-700. Retrieved from http://www.cs.upc.edu/~albarron/publications/2009/BarronNgramsECIR.pdf

Bay, H., Ess, A., Tuytelaars, T., & Gool, L. V. (2008). Speeded-up robust features (SURF). *Computer Vision and Image Understanding*, *110*(3), 346–359. doi:10.1016/j.cviu.2007.09.014

Bay, H., Tuytelaars, T., & Gool, L. V. (2006). SURF: Speeded Up Robust Features, *Proceedings of European Conference on Computer Vision*, 404-417.

Bayramoglu, N., & Alatan, A. A. (2010, August). Shape index SIFT: Range image recognition using local features. In *Pattern Recognition (ICPR), 2010 20th International Conference on* (pp. 352-355). IEEE.

Belarbi, M. A., Mahmoudi, S., & Belalem, G. (2017). PCA as Dimensionality Reduction for Large-Scale Image Retrieval Systems. *International Journal of Ambient Computing and Intelligence*, *8*(4), 45–58. doi:10.4018/IJACI.2017100104

Ben Ismail. (2017). A Survey on Content-based Image Retrieval. *International Journal of Advanced Computer Science and Applications.*

Bennett, R. (2005). Factors associated with student plagiarism in a post-1992 University. *Journal of Assessment and Evaluation in Higher Education*, *30*(2), 137-162. Retrieved from https://www.scribd.com/document/309860125/Bennett-2005-Factors-Associated-With-Student-Plagiarism-in-a-Post-1992-University

Bermejo, P., Gámez, J. A., & Puerta, J. M. (2014). Speeding up incremental wrapper feature subset selection with Naive Bayes classifier. *Knowledge-Based Systems*, *55*, 140–147. doi:10.1016/j.knosys.2013.10.016

Bezdek, J. C., Ehrlich, R., & Full, W. (1984). FCM: The fuzzy c-means clustering algorithm. *Computers & Geosciences*, *10*(2-3), 191–203. doi:10.1016/0098-3004(84)90020-7

Bhattacharya, R., & Pal, S. (2017, March 5). Deadly wheat blast symptoms enters India through Bangladesh border, Bengal Govt. burning crops on war footing. *Hindustan Times*. Retrieved from http://www.hindustantimes.com/kolkata/deadly-wheat-blast-symptoms-enters-india-through-the-bangladesh-border-bengal-govt-burning-crops-on-war-footing/story-3zoWQ0H7sdMU4HxQyzWUsN.html

Bheda, Joshi, & Agrawal. (2014). A Study on Features Extraction Techniques for Image Mosaicing. *International Journal of Innovative Research in Computer and Communication Engineering, 2*(3).

Bloch, I. (1999). On fuzzy distances and their use in image processing under imprecision. *Pattern Recognition, 32*(11), 1873–1895. doi:10.1016/S0031-3203(99)00011-4

Blum, M., Springenberg, J. T., Wulfing, J., & Riedmiller, M. (2012). A Learned Feature Descriptor for Object Recognition in RGB-D Data. *IEEE International Conference on Robotics and Automation (ICRA)*, 1298-1303. 10.1109/ICRA.2012.6225188

Bouaguel, W. (2015). *On Feature Selection for Credit Scoring*. Retrieved September 30, 2017 From https://www.researchgate.net

Brown, M., Szeliski, R., & Winder, S. (2005). Multi-image matching using multi-scale oriented patches. *Proceedings of IEEE Conference on Computer Vision and Pattern Recognition*.

Bull, J., Collins, C., Coughlin, E., & Sharp, D. (2001). *Technical review of plagiarism detection software report*. Luton: Computer Assisted Assessment Centre. Retrieved from https://www.researchgate.net/publication/247703683_Technical_Review_of_Plagiarism_Detection_Software_Report

Buruiana, F., Scoica, A., Rebedea, T., & Rughinis, R. (2013). Automatic Plagiarism Detection System for Specialized Corpora. *Proceedings of the 19th International Conference on Control Systems and Computer Science (CSCS)*, 77-82. Retrieved from https://www.researchgate.net/publication/251899410_Automatic_Plagiarism_Detection_System_for_Specialized_Corpora

Bustos, B., Keim, D., Saupe, D., Schreck, T., & Vranic, D. (2005). Feature-based Similarity Search in 3D Object Databases. *ACM Computing Surveys, 37*(4), 345–387. doi:10.1145/1118890.1118893

Camargo, A., & Smith, J. S. (2009). An image-processing based algorithm to automatically identify plant disease visual symptoms. *Biosystems Engineering, 102*(1), 9–21. doi:10.1016/j.biosystemseng.2008.09.030

Carneiro, G., & Jepson, A. (2004). Flexible spatial models for grouping local image features. *Proc. Conf. Comput. Vis. Pattern Recognit., 2*, 747–754. 10.1109/CVPR.2004.1315239

Carson, C., Thomas, M., Belongie, S., Hellerstein, J. M., & Malik, J. (1999, June). Blobworld: A system for region-based image indexing and retrieval. In *International Conference on Advances in Visual Information Systems* (pp. 509-517). Springer. 10.1007/3-540-48762-X_63

Ceska, Z. (2009). *Automatic Plagiarism Detection Based on Latent Semantic Analysis* (Unpublished Ph.D Thesis). University of West Bohemia.

Chamorro-Martínez, J., Medina, J. M., Barranco, C. D., Galán-Perales, E., & Soto-Hidalgo, J. M. (2007). Retrieving images in fuzzy object-relational databases using dominant color descriptors. *Fuzzy Sets and Systems, 158*(3), 312–324. doi:10.1016/j.fss.2006.10.013

Chanda, B., & Majumdar, D.D. (n.d.). *Digital Image Processing & Analysis*. New Delhi: Prentice Hall of India Pvt. Ltd.

Chandrasekhar, U., & Das, T.K. (2011). A Survey of Techniques for Background Subtraction and Traffic Analysis on Surveillance Video. *Universal Journal of Applied Computer Science and Technology, 1*(3), 107-113.

Chan, K. P., & Cheung, Y. S. (1992). Fuzzy-attribute graph with application to chinese character recognition. *IEEE Transactions on Systems, Man, and Cybernetics*, *22*(1), 153–160. doi:10.1109/21.141319

Chaudhary, P., Chaudhari, A.K., Cheeran, A.N., & Godara, S. (2012). Color transform based approach for disease spot detection on plant leaf. *International Journal of Computer Science and Telecommunications, 3*(6), 65-70.

Chen, D., Zhao, S., Zhang, L., Yang, Y., & Zhang, X. (2012, November). Sample Pair Selection for Attribute Reduction with Rough Set. *IEEE Transactions on Knowledge and Data Engineering*, *24*(11), 2080–2093. doi:10.1109/TKDE.2011.89

Chen, G., & Chen, L. (2014). Recommendation based on contextual opinions. In *International Conference on User Modeling, Adaptation, and Personalization* (pp. 61-73). Springer.

Chen, H., & Bhanu, B. (2007). 3D Free-form Object Recognition in Range Images using Local Surface Patches. *Pattern Recognition Letters*, *28*(10), 1252–1262. doi:10.1016/j.patrec.2007.02.009

Chen, Y.-K., & Wang, J.-F. (2000, November). Segmentation of Single- or Multiple-Touching Handwritten Numeral String Using Background and Foreground Analysis. *IEEE Transactions on Pattern Analysis and Machine Intelligence*, *22*(11).

Chen, Y., & Wang, J. Z. (2002). A region-based fuzzy feature matching approach to content-based image retrieval. *IEEE Transactions on Pattern Analysis and Machine Intelligence*, *24*(9), 1252–1267. doi:10.1109/TPAMI.2002.1033216

Cheung, K.-W., Yeung, D.-Y., & Chin, R. T. (2002, August). Bidirectional Deformable Matching with Application to Handwritten Character Extraction. *IEEE Transactions on Pattern Analysis and Machine Intelligence*, *24*(8).

Chitade, A. Z., & Dr.Katiyar, S. K. (2010). Colour based image segmentation using K-means clustering. *International Journal of Engineering Science and Technology*, *2*(10), 5319–5325.

Chong, M., Specia, L., & Mitkov, R. (2010). Using Natural Language Processing for Automatic Plagiarism Detection. *Proceedings of the 4th International Plagiarism Conference*. Retrieved from http://www.academia.edu/326444/Using_Natural_Language_Processing_for_Automatic_Detection_of_Plagiarism

Chowdhary, C. L., & Acharjya, D. P. (2016). Breast Cancer Detection using Intuitionistic Fuzzy Histogram Hyperbolization and Possibilitic Fuzzy c-mean Clustering algorithms with texture feature based Classification on Mammography Images. *AICTC'16 Proceedings of the International Conference on Advances in Information Communication Technology & Computing*. 10.1145/2979779.2979800

Chowdhary, C.L., & Acharjya, D.P. (2017). A Hybrid Scheme for Breast Cancer Detection Using Intuitionistic Fuzzy Rough Set Technique. *Biometrics: Concepts, Methodologies, Tools, and Applications*, 1195-1219.

Chowdhary, C. L. (2011). Linear Feature Extraction Techniques for Object Recognition: Study of PCA and ICA. *Journal of the Serbian Society for Computational Mechanics*, *5*(1), 19–26.

Chowdhary, C. L. (2016). A Review of Feature Extraction Application Areas in Medical Imaging. *International Journal of Pharmacy and Technology*, *8*, 4501–4509.

Chowdhary, C. L., & Acharjya, D. P. (2016). A Hybrid Scheme for Breast Cancer Detection Using Intuitionistic Fuzzy Rough Set Technique. *International Journal of Healthcare Information Systems and Informatics*, *11*(2), 38–61. doi:10.4018/IJHISI.2016040103

Chowdhary, C. L., & Acharjya, D. P. (2017). Clustering Algorithm in Possibilistic Exponential Fuzzy C-mean Segmenting Medical Images. *Journal of Biomimetics, Biomaterials and Biomedical Engineering*, *30*, 12–23. doi:10.4028/www.scientific.net/JBBBE.30.12

Chowdhary, C. L., Muatjitjeja, K., & Jat, D. S. (2015). Three-dimensional object recognition based intelligence system for identification. *International Conference on Emerging Trends in Networks and Computer Communications (ETNCC)*, 162-166. 10.1109/ETNCC.2015.7184827

Chuang, L. Y., Ke, C. H., & Yang, C. H. (2016). *A hybrid both filter and wrapper Feature Selection method for microarray classification*. Academic Press.

Clough, P. (Ed.). (2003). *Old and new challenges in automatic plagiarism detection*. National UK Plagiarism Advisory Service. Retrieved from http://ir.shef.ac.uk/cloughie/papers/pas_plagiarism.pdf

Clough, P., & Stevenson, M. (2011). Developing a corpus of plagiarised short answers. *Language Resources and Evaluation, 45*(1), 5-24. Retrieved from https://www.researchgate.net/publication/220147549_Developing_a_corpus_of_plagiarised_short_answers

Cosma, G., & Joy, M. (2008). Towards a definition of source-code plagiarism. *IEEE Transactions on Education, 51*(2), 195-200. Retrieved from https://www.researchgate.net/publication/3052950_Towards_a_Definition_of_Source-Code_Plagiarism

Cremers, D., & Soatto, S. (2005). Motion competition: A variational approach to piecewise parametric motion segmentation. *International Journal of Computer Vision, 62*(3), 249–265. doi:10.100711263-005-4882-4

Crops in India – GK notes in PDF. (2016). Retrieved from https://testbook.com/blog/crops-in-india-gk-notes-pdf/

Das, R., Thepade, S., & Ghosh, S. (2017a). Decision Fusion for Classification of Content Based Image Data. In Transactions on Computational Science XXIX (pp. 121-138). Springer Berlin Heidelberg. doi:10.1007/978-3-662-54563-8_7

Das, T. K., Acharjya, D. P., & Patra, M. R. (2014). Business Intelligence from Online Product Review - A Rough Set Based Rule Induction Approach. Proceedings of International Conference on Contemporary Computing and Informatics (IC3I- 2014), 800-803.

Das, R., & Bhattacharya, S. (2015a). A Novel Feature Extraction Technique for Content Based Image Classification in Digital Marketing Platform. *American Journal of Advanced Computing, 2*(1), 17–24. doi:10.5923/j.ac.20120201.04

Das, R., Thepade, S., & Ghosh, S. (2015b). Content based image recognition by information fusion with multiview features. *International Journal of Information Technology and Computer Science, 7*(10), 61–73. doi:10.5815/ijitcs.2015.10.08

Das, R., & Walia, E. (2017). Partition selection with sparse autoencoders for content based image classification. *Neural Computing & Applications*, 1–16.

Das, T. K., & Chowdhury, C. L. (2017). Implementation of Morphological Image Processing Algorithm using Mammograms. *Journal of Chemical and Pharmaceutical Sciences, 10*(1), 439–441.

Dave, N. (2015). Segmentation Methods for Hand Written Character Recognition, International Journal of Signal Processing. *Image Processing and Pattern Recognition, 8*(4), 155–164. doi:10.14257/ijsip.2015.8.4.14

Dawn, D. D., & Shaikh, S. H. (2016). A comprehensive survey of human action recognition with spatio-temporal interest point (STIP) detector. *The Visual Computer, 32*(3), 289–306. doi:10.100700371-015-1066-2

De Luca, A., & Termini, S. (1972). A definition of a nonprobabilistic entropy in the setting of fuzzy sets theory. *Information and Control, 20*(4), 301–312. doi:10.1016/S0019-9958(72)90199-4

Diao, R., & Shen, Q. (2012). FS with harmony search. *IEEE Transactions on Systems, Man, and Cybernetics. Part B, Cybernetics, 42*(6), 1509–1523. doi:10.1109/TSMCB.2012.2193613

Doan, T.N., & Poulet, F. (2014). Large-scale Image Classification: Fast Feature Extraction and SVM Training. *Advances in Knowledge Discovery and Management*, 155-172.

Dollar, P., & Lawrence Zitnick, C. (2015). Fast Edge Detection Using Structured Forests. *IEEE Transactions on Pattern Analysis and Machine Intelligence*, *37*(8), 1558–1570. doi:10.1109/TPAMI.2014.2377715 PMID:26352995

Do, M. N., & Vetterli, M. (2005). The contourlet transform: An efficient directional multiresolution image representation. *IEEE Transactions on Image Processing*, *14*(12), 2091–2106. doi:10.1109/TIP.2005.859376 PMID:16370462

Douaud, G., Smith, S., Jenkinson, M., Behrens, T., Johansen-Berg, H., Vickers, J., ... James, A. (2007). Anatomically related grey and white matter abnormalities in adolescent-onset schizophrenia. *Brain*, *130*(9), 2375–2386. doi:10.1093/brain/awm184 PMID:17698497

Dr. Dobb's Essential Books On Algorithms And Data Structures, Book 5. (1999). Miller Freeman, Incorporated.

Dubois, S. R., & Glanz, F. H. (1986). An autoregressive model approach to two-dimensional shape classification. *IEEE Transactions on Pattern Analysis and Machine Intelligence*, *PAMI-8*(1), 55–66. doi:10.1109/TPAMI.1986.4767752 PMID:21869323

Eakins, J. P., Boardman, J. M., & Graham, M. E. (1998). Similarity retrieval of trademark images. *IEEE MultiMedia*, *5*(2), 53–63.

Ebrahimi, M. A., Khoshtaghaza, M. H., Minaei, S., & Jamshidi, B. (2017). Vision-based pest detection based on SVM classification method. *Computers and Electronics in Agriculture*, *137*, 52–58. doi:10.1016/j.compag.2017.03.016

Eissen, S. M. Z., Stein, B., & Kulig, M. (2006). Plagiarism Detection without Reference Collections. *Proceedings of the 30th Annual Conference of the GesellschaftfürKlassifikatione.V.*, 359-366. Retrieved from http://www.uni-weimar.de/medien/webis/publications/papers/stein_2007a.pdf

ElAlami, M. E. (2011). A novel image retrieval model based on the most relevant features. *Knowledge-Based Systems*, *24*(1), 23–32. doi:10.1016/j.knosys.2010.06.001

ElAlami, M. E. (2014). A new matching strategy for content based image retrieval system. *Applied Soft Computing*, *14*, 407–418. doi:10.1016/j.asoc.2013.10.003

El-Latif, A. A. A., Li, L., Wang, N., Han, Q., & Niu, X. (2013). A new approach to chaotic image encryption based on quantum chaotic system, exploiting color spaces. *Signal Processing*, *93*(11), 2986–3000. doi:10.1016/j.sigpro.2013.03.031

Fan, J. L., Ma, Y. L., & Xie, W. X. (2001). On some properties of distance measures. *Fuzzy Sets and Systems*, *117*(3), 355–361. doi:10.1016/S0165-0114(98)00387-X

Farhangi, M.M., Soryani, M. & Fathy, M. (2012). Improvement the Bag of Words Image Representation Using Spatial Information. *Advances in Computing and Information Technology*, 681-690.

Feng, M. L., & Tan, Y. P. (2004). Adaptive binarization method for document image analysis. In *Multimedia and Expo, 2004. ICME'04. 2004 IEEE International Conference on* (Vol. 1, pp. 339-342). IEEE.

Flickner, M., Sawhney, H., Niblack, W., Ashley, J., Huang, Q., Dom, B.& Steele, D. (1995). Query by image and video content: The QBIC system. *Computer, 28*(9), 23-32.

Flickner, M., Sawhney, H., Niblack, W., Ashley, J., Huang, Q., Dom, B., ... Steele, D. (1995). Query by image and video content: The QBIC system. *Computer, 28*(9), 23-32.

Forstner, W., Dickscheid, T., & Schindler, F. (2009). Detecting interpretable and accurate scale-invariant keypoints. *Proceedings of IEEE 12th International Conference on Computer Vision*, 2256-2263.

Ganesan, P., & Rajini, V. (2014). Assessment of satellite image segmentation in RGB and HSV color space using image quality measures. In *Advances in Electrical Engineering (ICAEE), 2014 International Conference on* (pp. 1-5). IEEE.

Gao, R., & Wu, H. (2015). Agricultural image target segmentation based on fuzzy set. *Optik – International Journal for Light and Electron Optics*, 1-13. doi: 10.1016/j.ijleo.2015.09.006

Gath, I., & Geva, A. B. (1989). Unsupervised optimal fuzzy clustering. *IEEE Transactions on Pattern Analysis and Machine Intelligence, 11*(7), 773–780. doi:10.1109/34.192473

Gavhale, K.R., & Gawande, U. (2014). An overview of the research on plant leaves disease detection using image processing techniques. *IOSR Journal of Computer Engineering, 16*(1), 10-16.

Gevers, T., & Smeulders, A. W. (2000). Pictoseek: Combining color and shape invariant features for image retrieval. *IEEE Transactions on Image Processing, 9*(1), 102–119. doi:10.1109/83.817602 PMID:18255376

Gonzalez & Woods. (n.d.). *Digital Image Processing* (3rd ed.). Pearson Publication.

Grabner, H., & Bischof, H. (2006, June). On-line boosting and vision. In *Computer Vision and Pattern Recognition, 2006 IEEE Computer Society Conference on* (Vol. 1, pp. 260-267). IEEE. 10.1109/CVPR.2006.215

Grady, Furey, Pietrini, Horwitz, & Rapoport. (2001). Altered brain functional connectivity and impaired short-term memory in Alzheimer's disease. *Brain, 124*(4), 739–756. doi:10.1093/brain/124.4.739 PMID:11287374

Grady, McIntosh, Beig, Keightley, Burian, & Black. (2013). Evidence from functional neuroimaging of a compensatory prefrontal network in Alzheimer's disease. *The Journal of Neuroscience, 23*(3), 986–993. PMID:12574428

Grand-Brochier, M., Vacavant, A., Cerutti, G., Kurtz, C., Weber, J., & Tougne, L. (2015). Tree leaves extraction in natural images: Comparative study of preprocessing tools and segmentation methods. *IEEE Transactions on Image Processing, 24*(5), 1549–1560. doi:10.1109/TIP.2015.2400214 PMID:25667351

Gulhane, V.A., & Gurjar, A.A. (2011). Detection of diseases on cotton leaves and its possible diagnosis. *International Journal Image Processing, 5*(5), 590-598.

Guo, J. M., & Liu, Y. F. (2014). Improved block truncation coding using optimized dot diffusion. *IEEE Transactions on Image Processing, 23*(3), 1269–1275. doi:10.1109/TIP.2013.2257812 PMID:23591493

Guo, J. M., & Prasetyo, H. (2015a). Content-based image retrieval using features extracted from halftoning-based block truncation coding. *IEEE Transactions on Image Processing, 24*(3), 1010–1024. doi:10.1109/TIP.2014.2372619 PMID:25420264

Guo, J. M., Prasetyo, H., & Chen, J. H. (2015b). Content-based image retrieval using error diffusion block truncation coding features. *IEEE Transactions on Circuits and Systems for Video Technology, 25*(3), 466–481. doi:10.1109/TC-SVT.2014.2358011

Gutchess, D., Trajkovics, M., Cohen-Solal, E., Lyons, D., & Jain, A. K. (2001). A background model initialization algorithm for video surveillance. In *Computer Vision, 2001. ICCV 2001. Proceedings. Eighth IEEE International Conference on* (Vol. 1, pp. 733-740). IEEE. 10.1109/ICCV.2001.937598

Hall, E. L., Kruger, R. P., Dwyer, S. J., Hall, D. L., Mclaren, R. W., & Lodwick, G. S. (1971). A Survey of Preprocessing and Feature Extraction Techniques for Radiographic Images. *IEEE Transactions on Computers*. Retrieved from https://hubpages.com/technology/Image-Retrieval-Color-Coherence-Vector retrived on 25/09/2017

Han, B. (2015). Watershed segmentation algorithm based on morphological gradient reconstruction. *2nd International conference on information science and control engineering*. doi: 10.1109/ICISCE.2015.124

Han, J., & Ma, K. K. (2002). Fuzzy color histogram and its use in color image retrieval. *IEEE Transactions on Image Processing*, *11*(8), 944–952. doi:10.1109/TIP.2002.801585 PMID:18244688

Hansen, N. R., Reynaud-Bouret, P., & Rivoirard, V. (2015). Lasso and probabilistic inequalities for multivariate point processes. *Bernoulli*, *21*(1), 83–143. doi:10.3150/13-BEJ562

Hetzel, G., Leibe, B., Levi, P., & Schiele, B. (2001). 3D Object Recognition from Range Images using Local Feature Histograms. *IEEE Computer Society Conference on Computer Vision and Pattern Recognition*, *2*, II-394-II-399.

Hiremath, P. S., & Pujari, J. (2007). Content based image retrieval using color, texture and shape features. In *Advanced Computing and Communications, 2007. ADCOM 2007. International Conference on* (pp. 780-784). IEEE. 10.1109/ADCOM.2007.21

Hughes, J. F., Van Dam, A., Mcguire, M., Sklar, D. F., Foley, J. D., Feiner, S. K., & Akeley, K. (2014). *Computer Graphics Principles and Practice*. Pearson Education.

Hu, Q., Liu, J., & Yu, D. (2008). Mixed feature selection based on granulation and approximation. *Knowledge-Based Systems*, *21*(4), 294–304. doi:10.1016/j.knosys.2007.07.001

Hu, Q., Yu, D., Liu, J., & Wu, C. (2008). Neighborhood rough set based heterogeneous feature subset selection. *Information Sciences*, *178*(18), 3577–3594. doi:10.1016/j.ins.2008.05.024

Hu, Y. C., Lo, C. C., Chen, W. L., & Wen, C. H. (2013). Joint image coding and image authentication based on absolute moment block truncation coding. *Journal of Electronic Imaging*, *22*(1), 013012–013012. doi:10.1117/1.JEI.22.1.013012

Iosifidis, A., Tefas, A., & Pitas, I. (2013). Multi-view human action recognition: A survey. In *Intelligent Information Hiding and Multimedia Signal Processing, 2013 Ninth International Conference on* (pp. 522-525). IEEE. 10.1109/IIH-MSP.2013.135

Irani, Pise, & Phatak. (2016). Clustering Techniques And The Similarity Measures Used In Clustering: A Survey. *International Journal of Computer Applications, 134*.

Irtaza, A., Jaffar, M. A., Aleisa, E., & Choi, T. S. (2014). Embedding neural networks for semantic association in content based image retrieval. *Multimedia Tools and Applications*, *72*(2), 1911–1931. doi:10.100711042-013-1489-6

Jalab, H. A. (2011). Image retrieval system based on color layout descriptor and Gabor filters. In *Open Systems (ICOS), 2011 IEEE Conference on* (pp. 32-36). IEEE. 10.1109/ICOS.2011.6079266

Jalba, A. C., Wilkinson, M. H., & Roerdink, J. B. (2004). Morphological hat-transform scale spaces and their use in pattern classification. *Pattern Recognition*, *37*(5), 901–915. doi:10.1016/j.patcog.2003.09.009

Jang, J. S. (1993). ANFIS: Adaptive-network-based fuzzy inference system. *IEEE Transactions on Systems, Man, and Cybernetics*, *23*(3), 665–685. doi:10.1109/21.256541

Javed, K., Maruf, S., & Babri, H. A. (2015). A two-stage Markov blanket based Feature Selection algorithm for text classification. *Neurocomputing*, *157*, 91–104. doi:10.1016/j.neucom.2015.01.031

Jensen, R., & Shen, Q. (2004). Semantics-preserving dimensionality reduction: Rough and fuzzy-rough-based approaches. *IEEE Transactions on Knowledge and Data Engineering*, *16*(12), 1457–1471. doi:10.1109/TKDE.2004.96

Jiang, J., & Song, X. (2016). An Optimized Higher Order CRF for Automated Labeling and Segmentation of Video Objects. *IEEE Transactions on Circuits and Systems for Video Technology*, *26*(3), 506–516. doi:10.1109/TCSVT.2015.2416557

Jiang, X., Yi, Z., & Lv, J. C. (2006). Fuzzy SVM with a new fuzzy membership function. *Neural Computing & Applications*, *15*(3-4), 268–276. doi:10.100700521-006-0028-z

Jing, S. Y. (2014). A hybrid genetic algorithm for feature subset selection in rough set theory. *Soft Computing*, *18*(7), 1373–1382. doi:10.100700500-013-1150-3

Jing, X. Y., & Zhang, D. (2004). A face and palmprint recognition approach based on discriminant DCT feature extraction. *IEEE Transactions on Systems, Man, and Cybernetics. Part B, Cybernetics*, *34*(6), 2405–2415. doi:10.1109/TSMCB.2004.837586 PMID:15619939

Jing, Y., & Baluja, S. (2008). Pagerank for product image search. *Proc. WWW*, 307–316.

Johanyák, Z. C., & Kovács, S. (2005). Distance based similarity measures of fuzzy sets. *Proceedings of SAMI*.

Johnson, A. E., & Hebert, M. (1999). Using Spin Images for Efficient Object Recognition in Cluttered 3D Scenes. *IEEE Transactions on Pattern Analysis and Machine Intelligence*, *21*(5), 433–449. doi:10.1109/34.765655

Kalantidis, Y., Pueyo, L. G., Trevisiol, M., Zwol, R. V., & Avrithis, Y. (2011). Scalable Triangulation-based Logo Recognition. *Proceedings of the 1st International Conference on Multimedia Retrieval*, 20:1-20:7.

Kao, C. C., & Lin, H. Y. (2015). Performance Evaluation of Bit-plane Slicing based Stereo Matching Techniques. VISAPP, 365-370. doi:10.5220/0005260203650370

Kayaken. (2017). *Simple Taylor Swift Red Wallpaper Hd Burger King and Starbucks Join forces Against Mcdonald S*. Retrieved from: http://big5kayakchallenge.com/taylor-swift-red-wallpaper-hd/simple-taylor-swift-red-wallpaper-hd-burger-king-and-starbucks-join-forces-against-mcdonald-s/

Ke, Y., & Sukthankar, R. (2004). PCA-SIFT: A More Distinctive Representation for Local Image Descriptors. Computer Vision and Pattern Recognition (CVPR-2004), 2, 506-513.

Kekre, H. B., Thepade, S., Das, R. K. K., & Ghosh, S. (2013). Multilevel Block Truncation Coding with diverse color spaces for image classification. In *Advances in Technology and Engineering (ICATE), 2013 International Conference on* (pp. 1-7). IEEE 10.1109/ICAdTE.2013.6524718

Kekre, H. B., Thepade, S. D., Athawale, A., Shah, A., Verlekar, P., & Shirke, S. (2010). Energy compaction and image splitting for image retrieval using kekre transform over row and column feature vectors. *International Journal of Computer Science and Network Security*, *10*(1), 289–298.

Khan (2013). Image Segmentation Techniques: A Survey. *Journal of Image and Graphics, 1*(4).

Kim, W. Y., & Kim, Y. S. (2000). A region-based shape descriptor using Zernike moments. *Signal Processing Image Communication*, *16*(1), 95–102. doi:10.1016/S0923-5965(00)00019-9

Kóczy, L. T., & Tikk, D. (2000). Fuzzy rendszerek. TypoTEX.

Koenderink, J. J., & van Doorn, A. J. (1992). Surface Shape and Curvature Scales. *Image and Vision Computing*, *10*(8), 557–564. doi:10.1016/0262-8856(92)90076-F

Konstantinidis, K., Gasteratos, A., & Andreadis, I. (2005). Image retrieval based on fuzzy color histogram processing. *Optics Communications*, *248*(4), 375–386. doi:10.1016/j.optcom.2004.12.029

Korytkowski, M., Rutkowski, L., & Scherer, R. (2016). Fast image classification by boosting fuzzy classifiers. *Information Sciences*, *327*, 175–182. doi:10.1016/j.ins.2015.08.030

Krishnapuram, R., & Keller, J. M. (1993). A possibilistic approach to clustering. *IEEE Transactions on Fuzzy Systems*, *1*(2), 98–110. doi:10.1109/91.227387

Krishnapuram, R., Medasani, S., Jung, S. H., Choi, Y. S., & Balasubramaniam, R. (2004). Content-based image retrieval based on a fuzzy approach. *IEEE Transactions on Knowledge and Data Engineering, 16*(10), 1185–1199. doi:10.1109/TKDE.2004.53

Krizhevsky, A., Sutskever, I., & Hinton, G. E. (2012). Imagenet classification with deep convolutional neural networks. *Advances in Neural Information Processing Systems*, 1097–1105.

Krstajic, D., Buturovic, L. J., Leahy, D. E., & Thomas, S. (2014). Cross-validation pitfalls when selecting and assessing regression and classification models. *Journal of Cheminformatics, 6*(1), 10. doi:10.1186/1758-2946-6-10 PMID:24678909

Kumar & Shukla. (2017). Design and Analysis of CBIR System using Hybrid PSO and K-Mean Clustering Methods. *International Journal of Current Engineering and Technology*.

Largeron, C., Moulin, C., & Géry, M. (2011). Entropy based feature selection for text categorization. *ACM Symposium on Applied Computing*. 10.1145/1982185.1982389

Laske, C., Sohrabi, H. R., Frost, S. M., López-de-Ipiña, K., Garrard, P., Buscema, M., ... O'Bryant, S. E. (2015). Innovative diagnostic tools for early detaction of Alzheimer's disease by chrishtophLaske. *NCBI, 5*.

Lavania, S., & Matey, P.S. (2015). Novel method for weed classification in maize field using Otsu and PCA implementation. *IEEE international conference on computational intelligence & communication technology*, 534-537. doi: 10.1109/CICT.2015.71

LeCun, Y., Bottou, L., Bengio, Y., & Haffner, P. (1998). Gradient-based learning applied to document recognition. *Proceedings of the IEEE, 86*(11), 2278–2323. doi:10.1109/5.726791

Lee, Y. H., Kim, B., & Rhee, S. B. (2013). Content-based image retrieval using spatial-color and Gabor texture on a mobile device. *Computer Science and Information Systems, 10*(2), 807–823. doi:10.2298/CSIS120716035L

Leutenegger, S., Chli, M., & Siegwart, R. Y. (2011). BRISK: Binary Robust Invariant Scalable Keypoints. *Proceedings of IEEE International Conference on Computer Vision*, 2548-2555.

Li, Y., Miao, Z., Xu, Y., Li, H., & Zhang, Y. (2016). Combining Nonlinear Dimension Reduction and Hashing Method for Efficient Image Retrieval. In *Semantics, Knowledge and Grids (SKG), 2016 12th International Conference on* (pp. 126-130). IEEE

Liang, J., Wang, F., Dang, C., & Qian, Y. (2012, July). A Group Incremental approach to feature Selection Applying Rough Set Technique. *IEEE Transactions on Knowledge and Data Engineering*, 9.

Li, C. H., Huang, W. C., Kuo, B. C., & Hung, C. C. (2008). A novel fuzzy weighted c-means method for image classification. *International Journal of Fuzzy Systems, 10*(3), 168–173.

Li, F., Tran, L., Thung, K. H., Ji, S., Shen, D., & Li, J. (2015). A Robust Deep Model for Improved Classification of AD/MCI Patients. *IEEE Journal of Biomedical and Health Informatics, 19*(5), 1610–1616. doi:10.1109/JBHI.2015.2429556 PMID:25955998

Li, J., & Wang, J. Z. (2003). Automatic linguistic indexing of pictures by a statistical modeling approach. *IEEE Transactions on Pattern Analysis and Machine Intelligence, 25*(9), 1075–1088. doi:10.1109/TPAMI.2003.1227984

Lin, C. F., & Wang, S. D. (2002). Fuzzy support vector machines. *IEEE Transactions on Neural Networks, 13*(2), 464–471. doi:10.1109/72.991432 PMID:18244447

Lingras, P., & Peters, G. (2012). *Applying Rough Set Concepts to Clustering*. Springer-Verlag London Limited. doi:10.1007/978-1-4471-2760-4_2

Liu, C. (2013). A new finger vein feature extraction algorithm. In *Image and Signal Processing (CISP), 2013 6th International Congress on* (Vol. 1, pp. 395-399). IEEE. 10.1109/CISP.2013.6744026

Liu, S. S., Cai, W., Pujol, S., Kikinis, R., & Feng, D. (2014). Early Diagnosis of Alzheimer's Disease With Deep Learning. University of Sydney.

Liu, S., Cai, W., Liu, S., & Zhang, F. (2015). Multimodal Neuroimaging & Depression. Springer.

Liu, H., & Yu, L. (2005, April). Toward Integrating Feature Selection Algorithms for Classification and Clustering. *IEEE Transactions on Knowledge and Data Engineering, 17*(4), ●●●.

Long, F., Zhang, H., & Feng, D. D. (2003). Fundamentals of content-based image retrieval. In *Multimedia Information Retrieval and Management* (pp. 1–26). Springer Berlin Heidelberg. doi:10.1007/978-3-662-05300-3_1

Lowe, D. G. (1999). Object recognition from local scale-invariant features. *Proceedings of Seventh IEEE International Conference on Computer Vision, 2,* 1150-1157. 10.1109/ICCV.1999.790410

Lowe, D. G. (2004). Distinctive image features from scale-invariant keypoints. *International Journal of Computer Vision, 60*(2), 91–110. doi:10.1023/B:VISI.0000029664.99615.94

Lyon, C., Barrett, R., & Malcolm, J. (2003). *Experiments in Electronic Plagiarism Detection.* Computer Science Department, University of Hertfordshire. Retrived from http://homepages.herts.ac.uk/~comqcml/TR5.3.5.doc

Lyon, C., Barrett, R., & Malcolm, J. (2004). A Theoretical Basis to the Automated Detection of Copying Between Texts, and its Practical Implementation in the Ferret Plagiarism and Collusion Detector. *Proceedings of the Plagiarism: Prevention, Practice and Policies Conference.* Retrieved from http://homepages.herts.ac.uk/~comqcml/LyonPaperFerretx.pdf

Ma, J., Li, X., Wen, H., Fu, Z., & Zhang, L. (2015). A key frame extraction method for processing greenhouse vegetables production monitoring video. *Computers and Electronics in Agriculture, 111,* 92–102. doi:10.1016/j.compag.2014.12.007

Majumdar, D., Kole, D.K., Chakraborty, A., & Majumder, D.D. (2015). *An integrated digital image analysis system for detection, recognition and diagnosis of disease in wheat leaves.* doi: 10.1145/2791405.2791474

Mamdani, E. H., & Assilian, S. (1975). An experiment in linguistic synthesis with a fuzzy logic controller. *International Journal of Man-Machine Studies, 7*(1), 1–13. doi:10.1016/S0020-7373(75)80002-2

Mareeswari, S., & Dr, G. (2015). A survey: Early Detection of Alzheimer's Disease using Different Techniques. *International Journal on Computational Sciences & Applications, 5*(1), 27–37. doi:10.5121/ijcsa.2015.5103

Marinai, S., Gori, M., & Soda, G. (2005, January). Artificial Neural Networks for Document Analysis and Recognition. *IEEE Transactions on Pattern Analysis and Machine Intelligence, 27*(1), 23–35. doi:10.1109/TPAMI.2005.4 PMID:15628266

McCabe, D. (2002). Cheating: Why Students Do It and How We Can Help Them Stop. *American Educator.* Retrieved from http://www.aft.org/periodical/american-educator/winter-2001/cheating

Mehtre, B. M., Kankanhalli, M. S., & Lee, W. F. (1997). Shape measures for content based image retrieval: A comparison. *Information Processing & Management, 33*(3), 319–337. doi:10.1016/S0306-4573(96)00069-6

Meuschke, N., & Gipp, B. (2014). Reducing computation effort for plagiarism detection by using citation characteristics to limit retrieval space. In *Proceedings of the 14th ACM/IEEE Conference on Digital Libraries* (pp. 567–575). Retrieved from http://www.academia.edu/28340526/Reducing_Computational_Effort_for_Plagiarism_Detection_by_using_Citation_Characteristics_to_Limit_Retrieval_Space

Miao, D., Duan, Q., Zhang, H., & Jiao, N. (2009). Rough set based hybrid algorithm for text classification. *Expert Systems with Applications, 36*(5), 9168–9174. doi:10.1016/j.eswa.2008.12.026

Mihalcea, R., & Corley, C. (2006). Corpus-based and knowledge-based measures of text semantic similarity. *Proceedings of the Twenty-first National Conference on Artificial Intelligence (AAAI-06)*, 775–780. Retrieved from https://www.aaai.org/Papers/AAAI/2006/AAAI06-123.pdf

Min, F., Hu, Q., & Zhu, W. (2014). Feature selection with test cost constraint. *International Journal of Approximate Reasoning, 55*(1), 167–179. doi:10.1016/j.ijar.2013.04.003

Moeslund, T. B., Hilton, A., & Krüger, V. (2006). A survey of advances in vision-based human motion capture and analysis. *Computer Vision and Image Understanding, 104*(2-3), 90–126. doi:10.1016/j.cviu.2006.08.002

Mohler, M., & Mihalcea, R. (2009). Text-to-text semantic similarity for automatic short answer grading. *Proceedings of the 12th Conference of the European Chapter of the ACL (EACL 2009)*, 567–575. Retrived from http://www.aclweb.org/anthology/E09-1065

Mokhtarian, F., & Mackworth, A. K. (1992). A theory of multiscale, curvature-based shape representation for planar curves. *IEEE Transactions on Pattern Analysis and Machine Intelligence, 14*(8), 789–805. doi:10.1109/34.149591

Mookiah, M. R. K., Acharya, U. R., Lim, C. M., Petznick, A., & Suri, J. S. (2012). Data mining technique for automated diagnosis of glaucoma using higher order spectra and wavelet energy features. *Knowledge-Based Systems, 33*, 73–82. doi:10.1016/j.knosys.2012.02.010

Mortensen, E. N., Deng, H., & Shapiro, L. (2005). A SIFT descriptor with global context. *Proceedings of IEEE Computer Society Conference on Computer Vision and Pattern Recognition (CVPR 2005)*, 1, 184-190. 10.1109/CVPR.2005.45

Mulhemý, P., Leowþ, W. K., & Leeþ, Y. K. (2001). Fuzzy conceptual graphs for matching images of natural scenes. *IJCAI*, 1.

Nair, V., & Clark, J. J. (2004, June). An unsupervised, online learning framework for moving object detection. In *Computer Vision and Pattern Recognition, 2004. CVPR 2004. Proceedings of the 2004 IEEE Computer Society Conference on* (Vol. 2, pp. II-II). IEEE. 10.1109/CVPR.2004.1315181

Nedeljkovic, I. (2004). Image classification based on fuzzy logic. *The International Archives of the Photogrammetry, Remote Sensing and Spatial Information Sciences, 34*, 685.

Nigam, A., & Kushwaha, V. K. (2015). *Secure Transaction of Medical Images using bit plane slicing and integer wavelet transform approach*. Academic Press.

Nikkam, P. S., & Reddy, E. B. (2016). A Key Point Selection Shape Technique for Content based Image Retrieval System. *International Journal of Computer Vision and Image Processing, 6*(2), 54–70. doi:10.4018/IJCVIP.2016070104

Nixon, M. S., & Aguado, A. S. (2008). *Feature Extraction and Image Processing*. Elsevier.

Oberreuter, G., Lhuillier, G., Ros, S. A., & Velsquez, J. D. (2011). Approaches for intrinsic and external plagiarism detection - notebook for pan at clef 2011. *Proceedings of the Conference on Multilingual and Multimodal Information Access Evaluation (CLEF 2011) Labs and Workshop*. Retrieved from http://ceur-ws.org/Vol-1177/CLEF2011wn-PAN-OberreuterEt2011.pdf

Oreski, S., & Oreski, G. (2014). Genetic algorithm-based heuristic for Feature Selection in credit risk assessment. *Expert Systems with Applications, 41*(4), 2052–2064. doi:10.1016/j.eswa.2013.09.004

Otsu, N. (1979). A threshold selection method from gray-level histograms. *IEEE Transactions on Systems, Man, and Cybernetics, 9*(1), 62–66. doi:10.1109/TSMC.1979.4310076

Pal, S. K., & King, R. A. (1983). On edge detection of X-ray images using fuzzy sets. *IEEE Transactions on Pattern Analysis and Machine Intelligence, PAMI-5*(1), 69–77. doi:10.1109/TPAMI.1983.4767347 PMID:21869086

Panchal, Panchal, & Shah. (2013). A Comparison of SIFT and SURF. *International Journal of Innovative Research in Computer and Communication Engineering, 1*(2).

Papageorgiou, C. P., Oren, M., & Poggio, T. (1998, January). A general framework for object detection. In *Computer vision, 1998. sixth international conference on* (pp. 555-562). IEEE. 10.1109/ICCV.1998.710772

Papineni, K., Roukos, S., Ward, T., & Zhu, W. (2002). Bleu: a method for automatic evaluation of machine translation. *Proceedings of the 40th Annual Meeting on Association for Computational Linguistics,* 311-318. Retrieved from http://www.aclweb.org/anthology/P02-1040.pdf

Parekh, R. (2006). *Principals of Multimedia* (2nd ed.). Mc Graw Hill.

Patil, L. H., & Atique, M. (2014). A Multistage Feature Selection Model for Document Classification Using Information Gain and Rough Set. *International Journal of Advanced Research in Artificial Intelligence, 3*(11). Retrieved from www.ijarai.thesai.org

Patil, L. H., & Atique, M. (2015). *A Novel Feature Selection and Attribute Reduction Based on Hybrid IG-RS Approach. Springer International Publishing Switzerland.* Doi:10.1007/978-3-319-13731-5_59

Patil, L. H., & Atique, M. (2015). An Improved feature selection based on neighborhood positive approximation rough set in document classification. *International Journal of Soft Computing and Software Engineering, 5*(1), 13–30. doi:10.7321/jscse.v5.n1.2

Patil, S. B., & Dr.Bodhe, S. K. (2011). Leaf disease severity measurement using image processing. *IACSIT International Journal of Engineering and Technology, 3*(5), 297–230.

Pawlak, Z. (1991). *Rough set: Theoretical Aspects of Reasoning about Data.* Kluwer Academic Publishers. doi:10.1007/978-94-011-3534-4

Piccardi, M. (2004, October). Background subtraction techniques: a review. In *Systems, man and cybernetics, 2004 IEEE international conference on* (Vol. 4, pp. 3099–3104). IEEE.

Pixia, D., & Xiangdong, W. (2013). Recognition of greenhouse cucumber disease based on image processing technology. *Open Journal of Applied Science, 3,* 27-31.

Podpora, M., Korbas, G. P., & Kawala-Janik, A. (2014). YUV vs RGB-Choosing a Color Space for Human-Machine Interaction. In FedCSIS Position Papers (pp. 29-34). Academic Press.

Poursepanj, H., Weissbock, J., & Inkpen, D. (2013). Ottawa: System description for SemEval 2013 Task 2 Sentiment Analysis in Twitter. In SemEval@ NAACL-HLT (pp. 380-383). Academic Press.

Prasad, B. G., Gupta, S. K., & Biswas, K. K. (2001). Color and shape index for region-based image retrieval. *Visual Form, 2001,* 716–725.

Prewitt, J. M. (1970). Object enhancement and extraction. *Picture Processing and Psychopictorics, 10*(1), 15-19.

Qian, Y., Liang, J., Pedrycz, W., & Dang, C. (2011). An efficient accelerator for attribute reduction from incomplete data in rough set framework. *Pattern Recognition, 4*(8), 1658–1670. doi:10.1016/j.patcog.2011.02.020

Rahimi, M., & Moghaddam, M. E. (2015). A content-based image retrieval system based on Color Ton Distribution descriptors. *Signal, Image and Video Processing, 9*(3), 691–704. doi:10.100711760-013-0506-6

Ramirez-Ortegon, M. A., & Rojas, R. (2010). Unsupervised evaluation methods based on local gray-intensity variances for binarization of historical documents. In *Pattern Recognition (ICPR), 2010 20th International Conference on* (pp. 2029-2032). IEEE. 10.1109/ICPR.2010.500

Ramya, A., & Raviraj, P. (2014, March). Performance evaluation of detecting moving objects using graph cut segmentation. In *Green Computing Communication and Electrical Engineering (ICGCCEE), 2014 International Conference on* (pp. 1-6). IEEE. 10.1109/ICGCCEE.2014.6921413

Ramya, A., & Raviraj, P. (2013). A Survey and Comparative Analysis of Moving Object Detection and Tracking. *International Journal of Engineering Research and Technology*, 2, 147–176.

Ravi, K., & Ravi, V. (2015). A survey on opinion mining and sentiment analysis: Tasks, approaches and applications. *Knowledge-Based Systems*, 89, 14–46. doi:10.1016/j.knosys.2015.06.015

Reddy, K. D. (2013). *Plagiarism Detection using Enhanced Relative Frequency Model* (Unpublished M.Sc Thesis). Department of Computer Science and Engineering, National Institute of Technology Rourkela, India. Retrieved from http://ethesis.nitrkl.ac.in/5401/1/211CS3297.pdf

Ren, S., He, K., Girshick, R., & Sun, J. (2015). Faster R-cnn: Towards Real-time Object Detection with Region Proposal Networks. *Advances in Neural Information Processing Systems*, 91–99.

Rey-Otero, I., & Delbracio, M. (2014). Anatomy of the SIFT Method, *Image Processing. Online (Bergheim)*, 4, 370–396.

Roffo, G., & Melzi, S. (2016). Features selection via eigenvector centrality. Proceedings of New Frontiers in Mining Complex Patterns-NFMCP 2016, 1-12.

Roffo, G., Melzi, S., & Cristani, M. (2015). Infinite Feature Selection. *Proceedings of the IEEE International Conference on Computer Vision*, 4202-4210.

Rosenfeld, A. (1984). The fuzzy geometry of image subsets. *Pattern Recognition Letters*, 2(5), 311–317. doi:10.1016/0167-8655(84)90018-7

Rublee, E., Rabaud, V., Konolige, K., & Bradski, G. (2011). ORB: An efficient alternative to SIFT or SURF. *Proceedings of IEEE International Conference on Computer Vision*, 2564–2571.

Rui, X. A. D. W. I. (2005). Survey Of Clustering Algorithms. *IEEE Transactions on Neural Networks*, 16(3). PMID:15940994

Rui, Y., Huang, T. S., & Chang, S. F. (1999). Image retrieval: Current techniques, promising directions, and open issues. *Journal of Visual Communication and Image Representation*, 10(1), 39–62. doi:10.1006/jvci.1999.0413

Runeson, P., Alexandersson, M., & Nyholm, O. (2007). Detection of Duplicate Defect Reports Using Natural Language Processing. *Proceedings of the 29th International Conference on Software Engineering, ICSE'07*, 499-510. Retrieved from https://www.semanticscholar.org/paper/Detection-of-Duplicate-Defect-Reports-Using-Natura-Runeson-Alexandersson/0d459e3be20f7f529bc0d92d42fa63e60fc1e1ba

Russakovsky, O., Deng, J., Su, H., Krause, J., Satheesh, S., Ma, S., ... Fei-Fei, L. (2015). ImageNet Large Scale Visual Recognition Challenge. *International Journal of Computer Vision*, 115(3), 211–252. doi:10.100711263-015-0816-y

Saeys, Y., Inza, I., & Larrañaga, P. (2007). A review of Feature Selection techniques in bioinformatics. *Bioinformatics (Oxford, England)*, 23(19), 2507–2517. doi:10.1093/bioinformatics/btm344 PMID:17720704

Sanjay, G. (2016). A Comparative Study on Face Recognition using Subspace Analysis. In *International Conference on Computer Science and Technology Allies in Research* (p. 82). Academic Press.

Sanjaya, K.W.V., Vijesekara, H.M.S.S., Wickramasinghe, I.M.A.C., & Analraj, C.R.J. (2015). Orchid classification, disease identification and healthiness prediction system. *International Journal of Scientific and Technology Research,* *4*(3), 215-220.

Sankaran, S., Mishra, A., Ehsani, R., & Davis, C. (2010). A review of advanced techniques for detecting plant diseases. *Computers and Electronics in Agriculture, 72*(1), 1–13. doi:10.1016/j.compag.2010.02.007

Sannakki, S. S., Rajpurohit, V. S., Nargund, V. B., & Arunkumar, R. (2013). Disease identification and grading of pomegranate leaves using image processing and fuzzy logic. *International Journal of Food Engineering, 9*(4), 467–479. doi:10.1515/ijfe-2012-0241

Saravanan, R. (2012). ICTs for agricultural extension in India: Policy implications for developing countries. New India Publication Agency.

Sarraf, S., & Tofighi, G. (2016). Classification of Alzheimer's Disease Structural MRI Data by Deep Learning Convolutional Neural Networks. *arXiv,* 1–14.

Sarraf, S., & Golestani, A. M. (2016). A robust and adaptive decision-making algorithm for detecting brain networks using functional mri within the spatial and frequency domain. *IEEE International Conference on Biomedical and Health Informatics (BHI),* 1–6. 10.1109/BHI.2016.7455833

Schor, N., Bechar, A., Ignat, T., Dombrovsky, A., Elad, Y., & Berman, S. (2016). Robotic disease detection in greenhouses: combined detection of powdery mildew and tomato spotted wilt virus. *IEEE Robotics and Automation Letters, 1*(1), 354–360. doi: 10.1109/LRA.2016.2518214

Shaikh, S. H., Maiti, A. K., & Chaki, N. (2013). A new image binarization method using iterative partitioning. *Machine Vision and Applications,* 1–14.

Shalom, S., Shapira, L., Shamir, A., & Cohenor, D. (2008). Part Analogies in Sets of Objects. *1st Eurographics Conference on 3D Object Retrieva,* 33-40.

Shen, G. L., & Wu, X. J. (2013). *Content based image retrieval by combining color, texture and CENTRIST.* Academic Press.

Shen, Y., & Wang, F. (2011). Variable precision rough set model over two universes and its properties. *Soft Computing, 15*(3), 557–567. doi:10.100700500-010-0562-6

Shieh, H.-L. (2012). A Hybrid Clustering Algorithm Based on Rough Set and Shared Nearest Neighbors. In *Applied Mechanics and Materials* (Vol. 145, pp. 189–193). Trans Tech Publications.

Shilane, P., & Funkhouser, T. (2007). Distinctive Regions of 3D Surfaces. *ACM Transactions on Graphics, 26*(2), 7, es. doi:10.1145/1243980.1243981

Shukla & Vania. (2014). A Survey on CBIR Features Extraction Techniques. *International Journal of Engineering and Computer Science, 3*(12).

Singh, V., & Misra, A. K. (in press). Detection of plant leaf disease using image segmentation and soft computing techniques. *Information Processing in Agriculture.* doi:10.1016/j.inpa.2016.10.005

Sklansky, J. (1978). Image Segmentation And Feature Extraction. *IEEE Transactions on Systems, Man, and Cybernetics, 8*(4), 237–247. doi:10.1109/TSMC.1978.4309944

Smeulders, A. W., Worring, M., Santini, S., Gupta, A., & Jain, R. (2000). Content-based image retrieval at the end of the early years. *IEEE Transactions on Pattern Analysis and Machine Intelligence, 22*(12), 1349–1380. doi:10.1109/34.895972

Smith, J. R., & Chang, S. F. (1997, February). VisualSEEk: a fully automated content-based image query system. In *Proceedings of the fourth ACM international conference on Multimedia* (pp. 87-98). ACM.

Solomon & Breckon. (n.d.). *Fundamentals of Digital Image Processing*. John & Sons Wiley. *Ltd.*

Sonka, M., Hlavac, V., & Boyle, R. (2014). *Image processing, analysis, and machine vision*. Cengage Learning.

Sørensen, L., Igel, C., Liv Hansen, N., Osler, M., Lauritzen, M., Rostrup, E., & Nielsen, M. (2015). Early detection of Alzheimer's disease using MRI hippocampal texture. *Human Brain Mapping, Alzheimer's DiseaseNeuroimaging Initiative, 37*(3), 1148–1161. doi:10.1002/hbm.23091 PMID:26686837

Stevens, R. B. (1960). *Plant pathology, an advanced treatise* (vol. 3). New York: Academic Press. Retrieved from https://www.apsnet.org/edcenter/instcomm/TeachingArticles/Pages/DiseaseTriangle.aspx

Subrahmanyam, M., Maheshwari, R. P., & Balasubramanian, R. (2012). Expert system design using wavelet and color vocabulary trees for image retrieval. *Expert Systems with Applications, 39*(5), 5104–5114. doi:10.1016/j.eswa.2011.11.029

Subrahmanyam, M., Wu, Q. J., Maheshwari, R. P., & Balasubramanian, R. (2013). Modified color motif co-occurrence matrix for image indexing and retrieval. *Computers & Electrical Engineering, 39*(3), 762–774. doi:10.1016/j.compeleceng.2012.11.023

Tabakhi, S., Moradi, P., & Akhlaghian, F. (2014). An unsupervised Feature Selection algorithm based on ant colony optimization. *Engineering Applications of Artificial Intelligence, 32*, 112–123. doi:10.1016/j.engappai.2014.03.007

Takagi, T., & Sugeno, M. (1985). Fuzzy identification of systems and its applications to modeling and control. *IEEE Transactions on Systems, Man, and Cybernetics, SMC-15*(1), 116–132. doi:10.1109/TSMC.1985.6313399

Tangelder, J. W. H., & Veltkamp, R. C. (2008). A Survey of Content-based 3D Shape Retrieval Methods. *Multimedia Tools and Applications, 39*(3), 441–471. doi:10.100711042-007-0181-0

Tang, X., Liu, M., Zhao, H., & Tao, W. (2009). *Leaf extraction from complicated background*. IEEE. doi:10.1109/CISP.2009.5304424

Tang, Y. Y., Tu, L.-T., Liu, J., Lee, S.-W., Lin, W.-W., & Shyu, I.-S. (1998, May). Offline Recognition of Chinese Handwriting by Multifeature and Multilevel Classification. *IEEE Transactions on Pattern Analysis and Machine Intelligence, 20*(5).

Thepade, S., Das, R., & Ghosh, S. (2013). Performance comparison of feature vector extraction techniques in RGB color space using block truncation coding for content based image classification with discrete classifiers. In *India Conference (INDICON), 2013 Annual IEEE* (pp. 1-6). IEEE. 10.1109/INDCON.2013.6726053

Thepade, S., Das, R., & Ghosh, S. (2014). A novel feature extraction technique using binarization of bit planes for content based image classification. *Journal of Engineering.*

Thepade,S., Das, R. & Ghosh, S. (2015). A Novel Feature Extraction Technique Using Bi-narization of Bit Planes for Content Based Image Classification. *Journal of Engineering.* doi:10.1155/2014/439218

Thepade, S. D., Das, R. K. K., & Ghosh, S. (2013). Image classification using advanced block truncation coding with ternary image maps. In *Advances in Computing, Communication, and Control* (pp. 500–509). Berlin: Springer. doi:10.1007/978-3-642-36321-4_48

Thepade, S., Das, R., & Ghosh, S. (2015). A novel feature extraction technique with binarization of significant bit information. *International Journal of Imaging and Robotic, 15*(3), 164–178.

Thepade, S., Das, R., & Ghosh, S. (2017). Decision fusion-based approach for content-based image classification. *International Journal of Intelligent Computing and Cybernetics, 10*(3), 310–331. doi:10.1108/IJICC-07-2016-0025

Tian, Y., Wang, L., & Zhou, Q. (2011). Grading method of crop disease based on image processing, Springer. *IFIP Advances in Information and Communication Technology*, *369*, 427–433. doi:10.1007/978-3-642-27278-3_45

Tokarczyk, P., Wegner, J. D., Walk, S., & Schindler, K. (2015). Features, color spaces, and boosting: New insights on semantic classification of remote sensing images. *IEEE Transactions on Geoscience and Remote Sensing*, *53*(1), 280–295. doi:10.1109/TGRS.2014.2321423

Townsend, J. T. (1971). Theoretical analysis of an alphabetic confusion matrix. *Attention, Perception & Psychophysics*, *9*(1), 40–50. doi:10.3758/BF03213026

Toyama, K., Krumm, J., Brumitt, B., & Meyers, B. (1999). Wallflower: Principles and practice of background maintenance. In *Computer Vision, 1999. The Proceedings of the Seventh IEEE International Conference on* (Vol. 1, pp. 255-261). IEEE.

Triba, M. N., Le Moyec, L., Amathieu, R., Goossens, C., Bouchemal, N., Nahon, P., ... Savarin, P. (2015). PLS/OPLS models in metabolomics: The impact of permutation of dataset rows on the K-fold cross-validation quality parameters. *Molecular BioSystems*, *11*(1), 13–19. doi:10.1039/C4MB00414K PMID:25382277

Tripoliti, Fotiadis, & Argyropoulou. (2012). A supervised method to assist the diagnois and classification of the status of Alzheimer's disease using data from an FMRI experiment. *Brain*.

Tripoliti, E. E., Fotiadis, D. I., & Argyropoulou, M. (2008). A supervised method to assist the diagnosis and classification of the status of alzheimer's disease using data from an fmri experiment. *30th Annual International Conference of the IEEE*, 4419–4422. 10.1109/IEMBS.2008.4650191

Tsai, Y. H., Yang, M. H., & Black, M. J. (2016). Video segmentation via object flow. *Proceedings of the IEEE Conference on Computer Vision and Pattern Recognition*, 3899-3908.

Tversky, A. (1977). Features of similarity. *Psychological Review*, *84*(4), 327–352. doi:10.1037/0033-295X.84.4.327

Uguz, H. (2011). A two-stage feature selection method for text categorization by using information gain, principal component analysis and genetic algorithm. *Knowledge-Based Systems*, *24*(7), 1024–1032. doi:10.1016/j.knosys.2011.04.014

Valizadeh, M., Armanfard, N., Komeili, M., & Kabir, E. (2009, October). A novel hybrid algorithm for binarization of badly illuminated document images. In *Computer Conference, 2009. CSICC 2009. 14th International CSI* (pp. 121-126). IEEE. 10.1109/CSICC.2009.5349338

Valliammal, N., & Geethalakshmi, S.N. (2012). Plant leaf segmentation using non linear k-means clustering. *International Journal of Computer Science Issues*, *9*(3), 212-218.

Vani, K., & Gupta, D. (2015). Investigating the impact of combined similarity metrics and POS tagging in extrinsic text plagiarism detection system. *Proceedings of the 4ᵗʰ International Conference on Advances in Computing, Communications and Informatics (ICACCI)*, 1578-1584. Retrieved from https://www.deepdyve.com/lp/institute-of-electrical-and-electronics-engineers/investigating-the-impact-of-combined-similarity-metrics-and-pos-Z29pbXpVIw

Vania, C., & Adriani, M. (2010). Automatic external plagiarism detection using passage similarities. *Proceedings of the Conference on Multilingual and Multimodal Information Access Evaluation (CLEF 2010)*. Retrieved from http://ceur-ws.org/Vol-1176/CLEF2010wn-PAN-VaniaEt2010.pdf

Vemuri, P., Jones, D. T., & Jack, C. R. (2012). Resting state functional MRI in Alzheimer's Disease. *Alzheimer's Research & Therapy*, *4*(1). PMID:22236691

Vergara, J. R., & Estévez, P. A. (2014). A review of Feature Selection methods based on mutual information. *Neural Computing & Applications*, *24*(1), 175–186. doi:10.100700521-013-1368-0

Vidal, R., & Ma, Y. (2004, May). A unified algebraic approach to 2-D and 3-D motion segmentation. In *European Conference on Computer Vision* (pp. 1-15). Springer. 10.1007/978-3-540-24670-1_1

Viola, P., Jones, M. J., & Snow, D. (2003, October). Detecting pedestrians using patterns of motion and appearance. In *Null* (p. 734). IEEE.

Walia, E., Goyal, A., & Brar, Y. S. (2014). Zernike moments and LDP-weighted patches for content-based image retrieval. *Signal, Image and Video Processing*, 8(3), 577–594. doi:10.100711760-013-0561-z

Walia, E., & Pal, A. (2014). Fusion framework for effective color image retrieval. *Journal of Visual Communication and Image Representation*, 25(6), 1335–1348. doi:10.1016/j.jvcir.2014.05.005

Walia, E., Vesal, S., & Pal, A. (2014). An effective and fast hybrid framework for color image retrieval. *Sensing and Imaging*, 15(1), 93. doi:10.100711220-014-0093-9

Wang, D., Zhang, H., Liu, R., Lv, W., & Wang, D. (2014). t-Test Feature Selection approach based on term frequency for text categorization. *Pattern Recognition Letters*, 45, 1–10. doi:10.1016/j.patrec.2014.02.013

Wang, F., Liang, J., & Qian, Y. (2013). Attribute reduction: A dimension incremental strategy. *Knowledge-Based Systems*, 39, 95–1. doi:10.1016/j.knosys.2012.10.010

Wang, H. (2006, June). Nearest Neighbors by Neighborhood Counting. *IEEE Transactions on Pattern Analysis and Machine Intelligence*, 28(6). PMID:16724588

Wang, J. Z., Li, J., & Wiederhold, G. (2001). SIMPLIcity: Semantics-sensitive integrated matching for picture libraries. *IEEE Transactions on Pattern Analysis and Machine Intelligence*, 23(9), 947–963. doi:10.1109/34.955109

Wang, Y., Wang, S., & Lai, K. K. (2005). A new fuzzy support vector machine to evaluate credit risk. *IEEE Transactions on Fuzzy Systems*, 13(6), 820–831. doi:10.1109/TFUZZ.2005.859320

Warsi, M. A. (2012). The Fractal Nature and Functional Connectivity of Brain Function as Measured by BOLD MRI in Alzheimer's Disease. *Magnetic Resonance Materials in Physics, Biology and Medicine*, 25(5), 335–344. doi:10.100710334-012-0312-0

Wei, C. H., Li, Y., Chau, W. U., & Li, C. T. (2009). Trademark image retrieval using synthetic features for describing global shape and interior structure. *Pattern Recognition*, 42(3), 386–394. doi:10.1016/j.patcog.2008.08.019

Wei, J., Zhang, R., Yu, Z., Hu, R., Tang, J., Gui, C., & Yuan, Y. (2017). A BPSO-SVM algorithm based on memory renewal and enhanced mutation mechanisms for Feature Selection. *Applied Soft Computing*, 58, 176–192. doi:10.1016/j.asoc.2017.04.061

Wu, J., Cui, Z., Sheng, V. S., Zhao, P., Su, D., & Gong, S. (2013). A Comparative Study of SIFT and its Variants. *Measurement Science Review*, 13(3), 122–131. doi:10.2478/msr-2013-0021

Wu, K., & Yap, K. H. (2006). Fuzzy SVM for content-based image retrieval: A pseudo-label support vector machine framework. *IEEE Computational Intelligence Magazine*, 1(2), 10–16. doi:10.1109/MCI.2006.1626490

Wyman, B. T., Harvey, D. J., Crawford, K., Bernstein, M. A., Carmichael, O., Cole, P. E., & Jack, C. R. (2013). Standardization of analysis sets for reporting results from ADNI MRI data. *Alzheimer's & Dementia*, 9(3), 332–337. doi:10.1016/j.jalz.2012.06.004 PMID:23110865

Xuecheng, L. (1992). Entropy, distance measure and similarity measure of fuzzy sets and their relations. *Fuzzy Sets and Systems*, 52(3), 305–318. doi:10.1016/0165-0114(92)90239-Z

Xu, P., Wu, G., Guo, Y., Chen, X., Yang, H., & Zhang, R. (2017). Automatic wheat leaf rust detection and grading diagnosis via embedded image processing system. *Procedia Computer Science, 107*, 836–841. doi:10.1016/j.procs.2017.03.177

Yanli, Y., & Zhenxing, Z. (2012). A novel local threshold binarization method for QR image. *IET International Conference on Automatic Control and Artificial Intelligence (ACAI)*, 224-227. 10.1049/cp.2012.0959

Yao & Zhao. (2008). Attribute Reduction in Decision-Theoretic Rough Set Models. *Information Sciences, 178*(17), 3356-3373.

Yıldız, O. T., Aslan, O., & Alpaydın, E. (2011). Multivariate statistical tests for comparing classification algorithms. *Lecture Notes in Computer Science, 6683*, 1–15. doi:10.1007/978-3-642-25566-3_1

Yilmaz, A., Javed, O., & Shah, M. (2006). Object tracking: A survey. *ACM Computing Surveys, 38*(4), 13.

Yoshitaka, A., & Ichikawa, T. (1999). A survey on content-based retrieval for multimedia databases. *IEEE Transactions on Knowledge and Data Engineering, 11*(1), 81–93. doi:10.1109/69.755617

Yu & Brandenburg. (2011). Multimedia Database Applications: Issues And Concerns For Classroom Teaching. *The International Journal of Multimedia & Its Applications, 3*.

Yue, J., Li, Z., Liu, L., & Fu, Z. (2011). Content-based image retrieval using color and texture fused features. *Mathematical and Computer Modelling, 54*(3), 1121–1127. doi:10.1016/j.mcm.2010.11.044

Yu, G., & Morel, J.-M. (2011). ASIFT: An Algorithm for Fully Affine Invariant Comparison, *Image Processing. Online (Bergheim), 1*, 11–38.

Zadeh, L. A. (1965). Fuzzy sets. *Information and Control, 8*(3), 338–353. doi:10.1016/S0019-9958(65)90241-X

Zeiler, M. D., & Fergus, R. (2014). Visualizing and understanding convolutional networks. In *European conference on computer vision*. Springer International Publishing.

Zhang, D., & Lu, G. (2003). A comparative study of curvature scale space and Fourier descriptors for shape-based image retrieval. *Journal of Visual Communication and Image Representation, 14*(1), 39–57. doi:10.1016/S1047-3203(03)00003-8

Zhang, D., & Lu, G. (2004). Review of shape representation and description techniques. *Pattern Recognition, 37*(1), 1–19. doi:10.1016/j.patcog.2003.07.008

Zhang, H. Y., Leung, Y., & Zhou, L. (2013). Variable-precision-dominance-based rough set approach to interval-valued information systems. *Information Sciences, 244*, 75–91. doi:10.1016/j.ins.2013.04.031

Zhang, S. W., Shang, Y. J., & Wang, L. (n.d.). Plant disease recognition based on plant leaf image. *The journal of animal & plant sciences, 25*(3suppl.1), 42–45.

Zhang, S., Wu, X., You, Z., & Zhang, L. (2017). Leaf image based cucumber disease recognition using sparse representation classification. *Computers and Electronics in Agriculture, 134*, 135–141. doi:10.1016/j.compag.2017.01.014

Zhang, Y., Wang, S., Phillips, P., & Ji, G. (2014). Binary PSO with mutation operator for Feature Selection using decision tree applied to spam detection. *Knowledge-Based Systems, 64*, 22–31. doi:10.1016/j.knosys.2014.03.015

Zhou, R., Kaneko, S., Tanaka, F., Kayamori, M., & Shimizu, M. (2014). Disease detection of cercospora leaf spot in sugar beet by robust template matching. *Computers and Electronics in Agriculture, 108*, 58–70. doi:10.1016/j.compag.2014.07.004

Zhou, X.-D., Wang, D.-H., Tian, F., & Liu, C.-L. (2013, October). Handwritten Chinese/Japanese Text Recognition Using Semi-Markov Conditional Random Fields. *IEEE Transactions on Pattern Analysis and Machine Intelligence, 35*(10), 2413–2426. doi:10.1109/TPAMI.2013.49 PMID:23969386

Zhu, Q., & Shyu, M. L. (2015). Sparse linear integration of content and context modalities for semantic concept retrieval. *IEEE Transactions on Emerging Topics in Computing*, *3*(2), 152–160. doi:10.1109/TETC.2014.2384992

Zubarev, D. V., & Sochenkov, I. V. (2017). Paraphrased plagiarism detection using sentence similarity. *Proceedings of the International Conference on Computational Linguistics and Intellectual Technologies: Dialogue 2017*. Retrieved from http://www.dialog-21.ru/media/3965/zubarevdvsochenkoviv.pdf

Zwick, R., Carlstein, E., & Budescu, D. V. (1987). Measures of similarity among fuzzy concepts: A comparative analysis. *International Journal of Approximate Reasoning*, *1*(2), 221–242. doi:10.1016/0888-613X(87)90015-6

About the Contributors

Rik Das is an Assistant Professor, Department of Information Technology, Xavier Institute of Social Service, Ranchi, Jharkhand, India. He is a PhD (Tech.) in Information Technology from University of Calcutta, Kolkata, India and has completed his M.Tech. in Information Technology from the same University. Prior to this, he has done his B.E. in Information Technology from University of Burdwan, India. He takes keen interest in researching with Image Processing, Object Detection, Computer Vision, Deep Learning and Machine Learning. He has carried out collaborative research work with Institutions in India and abroad. Rik has multiple International research publications till date with reputed Publishers, namely, IEEE, Springer, Emerald, Inderscience etc. He is a reviewer for leading Journals, such as, Journal of Visual Communication and Image Representation, Elsevier, Transactions on Mutimedia, IEEE, LNCS Transactions on Computational Science, Springer etc. He is the receiver of "Certificate of Outstanding Contribution in Reviewing" conferred by Elsevier in cooperation with King Saud University. He has also chaired sessions in International Conferences on Image Processing. Rik is a part of academic fraternity for more than 14 years and has served significant Academic Institutions in India, including, Narsee Monjee Institute of Management Studies (NMIMS) (Deemedto-be-University), Mumbai, India, Birla Institute of Technology (BIT), Mesra, Ranchi, India and so on to name a few. He is a Resource person for UGC-HRDC Refresher Courses in Information and Communication Technology. Rik is always open to discuss new research ideas for collaborative research work and for techno-managerial consultancies.

Sourav De did his Bachelors in Information Technology from The University of Burdwan, Burdwan, India in 2002. He did his Masters in Information Technology from West Bengal University of Technology, Kolkata, India in 2005. He completed PhD in Computer Science and Technology from Indian Institute of Engineering & Technology, Shibpur, Howrah, India in 2015. He is currently an Associate Professor of Computer Science & Engineering in Cooch Behar Government Engineering College, West Bengal. Previous to this, he was an Assistant Professor in the Department of Computer Science and Information Technology of University Institute of Technology, The University of Burdwan, Burdwan, India since 2006. He served as a Junior Programmer in Apices Consultancy Private Limited, Kolkata, India in 2005. He is a co-author of one book and the co-editor of 3 books and has more than 25 research publications in internationally reputed journals, international edited books and international IEEE conference proceedings to his credit. He served as reviewer in several International IEEE conferences and also in several international editorial books. He also served as reviewer in Applied Soft Computing, Elsevier, B. V. He has been the member of the organizing and technical program committees of several national and international conferences. He has been invited in different seminars as an expert speaker. He is a co-author of a proposed book on soft computing. His research interests include soft computing, pattern recognition, image processing and data mining. Dr. De is a member of IEEE, ACM, Computer Science Teachers Association (CSTA) and IAENG, Hong Kong. He is a life member of ISTE, India.

Siddhartha Bhattacharyya did his Bachelors in Physics, Bachelors in Optics and Optoelectronics and Masters in Optics and Optoelectronics from University of Calcutta, India in 1995, 1998 and 2000 respectively. He completed PhD in Computer Science and Engineering from Jadavpur University, India in 2008. He is the recipient of the University Gold Medal from the University of Calcutta for his Masters. He is the recipient of the coveted National Award Adarsh Vidya Saraswati Rashtriya Puraskar for excellence in education and research in 2016. He is the recipient of the Distinguished HoD Award and Distinguished Professor Award conferred by Computer Society of India, Mumbai Chapter, India in 2017. He is the recipient of the coveted Bhartiya Shiksha Ratan Award conferred by Economic Growth Foundation, New Delhi in 2017. He received the NACF-SCRA, India award for Best Faculty for Research in 2017. He received the Honorary Doctorate Award (D. Litt.) from The University of South America and the South East Asian Regional Computing Confederation (SEARCC) International Digital Award ICT Educator of the Year in 2017. He also received the Rashtriya Shiksha Gaurav Puraskar from Center for Education Growth and Research, India in 2017. He has been appointed as the ACM Distinguished Speaker for the tenure 2018-2020.

* * *

Ramya A. has graduated M.E. in Computer Science & Engineering in KIT-Kalaignar Karunanidhi Institute of Technology, Coimbatore, Tamilnadu. Her area of interest is Image Processing & Video Surveillance. She has published many papers in International Conference and international Journals.

Mohammad Atique is presently working as Professor in Post Graduate Department of Computer Science & Engineering. He has more than 25 years of Teaching and administrative experience. He is Life Member of ISTE, New Delhi, Fellow IE Kolkata, Fellow IETE New Delhi and Senior Life Member of CSI, Mumbai. His work gets recognized by many National and International Journals. He is also reviewer of reputed National and International Journals. He is a recognized PhD supervisor for S G B Amravati University, Amravati. Currently 5 students are perusing PhD under him. His area of interest is Soft Computing,Operating System, Ad hoc Network, Delay tolerant network, data mining and Machine Intelligent etc. He has chaired many sessions and also delivered keynote addresses in National and International conferences, STTPs and refresher courses. He has successfully completed two Major Research Project sponsored by AICTE,New Delhi and UGC, New Delhi.

Mahua Banerjee is an Associate Professor in the Dept. of Information Technology at Xavier Institute of Social Service, Ranchi. She is a PhD from Indian School of Mines, Dhanbad. She has multiple research papers to her credit with reputed publishing houses.

Saugata Bose is an Assistant Professor of Computer Science and Engineering Department of University of Liberal Arts Bangladesh has over 10 years of teaching experience in tertiary education sector. His research interests embrace machine learning mostly.

Chiranji Lal Chowdary received the B.E. degree in computer science and engineering from the Jai Narain Vyas University, Jodhpur, India, in 2001, and the M.Tech. degree in computer science and engineering from the M. S. Ramaiah Institute of Technology (MSRIT) Bangalore, India, in 2008. He completed his Ph.D. in 2017 from VIT Vellore. In 2008, he joined the Department of Computer Science and Engineering, M. S. Ramaiah Institute of Technology, Bangalore, as a Lecturer. Since March 2010, he has been with the School of Information Technology and Engineering, VIT Vellore, where he was an Assistant Professor (Senior), became an Assistant Professor (Selection Grade) in 2014. His current research interests include digital image processing, medical imaging, computational intelligence and artificial intelligence. Mr. Chowdhary is a Life Member of the Indian Society for Technical Education (ISTE), Computer Society of India (CSI), and International Science Congress Association (ISCA).

R. P. Dahake is currently working as Assistant Professor in Department of Computer Engineering, MET's IOE Bhujbal Knowledge City, Nasik, Maharashtra, India. She has completed her Post Graduation in Computer Engineering from Govt. College of Engineering Aurangabad Maharashtra. She has presented papers at National and International conferences and also published papers in National and International Journals on various aspects of Computer Engineering and Networks. Her areas of interest include Computer Networks Security and Embedded Systems.

T. K. Das received Ph. D from VIT University, Vellore India in the year 2015 and M. Tech. from Utkal University, India in the year 2003. He is currently working as Associate Professor in VIT University, India. He has about 10 years' experience in academics, in addition to this he has worked in Industry in data warehousing domain for 3 years. He has authored many international journal and conference papers to his credit. His research interests include Artificial Intelligence, Data Analysis and Data Mining, Databases. He is associated with many professional bodies CSI, and ISCA.

C. Deisy is currently working as a Professor in Thiagarajar College of Engineering with 17 years of teaching experience, Madurai. Pursued Ph.D from Anna University on 2010. Published more than 60 papers in various reputed journals and conferences. Guiding more than 10 research scholars in different areas of research like Web Mining, Text Mining, Image mining.

Ezhilmaran Devarasan is currently working in the Division of Applied Algebra, School of Advanced Sciences, VIT University, Vellore. He received his Ph.D degree in Mathematics from the Alagappa University in 2011. He has more than eighteen years of experience in teaching and more than ten years of experience in research. His current research interests include Fuzzy Algebra, Fuzzy Image Processing, Data Mining and Cryptography. He has published more than sixty research article in peer-reviewed international journals.

Mercelin Francis is currently doing Research on Image Mining under Quality Improvement Programme, Anna university at Thiagarajar College of Engineering. Worked as an Assistant Professor at Marian Engineering College, Thiruvananthapuram with 12 years of teaching experience. Pursued my M.E. degree from Manonmaniam Sundaranar University, Tirunelveli.

Shyamrao Gumaste is presently working as Professor in Computer Engineering Department of MET's Institute of Engineering, BKC Nasik. Has Teaching Experience of more than 23 years. Area of Interest is applied algorithms and Soft Computing.

Tarun Jain is Assistant Professor in SCIT, Manipal University Jaipur.He Completed his M.tech degree in Information System (Dept. of Computer Engineering) from Netaji Subhas Institute of Technology, Dwarka, Delhi under the affiliation of University of Delhi (2013-2015). He Completed his B.Tech degree in Information Technology from H. R. Institute of Technology, Ghaziabad under the affiliation of G. B. T. U (2008-2012).His key research area are Machine Learning, Image Processing, Pattern Recognition etc.

R. R. Janghel is serving as an Assistant Professor in Department of Information Technology at National Institute of Technology Raipur. He did Ph.D. from Indian Institute of Information Technology and Management Gwalior and M.Tech from National Institute of Technology, Raipur (C.G.) in 2007 and B.Tech from Rungta College of Engineering and Technology, Bhilai (C.G) in 2005. He secured first position in his post-graduation from NIT Raipur. His areas of research include Deep Learning, Machine Learning, biomedical Healthcare System, expert systems, neural networks, hybrid computing and soft computing. He has numerous publications in various international journals and conferences.

Rose Bindu Joseph P. is currently completing her Ph.D. at VIT University, Vellore, India. She has more than 10 years of experience in academia. She has qualified NET by CSIR-UGC for lectureship. Her research interests include applied mathematics, machine learning, soft computing and artificial intelligence.

Madan Kharat is presently working as Professor and Head in Department of Computer Engineering, MET's Institute of Engineering, BKC Nasik, with total Teaching Experience of more than 25 years. Area of Interest is Wireless Sensor Networks and Networking.

Ritambhra Korpal has over 25 years of teaching and Industry experience with over 20 years of experience in teaching/guiding research projects. Research interests include Natural Language Processing, Machine learning, data mining and other related technologies. Guides various research projects like Intelligent Answering Machine, Plagiarism detection in monolingual text. Developed a new clustering technique which tries to overcome the inherent drawbacks of K-means clustering.

Komal Kumari is pursuing PGDM-IT, currently in final year, coauthored e-book Recent Trends and Techniques in Content Based Image Classification- ISBN 10: 6202029374 with Lap Lambert Publications, Interest areas: market research, image classification, analytics, digital marketing.

Shishir Mayank is a final year student of Post Graduate Diploma in Management (Information Technology). He is an avid reader and has expertise in GIS.

K. V. Metre is working as an Associate Professor at MET's Institute of Engineering, Nashik, Maharashtra, India. She has completed her BE from VNIT, Nagpur and post graduation in Computer Engineering from Dr. Babasaheb Ambedkar Technological University, Lonere. She has completed Ph.D. from RTM

Nagpur University. She has presented and published the research papers at National and International conferences and Journals. Her areas of interest include Database, Algorithms, Theory of computation etc.

Raviraj Pandian completed his doctorate degree in Computer Science and Engineering in the area of Image Processing. He holds a position of Professor in the department of Computer Science & Engineering, GSSS Institute of Engineering & Technology for Women, Mysore. He has 13 years of teaching and research experience. He has published more than 50 papers in International journals and conferences. He serves as an Editorial Board Member and Reviewer for more than 15 International Journals. He is also a life member of professional bodies like ISTE, CSI etc. He has guiding the Ph.D. research scholars in the areas of Image Processing, Pervasive & Cloud computing, Datawarehousing and Robotics etc. He has reviewed lot of articles in International conference proceedings and journals etc.

Leena Patil is presently working as Associate Professor in the Department of Computer Science and Engg.,Priyadarshini Institute of Engineering and Technology, Nagpur. She has more than 15 years of Teaching and administrative experience. She is Life Member of ISTE, New Delhi and Life Member of CSI, Mumbai. Her work gets recognized by many National and International Journals.

Ritika Selot is currently pursuing PGDM-IT from Xavier Institute of Social Service, Ranchi with the stream of Information Technology. She has received a job offer from Tata Consultancy Services in the grade CY1 and with a profile of Management Trainee. She is an aspiring candidate and having a zeal to attain future organisation goals.

S. N. Singh is the Head of the Department, Information Technology, Xavier Institute of Social Service. He has over 30 years of Teaching and Research Experience.He has got several research articles in reputed international journals and conferences. He has also delivered many invited lectures in well known Universities and colleges. Dr. Singh is a member in Professional Bodies and Recruitment Bodies of Birla Institute of Technology, Meshra, Ranchi, Central University of Jharkhand, Ranchi University and Jharkhand Rai University. He is a resource person for JPSC, Ranchi and Academic Staff Training College, Ranchi University, ICFAI University and Jharkhand University.

Madhumita Singha (Neogi) is associated as a faculty member with Xavier Institute of Social Service, Ranchi. She has got several International Publications to her credit with reputed publishing houses. Dr. Singha (Neogi) is open for research collaboration and consultancies.

Vivek Verma is working as an Assistant Professor at the School of Computing & Information Technology Manipal University Jaipur, India. His key research area is Image processing, Natural Language Processing, HCI etc.

Prashant Yawalkar is presently Working as a Associate Professor at MET Institute of Engineering, Bhujbal Knowledge City, Nasik. Completed graduation in computer Engineering from SSVPS College of Engineering, Dhule, Post Graduation in Computer Engineering from WCE Sangli. Presently Pursuing PhD from SPPU Pune. Total Teaching Experience of 21 years. Area of Interest is Image Processing, Soft Computing.

Index

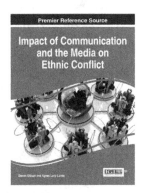

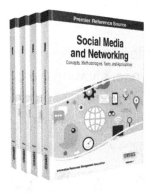
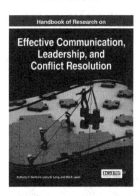

Stay Current on the Latest Emerging Research Developments

Become an IGI Global Reviewer for Authored Book Projects

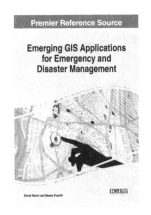

The overall success of an authored book project is dependent on quality and timely reviews.

In this competitive age of scholarly publishing, constructive and timely feedback significantly decreases the turnaround time of manuscripts from submission to acceptance, allowing the publication and discovery of progressive research at a much more expeditious rate. Several IGI Global authored book projects are currently seeking highly qualified experts in the field to fill vacancies on their respective editorial review boards:

Applications may be sent to:
development@igi-global.com

Applicants must have a doctorate (or an equivalent degree) as well as publishing and reviewing experience. Reviewers are asked to write reviews in a timely, collegial, and constructive manner. All reviewers will begin their role on an ad-hoc basis for a period of one year, and upon successful completion of this term can be considered for full editorial review board status, with the potential for a subsequent promotion to Associate Editor.

If you have a colleague that may be interested in this opportunity,
we encourage you to share this information with them.

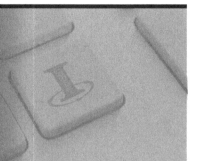

Printed in the United States
By Bookmasters